T0368406

KINGS PARK
PSYCHIATRIC CENTER:

A JOURNEY THROUGH HISTORY

BOOKS BY JASON MEDINA AVAILABLE
THROUGH XLIBRIS

No Hope for the Hopeless at Kings Park (2013)
The Diary of Audrey Malone Frayer (2014)
A Ghost in New Orleans (2015)
The Manhattanville Incident (2018)

OTHER BOOKS BY JASON MEDINA

Ghosts and Legends of Yonkers (2015)
A Night at the Shanley Hotel (COMING SOON!)

KINGS PARK
PSYCHIATRIC CENTER:

A JOURNEY THROUGH HISTORY

Volume II

JASON MEDINA

Library of Congress Control Number: 2018901630
ISBN: Hardcover   978-1-5434-8359-8
               Softcover   978-1-5434-8358-1
               eBook   978-1-5434-8357-4

Cover photography by Jo-Ann Santos-Medina, and interior cover photo by Jason Medina.

Print information available on the last page.

Rev. date: 03/26/2018

TRIBE.

To order additional copies of this book, contact:
Xlibris
1-888-795-4274
www.Xlibris.com
Orders@Xlibris.com
773775

Contents

Section V: The Structures

Addendum III: KPPC Building Chart

Section VI: Getting Around The Hospital

Section VII: The End of an Era

What sane person could live in this world and not be crazy?
–Ursula K. Le Guin (author and poet), *The Lathe of Heaven*, 1971

SECTION V

The Structures

CHAPTER 10

Building Groups

Divided into Groups

Why is it that when one man builds a wall, the next man immediately needs to know what's on the other side?
–George R. R. Martin (author), *A Game of Thrones*, 1996

M OST STATE HOSPITALS were constructed using a group system in which groups of buildings would be constructed one group at a time starting with the most important buildings. In an ideal situation, the first group should generally consist of a reception building and a convalescent building. The second group of buildings should be for those cases that are acute surgical cases and patients that are incurable. These two groups should be geographically close to one another. The administration building, superintendent's residence, staff houses, and nurses' homes should be near these groups. It would be even more fitting if these buildings were to exist between the first two groups and the third group, where the chronic and disturbed cases are housed. The fourth group should be for epileptic cases.

Each group should have its own kitchen and dining facilities, unless one that is suitable for the entire hospital can be centrally located. A power plant, sewage disposal plant, amusement hall, chapel, and morgue should also be centrally located. A water supply should be located at a place of convenience.

Like most other state hospitals, many of the buildings at the Kings Park Psychiatric Center were separated into building groups in accordance with their main purposes or general locations. There were several groups of buildings that existed at the hospital ranging from three buildings in one group to twenty-one buildings in the largest group.

There were times when expansion was a high priority as a way of dealing with overcrowding at the smaller cottages and buildings. The resolution was to add new groups of buildings to help alleviate the congested conditions. In the beginning, there was so much land to choose from, and the location near the river and the Long Island Sound made it ideal for the delivery of building supplies. There was a matter of avoiding the marshlands and trying not to destroy too many valuable fields of crops that could be cultivated, but on occasion, decent farmland had to be sacrificed. This was the case with the construction of several building groups at Kings Park.

Generally, most of the buildings in each group were built around the same time as the other buildings of that same group. In a few cases, there were buildings built much later on, which were later added to the already existing groups, sometimes as an annex. As a rule, the buildings from each group were built as close to one another as possible to provide easy access for the patients to the communal dining and recreational areas of the group.

In some cases, there was a tendency to make the buildings of a group identical to one another. This was mainly done for convenience, since it made designing and building them simpler.

It also helped to distinguish the buildings of one group from those of another. For example, most of the patient cottages from Groups 2 and 3, built simultaneously, resemble each other down to the octagon-shaped dayroom additions, added a few years after their construction. In other groups, some of the buildings were mirror images of each other, such as Buildings 41 and 43 of Group 4.

There were corridors that linked a few buildings from certain groups together. The Kirkbride buildings of Group 1 had beautiful solariums that connected the buildings occupied by female patients. Patient buildings were linked to the kitchen and dining facilities at Group 3 and the Veterans' Group via breezeway corridors. Other buildings were connected in such a way that they appeared to be one large building, such as the buildings of the second Group 4, often referred to as the Quad. There were also miles of underground steam tunnels that connected most of the buildings to one another. These various connections definitely made transporting patients much easier during harsh weather conditions.

Some of the building groups stood out because they were completely different from the other groups. Not all of the groups housed patients. The farm buildings did not house patients, nor did the unofficially dubbed Group 6, which was actually the homes of the workers who resided off grounds. It was their personal joke to refer to their homes as Group 6 of the hospital.

Prior to the 1970s, when the buildings were officially numbered as they are today, most people often referred to them by their group designation or ward number. Letters were also used to identify the buildings in some cases. The Veterans' Memorial Hospital Unit is a perfect example of how that system was utilized. Many former employees refer to the buildings by their letter designations rather than by the building numbers.

Not every building was part of a specific group. Most of the support structures such as workshops, storage sheds, and garages did not belong to building groups. Beginning in 1939, the buildings that were constructed did not belong to any such building group.

Aerial of Buildings 7 & 21-23 from April 10, 1976

The era of building groups had come to an end during the early 1930s. Otherwise, Buildings 7 and 21–23 would have certainly been numbered as a group when they were added, despite being added decades apart. They were the last "group" of large patient buildings to be added from 1957 to 1970.

The first groups that will be mentioned in this chapter were not official building groups, but they were divided into groups.

The Early Structures

With grass, birch trees, country dirt roads, and flowering bushes surrounding these early buildings, the reason for the 'park' in Kings Park is quite evident.

—Leo Polaski (author and historian), *The Farm Colonies: Caring for New York City's Mentally Ill in Long Island's State Hospitals*, 2003

The earliest structures were the six temporary one-story wooden pavilions that were built from the fall of 1886 to spring of 1887. These structures were erected near the Bécar Mansion on the site near where the director's mansion would someday be built. This unofficial group of buildings was only intended as temporary housing for the patients until permanent cottages could be built nearby.

The first of these permanent cottages was built under the cottage plan from 1888 to 1889. By this time, there were 698 patients crammed into these small cottages. It was obvious more were needed. As of 1893, there were twenty two-story wood-framed cottages. The newly constructed Kings Park Boulevard divided them in half with male cottages on the west side and females on the east side. Each of the patient cottages could accommodate up to forty patients comfortably.

Of the ten cottages situated on either side of the boulevard, one was for the first assistant physician and another for the attendants, and a third was used as a hospital cottage. For the females, it was Cottage 24, while for the males, it was Cottage 28. There was also a separate dining hall for each side. A few staff members were forced to reside on wards with patients until better accommodations could be provided.

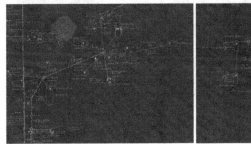 

Blueprints of the male cottages   Blueprints of the female cottages

In the meantime, the six temporary buildings were still being used, as patients and staff were crammed into both the temporary buildings and the cottages.

Continuously increasing overcrowded conditions led to the construction of larger two-story patient ward buildings. In 1891, construction began on four brick U-shaped buildings, which were allegedly the first fireproof buildings erected on the grounds. Two of these buildings were built on the east side of the boulevard, while the other two were built on the west side. These new structures were Buildings A–D.

The new brick buildings were ready for patients by 1894, although improvements and additions would continue for the next few years. Each of these housed both patients and staff members, who were finally able to vacate the temporary structures. Building

A would also serve as the new administration building, while Building B became the medical and surgical building. A nursing school was established at Building C, along with a photo lab for the hospital's official photographer. The pathological laboratory was located in Building D.

View of Buildings C & B with cottages, circa 1924

New kitchen buildings were added too. One was built behind Buildings A and B, while the other was behind Buildings C and D. These kitchens soon took over feeding the patients of the nearby cottages as well. Buildings A–D each had its own one-story dining hall located at the rear of the buildings.

From 1897 to 1898, pantries and dining areas were established in the women's cottages, freeing up their kitchen and dining hall to be used solely as an amusement hall. In time, the same was done with the male cottages. This allowed patients to dine conveniently without having to leave their cottages, especially at times when the weather was harsh. It also provided a cozier atmosphere.

Aerial of boulevard from April 21, 1984

From the 1920s to 1930s, most of the early cottages were removed to make room for the construction of newer improved buildings. Buildings A–D continued to be used until the

1970s. Buildings B–D were finally abandoned and demolished by 1976. Building A lasted another few months before joining the rest of its former neighbors, thus marking the end of the earliest patient buildings of the hospital. Larger brick buildings replaced them. Today, old photos, documents, and memories are all that allow them to be acknowledged as a part of history.

The Dairy Farm and Piggery

"Comrades!" he cried. "You do not imagine, I hope, that we pigs are doing this in a spirit of selfishness and privilege? Many of us actually dislike milk and apples. I dislike them myself. Our sole object in taking these things is to preserve our health. Milk and apples (this has been proved by Science, comrades) contain substances absolutely necessary to the well being of a pig. We pigs are brainworkers. The whole management and organization of this farm depend on us. Day and night we are watching over your welfare. It is for your sake that we drink the milk and eat those apples."

–George Orwell (author), *Animal Farm*, 1945

This bulk of the farm buildings was built along the west side of Old Dock Road, later known as the Dairy Road, in the area behind the Group 1 buildings just north of the William T. Rogers Middle School playing field. These buildings consisted of a dairy barn with several silos, a horse barn, a chemical feed house, a root cellar, a slaughterhouse, two piggery structures, and a hennery. These buildings were built from 1889 to 1943.

The dairy barn was the first to be erected, followed by three silos, a stable, the

Aerial view of the farm & piggery, circa Sept. 1927

slaughterhouse, and the first piggery. The hennery was added in the early 1910s. It was the only structure located away from the rest of the farm. It was built on the other side of the hospital grounds near the superintendent's residence. Apparently, the superintendent liked his eggs fresh in the morning.

When the hospital was established as a county farm, it was quite evident the farming structures would play a large role in sustaining its long-term existence. Almost two hundred acres of fields waiting to be cultivated, several different orchards with fruit to be picked, thick woodlands that had to be cleared, and marshes that would have to be filled surrounded the land of the county farm. Through the efforts of daily farmwork, the hospital was capable of supplying its own food throughout its early years, which helped to make it a self-sufficient community. The farm's continued existence relied heavily on patient occupational and recreational therapy programs.

Sometime in the early part of 1940, there was a destructive fire that caused many of the farm buildings to burn to the ground. This was the main problem with having buildings built so close together. If one went up in flames, they all tended to go down in the blaze.

New farm buildings were immediately erected to replace the ones that were lost. By 1941, a longer dairy barn and several new silos were built. A two-story concrete horse barn was built behind it. A new slaughterhouse was also built by 1943. While the piggery had not been damaged by fire, it had also been replaced.

Aerial view of the farm &
piggery, circa 1964

The slaughterhouse & dairy barn

The farm buildings were gradually phased out during the late 1950s, and farming operations ceased in the early 1960s. A few of the farm buildings remained in use for storing food and grounds maintenance equipment. They were not abandoned until the hospital closed.

Dairy farm on April of 1975

Once this group of buildings was finally abandoned, the buildings were gradually swallowed up by an overgrowth of trees, bushes, weeds, and tall grass. By December 2012, this entire area was cleared away, and its buildings were demolished. Only one lonely structure remains isolated in the woods, although it is merely a few walls with a doorway and no roof, surrounded by an old barbed wire fence.

Dairy farm buildings on Nov. 7, 2011

Farm area during demolition phase on Dec. 19, 2012

Farm close-up during demolition phase

Closed gate at farm during demolition phase

Closed gate at former farm area on June 20, 2016

The former farm area reclaimed by nature on June 20, 2016

Main Building Groups

By the 1930s, . . . the State had realized that the great increase in the number of patients being cared for in their mental hospitals on Long Island could only be met by the erection of large structures. Such buildings were efficient, because all similar services could be placed together and staffed with fewer employees than if they were scattered around the campus; and economical, because one large structure costs less to build than several smaller ones of the same aggregate size; and also effective, because having the capacity of the large buildings would allow the State to finally catch up, they believed, with chronic overcrowding.

–Leo Polaski (author and historian), *The Farm Colonies: Caring for New York City's Mentally Ill in Long Island's State Hospitals,* 2003

The following building groups range from Group 1 to 5 and include the Veterans' Memorial Hospital Unit. These were the actual building groups that existed at the hospital. I have also included the unofficial Group 6. The initial construction on these groups began shortly after the Kings County Farm and Asylum was taken over by the state and the name of the hospital was changed to the Long Island State Hospital at Kings Park.

The first group to be built did not have a particular name or number. It was simply called the Group. Only after the addition of the next two groups several years later did it become known as Group 1. Based on the Kirkbride Plan design, it was a continuous ward structure with buildings that were connected to each other via corridors and underground tunnels. There were ten multistory brick buildings in this group. In 1898, the group opened to house approximately one thousand patients, thus significantly relieving the overcrowded conditions of the early cottages.

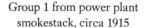

Group 1 from power plant
smokestack, circa 1915

View of Groups 3 & 2 from the
smokestack, circa 1925

A little more than a decade later, Groups 2 and 3 were added. Each of these two groups consisted of two two-story male and female buildings with their own kitchen and dining hall building. The buildings were connected via the underground tunnels. Upon their completion, chronic cases were placed within these new buildings.

Construction on Group 4 began immediately upon the completion of Groups 2 and 3. It consisted of long one-story patient wards that were built away from the main patient population because this group would be used to care for patients with contagious diseases such as tuberculosis.

During the 1910s construction of these three additional groups, the contractors hired immigrant laborers to do much of the work. These workers were camped out on the grounds for the duration, which lasted about five years. During that time, there were a few issues that arose regarding their behavior.

Some of these workers had very little respect for property. They trespassed in gardens belonging to neighboring private residences. At times, they wandered into hospital buildings in which they had no business. There were a few incidents of theft that took place. Alcohol was brought onto the grounds and consumed heavily. At night, women were being snuck into the workers' tents. There were even cases of assaults. Two stabbings occurred in disputes over women.

It was a tremendous relief to the superintendent and the hospital staff when the work on these three groups was completed. It would be at least another decade before there would be another large construction project at the hospital. This would be when the Veterans' Group was added.

Before that, there was Group 5, which became an official group during the early 1930s. Building 2 had been built about ten years earlier. Only after the addition of Buildings 1 and 3 did this become a group. It was the last of the building groups numbered from 1 to 5 to be built.

Right around the same time, the original buildings of Group 4 were demolished and replaced by three new four-story brick buildings. These connected buildings would serve as the new Group 4.

The Veterans' Group was the largest group of buildings constructed for the state hospital. It encompassed most of the northern section that is now a large portion of the Nissequogue River State Park. It was built around the older buildings of Group 3. Those buildings were incorporated into the Veterans' Group, which was officially known as the Veterans' Memorial Hospital Unit. The buildings of this group were added from the 1920s to 1930s.

Each of these building groups was built with one common goal in mind. They were meant to alleviate overcrowding at the hospital, but it was never a permanent solution. In time, the new buildings not belonging to any group were added. They would also become overcrowded. It was a never-ending battle for most of the twentieth century.

Bird's eye view of the KPSH   Aerial view of the KPSH, circa 1947
on Sept. 23 1947

In the following pages, each group has been listed individually, along with a detailed description.

Group 1 (the Group):

A bird's eye view of Male and Female Cottages at Group, K. P. S. H.

1909 postcard looking south at Group 1

Buildings 4A–J made up what became the first building group of the hospital. Construction began in the spring of 1897 and was completed during the winter of 1898, utilizing the Kirkbride Plan at a cost of about $500,000. This was the first large-scale construction project started by the state after taking over the hospital two years earlier. This group was situated on the west side of Kings Park Boulevard, north of the lower reservoir. Most of the structures were two-story brick buildings with attics and basements. The dayrooms of the wards were located on the ground floors of each building.

This group opened on a Thursday evening, December 29, 1898, with a reception party given by the officers of the hospital. Many of the guests arrived from Brooklyn. They were greeted by staff and given a tour of the main structure before being ushered into a large dining area in one of the solariums. There were music, dancing, and refreshments. The party went on until around two in the morning. Members of the press covered the event, and it appeared in newspapers over the following days.

In the earlier days, most employees referred to these buildings by using their respective ward numbers, which were Wards 41–49. Much later, these buildings were numbered from 111 to 120.

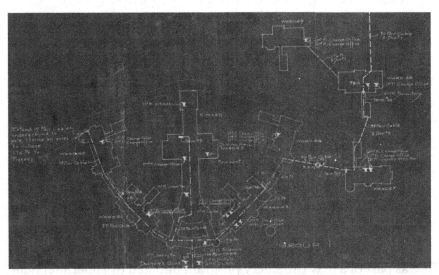

Blueprints showing the layout of Group 1

Building 111 (4A) was the administration building of the group. It stood at the front central portion of the group and faced the boulevard. To the left of Building 111 (4A) were Buildings 112 (4B) and 113 (4C). On the opposite side, to the right, were Buildings 114 (4D) and 115 (4E). These four buildings extended the wings of the central building, forming a U shape. Directly behind Building 111 (4A) were Building 116 (4F), followed by Building 117 (4G), which was the kitchen and dining hall of the group. All three were connected. On the north side of East Third Street, across from these connected buildings, were the only three separate buildings of the group, 118 (4J), 119 (4I), and 120 (4H).

Kings Park State Hospital (Group 1), circa 1932

Panoramic view of Group 1, circa 1932

These buildings had been built to ease the burden of the smaller overcrowded cottages. As soon as the group opened, nine hundred patients were transferred here. Most of them were from Brooklyn. There were 275 males and 625 females. Right from the start, the females made up the majority of patients of this group. Eventually, Group 1 housed approximately five hundred male patients and five hundred female patients, but within a few years, it housed the greater part of the female patient population. The females were housed in the connected portion, while males of the group were kept in the three detached buildings.

By 1899, the group had fire alarms installed, and each building was equipped with portable fire extinguishers, which was a first for the hospital. The buildings of this group also had fire escapes. It was part of a new fire safety program initiated by superintendent Oliver M. Dewing. In the event of a fire, the boiler house would sound its whistle the same number of times as the signal box that gave out the first alarm.

Two rustic summerhouse gazebos were erected in small groves near this group. The first was built in 1901. It was located on the west side of the boulevard, north of Building 111 (4A). The second was built next to Building 119 (4I) in 1908. Both had built-in seats, where patients and employees could sit comfortably and enjoy the day.

During the first few years, after the group was built, an auxiliary boiler house was built and used to supply heat because the hospital's electric heating plant (Building 59) was too far away to provide a sufficient amount of heat. The railroad spur had an extension and a trestle that stopped here to deliver coal.

After the superintendent made requests to the state, a new power plant and boiler house were built near the current power plant location. This new centralized location was more suitable for all of the patient buildings at the hospital. The temporary boiler house near Group 1 was subsequently removed.

In 1913, the wooden steps leading to Group 1 from the boulevard were rebuilt using concrete. This is something that was being done at many of the old buildings because the old wooden steps had become worn out and dangerous.

By the 1960s, the entire group had become worn out and dangerous. These buildings were closed by 1966. The buildings of Group 1 would eventually succumb to flames, marking their ultimate end. After these buildings were abandoned, they sat forgotten until a series of fires during the early 1970s led to their inevitable demolition. The first building razed was Building 115 (4E), which housed Ward 44. Afterward, a large fire destroyed most of the group. The fires in each case were likely the result of arson. By 1973, all of these buildings were gone.

Fire destroying Building 115, circa early 1970s

Building 112 of Group 1
burning at night, circa 1972

Building 112 of Group 1
burning at night, circa 1972

Building 112 not long after
the fire, circa 1972

Building 112 side view not long
after the fire, circa 1972

Building 112 side view, circa 1972

Rear of Group 1 not long
after the fire, circa 1972

Rear of Group 1 buildings with fire
escape prior to demolition

Destroyed Group 1 building

Today, all that remains of Group 1 is an empty field of grass, former overgrown grassy parking lots, and dead-end tunnels made of bricks hidden away beneath the surface.

Group 2 (Adolescent Unit/Mental Retardation Unit)

Aerial view of Group 2, circa 1957

At the time this group was added, the hospital was using a larger cottage design with the intention of housing about three hundred patients in these structures. While most of the brick buildings at the hospital were built using red bricks, these were constructed with yellow bricks. This group was built at the same time as Group 3, which was identical in design. Both groups were intended to house chronic cases. The bedridden patients from Wards 45 and 48 were the first to be placed here on the ground floors.

Group 2 consisted of Buildings 122–124 and their annex, Building 40. Buildings 122–124 were the oldest buildings of the group, built from 1910 to 1912 at the cost of $358,242, while Building 40 was added years later, in 1932. All buildings of the group were connected at basement levels through underground tunnels. This group was situated on the north side of St. Johnland Road and at the west side of Kings Park Boulevard atop a hill that overlooked the electric heating plant (Building 59) and original laundry (Building 33). The location had previously served as a ten-acre farming field. Buildings 122–124 were originally known as Buildings 54A–C. Wards 50–54 were located within the two main buildings.

Blueprints showing the layout of Group 2

From 1915 to 1916, a two-story octagon-shaped addition with a basement was added to the south side of Building 122 at the rear. At first, a similar extension was planned for Building 124 but was never built because of the building's proximity to the edge of the hill at the front and rear of the building. Tons of

Aerial view of Group 2, circa 1947

landfill would have been required to support the addition, and the road would have needed adjusting.

Group 2 closed down temporarily during the early 1950s for renovations. During this time, the porches were all rebuilt, slightly changing the appearance of the two main buildings. When the group was reopened, it became home to the Adolescent Unit. Building 122 housed females, while the males were in Building 124. The children's ward was moved to Building 40. A playground existed behind these buildings.

During the mid-1960s, the adolescents and children were relocated to Building 22. At this time, this group underwent extensive renovations. The buildings got a complete overhaul, including new plumbing, brightly colored paint, improved masonry, electrical fixtures, and the installation of electric outlets.

In January 1974, this group reopened as the new Mental Retardation Unit (MRU). By this time, all window bars were removed so the new patients would not feel as if they were in a prison. The first eighteen patients, ranging from 7 to 28 in age, arrived by bus from Willowbrook. The worst of the patients were placed into Building 122.

Mentally handicapped patients from the Willowbrook State School and Hospital in Staten Island were relocated here after an investigation by investigative reporter Geraldo Rivera revealed the harsh treatment and abuse of patients. Willowbrook was ultimately shut down in 1987. Other patients were moved here from the Suffolk Developmental Center, which was located in Melville.

The Suffolk Developmental Center eventually took administrative control of the unit in the late 1970s. During this time, the ward numbers were renumbered from Wards 50–54 to Wards 851–855, respectively.

About a year before the Group 2 buildings closed, some of the interiors were repainted. This was a sporadic practice that was done at the hospital toward its final years when it came to buildings with reuse potential. When the group closed to patients in 1980, most of its patients were sent back to the Suffolk Developmental Center, later renamed as the Long Island Developmental Center. It closed in 1993 and was promptly demolished two years later. Its 1,300 patients were sent to Pilgrim Psychiatric Center.

For a couple of years afterward, the group housed a day care center at Building 40 for the children of the employees. The rest of the buildings remained unused. Eventually, the day care center was relocated, and the entire group was abandoned.

The buildings of Group 2 were among the oldest buildings still in existence at the abandoned hospital, and they looked it. Building 124 was the first to go after it was destroyed by arson during the mid-1990s and demolished about a year later. Over the next two decades, Buildings 122 and 123 were on the verge of collapse. This made them a danger for anyone who dared to enter. The floors were unsafe to walk across. Ceilings were literally hanging by threads.

Aerial view of Buildings 122 &
123 with 40 behind them, 2007

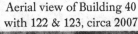

Aerial view of Building 40
with 122 & 123, circa 2007

Aerial view of Building 123 with
40 behind it, circa 2007

Aerial view of Buildings
40 & 123, circa 2007

By late July 2012, the area around these buildings was cleared out to begin the demolition process. Demolitions on Buildings 122 and 123 finally began in September of that year. By the end of the month, these buildings were mostly gone. A later visit in December showed only piles of rubble remained from the two buildings. Now, you cannot even tell they were there. Only

Building 40 still stands abandoned and alone. So far, there are no known plans for the last building of Group 2.

Road to Building 122 during
demolition phase on Sept. 5, 2012

Building 122 being demolished
on Sept. 5, 2012

Building 123 being demolished
on Aug. 14, 2012

Demolition equipment at
Building 123 on Aug. 14, 2012

Building 40 remained after the
demolitions, circa April 16, 2013

Group 2 on July 30, 2013

Group 3

This group originally consisted of Buildings 137, 143, and 147, becoming the oldest buildings of the twenty-one buildings of the

Veterans' Memorial Hospital Unit. The three buildings of Group 3 were built from 1910 to 1912 on a twenty-five-acre farming field along Sound View Court at the northern end of the hospital. Built at the same time as the buildings of Group 2, both groups were intended to house a total of up to six hundred chronic patients that were generally bedridden and helpless from Wards 45 and 48 of Group 1.

| View of Group 3 from the power plant smokestack, circa 1925 | Patiky brothers at reservoir during winter 1915-1916 |

There were large octagon-shaped additions added to the front entryways of Buildings 143 and 147 from 1915 to 1916, similar to the one added to Building 122 of Group 2.

Building 136 (73L) was added to Group 3 as construction began on the Veterans' Memorial Hospital Unit during the mid-1920s. The new building served as a medical and surgical building for the group. Two breezeway corridors were built, linking it to Building 137, which was the kitchen and dining hall of Group 3. The original buildings of Group 3 were incorporated into the new Veterans' Group and renumbered as Buildings 137 (73M), 143 (73S), and 147 (73W).

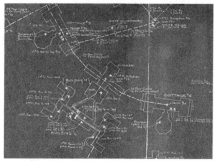

Blueprints showing the layout of Group 3, after addition of Building 136 (L) Aerial view of Buildings 136 (L) & 137 (M), circa 1967

Group 3 had been known as Buildings 73A–C prior to the addition of the Veterans' Group buildings.

Buildings 143 (73S) and 147 (73W) were demolished during the early 1980s, while Buildings 136 (73L) and 137 (73M) were abandoned when the hospital closed. They are still standing today as part of the Nissequogue River State Park, although they could be marked for demolition soon. Currently, Building 137 (73M) is the oldest building of the group remaining.

Aerial view of Buildings 136 (L) & 137 (M) on March 6, 1988 Aerial view from 2013

Veterans' Group (Veterans' Memorial Hospital Unit)

Aerial view of Veterans' Group on Nov. 6, 1951

This group has sometimes been referred to as Group 3, although it was actually Group 3 that was added to this large group. For this reason, I have listed it after Group 3.

The First World War had a powerful and lasting effect on everyone it touched. Never before had such a devastating war been fought on such a large scale. With the casualties in the millions, it was, for its time, the deadliest conflict in human history.

There are few things that can compare to the horrors those soldiers must have experienced while in battle. Not everyone is capable of dealing with the stress involved. At the time, there was no such term as "post-traumatic stress." Instead, it was known as shell shock.

After the war ended, there were 710 veterans with various forms of mental illness admitted to state hospitals from July 1919 to June 1920. There were only 287 admitted in the previous year. The largest increase in numbers took place at Kings Park and Central Islip, and especially at the US Public Health Service Hospital at Dansville. At Kings Park, there were 57 veterans admitted in 1919, and by the next year, the number increased to 109. Over at Central

Islip, the number went from 52 in 1919 to 131 in 1920; while at the US Public Health Service Hospital, the numbers climbed dramatically from a mere 17 admitted in 1919 to 222 admitted during the next year.

This was a significant amount of veterans, and it drew the attention of the right people. It became apparent how beneficial it could be to have a specialized unit dedicated to the needs of these soldiers.

The federal government cooperated with the state hospitals in the treatment of its veterans. The Veterans' Bureau worked efficiently with the staff at Kings Park to treat veterans in 1921.

In the mid-1920s, Sen. George Lincoln Thompson of Kings Park provided considerable funding for the expansion of the hospital, which went directly toward the creation of the Veterans' Memorial Hospital Unit. His actions helped create jobs for the construction of the group as well as new lifetime employment opportunities at the hospital.

Veterans' Group under construction on July 13, 1925

This magnificent group consisted of twenty-one buildings, which were numbered as Buildings 125 (73A)–147 (73W). It was the greatest number of buildings ever erected at the hospital within the same period. The buildings of Group 3 were included as the Veterans' Group was constructed around them. The eighteen newer buildings were built between 1923 and 1931 at a cost of $2,682,702 and were intended to house up to eight hundred patients or more.

A state hospital map from 1912 identified the older buildings of Group 3 as Buildings 73A–C, hence the number designation used for the new group built around them. This large group of buildings was located north of St. Johnland Road, past the boat basin at the end of the boulevard. These buildings made up almost the entire northern section of the hospital, which bordered the Long Island Sound at Kings Park Bluff and the Nissequogue River at Jones Point.

Artists' rendition of how it was intended to look, circa 1923

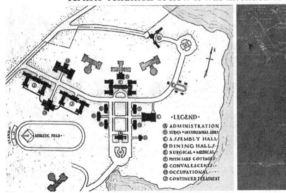

Map from 1923 showing proposed layout for Veterans' Group

Blueprints showing the layout of the Veterans' Group

Buildings 145 (73U) and 146 (73V) were meant to be a part of this group but were never built. The numbers reserved for these two structures were never reused. I am uncertain as to why they were not built, but my guess is that it had to do with insufficient funding or a last-minute change in plans.

An opening and dedication ceremony was held on September 24, 1927. ov. Alfred E. Smith was in attendance, along with many dignitaries from the military, federal, state, and local government. When this group of buildings opened, it became the first state-operated mental health facility dedicated solely to war veterans, an idea that was heralded as one of the most significant events in the history of the state hospital system.

Veterans' Group dedication ceremony at Building 136 (L), Sept. 1927

Prayer by Rev. John York at dedication ceremony on Sept. 1927

Major Gen. W.H. Haskell at dedication ceremony on Sept. 1927

Major Gen. Haskell unveils dedication tablet, Sept. 1927

The first nineteen veterans to be admitted were those of the Indian Wars and the Spanish-American War. Within the next few months, another fifty arrived from Manhattan State Hospital and one hundred more from Central Islip. They were split up and admitted into Buildings 136 (73L), 138 (73N), and 140 (73P).

Dedication tablet on display at the Kings Park Heritage Museum

By 1954, there were 1,480 veterans committed to this group. It was the most veterans the hospital would ever have. This number included a veteran from the Indian Wars, twenty-three veterans from the Spanish-American War, 844 from World War I, and 612 from World War II. There were another five hundred convalescents. This group made up almost 15–20 percent of the patient population.

This Veterans' Memorial Hospital Unit was the primary psychiatric center for New York's war veterans until the late 1970s. It provided treatment, recreation, and occupational therapy specifically suited toward their interests and experience.

These buildings were not only used for veterans. Throughout most of their time in use, there really were not many patients that were veterans. The majority of veterans were usually admitted in conjunction with times of war. Considering how overcrowded the rest of the hospital buildings were, it was necessary to use whatever space was available.

Almost half of the buildings from this group were residential buildings for employees of the hospital. These structures were two-family or four-family homes. They consisted of Buildings 126 (73B) to 134 (73J). Home T, a three-story brick building, was used to house hospital attendants.

One building of the group was used as a building for sick employees. Two of the buildings were kitchen and dining halls. There was even a building that became the main administration building of the hospital for many years. That was Building 125 (73A).

Aerial view from 1955

Veterans' Group administrative
offices & staff residences, circa 1967

Several years after the psychiatric center closed, the northern section of the hospital where this group of buildings is located was converted into the Nissequogue River State Park. Most of the buildings on that side of the grounds are currently abandoned, but the New York State Office of Parks, Recreation and Historic Preservation still uses a few for clerical, maintenance, and storage purposes. Building 125 (73A) has become the main office of the park.

The park is open to the public, including Tiffany Field, with exception to 2010, when New York State governor Paterson decided to shut down numerous state parks as a means of saving money. He did this at the expense of many townspeople, children, and out-of-town visitors who often look forward to enjoying a nice sunny day at the beautiful Nissequogue River State Park.

A few of the old doctors' cottages were demolished in June 2016. It is planned that only two will remain. Building 130 (73F) will be transformed into a new comfort station for the park's visitors, and Building 132 (73H) will be turned into a small museum dedicated to preserving the history of the hospital. By September, Buildings 135 and 142 were also razed.

Looking north towards doctors'
cottages on Dec. 22, 2011

Doctors' cottages on May 11, 2011

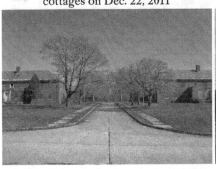

Buildings 126-129 on April 19, 2016

Quadrangle between Buildings
126-129 on June 20, 2016

Fence surrounding cottages,
circa April 2016

Doctors' cottages on April 19, 2016

Dumpsters outside of cottages
on April 19, 2016

Demolitions begin on doctors'
cottages in June of 2016

Looking into the basement of
Building 134 (J) on June 20, 2016

Building 135 (K) on June 20, 2016

Group 4 (TB Camps)

During the early 1900s, two of the first cottages built on the grounds were converted for the care of patients with tuberculosis (TB). These were Female Cottage 24 (I) and Male Cottage 28 (D), which were originally used as infirmary cottages. The state hospital at Kings Park was one of the very first institutions in New York to segregate its TB patients in such a manner, although soon there was a need for more TB cottages because of a steady increase in the amount of female patients inflicted with the illness. To fill that need, Female Cottages 22 (G) and 23 (H) were converted into additional TB cottages, along with Male Cottage 30 (H).

In 1911, the amount of patients with TB had more than doubled. The TB population increased from sixty to one hundred patients in 1910 to 225 patients by October 1911. The majority of the patients with the illness remained female. Eventually, it became necessary to begin planning for a much larger unit that could replace the five small cottages and house up to one thousand patients.

Originally made up of a series of three one-story cottages, the new TB wards were built from 1912 to 1913 on a twenty-acre meadow near the dairy farm, along the west side of Old Dock Road. They were numbered as Buildings 3A–C and were also known as the TB camps. This group became home to Wards 60–65.

Tuberculosis cottages
on Feb. 20, 1925

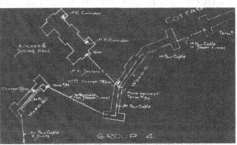

Blueprints showing the layout
of original Group 4

These cottages opened on March 25, 1913, with the intention of housing up to 250 patients. This new group fell short of the original goal, but it would have to suffice.

In the same year these cottages opened, there was a small fire that began when one of the contractor's workers threw a hot match onto some wood shavings. Fortunately, the fire was noticed and speedily extinguished before any great damage could occur.

In 1915, new awnings were added for these cottages. A kitchen and dining hall were finally built between 1922 and 1923. They were not added sooner because of

New Group 4 construction on July 14, 1934

a lack of state funding and supplies, partially as a result of the war effort for World War I.

Over the next couple of years, these wards filled up quickly taking in patients from Manhattan and Brooklyn. Soon, it became necessary for a new addition. Superintendent William C. Garvin made several requests for an additional building that could house up to two hundred patients, but this request was not fulfilled.

Several years later, the TB patients were transferred to a modern brick colony at Central Islip State Hospital. Afterward, these cottages were abandoned. During the early 1930s, a new Group 4 was built to replace this old group. As these new buildings were erected, the old ones were demolished. By 1934, the old Group 4 was gone.

Group 4 (the Quad)

Buildings 41–43 were built as the new Group 4. They replaced the TB cottages between the years 1932 and 1934 at a cost of $1,729,954. This group officially opened on December 1, 1936. These four-story brick buildings are all connected to each other and are sometimes referred to by urban explorers as the Quad because of the group's shape with its four sets of corner wings. Building 41 is set upon the edge of a hill looking

Group 4A Wards 101 to 108
Group 4B Wards 109 to 116
Group 4C Wards 117 to 122
Group 4D Wards 123 to 128

Aerial view of Group 4,
circa 1950s-1960s

down from the west side of Old Dock Road. Behind this building is the X-shaped Building 42, which served as the kitchen and dining hall for the group. Building 43 sat at the rear of the group, behind Building 42. The patients were housed in both H-shaped Buildings 41 and 43 on Wards 101–128.

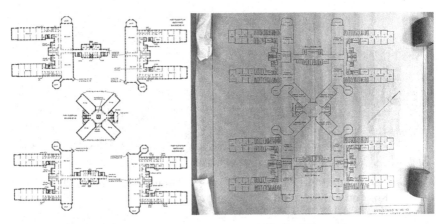

Floor plans showing
Buildings 41-43

Group 4 floor plans

In 1953, a Children's Unit was established here. It was later relocated to Building 40 of Group 2.

On December 4, 1974, a new mobile canteen service cart was unveiled, specifically for use at Group 4. Built by the storehouse crew, this was organized for patients that were unable to go to the community store building. It was a very thoughtful and much-appreciated innovation.

Approaching Group 4 from Old
Dock Road on Dec. 19, 2012

Group 4 at sunset on Nov. 25, 2011

Group 4 from across Old Dock
Road on April 16, 2013

Group 4 on April 16, 2013

Group 4 from the top of Building 93 on March 27, 2013

This group of buildings was closed in 1992. Ever since it was abandoned, this group has attracted large numbers of trespassers. Because of its close proximity to the road, isolated location, and easy accessibility to the underground tunnel system, it is no surprise. These buildings are quite fascinating and have a unique design.

At this time, there are no plans to demolish this group. It would surely be an expensive project to undertake because of the group's size and abatement process that would be involved. However, the tunnel access has become limited to the nearby power plant after recent demolitions from the past few years. Trespassing is still a major concern.

Aerial view looking north
at Group 4, circa 2007

Aerial view of Group 4, circa 2007

Group 5

Buildings 1–3 were all located on the east side of Kings Park Boulevard, and together they made up the buildings of Group 5. They were built from 1919 to 1934 at a cost of $1,172,296 with Building 2 being the oldest of the three. Building 1 served as the male reception building and housed Wards 93–100, while Building 2 was the female reception building and home to Wards 66–71. Building 3 was built to house staff members and was also the administration building of the group.

Aerial view looking east at
Group 5, circa 1957

Aerial view of Group 5,
circa March 1962

During the early 1930s, a kitchen and dining hall were built into the rear portion of Building 2. An underground tunnel connected the two patient buildings so that they could share the dining area.

Connecting tunnel beneath
Buildings 1 & 2 on Feb. 7, 2015

Building 2, being the oldest of the three, was the first to be demolished. It was abandoned in the early 1980s and used for fire practice by the Safety Department. By 1985, it had been demolished. Rubble from the building can still be found in the woods, where it once stood. The underground tunnel that once connected Building 1 to Building 2 now leads to a dead end.

Shortly before the hospital closed, Building 3 was abandoned. Afterward, Building 1 was one of the only buildings on the property that still housed patients long after the hospital closed. It was under the administration of Pilgrim Psychiatric Center.

At the end of 2012, Building 1 was closed and its patients were transferred to Pilgrim Psychiatric Center. There were plans for the Department of Environmental Conservation (DEC) to reuse this building, but that never happened.

Buildings 3 & 1 during winter on March 9, 2015

Instead, the building was abandoned.

Both remaining buildings of the group stand empty across from each other. With each passing day, the condition of each worsens. Vandals have destroyed much of the interior of Building 1. Soon enough, it will look as bad as its sister building.

Group 6

There was never really a Group 6. During the later years of the psychiatric center's existence, the employees often referred to their homes that were located off grounds as Group 6. It was merely an inside joke among themselves. They would say they are going to Group 6 when they were going home.

Employee Kate Newcomb
with Mrs. Nathan on a sled

Employees' cruise, circa 1980

I was lucky enough to learn about this private joke, since it was never written on any official documents. It is the recollections like that, that are unique and not known to everyone that I like to note. I thought it was worth mentioning for those former employees who read this book, as just a little something to spark some old memories.

For the record, during the earlier times, most of the doctors and nursing staff actually resided on the grounds of the hospital in the various cottages and residential staff buildings such as Buildings 3, 18, 19, 34–37, 49, 67, 74, 77–79, 90, 95–101, 126 (73B)–134 (73J), and 144 (73T). For a while, it was even required. Some of these structures are still standing today, although they are abandoned. A few have been scheduled for demolition in the next coming year or so.

CHAPTER II

The Buildings

First Temporary Buildings

No photos of the three small wooden shacks which housed the first 55 patients sent from Flatbush to Kings Park in 1886 have been found.
—Leo Polaski (author and historian), *The Farm Colonies: Caring for New York City's Mentally Ill in Long Island's State Hospitals,* 2003

IN THE EARLY fall of 1886, Alderman James W. Birkett promised he could have the first two out of sixteen cottages built within three weeks time once the materials were available and on site. It would end up taking much longer. The overcrowding situation had become so critical at Kings County that the need to create temporary structures at the new county farm for the immediate intake of Kings County's chronic patients became necessary.

It was decided to use contractors from Kings County for the construction of the new buildings at the county farm. A contract was put out for someone to provide the materials required to build five temporary wood-framed buildings. This contract was awarded to a contractor by the name of Charles Hart, who was to have these five shelters erected within thirty days.

President pro tempore John Y. McKane of the Supervisors' County Farm Committee refused to sign the contract awarded to Alderman Birkett on the grounds that the Board of Charities Commissioners submitted defective plans. The contract called for the cottages to be erected upon posts rather than bricks, which would be more reliable.

As of September, there were still no new structures, but the first fifty-five patients had already arrived. Of that amount, there were only twenty-three female patients and thirty-two men. The patients were temporarily housed in a preexisting farmhouse until the temporary buildings could be erected.

As of October 16 of that year, not one of the contractors had begun working. Four days later, another contract was drawn up for furnishing the materials and labor for the complete erection of two physicians' residences and two additional frame cottages on the county farm. This contract also went to Alderman Birkett in the amounts of $4,500 and $4,200, respectively, because of the delays of his previous work contract.

On the afternoon of October 21, members of the board of supervisors met to discuss the unsigned contract. The matter also passed before the County Farm Committee.

By November 1886, construction had finally begun at the cost of $20,000. The first three temporary buildings were built near the former mansion of Noel J. Bécar to accommodate two hundred patients. One housed females, another housed males, and the third served as a dining hall.

The Bécar Mansion existed as part of the farm at the time of the Kings County purchase. It was built sometime prior to 1837 and was one of the oldest houses in St. Johnland. After the purchase was made, this house was refurbished and converted into a temporary administration building. The medical superintendent's office was located here, where it remained for several years until more suitable premises could be erected.

By the early 1900s, the Bécar Mansion would later serve as the superintendent's residence. It would remain so until Building 67 was built to replace it in 1939.

Toward the end of 1886, contractor Hart's first three building frames were taking shape as they were fairly boarded up and covered. These temporary structures were clustered tightly around the Bécar Mansion. By December 15, they were occupied.

While the first three were completed generally on time, Hart had not yet completed the other two temporary buildings he was hired to build. They would not be ready until the early part of March 1887.

By then, there were nearly two hundred patients crowded into these small, primitive temporary structures, which were at their maximum capacity. The need for adequate patient wards became a top priority. Soon, a sixth temporary building had to be added.

None of these one-story pavilions had a proper heating system. They were designed for temporary use only, so they had to be heated using stoves protected by wire netting.

Finally, construction had begun on sixteen permanent cottages for patients and employees near the new boulevard in 1888. These cottages were intended to replace the six temporary structures. However, as the cottages began to open and fill up with patients, they quickly became overcrowded.

The six temporary buildings were immediately put to use as backup wards. There were no bathrooms for the men, so they had to walk to the new cottages to bathe. Soon, construction began on new brick buildings because the cottages were filling up too fast. By 1893, there were still 150 patients housed within the temporary buildings, one hundred female and fifty male. It remained so until Buildings A–D opened a year later. These new larger buildings eased the burden of the smaller cottages and temporary buildings, providing some relief to the hospital.

By 1894, the temporary buildings were vacated and ready to be taken down. They were finally demolished by 1896. The wood from these structures was then used to construct other buildings for the hospital.

To the best of my knowledge, there are no known photographs of the temporary buildings; nor do they appear on any map known to me. I was very lucky to learn of their exact location thanks to an old newspaper article from the *Brooklyn Daily Eagle*.

While these temporary buildings are the main buildings known to local historians, there were other structures that were only on the grounds for a short time worthy of note. They were not necessarily temporary, but they did not last once the county farm was established.

In 1898, an old farmhouse formerly belonging to future head farmer Warren W. Conklin was demolished. It was located near the canal and had been built sometime between 1858 and 1873. Another house built around the same time and formerly belonging to Sidney Smith was refurbished to serve as the assistant steward's residence. It remained in use until the early 1930s, and then it was demolished. This house was numbered as the original Building 56.

There was also a very old farmhouse located on the east side of Old Dock Road, which at this time was called the Dairy Road. The house was built prior to 1837 and stood across from where Shanahan's restaurant is currently located. It belonged to

1909 Belcher Hyde map showing hospital property

Capt. John H. Smith, but it was abandoned when the property was

purchased by Kings County in 1885. The house was torn down in 1899 with the help of a squad of patient laborers. Its bricks were recycled by the hospital for other purposes, while the lumber was set aside because it was rotted and useless. The cellar was filled in and covered, erasing any physical trace of this structure.

Based on maps from 1909 to 1917, there was an unknown house on the south side of East Main Street/Route 25A that stood on the site of the current firehouse parking lot, to the east of the railroad station. This may have been part of the former Charles Halleck (Hallock) property that was purchased in 1885. The house was no longer standing when the firehouse was built in 1924. In 1909, a seven-hundred-foot picket fence that stood around the hospital property near the Kings Park Railroad Station was rebuilt. The house mentioned was within this area.

There was also a temporary laundry building and a temporary boiler house for the buildings of Group 1.

The Kings County Farm Cottages

Kill out the Lunatic Asylum and develop the home!
–Dr. John S. Butler (doctor) to Frederick Law Olmsted
(landscape architect), 1872

Veterans' Group donkey
engine on June 8, 1925

By September 16, 1886, Kings County drew up a contract to erect sixteen cottages at the county farm. They were soliciting for a company to do the job, which included providing the materials and erecting a small boiler house with two boilers, as well as a steam-powered donkey engine to be used for logging. Architect Richard B. Eastman designed the cottages and would act as chief architect overseeing the project on site.

On October 7, Alderman James W. Birkett secured the contract for erecting the cottages. Two cottages were to be built at once according to the contract. The contract for the donkey engine and two boilers was awarded to a company by the name of Smith Brothers. The estimated cost of the cottages was $114,400, while the engine and boilers would cost $8,500.

Alderman Birkett hastily promised to complete the first two cottages within three weeks but was unable to fulfill that promise.

In 1888, after two years, the first two cottages of the sixteen that were proposed were finally built to accommodate male and female patients. The next to be ready was a staff house, which was completed at the start of 1889. The other cottages soon followed, and by the end of January, they were fully furnished. Two cottages were reserved for males and females with tuberculosis to isolate them from other patients.

Before the cottages could be occupied, suitable arrangements had to be made to keep them properly heated during the winter. The first boiler house built had to be condemned because of faulty construction work, and a new one had not yet been constructed. It was one of many setbacks.

There was a bathroom on each floor of every cottage with iron bathtubs and porcelain lining. The bathtubs were left filled with water overnight, and pails were stored nearby ready to use in case of a fire. In addition, there were three hand grenades on each floor that could be used for firefighting purposes.

When Kings County started sending patients to occupy these cottages, they sent about thirty to thirty-five at a time on a weekly basis. This was done until the new cottages were fully occupied as a way of gradually easing overcrowded conditions at Flatbush.

The conditions at Flatbush were still over the maximum capacity. The only viable solution was to erect more buildings at the county farm.

An inspection of the sixteen cottages revealed the absence of wire guards on the second stories, which were supposed to have been added. Only two of the cottages were equipped with fire escapes. That would later change as fire escapes would have to be added to each.

These wood-framed cottages were constructed hastily and set upon brick pillars without basements. The fact that there were no basements meant there was no proper ventilation beneath the structures, which caused the wood to deteriorate rapidly. Throughout the winter, dirt constantly washed under the cottages, exposing the steam and water pipes. This caused frequent cold conditions within the cottages. It quickly became clear these cottages were not built to last.

Porches were built on the ground level of each cottage to allow patients to sit outside whenever the weather was pleasant. The porches were equipped with storm shelters, which made it possible to leave windows open on rainy days without fear of water getting inside while also providing shade during sunny days.

Basements were added to most of the cottages by the early 1890s after underground steam tunnels were built. The steam from the tunnels only caused the wood to deteriorate faster. As a result, the basements were fitted with concrete over the next couple of years. In 1906, concrete foundations were added underneath most of the cottages with the exception of Male Cottages 30 (F) and H and the male dining hall. These were left out because of insufficient funding.

While it would have been quite simple to build more cottages as needed, it would have merely been a temporary solution. There was no telling how long it would be before constant repairs would have to be made. The cottages held a

Kings Park Heritage Museum - www.KingsParkMuseum.com

Cottages from the smokestack, circa 1924

limited number of patients and became overcrowded too easily. It was just a matter of time before larger buildings would be needed.

As a solution, Buildings A, B, C, and D were added. The patient capacity of these new structures was much better than the smaller cottages. Patients were gradually relocated to the larger wards until they were filled to capacity. In 1898, the ten additional buildings that formed Group 1 were built to further help with overcrowding.

The times were changing. More patients meant the need for an amusement hall was greater than ever. The female dining hall was converted for this purpose. In 1897, dining rooms were set up throughout the female cottages, where they could dine without the need for venturing outside. This worked out so well, the same was later done with the male cottages, although not until after 1898.

By 1899, most of the hospital's structures were fitted with electricity, fire alarms, new plumbing, bathrooms, and spray baths. More cottages were added. In 1906, many had fly screens installed at a cost of $1,054.20, much to the comfort and satisfaction of the employees and patients, who were sick and tired of mosquitoes and flies. In addition, the locks of most structures were changed to fit one master key. This certainly made it easier than carrying an entire set of keys.

More building groups were added from 1910 to 1915. These became Groups 2–4. By this time, some of the older cottages were in really poor shape with Female Cottage 20 (E) being the worst. In 1909, two coats of white paint were used on twenty of the cottages. That only provided a better appearance. Within a year, the ceilings were dropping down in pieces.

In 1912, wrought iron fire escapes were finally installed on fifteen of the older cottages. Materials were allowed

Employees assigned
to the cottages

to change all doors from opening inward to opening outward for fire safety reasons. Repairs were made whenever feasible, and the cottages were repainted every few years. Concrete steps replaced old wooden stairs leading up to the porches. Four cottages occupied by male patients were rewired from 1919 to 1920.

However, despite any improvements made, it became evident the Kings Park State Hospital could not go on using these old cottages, let alone build new ones. The constructing of buildings at the hospital had gradually undergone a transition from lumber and nails to brick and concrete.

By 1924, the first of the early cottages had been removed with more to follow in the next decade. These first few were mainly the female cottages, although almost all were gone by 1939, clearing the way for larger structures. Only about three cottages lasted until the early 1950s, by which time a new laundry building was built on the same spot.

Some of the remaining cottages were reassigned new building numbers. The following list mainly consists of the male and female cottages.

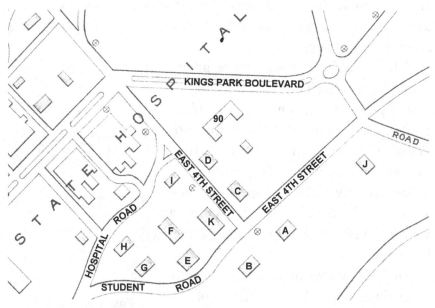

Modified 1923 Belcher Hyde map showing female cottages

Female Cottage A (Cottage 1)

Built from 1888 to 1889, this cottage served as a staff house. It was the third cottage completed, per contract. Also known as Cottage 1 (A), it only housed female employees of the hospital. It was located on the east side of East Fourth Street near the entrance to Student Road.

Staff House A (1), circa 1910-1920s

In 1920, this cottage was renovated and converted into a four-family home. Three new bathrooms were added, providing each suite with its own bathroom.

This cottage was demolished in 1939 so that new cottages could be built as Building 18. (*See Building 18.*)

Female Cottage B (Cottage 17)

This cottage was designated as Cottage 17 (B). Along with Male Cottage 25 (A), it was one of the first two cottages constructed in 1888. Located at the east side of the intersection for East Fourth Street and Student Road, it housed female patients on Ward 17. (*See Male Cottage A.*)

Cottage 17 (B) was condemned in 1939 and demolished soon afterward. Later that year, the site became a parking lot for the newly built cottages of Buildings 18 and 19. (*See Buildings 18 and 19.*)

Female Cottage C (Cottage 18):

Cottage 18 (C) was built from 1888 to 1889 and housed female patients on Ward 18. It stood on the northwest corner of East

Fourth Street and Student Road behind where Macy Home (Building 90) would later be built. (*See Building 90.*)

Cottage 18 (C) was one of the first three cottages to be demolished sometime between 1927 and 1931, after the patients were moved to larger facilities.

Female Cottage C (18)

Female Cottage D (Cottage 19)

Built from 1888 to 1889, Cottage 19 (D) housed female patients on Ward 19. It stood on the north side of East Fourth Street behind Macy Home. In 1897, a dining room and pantry were added. (*See Building 90.*)

This was one of the first three cottages that were demolished between 1927 and 1931.

Female Cottage E (Cottage 20)

This cottage was built from 1888 to 1889, and it housed female patients on Ward 20. It stood on the west side of Student Road and was known as Cottage 20 (E).

In 1897, this cottage was overhauled extensively and partially rebuilt. In

Female Cottage E (20)

1903, an electric diet kitchen was installed. Two years later, rain baths were installed.

This cottage was demolished in 1939, shortly after being condemned.

Female Cottage F (Cottage 21)

Cottage 21 (F) was built from 1888 to 1889, and it housed female patients on Ward 21. It was located near Student Road behind Buildings A and B. New cement steps and a platform were built for it in 1911. (*See Buildings 8 and 9.*)

Female Cottage F (21), as seen from St. Johnland Road, 1925

Female Cottage F (21)

This cottage was demolished sometime between 1927 and 1931, along with Cottages 18 and 19. They were the first of the early cottages to be removed. (*See Female Cottages C and D.*)

Female Cottage G (Cottage 22):

Cottage 22 (G) was built from 1888 to 1889 on the west side of Student Road. It housed female patients on Ward 22.

In 1897, this cottage was overhauled extensively and partially rebuilt. During this time, a dining room and pantry were added. In 1908, this cottage was converted

Female Cottage G (22) & planted trees east of Student Road

and used to treat patients with TB. New cement steps and a platform were added three years later.

After the TB wards of Group 4 were established in 1913, all TB patients were relocated there from the cottages. (*See Building 3.*)

This cottage was demolished in 1939, shortly after being condemned.

Female Cottage H (Cottage 23)

Cottage 23 (H) was built from 1888 to 1889. Located near Student Road behind Building B, it housed female patients on Ward 23. (*See Building 9.*)

In 1897, it was renovated and partially rebuilt. These extensive renovations included the addition of a dining room and pantry. In 1908, this cottage was

Female Cottage H (23) TB Ward, circa 1924

converted for the treatment of female TB patients because additional wards were needed. However, once the new TB wards of Group 4 were completed and opened in 1913, all TB patients were relocated there. (*See Building 3.*)

In 1939, this cottage was condemned and demolished later in the year.

Female Cottage I (Cottage 24)

Built from 1888 to 1889, Cottage 24 (I) was originally used as a hospital cottage for female patients. It was home to Ward 24 and was located near Student Road behind Building A. (*See Building 8.*)

Female Cottage I (24)

In 1897, a dining room and pantry were added. Rain baths were installed in 1905.

Sometime around 1901, this cottage was converted for the treatment of female TB patients, along with Male Cottage 28 (D), which treated males. By 1908, it became necessary to use more cottages for the same purpose. Cottages 22 (G), 23 (H), and 30 (F) were converted into additional TB wards for male and female patients. Fly screens were eventually installed on the windows of all cottages to keep flies and mosquitoes from bringing in more diseases. (*See Male Cottages D and F, and Female Cottages G and H.*)

In 1911, the overcrowding had become so out of control that there were ninety-eight employees sleeping in this cottage, which still housed TB patients at the time. In 1913, a small wood-framed shed was erected behind this cottage for the storage of ward supplies and soiled linen. When improved TB wards at Group 4 opened later that year, all patients with TB were moved there and cleared out of the cottages. (*See Building 3.*)

In 1939, Cottage 24 (I) was condemned, abandoned, and then demolished, along with its shed.

Female Cottage J

This was the first assistant physician's house, also known as the assistant director's residence. Built from 1890 to 1892, this cottage stood on the southeast corner of East Fourth Street and St. Johnland Road. Extensions were added during the next few years with major changes to the interior by the 1950s. It was later renumbered as Building 49. (*See Building 49.*)

In 2000, a fire destroyed most of it, and it was torn down a year later.

Female Cottage K

This was the female dining hall, which later became the amusement hall or assembly hall. It was built in 1889 and located on the south side of East Fourth Street. A concrete foundation was added in 1908, as the building was originally built upon brick pillars. Years later, it was numbered as Building 48. (*See Building 48.*)

Female Cottage K (Dining Hall/Assembly Hall)

Female Cottage K (Dining Hall/ Assembly Hall), circa Feb. 1925

Food was cooked in Building 50, the main kitchen, and delivered here for the first few years. After it ceased to be a dining hall, the food was sent to the female cottages instead, where dining rooms had been established. By 1912, the food for the females was cooked at the nearby kitchen for Buildings A and B. (*See Buildings 38 and 50.*)

This building was demolished at around 1932.

Modified 1923 Belcher Hyde Map showing male cottages

Aerial of male cottages from smokestack, circa Feb. 20,1925

Male Cottage A (Cottage 25)

Cottage 25 (A) was one of the first two cottages to be completed by the end of 1888, along with Female Cottage 17 (B). It housed Ward 25 for male patients and was located on the north side of West

Fourth Street to the west of Kings Park Boulevard. (*See Female Cottage B.*)

In 1905, the stairs were rebuilt. On November 16, 1911, there was a small fire within. A lot of clothing was lost because of this fire, which was not deemed arson.

The cottage was later renumbered as Building 27. It was demolished between 1938 and 1939, prior to the construction of Building 93. (*See Buildings 27 and 93.*)

Male Cottage A (25), circa Feb. 20,1925

Male Cottage B (Cottage 26)

Built between 1888 and 1889, Cottage 26 (B) housed male patients on Ward 26. It was located north of West Fourth Street on the east side of Industrial Road.

Male Cottage B (26), circa 1913

Male Cottage B (26), circa Feb. 20,1925

This cottage was later renumbered as Building 20. It was demolished around 1952–1953, shortly before Building 94 was built at the same location. (*See Buildings 20 and 94.*)

Male Cottage C (Cottage 27)

Cottage 27 (C) was built from 1888 to 1889 and was home to Ward 27. It was located south of West Fourth Street on the east side of Industrial Road.

It was the first of the male cottages to be demolished between 1932 and 1934.

Male Cottage C (27), circa Feb. 20,1925

Male Cottage D (Cottage 28)

Built from 1888 to 1889, this cottage was originally used as a hospital cottage for male patients. Ward 28 was located here. Cottage 28 (D) stood on the south side of West Fourth Street east of Industrial Road. In 1897, a dining room and pantry were provided within.

Male Cottage D (28), circa Feb. 20,1925

By 1901, this cottage was being used to treat male patients with TB, while Female Cottage 24 (I) housed infected female patients. Building 25, the Isolation Cottage, was added as an annex to this cottage and used as a Quarantine Ward. In 1908, new entrance steps and a platform were added to Cottage 28 (D). Additional TB wards were established at three other cottages during the same year because of the growing number of patients with TB. After the Group 4 TB wards opened in 1913, all patients with TB were moved there, freeing up the five male and female cottages for other purposes. (*See Female Cottages G–I, Male Cottage F, and Buildings 3 and 25.*)

Later in 1913, this cottage was renovated into an occupational therapy workshop, along with Cottage 30 (F).

It is very likely Cottage 28 (D) could have later been used to establish the first children's ward. A boys' cottage was established for patients with encephalitis in February 1924. Another cottage was later used for girls. Presumably, these cottages stood near each other, which means the other cottage could have been Cottage 30 (F). If you look closely at the photo of Cottage 28 (D), which was taken in 1925, you can see what appears to be a swing set on the east side of the building.

This cottage remained in place until 1939, when it was condemned and demolished. It had already been abandoned a few years earlier. The children's ward had been relocated around the same time. In 1936, the girls were sent to the new Group 4 buildings, while boys went to Group 2. (*See Buildings 41–43 and 124.*)

Male Cottage E (Cottage 29)

Built from 1888 to 1889, Cottage 29 (E) housed male patients on Ward 29. It was located on the west side of Industrial Road behind Building C. (*See Building 11.*)

In 1897, a pantry and dining room were added. For several years, there was also a staff laundry room in this cottage. This was because the

Male Cottage E (29), 1913

laundry building had become so crowded with equipment that there was no room to establish a separate room for staff use. (*See Building 33.*)

This cottage was later renumbered as Building 14. It was condemned and demolished in 1939. (*See Building 14.*)

Male Cottage F (Cottage 30)

Cottage 30 (F) was built from 1888 to 1889. It housed male patients on Ward 30. It was east of Industrial Road and just north from the rear of Building C. (*See Building 11.*)

This cottage was enlarged in 1897. A pantry and dining room

Male Cottage F (30), circa Feb. 20, 1925

were also added, and a new tin roof was installed the following year. For a short time, this cottage served as an employees' kitchen and dining area until a more suitable structure could be built for that purpose. (*See Building 50.*)

In 1905, a new rain bath was installed. Three years later, new cement steps were built. In the same year, this cottage was converted into a second male ward for TB patients. A sixteen-by-forty-foot sun veranda was added a year later in 1909.

Once the new TB wards of Group 4 were opened in 1913, the cottages previously used to house TB patients were reopened for other purposes, including this cottage. Cottages 28 (D) and 30 (F) both became occupational therapy workshops. (*See Male Cottage D.*)

It is possible this cottage may have been used as a children's ward, along with Cottage 28 (D), from 1924 to 1936.

This cottage was later renumbered as Building 13. In 1939, it was condemned and subsequently demolished. (*See Building 13.*)

Male Cottage G

Built in 1889, this cottage served as the staff house for the males, and it housed male employees. Like the female staff house, there were no patients residing in this house. It stood on the north side of West Fourth Street. In 1906, a one-story extension was added.

Male Cottage G, circa Feb. 20, 1925

According to a map from 1912, this cottage was later numbered as Building 29. In 1913, there was a fire in the kitchen caused by heat from the range stove, which burned the floor and beams beneath it. This cottage was demolished sometime around 1952–1953 to clear the way for construction of a replacement laundry building (Building 94). (*See Buildings 29 and 94.*)

Male Cottage H

This cottage was built from 1895 to 1896 on the west side of the boulevard south from West Fourth Street. It was first used as the acting general superintendent's residence in 1896. Electrical lighting was added that year for his convenience.

Male Cottage H, circa 1924

Male Cottage H during the winter of 1924

Superintendent Oliver M. Dewing used this house during his first few years of residing on the grounds until the Bécar Mansion could be refurbished to serve as his new residence. (*See Building 67.*)

In 1901, Cottage H became the home of the resident steward. Cement steps were constructed in the front and rear in 1908. By the early 1930s, this cottage was numbered as Building 33 after the original laundry building no longer used that number designation. This cottage was demolished a decade later in the early 1940s. (*See Building 33.*)

Male Cottage I (Cottage 31)

Built from 1888 to 1889, Cottage 31 (I) housed Ward 31 and was used for male patients. It stood on the west side of the boulevard behind Cottage 32 (K). In 1908, a garden was established in front, behind the Employees' Clubhouse. A rustic gazebo was built behind Cottage 31 (I). (*See Male Cottage K, Male Cottage I Gazebo, and Building 32.*)

The state hospital had become so overcrowded by 1911 that there were ninety-eight employees sleeping in this cottage despite the new nurses' home that was built a few years earlier. The hospital was in need of a home for attendants, although it would not get one until the creation of the Veterans' Group. (*See Buildings 34, 73, and 144.*)

In 1939, it was condemned and abandoned. It was demolished around the same time that Building 93 was being built. This cottage should not be confused with Building 31, which was the bowling alley. During the 1920s, the bowling alley was built directly in front of this cottage. (*See Buildings 31 and 93.*)

Postcard of Male Cottage I with gazebo

Male Cottage I Gazebo

Built in 1908, this rustic wooden gazebo stood right behind Male Cottage I as a summerhouse for male patients. It was made using cedar poles. It was taken down sometime around 1922–1924.

Male Cottage J

Male Cottage J was the male dining hall built in 1889. It stood on the west side of the boulevard on the future site of Building 93. In 1898, one of its rooms was converted into a laundry for medical officers, since the building was no longer being used as a dining hall. By this time, all of the male cottages had dining rooms established within. (*See Building 93.*)

When this building was built, it was built upon brick pillars. A concrete foundation was not added until 1907–1908.

Male Cottage J (Dining Hall), circa 1924

Originally, food was prepared at Building 50 and delivered here. After it ceased to exist as a dining hall, the food was sent to the cottages. By 1912, the food for males was cooked at the nearby kitchen for Buildings C and D. By this time, this building was numbered as Building 31. (*See Buildings 12, 31, and 50.*)

It was demolished around 1938–1939 for the construction of Building 93.

Male Cottage K (Cottage 32)

Cottage 32 (K) was built from 1895 to 1896 to house male night attendants. It was also home to Ward 32, although there were no patients residing here. It stood just north of Building C in front of where Building 93 was later built on the west side of the boulevard. In 1899, it was converted into the Employees' Clubhouse and numbered as Building 32. It reopened in 1900. Several years later, it was renovated again, this time into a community store. (*See Buildings 11, 32, and 93.*)

It was demolished in 1975.

Hospital Buildings

The sun was prying up the clouds and lighting the brick front of the hospital rose red.

–Ken Kesey (author), *One Flew Over the Cuckoo's Nest,* 1962

Throughout the many years the Kings Park Psychiatric Center has existed, there have been nearly two hundred buildings and cottages built upon the hundreds of acres that make up the property. At first, the majority of buildings were built along what became Kings Park Boulevard until construction efforts began to spread out to other parts of the grounds, changing the landscape in the process.

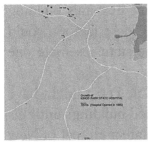  

| 1870s growth of KPSH, created in 2009 by David M. Flynn | 1890s growth of KPSH, created in 2009 by David M. Flynn | 1930s growth of KPSH, created in 2009 by David M. Flynn |

Before new buildings could be constructed, the money for them had to be acquired. Every year, the superintendent submitted an annual report to the state, and in this report, he would make requests for funding to build new structures. Sometimes these requests were approved, while other times they were denied, depending on the state's financial situation. Based on the importance of the buildings, the superintendent might have had to put in his request more than once until such funding was granted.

For example, before Building 83 was built as a firehouse, medical superintendent William A. Macy spent several years requesting funds to build a decent firehouse that could house up to ten firemen and all of the hospital's firefighting equipment. He also had to wait a few years before funds were allowed for the much-needed construction of Groups 2, 3, and 4. The first Group 4 did not get a kitchen building until several years later.

Aside from these requests for extra funding, there was a net amount that was given each year to pay for the regular operations of the hospital. However, it was not nearly enough to cover the construction costs of multiple buildings, which could range from thousands to millions of dollars depending on the era in question.

Once a sufficient amount of funding was granted by the state, arrangements were made usually with the state architect, who designed the many buildings that were then built using different contracting companies with help from a labor force that sometimes included the patients. Very often, other existing hospitals' building plans were used to assist with the design. These factors would explain why many hospital buildings in the state resemble one another.

It is possible that state architect Isaac Gale Perry might have designed some of the earlier state-constructed buildings until his passing in 1904. He is considered the first state architect of New York. A few of the designs he is known for are the New York State Inebriate Asylum, the New York State Armory in Poughkeepsie, and the First National Bank of Oxford, New York. Another state architect of that time was George Lewis Heins, who often worked together with Christopher Grant LaFarge. They are mostly known for their work with the Cathedral of St. John the Divine in Upper Manhattan, which is across the street from St. Luke's Hospital, a hospital founded by Rev. Dr. William A. Muhlenberg, founder of the Society of St. Johnland. Of course, there was also Richard B. Eastman, who served as chief architect during the first years prior to the takeover by the state. He designed almost all of the first cottages and buildings until 1895. Lewis F. Pilcher was the state architect charged with completing Buildings A–D after the state took over.

According to the annual report from 1904, there was a house that was referred to as the Kirby house. James Kirby resided in this house. He was the master of transportation in charge of wagons, carriages, and horses at the main stable. I believe his house was one of the homes located on Upper Dock Road, which were numbered as Buildings 74–77. It is uncertain which one. In 1904, a few rooms in the "Kirby house" had been painted. The house served as Kirby's home from 1890 until sometime after 1904.

Prior to and after the onset of World War I, medical superintendent Macy made numerous requests for new buildings to use as an administration building, an employees' residence, new farm buildings, a firehouse, and more fireproof patient wards. However, from 1916 to 1918, there would not be enough building materials because of conservation for the war effort. Most materials went into making vehicles, weapons, and supplies for the military. This was also the case during the time of the Second World War. During both wars, the hospital suffered from overcrowding that would not be eased soon enough.

Aerial view of the KPSH, circa 1940

In the decades prior to World War II, many new buildings were constructed. The Veterans' Memorial Hospital Unit was added from 1923 to 1932, which included Buildings 125–144 and 147. Buildings 145 and 146 were never built. In the 1930s, there were several other buildings added such as Buildings 1, 3, 15, 18–19, 32, 35–37, 40–44, 53, 62, 65–67, 91, and 93.

Many of these buildings were built as part of the Work Projects Administration (WPA), which was a project created under Pres. Franklin D. Roosevelt's administration. It was the largest and most ambitious American agency in connection with the president's "new deal" policy. It lasted from 1935 to 1943 and, at its peak in 1938, provided employment for three million men and women.

| Smithtown Topographical Geological Survey map, circa 1947 | Aerial photo indicating razed structures from 1960s-1980s, circa 1986 |

Finally, by the 1960s, the overcrowding began to subside, and the need for more buildings became unnecessary. Instead, buildings were gradually being abandoned. Within a decade, all of Group 1 was abandoned and demolished. Buildings A–D would follow shortly afterward.

Eventually, the hospital closed, and most of its buildings were abandoned. Over the past few years, some have been razed. Despite this, many of these old buildings still stand almost like a monument to what has become an unsung part of Long Island's history.

I have managed to uncover as much information as I could in my years of research to find the names, locations, number designations, purposes, and significant dates for mostly every building ever built on the grounds. I even acquired tentative designs for buildings that were never built.

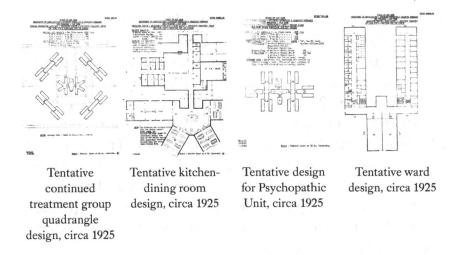

| Tentative continued treatment group quadrangle design, circa 1925 | Tentative kitchen-dining room design, circa 1925 | Tentative design for Psychopathic Unit, circa 1925 | Tentative ward design, circa 1925 |

There are building floor plans that exist, which can be found at the Kings Park Heritage Museum and published in John Leita's 2007 book, *L. I. Asylums Revealed: Kings Park Psychiatric Center.* During my research, I have found many minor errors and inconsistencies on the data sheets of these floor plans, which were printed during the 1960s. When the State of New York Office of General Service originally prepared these floor plans, thorough research was not conducted using the state annual reports. The errors mainly consist of incorrect dates. I have included many of the floor plans in this book. I will provide the data myself, along with a history of each building.

According to the floor plan data sheets for Buildings 123 and 124 of Group 2, the construction dates are incorrectly stated as 1915. This error has been repeated over the years at museums, in the libraries, and on documents. Both of these buildings were completed and opened by the spring of 1912, according to the hospital's annual report, prepared by medical superintendent Macy later that year. He further mentions the use of these "new" buildings in the reports of the years that followed while also indicating any additions made. Group 2 was in fact completed at the same time as Group 3, but the data sheets list Group 3 as being completed first, which does not make sense based on their numbering. It is a documented fact that both groups already had patients in them by late spring of 1912. As further proof, former Group 2 employee Barry Charletta can recall seeing names scratched into the elevator wall of Building 123 that predated 1915.

Another error was the date of construction for Building 78, a house better known as the White House. The data sheet states it was built in 1890. Based on the same annual report mentioned a moment ago, it was built in 1912. There were several houses nearby that were all built in 1890, so perhaps this might have been an innocent mistake. There are several more mistakes as well.

Unfortunately, I could not gain access to as many annual reports as I would have liked. They are difficult to acquire. I tried my best to compensate without them based on a vast collection of detailed maps and aerial photography available to me.

Of course, some maps are incomplete and do not show every structure that existed during the date on the map. This was the case with several small structures that may have been overlooked such as tool sheds, greenhouses, and summerhouses (gazebos).

For several years, information on a few structures eluded me, but a few months prior to the publication of this book, I acquired a useful map from 1912 through my contact, Joe Galante, at the Pilgrim Psychiatric Center Museum. This map filled in the missing pieces of the puzzle, allowing me to match mostly every building with a number while enabling me to understand the chaotic numbering system used over the years.

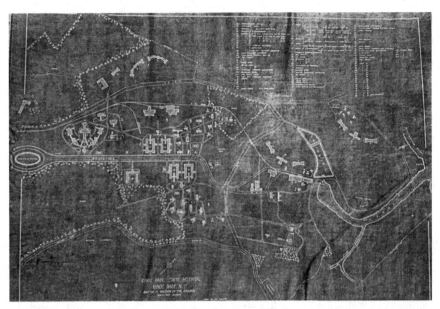

KPSH map, June 1912

Originally, the ward numbers were used to identify the early cottages. Buildings with a specific purpose such as the barge, blacksmith and wheelwright shop, locksmith, or oil house were called by those names. The first numbering system marked each structure in order, from left to right, on the early maps that showed the location of each building. Any buildings already identified by certain numbers were simply marked by said number on later maps. The rest were listed according to how they were spread out across the map. Sometimes numbers were reused to identify other buildings depending on how the map was set up and when those buildings existed.

In many cases, some buildings retained their numbers. A few examples are Buildings 50–52 and 67–71, which have always been identified by the same numbers on every map they appeared on dating back to the 1912. Prior to that, they were identified by their purpose, not numbers. A few buildings were identified using letters. From the 1920s to 1930s, many new buildings were erected, while old ones were removed. As new maps were made, new numbers were assigned to identify the buildings. Occasionally, numbers were reused after they were no longer in use by previous buildings.

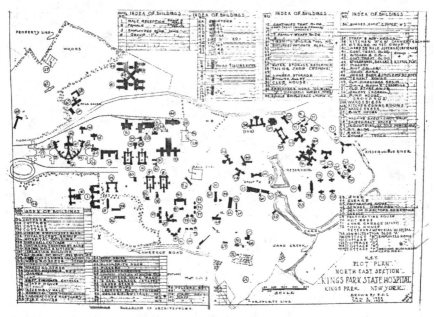

KPSH Key Plot Plan, circa 1954

I created a list to keep track of each building using names, numbers, and letter designations. The list directly follows this chapter. Over the years, it has grown, as I have updated it several times, especially after reading the annual reports and studying various state hospital maps. I have done my best to acquire the most accurate information possible. I feel quite confident with my findings and can assure that this book contains the most complete and accurate list of the

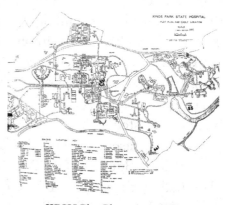

KPSH Plot Plan, circa 1970

hospital's buildings in existence based on the numerous resources at my disposal, including documents, books, maps, photographs, and websites.

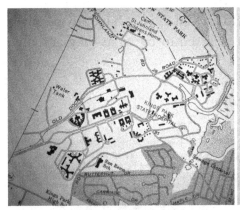 

| Smithtown Geological Survey map, circa 1972 | Smithtown Geological Survey map, circa 1979 |

Although the majority of buildings are gone now, there are still more than fifty structures standing. Most of these are abandoned and closed to the public. Some await their demise.

Throughout the buildings are rusted gurneys, beds, cabinets hanging off the walls, dishwashing machines, dusty old lockers, fallen ceiling tiles, graffiti-covered walls with chipping paint, piles of stacked chairs, outdated medical equipment, smashed bathroom sinks, cracked mirrors, broken windows, pieces of pipe insulation and covering, leftover clothing, paintings, murals, beer cans and bottles, and scattered documents and paperwork soaked in rainwater, beer, or urine.

The oldest surviving structure dates back to the 1890s. It was initially used as a pumping station for the wells, which fed water to the main pump house, Building 60. This particular structure never had a number to my knowledge. Because of its proximity to the boathouse, it has been listed as Building 55.1.

As you read this chapter, keep in mind there will be buildings that can be identified by more than one number. Rather than repeat the full description and history for both numbers, I will only describe the building in great detail once. If a building is mentioned again, I will briefly describe it and refer you to its more commonly used building number.

First, I have listed the structures that did not have any number designations and were mainly referred to by what they actually were.

Bandstands and Music Pavilion

A rather simple-looking music pavilion was erected near the amusement hall in 1897. It was used for outdoor performances to entertain the patients.

In 1906, two octagon-shaped wooden rustic bandstands were built. One was on the north side of East Fourth Street across

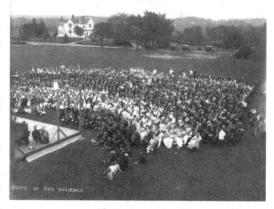

An audience at the music pavilion with 49 in background

from the amusement hall, and the other was on the west side of the boulevard just south of West Fourth Street near the steward's house. Female patients generally used the one near the amusement hall, while the other was mainly for men. Lighting was installed on the female bandstand on the same year it was built. Lighting was not added to the male bandstand until a year later.

These structures did not have number designations. They were all demolished by 1925.

The Barge

The barge was located at the marina along Canal Road. Originally just a flatbed barge, it is quite similar to those first used as early as the late 1800s for transporting coal via the canal to the power plant's boiler house and also for the transportation of building materials used for the construction of the earliest buildings. This was before the hospital's railroad spur was built.

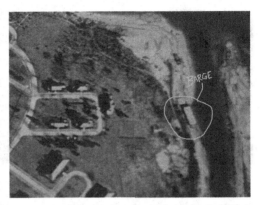

Aerial photo of the beached barge from March 1962

As of the late 1950s, this particular barge lay beached along the south bank of the canal. At one time, it belonged to Grumman, a company well known for its work in aviation. For several years, it remained a forgotten, dirty, and smelly wreck.

On August 8, 1966, the Nissequogue Yacht Club/Kings Park State Hospital Employees Inc. purchased it for the sum of $300. This was a separate club from the boat club that used the boathouse. The barge was cleaned up and moved to its longtime location at Jones Point across the canal from the boathouse. Within that first year, a fabulous clubhouse was built onto the deck. (*See Building 55.*)

The yacht club used the barge clubhouse exclusively for several years. It was beautifully decorated on the inside. It included a full-sized kitchen, a bathroom, a fancy wraparound bar, an icemaker, and a dance floor. Many private functions were held here.

The barge, circa 2000s

The interior facing toward the bow, courtesy of Dave Rockenberry

The interior facing the stern, courtesy of Dave Rockenberry

Blackboard messages in the barge, courtesy of Dave Rockenberry

After the hospital closed, the yacht club continued to use the barge clubhouse until the Office of Mental Health became aware of the activities. The yacht club argued that they had every right to use the barge they purchased, while the state claimed it was on their land and off limits. The fight was taken to court, where a judge closed down the yacht club permanently to avoid any further issues.

Park employee near the entrance
of the barge on May 11, 2011

Looking at the barge from
the pier, circa May 2011

View showing the battered
condition of the barge from 2011

The road to the barge is closed
during Dec. of 2011

The abandoned barge became a part of the Nissequogue River State Park by default when that side of the hospital where the canal and boat basin are located was turned over to the New York State Office of Parks, Recreation and Historic Preservation.

For a while, the barge was still in use by the park. When Hurricane Sandy struck in the fall of 2012, it caused some damage to the structure. By the end of January 2013, a demolition crew finished the job.

Demolition vehicles near the
barge on Jan. 23, 2013

Demolition of the barge in Jan. 2013

Former location of the barge
from the pier on Sept. 15, 2014

Facing north toward the former site
of the barge on Sept. 15, 2014

Bird Watching Shelter

This one-story, three-sided, wood-framed structure with a slanted roof was added soon after the Nissequogue River State Park opened in 2005. It stands along the old Pickle Road on the south side of the former upper reservoir, now a bird sanctuary.

Facing east on Pickle Road toward the bird watching shelter, 2013

Bird watching shelter on Aug. 31, 2013

Blacksmith and Wheelwright Shop

The first blacksmith and wheelwright shop was constructed in 1896 using lumber recovered from the original temporary buildings. It stood behind the electric heating plant. There are no photos of this structure. It only lasted five years before it was demolished and replaced by a new shop. (*See Building 59.*)

Aerial photo from 1931 showing recently cleared rectangular patch of land at the center of the image

In 1901, the second blacksmith and wheelwright shop was built to replace the first. It was a corrugated iron structure that was also located in the same area. This structure might have stood a little further east in the woods. There is a rectangular empty patch of land that can be seen in an aerial photo from 1931, which was eventually used for a tennis court.

This shop was moved to a new location near the new power plant, Building 6, in 1915. This third blacksmith and wheelwright shop was numbered as Building 36. (*See Buildings 6 and 36.*)

Garbage Burning House

According to the hospital's annual report from 1907, there was a small structure that was utilized as a garbage house. The tinsmith shop built it in 1901. It is unknown exactly where this small structure was located, but it was likely somewhere near the barge at Jones Point. That area was used as a dumping ground during the early years. Once the sewage disposal plant was built at that location during the 1930s, there was no need for any garbage burning houses or dumping grounds.

Years later, there were actually several locations that became secret dumping grounds for the hospital. One such area is located in the woods across from the Potter's Field Cemetery. There were other piles near every group of buildings. Occasionally, after a building was demolished, a pile of furniture and rubble was left behind. This was the case with Building 2 and some of the older structures. Today, there are still scattered piles of junk hidden in the woods around the grounds. (*See Building 2.*)

Remains of an abandoned car behind the laundry building in 2008, courtesy of Max Neukirch, Jr.

The same car from a different angle, courtesy of Max Neukirch, Jr.

Another pile of junk, circa 2008, courtesy of Max Neukirch, Jr.

A pile of junk in the woods near the cemetery road on Nov. 7, 2011

Garbage Storage Shed

This is one of the smallest structures on the entire complex. It was a one-story concrete storage shed with a bunker-like cellar that was only accessible from an opening on its east side. It was built sometime around 1923–1931, in connection with the Veterans' Memorial Hospital Unit, and used for storing garbage. (*See Building 73.*)

Only the cellar remains today. It can be found along the upper portion of the Greenbelt Trail in the wooded area behind Building 132, slightly to the south.

Aerial view of Veterans' Group, circa 1947

Concrete cellar on May 11, 2016   Interior of concrete cellar

Locksmith

This was a small structure built in approximately 1890–1892. It stood at the rear of the male dining hall. It was demolished around 1938–1939 for the construction of Building 93. The locksmith shop was relocated to Building 57 and then to Building 5 during the mid-1950s. (*See Male Cottage J and Buildings 5, 57, and 93.*)

Oil House

Built from 1908 to 1909, this building was located near the main power plant area next to the soap house. It was used to store oil drums. To my knowledge, this particular oil house did not have a number designation, although it might have been a replacement for the original Building 65. It was one of several oil houses to exist. (*See Buildings 6, 7, and 65.*)

Oil house with Building 57 in the background, circa 1925

One of the earlier oil houses was Building 65, according to a map from 1912. It was built around 1890 and removed sometime before 1915. There was also an oil house numbered as Building 21, which was built from 1905 to 1906. Most of the oil houses were demolished by 1935 after the construction of a new storehouse (Building 44). (*See Buildings 21 and 44.*)

Nissequogue River State Park Guardhouse

When the Nissequogue River State Park was established in 2000, this small one-story wood-framed structure with a gable roof was built to serve as a guardhouse at the entrance of the park. It is located on the boulevard just north of St. Johnland Road at the center of the road between north and southbound traffic.

During normal park seasons from summer until fall, there is a park employee posted inside. It is free to enter on foot, and there are no fees for vehicles during the winter and spring. However, during the summer and fall, vehicles must pay a fee to enter.

The guardhouse on May 3, 2011   The guardhouse on Aug. 3, 2012

Reservoir Valve Box Houses

From 1896 to 1897, the dam near the upper reservoir was rebuilt, and a one-story brick valve box shed was added on the west wall of the dam that now supports the boulevard road. The shed basically consists of three brick walls and a concrete slab for a cover. When this reservoir was no longer in use, this structure was abandoned.

The upper reservoir valve box, circa 1920s

The same area in 2010

The reservoir valve box
on April 19, 2016

In 1905, the area around the lower reservoir was graded extensively to make it much higher. This valve box was built soon afterward at the top of the access stairs on the northern side of the reservoir, which was located on the boulevard just north of Flynn Road. It was roughly a ten-by-ten-square foot one-story wood-framed building with a hip roof. It did not have a number designation.

By the mid-1920s, it was abandoned and filled with dirt. The valve box house was removed sometime after 1931. An oval-shaped grassy field was created in its place. The flagpole was set at the center, where it stood proudly for many years. Soon, a signpost was also added with a map of the hospital buildings.

Today, the field is fairly empty.

Lower reservoir valve box house   The former site of the lower
                                                    reservoir, as seen on June 20, 2016

Steamroller Garage

In 1905, a shed was built to store the hospital's steamroller. The location was not mentioned in the annual report of that year, but there were several small garages that existed near Industrial Road. This could have been one of them. It might have also been located near the main stable east of the boulevard on the north side of St. Johnland Road.

It was no longer necessary by 1939 after a long truck garage was built. (*See Building 62.*)

Stenographer's House

This was a house on the bluff that was built in 1890 on the other side of Upper Dock Road from the hospital grounds. It belonged to the superintendent's stenographer, who, at one time, was a woman named Mrs. Ash. It appears on a 1920s blueprint of the Kings Park State Hospital. However, it must have been either sold or torn down by the 1930s because it is no longer included on any other map.

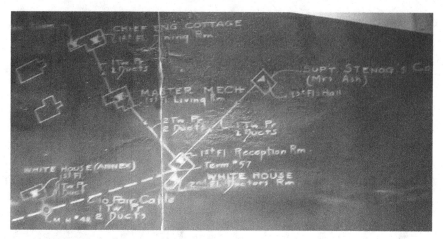

Blueprint showing the stenographer's house

Superintendent's Greenhouse

There was once a small greenhouse in the same area of the first superintendent's residence on the west side of the boulevard. It never had a number designation. Constructed in 1896, it was the very first greenhouse to be erected on the grounds. (*See Male Cottage H.*)

Unfortunately, it burned to the ground at around 12:30 a.m. on December 10, 1898. At the time, there was no fire department or alarms set in place. An overheated furnace supposedly caused the fire.

The fire prompted superintendent Dewing to take measures against another such incident occurring. Within a year, there was a new fire alarm system installed on the grounds.

Temporary Laundry

After a fire occurred at the laundry building in 1906, two small houses about eight-foot square in size were built near Wards 45 and 48 of Group 1 to store soiled clothing. In January 1907, temporary laundry facilities constructed of boards and tar paper were hastily set up at the cost of $11,066.34. That price did not include any additions, extensions, or laundering equipment. Inside were six double-geared metallic washers, eight washtubs, and four centrifugal extractors. An old 25-horsepower engine that was not being used had been installed to operate this machinery. Just to be on the safe side, ten fire extinguishers were also placed within this structure. (*See Buildings 33, 45.1, and 48.1.*)

Once Building 5 was completed in 1910 to take over as the new laundry building, this temporary structure was abandoned and removed. Its location was never mentioned on the annual reports, and it does not appear on any maps during that time. It was likely located near the old laundry building. (*See Building 5.*)

Watchman's Gatehouse

In 1897, a small gatehouse was built at the entrance to the boulevard near East Main Street/ Route 25A on the east side of the road. It was used for the boulevard watchman as a sort of guardhouse. This structure was painted in 1904.

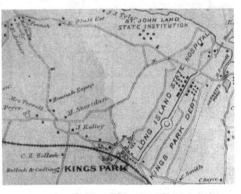

West Sayville Maritime Museum map, ca 1897, showing Watchman's house

In 1925, a new fire alarm was placed outside of this structure. It was demolished by 1930. There are no known photographs of it, but it can be seen on a map from 1897.

Building 1

Building 1 served as the male patient reception building and was located on the east side of Kings Park Boulevard at the south side of East Third Street. Construction began in April 1930 and lasted until sometime in 1931. There was still improvement work being done inside and around the building until the summer of 1933. The building finally opened for patients in 1934. This two-story brick building with a basement housed Wards 93–100 in four long wings as part of Group 5. A dentist office was located here as well. There was an elevator at the rear central portion of the building. A tunnel in the basement connected this building to the kitchen section of Building 2. (*See Building 2.*)

Building 1 during the summer of 1993

Maintenance on Building 1, not long after its construction, Aug. 7, 1933

BASEMENT FLOOR PLAN
BUILDING NO. 1

KINGS PARK STATE HOSPITAL
DEPARTMENT OF MENTAL HYGIENE

Building 1 floor plan (basement)

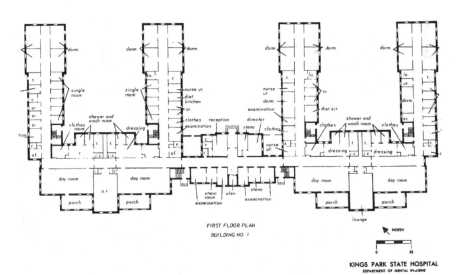

FIRST FLOOR PLAN
BUILDING NO. 1

NORTH
0   32

KINGS PARK STATE HOSPITAL
DEPARTMENT OF MENTAL HYGIENE

Building 1 floor plan (first floor)

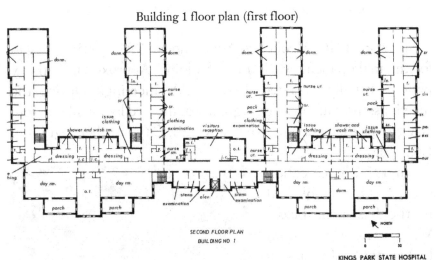

SECOND FLOOR PLAN
BUILDING NO. 1

NORTH
0   32

KINGS PARK STATE HOSPITAL
DEPARTMENT OF MENTAL HYGIENE

Building 1 floor plan (second floor)

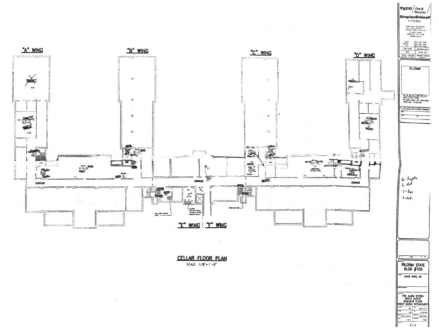

Map indicating locations of fire alarms in the basement of newly
renumbered "Building 700" of Pilgrim State Psychiatric Center

In April 1946, Alcoholics Anonymous (AA) meetings began
for the male patients within this building. Approximately thirty
patients usually attended these weekly meetings. During the
meetings, the patients were regularly addressed by members from
AA groups that came in from New York City or other regions of
Long Island.

In 1953, a recreation area was established in the basement below Ward 94. This room had a pool table and a ping-pong table. Patients and employees would sometimes play against each other.

The storage shed behind Building
1 on April 16 2013

By the 1980s, this building only admitted male patients from Huntington and Smithtown.

After the rest of the hospital was shut down in 1996, this building was used to house patients until they could later be transferred to the nearby Pilgrim Psychiatric Center. Known as the Residence by the Sound, it was later turned into a group home and halfway house for chronic patients. It became Building 700 of Pilgrim Psychiatric Center.

It was around this time when a wooden shed was erected behind the building. It was used to store grounds-keeping tools, athletic equipment, and other typical backyard necessities.

During the last few years that Building 1 was open, it had one of the only active parking lots on the vastly abandoned hospital grounds. It was accessible by public transportation. A bus stop was located along the boulevard entrance to the parking lot. Since being abandoned, use of this bus stop was discontinued.

Cars in the parking lot on June 22, 2010   The Residence by the Sound
                                             sign on April 16, 2013

I am proud to say this is the only building that I ever had the luck of visiting while patients were still being housed here. Although it was a very short visit, I was able to see patients walking around inside and in front of the building. I even had a brief casual conversation with an elderly male patient. He seemed quite friendly and told me that he loved going to the beach.

Building 1 housed patients until closing in November 2012. The Department of Environmental Conservation (DEC) had plans to take over the building, but those plans fell through, and the building was abandoned.

There were security cameras actively monitoring the front, rear, and interior of the building. They relayed signals to monitors located inside of the building. At night, the interior lights used to remain on, which helped keep trespassers away.

In the early part of 2013, there was talk of renovations for governmental use, but once more, that never happened. Soon, the lights were no longer turned on, and the cameras stopped working. Trespassers began to take over. It was the beginning of the end for this building.

Building 1 from the parking lot on March 27, 2013

Shelter in front of Building 1 on April 16, 2013

The entrance of Building 1 on April 16, 2013

Facing west in front of Building 1 on April 16, 2013

The handicapped side door of
Building 1 on April 16, 2013

The rear door of Building
1 on April 16, 2013

As time goes by, its condition has worsened because of constant vandalism. Any possibility of reusing this building quickly slips away with time. In less than a year of it being abandoned, vandals had literally destroyed the interior of this building. I have included several photos of the interior while it still looked presentable.

A patient seating area at the rear
porch of Building 1 on April 16, 2013

Peeking into the backdoor
window on April 16, 2013

Second floor ward on Feb. 7, 2015

Building 1 hallway on Feb. 7, 2015

The kitchen area on Feb. 7, 2015   Basement corridor on Feb. 7, 2015

This was not the first building to be listed as Building 1. According to a state hospital map from 1912, the first building identified as Building 1 was actually the piggery. Before it was built, the pigs were kept in sheds. The piggery was built from 1897 to 1898.

It was later renumbered as Building 45. (*See Building 45.*)

Building 2

Building 2 was the female patient reception building. Construction began in 1919 on the first building of the future Group 5. There was a delay with the completion because of the laying of the linoleum. The building would not be opened until 1923. This three-story E-shaped Georgian Revival brick building was designed to house up to two hundred acute female patients in need of long-term care. It had four three-story white wooden columns at the front central portion of the building and balconies on the upper floors that faced the front. There was also an attic and a basement. The roof had a hip roof design. An elevator was situated at the rear section of the building, and handicap ramps in the west wing went from the basement up to the third floor. While a few other buildings had exterior handicapped ramps, this was the only building to have such ramps on the inside with access to each floor. This building stood behind Building 1 east of the boulevard on the north side of East Second Street. It housed Wards 66–71.

Building 2 was very similar in design to a new group of buildings that were constructed around the same time at Central Islip State Hospital.

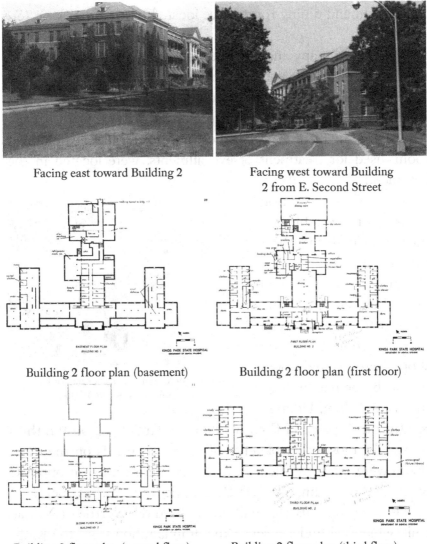

Facing east toward Building 2

Facing west toward Building 2 from E. Second Street

Building 2 floor plan (basement)

Building 2 floor plan (first floor)

Building 2 floor plan (second floor)

Building 2 floor plan (third floor)

In the beginning, food was prepared in another nearby building and brought over to Building 2, but in 1930, a full kitchen extension was added at the rear of the building, while a home economics room was established on the second floor. A connection was made to its neighbor, Building 1, through the basements via an underground tunnel. Afterward, Building 2 served as the kitchen and dining area for the female and male patients of Group 5. Both the kitchen and dining room were located on the first floor. (*See Building 1.*)

Different therapy and treatment rooms were located down in the basement. There was a room for hydrotherapy, which was across from the electrotherapy room. About ten large tubs were located on the second floor for prolonged baths, but they were removed by the 1930s. An x-ray room and an ophthalmic treatment room, used for treatment of eye ailments, were located in the basement.

In 1957, recreation areas were established on the second and third floors. A library and classroom were also located on the third floor, along with occupational therapy rooms. Beauty shops were located down in the basement and on the second floor. Doctors

Photo looking at the upper balconies of Building 2, circa 1960s-1980s

resided on the second floor, while attendants lived on the third floor. Like most other patient buildings, the wards on the three floors were arranged identically. There were wards on opposite wings of the building on each floor aside from the basement.

During the 1960s, this building housed the Northeast Nassau Unit, which fell under a separate administration from the Kings Park State Hospital. The unit had a separate director and staff.

By 1983, this building was vacant. It was then used for firefighting practice by the hospital's Safety Department. Its charred remains were soon demolished around 1984–1985. The rubble was buried on the exact same spot where the building stood, which was common practice. All that remained was an empty space on the grass where it once stood and the underground tunnel that still connects to Building 1, although access to Building 2 has been sealed off.

Building 2 firefighter
practice, circa 1980s

FD "cherry picker" ladder at second
floor of Building 2, circa 1980s

Rear of Building 2, after the fire

West side of Building 2, after the fire

Looking into three broken windows

Another photo showing fire
damage to Building 2

As with Building 1, there was another Building 2 before this one was built. The original Building 2 was the first dairy barn, also referred to as the cow barn. It was erected in 1889, although this structure does not appear on any maps until 1909. It was mentioned in an annual report from 1896, in which it is referred to as the stockyard barn.

Panoramic view of dairy barn, circa 1913

| Cows in the dairy barn, circa 1910s | Dairy barn interior, circa 1910s | Inside the slaughterhouse, circa 1910s |

Over the next few years, there were additional structures built adjacent to the larger cow barn. Based on the annual report from 1896, a large brick-and-cement cistern was built at the dairy farm next to the cow barn for the storage of water. In 1897, a slaughterhouse was the next structure to be added next to the cow barn, along with a large shed suitable to be used as a stable. Inside the slaughterhouse was a 25-horsepower engine that was used to cut feed and grind bones. In 1898, a galvanized water tank and a new silo were added. The new water tank replaced the cistern, which was then removed. There are no photos of it. Another silo was added at the end of 1901, along with an extension to the cow barn, adding several more accommodations for cows. By 1902, five new automatic watering devices were installed at the barn. In 1910, the wood floor on the second floor of the barn, which was in very poor condition by this time, was repaired. The roof of the barn was repaired in 1912 after being struck by lightning.

In 1940, a new dairy barn was constructed to replace this one after these structures were all destroyed by fire earlier in the year. (*See Building 47.*)

Building 3

Building 3 was originally used to identify the first Group 4 buildings, where the tuberculosis wards were located, as Buildings 3A–C. These initial three structures were one-story wood-framed buildings with attics built from 1912 to 1913 and housed Wards 60–65. New awnings were added in 1915. Each building accommodated approximately two hundred patients and mainly consisted of female patients. A kitchen and dining hall brick building and small storage house next to it were built from 1922 to 1923. The ten-year delay was mainly due to state funding of the war effort during World War I.

TB Cottages facing north to the LI Sound, circa 1913-1915

TB Cottages, circa 1913-1915

TB Cottages & pumpkin
field on Sept. 10, 1917

Eventually, these infectious patients were relocated to a more appropriate facility at Central Islip State Hospital. After these buildings were abandoned, the current Building 3 acquired the number. From 1932 to 1934 the original Group 4 was demolished and replaced by the current Group 4 buildings. (*See Buildings 41–43.*)

Patients at Ward 60, circa June 1915

Tubercular Ward, circa 1910s

TB Wards kitchen, circa 1920

Dining room, circa 1910s

The replacement Building 3 is a two-story rectangular brick building with a basement and an attic, which was built from 1931 to 1934. The roof is a slate hip roof Georgian Revival surmounted by two white-louvered cupolas. The front and rear entrances are both similar in design. Known as Home U, this building was added to Group 5 to serve as an administrative building for the group. Offices for the Employee Assistance Program (EAP), Civil Service Employees Association Union (CSEA), Public Employees Federation Union (PEF), general information, and management were located within.

Building 3 under construction on July 3, 1931

Building 3 nursing administrative offices

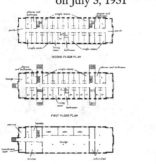

Building 3 floor plans

Boulevard sign for Buildings 1 & 3 on June 22, 2010

It still stands across from Building 1 on the north side of East Third Street, partially covered by trees. Both buildings are abandoned.

Building 3 from parking
lot on Jan. 23, 2013

Building 3 on Jan. 23, 2013

Building 3 west entrance
on April 16, 2013

Building 3 east entrance
on April 16, 2013

East side of Building 3 on July 30, 2013

Basement room on April 16, 2013

Building 4 (Group 1/Buildings 4A–L/Buildings 111–120)

This was not a single building but an entire group of buildings called Group 1. It was the first group of buildings built after the state took over. They were designated as Buildings 4A–J but were also later numbered as Buildings 111–120. They were built from 1897 to 1898 on the west side of Kings Park Boulevard using the

Kirkbride Plan. At the time, most state hospitals were using the popular building plan. The majority of buildings in this group were connected, forming a semicircle with the main administrative offices of the group at the center, facing the boulevard. This group consisted of Wards 41–49, also called Cottages 41–49. After these buildings were built, many employees simply referred to them as the Group. (*See Buildings 111–120.*)

No. 9—West End of Group, Kings Park State Hospital, N. Y.   T. J. McCARTHY

Postcard of Group 1 facing north, by T.J. McCarthy

This group of buildings had two summerhouse gazebos, which were designated as Buildings 4K and 4L. The first of these rustic gazebos was built in 1901. Seating was made available for patients and employees to enjoy the outdoors while protected by shade. It was located in a grove near west side of the boulevard north of the group's administration building. In 1908, the second gazebo was built in the grove next to Building 119 (4I), which housed Ward 48. Both were removed shortly before Building 15 was built in 1939. (*See Building 15.*)

Summerhouse 4K, circa 1905   Summerhouse 4L, circa 1913

Group 1 was abandoned by the mid-1960s and burned down by vandals in 1972. The skeletal remains of the group were eventually demolished by the mid-1970s, leaving behind only an empty patch of land in their place.

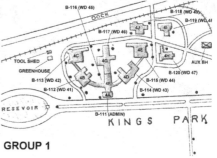

Aerial photo of Group 1   Modified Belcher Hyde map from 1906
from April 30, 1972   indicating the structures of Group 1

Buildings 16 and 17 would have been larger patient ward buildings meant to replace them, but they were never built. To this day, nothing has ever been built on this site. (*See Buildings 16 and 17.*)

Building 4.1

Built in the late winter of 1900–1901, this was a small temporary boiler house with four small iron smokestacks. It was hastily built using flimsy boards covered with tar paper to surround a boiler plant that would serve as an auxiliary boiler house for the buildings of Group 1 because the heating plant was too far away to adequately supply heat. It stood north of the group where the south wing of Building 15 is now located. Within a year of its construction, the railroad spur was extended to reach it, and a wooden trestle was erected. Both were completed by 1902. (*See Building 4.*)

During the first year or so, there was a considerable amount of difficulty keeping this building from flooding whenever there were heavy rains. The building had to be properly sealed and protected from such further occurrences; hence, the boards and tar paper were added to protect the boiler from the weather. In 1903, drains were put in to avoid flooding.

A year later, repairs were made to the four iron smokestacks, and a new addition was added to make room for two old boilers from the main boiler house. The building was enlarged again by the next year. In 1907, the four high temperature (HT) boilers were retubed, and the fireboxes for each were repaired. Within two years, a new 150-horsepower horizontal tubular boiler was purchased, replacing the two older 100-horsepower boilers that came from Building 59. The walk along the trestle was also extended during the same year, and an extension bell was installed. (*See Building 59.*)

Despite all the work put into it, this boiler house was removed in 1912. Once Building 6 became fully operational as the new power plant in 1910, it was no longer necessary to maintain an extra boiler house. The new tubular boiler was transferred to the boiler house of Building 6. The trestle and the portion of the spur that extended to the auxiliary boiler house were removed sometime later. There are no known photographs of the Group 1 boiler house. The only information available came from numerous annual reports of the hospital starting with 1901 and ending with 1912. I have indicated its location on the previous modified Belcher Hyde map. (*See Building 6.*)

Building 4.2

This was a small structure used to store a fire hose reel, which was located at Group 1. It was built in 1901. It was likely removed in 1925 after a firehouse was built. (*See Buildings 4 and 83.*)

Building 4.3

In 1906, a small greenhouse was built west of the boulevard and lower reservoir in the lower garden, which was situated in the hollow on the south side of West Second Street south of Group 1. It became known as the lower greenhouse. It stood directly across from Building 113 (4C), which housed Ward 42. In 1899, a chimney was built for the greenhouse. In 1908, a new bench was added, and the greenhouse was reglazed and painted. (*See Buildings 4 and 113*)

This greenhouse only appears on two maps from 1917 to 1947. Its location is indicated in the previous modified Belcher Hyde map. The lower garden is only barely noticeable in aerial photography from 1927, while the greenhouse cannot be seen at all. It was demolished between 1947 and 1950. There are no known photos of this structure.

This greenhouse did not have an official number designation, so I assigned one for the purpose of easier identification.

Building 4.4

This was a small wood-framed toolhouse that was located in the lower garden south from Group 1. Built around 1898, it stood next to the lower greenhouse. It was demolished either in the later part of 1908 or in the early part of 1909. By 1909, a new toolhouse had replaced it. (*See Buildings 4, 4.3, and 4.5.*)

Building 4.5

This was a small sixteen-by-thirty-nine-foot brick toolhouse. It replaced the wooden toolhouse in the lower garden, which was south of Group 1. Its location has been indicated in the previous modified Belcher Hyde map. It was built in 1909 next to the lower greenhouse using bricks from the fire-damaged laundry building. It had a small bathroom. (*See Buildings 4, 4.3, and 33.*)

It was likely demolished around 1947–1950.

Building 5

Building 5 was a one-and-a-half-story brick building built from April 1909 to 1910 to replace the original laundry building after a fire destroyed much of it in 1906. Its windows were segmental arch designs with articulated brick openings. It was located on the west side of Industrial Road between Old Dock Road and Kings Park Boulevard. Its construction was delayed because of faulty bricks that were used. According to the contract, it should have been completed in a few months' time, but that was not the case. (*See Building 33.*)

Looking toward Building 5 from Industrial Road, circa 1930s

Building 5 from the same angle, circa 1970s

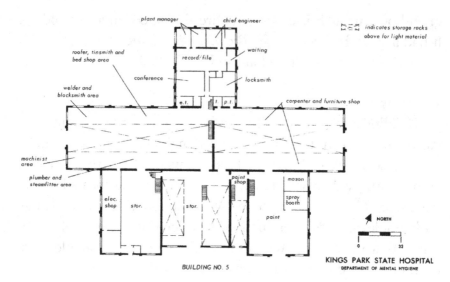

Building 5 floor plan

Before construction even began, there was a temporary laundry building that was being used for about two years. It was located near Group 1. Once Building 5 was completed, this temporary laundry was removed, and all of its machinery and equipment were transferred to the new laundry building.

There were rumors that this building was once a temporary power plant. Based on the information from over forty annual reports, which include the planning and early construction of this building, it is safe to say these rumors are false.

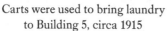

Carts were used to bring laundry to Building 5, circa 1915

Piles of laundry on June 2, 1925

An increase in the amount of
laundry is evident on July 26, 1949

Laundry washing room,
circa 1910s-1920s

Laundry washing room on June 2, 1925

Clothes were hung to dry
in the drying room

Cabinet dry room on June 2, 1925

Clean laundry sorting room, circa 1920

The ironing room

Posing for a photo, while
the irons heat up

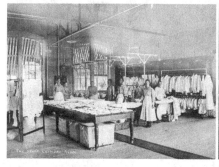

Staff ironing room

Flatwork ironers on June 2, 1925

Sorting out the laundry, so it can
be picked up and sent to wards

Maintenance employees outside
Building 5, circa 1920s

Building 5 was used as the laundry building for nearly forty-five years. Sometime around 1953, there was a terrible fire in the sorting room. There were no serious injuries, but the room was gutted. This was during the same year Building 5 was replaced by a new laundry building. (*See Building 94.*)

Building 5 was converted into several different maintenance and engineering workshops that were once located in much older buildings. These workshops included a blacksmith, locksmith, tinsmith, carpentry, paint shop, masonry, plumbing, electrical, and the offices of the chief engineer and plant manager. The interior was rehabilitated from 1967 to 1968. By 1978, the building was more commonly known as the Lock Shop. Supplies were also stored here on the second floor.

Maintenance employees outside Building 5, circa 1957

Rear of previous photo listing names of employees in photo, circa 1957

Hospital truck parked in the garage

Hospital truck in Building 5

Inside the old laundry building　　　　Stacked crates & shelves

File cabinets　　　　　　　　Two employees hard at work

Years later, the building was converted once more, but this time into a wood shop. A new addition was added in 1988. Another one was added between 1990 and 1992, along with a nearby storage pyramid for storing sand and salt. (*See Building 5.1.*)

Aerial photo from March 6, 1988　　　　Aerial photo from March 4, 1990
showing a new addition

Toward the end of the hospital's run, this building was where the building planners worked. Outside contracts were managed here as well. At one time, all old building plans, blueprints, and hospital maps were kept here. Today, the building is pretty much empty.

After a study was conducted in 2002, it was proposed to use this building as an extension to the Kings Park Heritage Museum with access from both Orchard and Industrial Roads. It did not happen.

The steam tunnel beneath it goes south past Building 15 and leads to a dead-end tunnel from the old Group 1 buildings. It also used to go north to the steam pipe junction room, but that structure was demolished in 2012. However, a tunnel still leads to Building 93. (*See Buildings 4, 6, 15, and 93.*)

Building 5 as seen from Building 93 on March 27, 2013

Building 5 on May 11, 2011

The Hike & Bike Trail sign on Sept. 9, 2011

Puddle on the south side of Building 5 on Nov. 7, 2011

The old workshop on Oct. 24, 2011   Daytime view of an old
workshop on April 17, 2016

Rusted metal storage shelves   Drawer filled with screws, nails, &
on Oct. 24, 2011   other misc. items on Oct. 24, 2011

Building 5.1 (Salt Shed/Sand Pyramid)

The salt shed, or sand pyramid, was used to store sand/salt to use during the wintertime when the roads became icy. It was added sometime around 1990–1992 near the parking lot for Building 5 where the workshops were located. (*See Building 5.*)

Sand pyramid

Aside from a large pile of dirt, it stood empty for many years. It was finally demolished by the end of August 2012.

Sand pyramid on May 11, 2011

Interior of the sand pyramid, circa April 2011

Looking up toward the   Former site of the sand
ceiling, circa April 2011   pyramid on Sept. 5, 2012

Building 6

This structure was the second power plant to be utilized on the hospital grounds. Built from 1908 to 1910, it was a one-story brick building with a flat built-up roof. It replaced the heating plant (Building 59), which was too distant from most of the buildings. At the time, the majority of buildings were south of St. Johnland Road. It became necessary for a new power plant with a more centralized location that could easily supply power and heat to all of the buildings. Building 6 was constructed east of Old Dock Road, along the railroad spur tracks and across from where Group 4 would be built on the west side of Industrial Road. It was superintendent William A. Macy who selected the new location. (*See Buildings 3 and 59.*)

Power plant with trestle and old power plant smokestack in background, circa 1913

Second power plant, circa 1920

A coal shed was built as part of the building adjacent to it with a capacity for two thousand tons. At around the same time, a wooden railroad trestle was built extending from the spur, which stopped between both structures.

In 1911, a bolt of lightning struck the chimney. A four-point lightning rod was installed to avoid such occurrences from happening, again. Until a new firehouse was erected several years later, there were at least two hospital firemen residing in this structure.

This building had twelve 150-horsepower HT boilers and a single 215-foot tall smokestack atop the central area of the building. During its construction, the vacuum pumps from the heating plant were moved here, while the vacuum pumps from the Group 1 auxiliary boiler house were moved to the heating plant. In 1913, an extension was added to the new boiler house to fit more boilers. Three 300-horsepower water tube boilers were installed. Two three-hundred-kilowatt turbine generators, a large air compressor, and a switchboard were installed in the new dynamo room, which was also part of the extension. In addition, two turbine main water supply pumps and two turbine feed-water pumps for the boilers were installed. A booster pump was added in 1915. (*See Buildings 4.1 and 59.*)

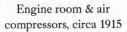

Engine room & air compressors, circa 1915

Engine room control panel, circa 1915

The hospital was in need of new boilers by 1920, as there had been no new additions for a few years. More water tube boilers were preferred. Five of the existing boilers got excessive use during the wintertime. While they were large, they were considerably overworked. The reserve boilers were a few old pressure boilers that had not been used in a long time and could only provide steam to the heating mains.

Inspector of buildings and engineering Charles B. Dix suggested that the power plant be equipped with oil-burning apparatus to reduce the cost of labor. Within a year, it was suggested a new smokestack and powerhouse be built. That became the adopted solution.

During the mid-1920s, a new boiler house was built with twin smokestacks as Building 84 in connection with this power plant. About ten years later, the old smokestack was removed. More coal would be required for the twin smokestacks. This came at an inconvenient time. There was a major coal strike in Alabama in 1920, which led to an increase in the price of coal. (*See Building 84.*)

In 1939, a small one-story brick addition was added to serve as a steam pipe junction room. (*See Building 85.*)

In time, this power plant was replaced by a larger, more productive power plant constructed just on the opposite side of the railroad spur closer to Old Dock Road. The old power plant was abandoned. It was demolished in 1968, along with its twin smokestack boiler house. (*See Building 29.*)

All that remained was the steam pipe junction house, which served as the main distribution area for steam. This structure had to be partially rebuilt in 1968 after the demolition, as it was still needed. It was originally numbered

The last Building 6 with Building 29 in the background

as Building 85, but after the old power plant was demolished, it adopted that building's former number designation.

After being abandoned for many years, this structure was demolished toward the end of August 2012, along with the old concrete railroad trestle pillars and salt shed. The demolition of this building also meant many of the underground tunnels would now be sealed from one end, limiting tunnel access to the power plant (Building 29).

Building 7

Building 7 was built from 1966 to 1967 on the north side of East First Street and Roundtree Road. Designed by Harry M. Price, this thirteen-story building was used as the new medical and surgical building complete with a clinic, laboratories, surgical rooms, x-ray facilities, and, most notably, a new modernized morgue on the first floor, which replaced the old one in Building 82. This would be the last medical and surgical building ever to be built for the hospital. It had a service elevator and a freight elevator at the central portion of the building. (*See Building 82.*)

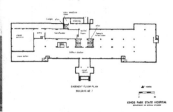

Building 7, circa 1970s   Footbridge going over parking lot to Building 7   Building 7 floor plan (basement)

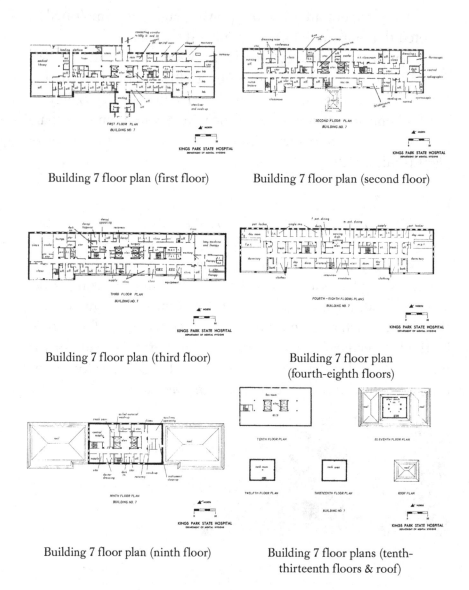

Building 7 floor plan (first floor)

Building 7 floor plan (second floor)

Building 7 floor plan (third floor)

Building 7 floor plan
(fourth-eighth floors)

Building 7 floor plan (ninth floor)

Building 7 floor plans (tenth-
thirteenth floors & roof)

By the time this building opened, there were already rumors about the hospital possibly closing. There were only a few buildings still in use, while most of the others were gradually being abandoned. The construction of this building was the state's way of showing its confidence that the hospital was here to stay. It became a big deal for the people of Kings Park to watch this tall building being erected. The governor even made an appearance during the dedication ceremony. To this day, it is the tallest building in Kings Park.

Upon opening, the nursing school was relocated from Macy Home to Building 7, where it would remain for a decade until the final class graduated in 1976. The office of the monthly newspaper was also relocated here from Macy Home. (*See Building 90.*)

There was a fallout shelter in the basement. The administrative offices were located on the lower three floors, while physically sick patients were kept on floors four to eight on Wards 229–238. There were two operating rooms on the ninth floor. The last few floors were mostly maintenance areas. There was also a professional library for use by employees, which was open from Monday through Friday.

The operating room was only used for surgical operations for the first few years. All surgeries were later conducted at Central Islip Psychiatric Center until the mid-1970s, when all surgery was discontinued there as well. In the end, it became more cost-effective to send patients to the local hospitals.

A long one-story brick corridor was constructed to connect Building 7 to its neighbors, Buildings 21 and 22. This breezeway corridor was located on the ground floor and was connected to the rear of the building. The buildings are also connected via the underground tunnel system, which can only be accessed through a manhole in the basement of Building 7. (*See Buildings 21 and 22.*)

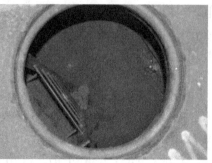

Breezeway connecting to Buildings
21 & 22 on March 9, 2014

Manhole in the basement used to
access tunnels, circa Nov. 7, 2011

In its final years of operation, Building 7 was used only as an administrative building. It became the last administration building of the hospital. During this time, its sister building, located at the Central Islip facility, served the medical and surgical needs of the KPPC. In these later years, geriatric patients were admitted through this building.

Building 7 employees pose for
a group photo in the lobby

Employees in a classroom

X-Ray Department at Christmas time   Assemblyman Bob Wertz & Director
                                       Alan Weinstock, 8th Fl, Nov. 1996

The building closed in 1996 when the hospital closed. Years afterward, the power continued to run from the basement up to the roof to a small structure commonly referred to by urban explorers as the Cube, which actually contained the water tank of the building. Technically, the actual water tank only consisted of the top two levels of this portion of the building. The power was being used to keep an active motion sensor security system going that alerted police and security personnel using an ear-piercing high-pitch siren whenever trespassers illegally entered the uppermost portion of the building. The sensors were situated above the lowest roof landing. The siren could be heard from all across the property, especially in the dead of night, which is when it tended to go off the most. At some point, clever trespassers found a way to disable the alarm system. It was never reactivated.

Building 7 on Nov. 7, 2011   The front of Building 7 on July 11, 2011

The rear of Building 7 on July 11, 2011

Rear loading dock on July 11, 2011

The basement on July 11, 2011

One of the main corridors
on July 11, 2011

Large room on the ground
floor on July 11, 2011

The same room on March 9, 2014

X-Ray Department on March 9, 2014   Patient ward on March 9, 2014

Although the building is abandoned, it is one of the most high-risk buildings because of constantly breached security systems, trespassers, vandals, and arsonists. This building has not been deemed structurally unsound, which means the police can enter if necessary.

In 2010, there was a fire that was started in a second-floor occupational therapy room in the rear. The fire caused significant damage to the second and third floors, but the building's structural integrity was not compromised, and no one was injured. However, the halls and rooms of that area remain charred and blackened from the fire and smoke, giving that section of the building a dark, eerie feel to it.

Fire damage on the rear of the   The room where the fire
building on July 11, 2011   began on Nov. 7, 2011

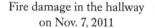

Fire damage in the hallway
on Nov. 7, 2011

Fire damage on the elevator
doors, on Nov. 7, 2011

On August 2, 2015, there was another fire near the loading dock in the breezeway that connects to Buildings 21 and 22. The fire, which began shortly before 2:57 p.m., was quickly extinguished. During the same year, someone started a fire at the front entrance in the late night hours on September 23.

Fire damage to the main
entrance on Oct. 5, 2015

Damage to the lobby on Oct. 5, 2015

Recent plans included the demolition of the cube/water tank atop the building. There was controversy about the state's plans to only demolish this portion of the building, which had become an eyesore to the community because of graffiti that could be seen for miles. Some said it was a waste of time and money because it could have been cleaned and access to the roof could have been blocked. Some preferred they demolish the entire building rather than one small portion on the roof that could later make the building structurally unsafe. The cube was ultimately demolished in 2017.

Graffiti on "The Cube" on June 20, 2016

Before this one, the original Building 7 was a small soap factory known as the soap house. It was built in 1902. At first, this structure stood somewhere near the original laundry building, but it was moved next to the second laundry building in 1911. For many years, soap for the hospital was made here using grease collected from the kitchens and piggery. It made an average of over thirty-five thousand pounds of soap a year. (*See Buildings 5 and 33.*)

Soap house

The soap house was demolished in the 1930s after a new storehouse was built. (*See Building 44.*)

Buildings 8–11 (Buildings A–D)

Work began on Buildings A–D in 1891 under the leisurely supervision of contractor John H. O'Rourke. They were supposed to be completed by 1892 but were nearly two years behind schedule. At the end of August 1892, a contract was awarded to the Thompson-Houston Electric Company for the electric illumination of Buildings A–D, which had not yet been finished.

These were the first allegedly fireproof brick patient ward buildings to be built at the hospital and were located along the boulevard. Buildings A and B stood on the east side of the road, while Buildings C and D were on the west side.

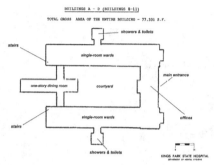

Postcard from 1905 showing Buildings D & C facing north

Modified floor plan for Buildings 8-11

Since the main portions had already been finished, these buildings were expected to open at the end of 1893. Instead, they were not opened until the following year. Patients were hastily placed inside to relieve the burden of the much smaller cottages and temporary buildings. There was still much work to be done in regard to building improvements. The work was not completed until 1897 because of the fact that when the buildings were started, the hospital belonged to Kings County. By the time the state took over in 1895, it also took on the responsibility of completing these four buildings. Building A was the first to be finished.

While they were later numbered as Buildings 8–11, they were almost always known as Buildings A–D.

Facing north on the boulevard toward Buildings A & B, circa 1913

Buildings A–D were practically identical to one another in design. Each was a two-story U-shaped, hip-roofed brick building. All had front porches with storm shelters over them, unfinished attics, and basements. At the rear of each was a single-story dining hall situated at the

Building B dining room, circa 1916

open end of an inner courtyard. Summerhouses, or gazebos, were later added at the center of each courtyard. The corridors on either side of the courtyards consisted of thirty-eight single rooms, along with three rooms for attendants and a large sitting room. It was the same layout on the second floors. Each corridor also had a bathroom with tiled flooring, while the bathtubs were galvanized iron. For some reason, they were not lined with porcelain, which was preferred.

In 1897, new sculleries were added in the basements to serve the dining halls above and for dishwashing. In 1899, there were sixteen spray baths added to these buildings, four for each. The buildings were later connected to an underground tunnel system through their basements. New gutters were added to the buildings in 1903.

The hardwood floors of the corridors were cold and slippery. At first, blankets had been laid out on the floors of the entrance lobbies to prevent them from being scratched by visitors. Rugs woven by the patients would later replace these blankets.

A two-story piazza was built onto the west side of Building B in 1903. In 1906, small octagon-shaped sun verandas were added to Buildings B, C, and D. Each had awnings over them to provide shade. The additions of these new sunrooms allowed for them to be utilized as dayrooms. This freed the old dimly lit dayrooms so they could be used as dormitories instead, helping to ease the overcrowded wards of these buildings.

Bldg. "C" and "D" K. P. S. H.

Postcard showing Building D & C with new verandas

Soon after, a few patients attempted to escape from Building B. Window guards had to be installed at each veranda about a year later to prevent any further attempts. By the 1920s, the octagon portion was removed from Building B. Another change that was made to prevent escapes was when the verandas of all three buildings were sealed and converted into solariums.

Electric diet kitchens were allowed for acute services in Buildings B and C. They were installed in 1904. In the same year, the plumbing was renewed in Buildings A, C, and D. In 1909, the hydraulic elevators located in the dining halls were overhauled. There were additions made to all four buildings in 1937. In 1959, recreation areas were added in each of these buildings. The steel fire escapes, which had been installed during the late 1890s, were replaced with new ones in 1966.

Fire escape at the side of one building   Ward sitting room

The patients within these four buildings resided in single-occupancy seclusion rooms rather than open wards. Single patient rooms were more commonly found at asylums than regular medical hospitals. Each of these buildings was actually home to four large patient wards. Wards 1–4 were located in Building A, while Wards 5–8 were in Building B. Across the boulevard, Building C housed Wards 9–12, and Building D housed Wards 13–16. By 1909, the partitions at Wards 3, 4, 6, 8, 10, and 15 were torn down to create small dormitories. New electrical fixtures were installed in all four buildings, and the electrical wiring was straightened and reconnected.

The patients were not the only ones residing in these new large buildings. Attendants resided at the ends of the wards, while the doctors lived at the central portion of each building. There were also small apartment suites located inside of Buildings B and C for the doctors.

In 1913, two small frame buildings were erected behind Buildings A and B to serve as storage rooms for ward supplies and soiled linen.

Building A, also Building 8, became the main administration building of the hospital for many years, although it also housed patient wards. In 1896, a medical library was established here for the staff. In 1897, a clerk's lavatory, linen room, locksmith workshop, and storeroom were added to the basement, while a drug room was established in the basement. In 1902, the drug room was moved to the first floor near the lobby, while the linen room became the main linen room of the hospital for several years.

Robert Feather postcard of
Building A, circa 1900-1910s

T.J. McCarthy postcard of
Building A, circa 1905-1906

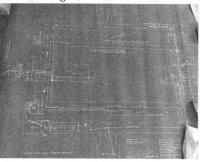

Building A basement blueprint

Building A first floor blueprint

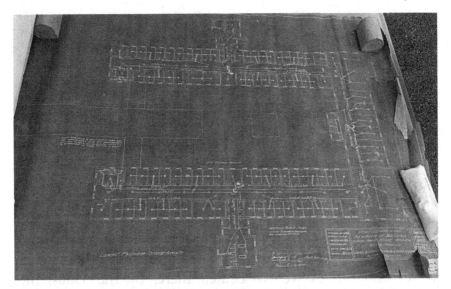

Building A second floor blueprint

The superintendent and his officers all had offices within this building. The steward's office was among these offices. For several years, the valuable personal property belonging to patients and hospital records were kept here in a wooden cupboard until better accommodations could be made. In 1905, the engineering department built new patients' record cases.

In 1903, a cement walk was laid out in the basement of Building A, considering the basements of these four buildings only had dirt floors when they were built. This improvement was very much needed because there was a lot of foot traffic down there. Patients and employees were constantly kicking up the dirt when they walked through the basement. Now that would change.

In 1909, a new concrete porch was built at the front to replace the wooden one. By 1912, a vestibule was added.

Building A, by Peter
Hildenbrand, circa 1920s

Employees on the front steps
of Building A, circa 1924

The administrative offices remained in Building A until 1927. When Macy Home was completed and opened in 1919, some of the clerical offices were relocated there. By the 1930s, the administration building of the Veterans' Memorial Hospital Unit became the administration building for the entire hospital. Building A was still used for additional administrative purposes. The hospital's main telephone operators remained here for many years afterward. (*See Buildings 90 and 125.*)

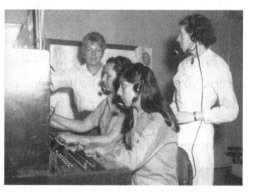

Building A telephone switchboard operators

In October 1953, Alcoholics Anonymous meetings were started for the female patients. They were held here twice per month. During the first few years, there was an average of ten patients in attendance. That number gradually increased over time.

Sometime after the 1950s, the pharmacy in this building was relocated to the basement of Building 93, which stood directly across the boulevard. (*See Building 93.*)

Building A had more than one fire throughout its existence, yet these buildings were intended to be fireproof. Sometime around

1905, there was a fire up on the cupola, caused by lightning. At the time, there were no electrical lights in the attic, which made dealing with the fire quite difficult. On January 30, 1907, a fire began in the stockroom of the linen room. It was caused by defective electrical wiring insulation. The loss totaled $1,450.

Building B, or Building 9, stood between Building A, which was just to its north, and the firehouse, which was on its south side. Inside were an operating room, therapy rooms, an office used by the treasurer, and the hospital's very first Adolescent Unit. Aside from housing patients, it served as the medical and surgical building for the hospital until Building 136 was constructed specifically for that purpose. (*See Buildings 83 and 136.*)

4—Building "B," Kings Park State Hospital, N. Y.

T.J. McCarthy postcard of
Building B, circa 1905-1906

Building B by Peter
Hildenbrand, circa 1924

The Burleson Hardware Company installed new plumbing and spray baths in Building B in 1903. Four years later, improvements were made to the operating room, and a new bay window was installed to allow for plenty of natural light.

The plumbing and electrical shops were temporarily located in the basement at the rear of this building under the dining room. This was only meant to be temporary, as having these shops on the premises was a danger because they were fire hazards. These two shops were moved into a new shop by 1912. (*See Building 57.*)

In 1909, a day school was established during the afternoons for the patients on Ward 7. A certified teacher was employed to teach those willing to attend. The numbers were low at first, but within a few years, more and more patients participated.

On December 27, 1914, there was a fire in Building B, which destroyed a lot of clothing.

As previously mentioned, Buildings A and B were across the boulevard from Buildings C and D, which were situated between Buildings 15 and 93. Because of being numbered in clockwise order, Building C became Building 11 rather than Building 10. Building D was numbered as Building 10 instead. (*See Building 15.*)

In 1897, a shoe shop was established in the basement of Building C. In 1899, a new staircase leading up from the boulevard was built. This building was home to the School of Nursing during its earliest years. A new lecture room was established in 1913. After Macy Home opened in 1919, the nursing school was relocated there. There was more space and no patients to distract the students from their studies. The ophthalmologist had an office at the center of Building C on the second floor. A dental office and sewing room were also located in this building, as well as a bowling alley, which was in the lower northwest wing at the rear of the building. In 1920, the service pipes for hot and cold water connected to the four wards in this building were renewed.

Building C by Peter Hildenbrand, circa 1924

Building C with Building 93, circa 1940s

Two female employees in front of Building C

At one time, hospital photographer Peter Hildenbrand had a one-room photo lab on the second floor of Building C. One of his tasks was to photograph the patients from the front and their profiles in a fashion quite similar to police mug shots. For a brief time, he was also responsible for fingerprinting newly admitted patients.

Building D was just south of Building C and north of Building 15. In 1897, a pathological laboratory was established within Building D. A bowling alley was added to the lower level in 1901. In 1909, concrete steps replaced the wooden steps in front of this building.

Postcard of Building D, incorrectly marked as Building C

Building D, circa 1913

On February 8, 1919, at two o'clock in the morning, there was a fire in the bowling alley of Building D, which was primarily used by employees. The fire began in a closet after a careless employee threw away a lit match or cigarette. The damage totaled one hundred dollars.

In 1939, Work Projects Administration (WPA) workmen renovated this building as part of a project created under Pres. Franklin D. Roosevelt's administration.

A small brick building stood behind Buildings C and D, which served as their kitchen. This was Building 12. Another brick building was located behind Buildings A and B serving as their kitchen. This was Building 38. At one time, the patients from the cottages used to get their meals from these kitchens. (*See Buildings 12 and 38.*)

By the late 1960s, these buildings were past their prime. The floors were starting to separate from the walls in some places. Ultimately, Buildings B–D were condemned as fire hazards and abandoned.

Aerial photo of A-B & C-D by King Pedlar, circa Feb. 1968

Building A, circa 1960s-1970s   Building C, circa 1960s-1970s

When these buildings were no longer used, some did not consider it a loss. The State of Charities had always viewed these buildings as being unsuitable to house patients with their long uninviting wards arranged in a single-room system. They felt these buildings were ill adapted for the caring of recoverable cases. It seemed more like an apartment building or hotel than a hospital ward.

All three abandoned buildings were demolished between 1975 and 1976, along with the kitchen for A and B. This was during a demolition phase that included Buildings 31 and 32, which were demolished first in 1975. By this time, the kitchen for C and D was already gone. (*See Buildings 31 and 32.*)

Bulldozer demolishes the old Clubhouse next to Building C, circa 1975

Building A was also in bad condition, so it was partially closed. Only the telephone switchboard operators were occupying the building throughout the early 1970s. There was a plan to relocate the system to Building 22, but, first, preparations needed to be made. (*See Building 22.*)

However, on March 16, 1976, there was a fire that began on the second floor of Building A in the telephone switchboard equipment room. As a result, much of the roof and interior of the north wing was destroyed, but no one was seriously injured, mainly since the building had already been mostly abandoned by this time. The telephone system experienced many problems because of the fire. For several weeks, no calls could be made to outside lines, and certain intrahospital connections could not be made.

Aerial photo from April 30, 1972   Aerial photo from April 10, 1976

Fire blazes in the northwest corner of Building A on March 16, 1976   Kings Park FD uses their "cherry picker" to fight the fire on March 16, 1976

Firefighter on a ladder, as Building A burns on March 16, 1976

Building A fire on March 16, 1976, as seen from Macy Home

The front of Building A, after the fire on March 16, 1976 The front of Building A, after the fire on March 16, 1976

Viewing the damage from West Fourth Street on March 16, 1976

Despite the fire, the building remained open until the telephone switchboard operators could be relocated to Building 22's first floor. By summertime of that year, the building had been abandoned and demolished.

The demolished buildings were buried within their own basements. This also blocked off any access to the basements by way of the underground tunnels, which had already been sealed off. Only empty fields of grass remain where these structures once stood, but if one looks closely enough, the building foundations can be found sticking out of the grass in some areas. From the top of Building 93, you can make out the faint outlines of these buildings on the ground.

Lasting impressions made by Bldgs   Impressions made by Bldgs A &
A-D, during the winter of 2007   C-D, during the winter of 2007

Fragments of Building B at the Pilgrim Psychiatric
Center Museum on November 4, 2015

Building 12

There were two buildings that were identified with this number designation. Both have been gone for a good many years.

The first Building 12 was the mist house, or hothouse, which was basically a large one-and-a-half-story wood-framed greenhouse with a gable roof that was built on a hillside in 1897 using wood recovered from when the six temporary buildings were torn down. It was two hundred feet long, and a garden was established around the west side of it. This was the second greenhouse to exist on the hospital grounds.

Interior of original Building 12 mist house, circa 1910s

It was located in the area where the main power plant would later be built behind Building C on the east side of Industrial Road. The structure was renewed in 1904. Two years later, it was glazed and painted, and a new potting house was built for the florist. (*See Building 11.*)

Unfortunately, the garden next to it had to be removed in 1908 because of the construction of a new power plant on that site (Building 6). The garden was relocated next to Male Cottage 31 (I). It was considered moving this greenhouse to the lower garden south of Group 1, but that did not happen. There was already a two-year-old greenhouse there by that time anyway. (*See Male Cottage I and Buildings 4, 4.3, and 6.*)

In 1918–1919, this greenhouse was repaired. It was eventually taken down around 1938–1939. At that point, a much larger greenhouse was built to replace this one on the other side of St. Johnland Road. (*See Building 65.*)

The next structure, which was numbered as Building 12, was a two-story brick building with a hip roof that served as the kitchen for Buildings C and D. At first, it was simply referred to as the kitchen for C and D, but in due time, it became the next Building 12, since it was near the previous one and it served Buildings 10 and 11. This building was built from 1896 to 1897 at the same time as those buildings and was situated in the middle of both buildings at their rear.

Building 12 kitchen for
Buildings C & D, circa 1913

Aerial view close-up with
Buildings C & D, circa 1947

In 1908, a new rear porch and platform were built to act as a boardwalk for easier access, and the hydraulic elevator was overhauled a year later. In 1913, a new refrigeration machine was installed. A new cement platform and steps were built at the rear of the building in 1914 to replace the old wooden stairs and platform that were already worn out.

Sometime after March 1957, this building collapsed onto the east side of Industrial Road. By 1959, most of the wreckage was cleared away, but the last bits of rubble did not get removed until the early 1960s.

Boardwalk support beams
on Nov. 7, 2011

Former site of Building
12 on April 17, 2016

Building 12.1

This one-story concrete structure was an annex to the kitchen for Buildings C and D. It was built sometime around 1908–1914. All that is known about this structure is that it was used for storage. (*See Buildings 10–12.*)

| Concrete annex to Building 12 on April 17, 2016 | Interior of concrete annex to Building 12 on April 17, 2016 |

It remains abandoned on the east side of Industrial Road.

Building 13

According to a map from 1912, Building 13 was one of the early male cottages, also known as Male Cottage 30 (H). It was built from 1888 to 1889 and was home to Ward 30. (*See Male Cottage F.*)

It was demolished in 1939.

Building 14

According to a map from 1912, Building 14 was Male Cottage 29 (E). It was built from 1888 to 1889 and housed Ward 29. The staff had a laundry room in this building for a few years. (*See Male Cottage E.*)

This cottage was demolished in 1939.

Building 15

Building 15, known to urban explorers as Wisteria House, was constructed from 1939 to 1941. It is a three-story E-shaped brick building with an elevator, which is situated on the west side of the boulevard north of Group 1 and across from Group 5. It has a hip roof design with a Georgian Revival feel. There are indoor brick porches that face the front of the building on all three levels at either side of its one-story segmental arch-design entrance. This building originally housed only male patients on Wards 60–65. At one time, it was used for the placement of the most dangerous patients of the hospital. Ward 65 was specifically used for criminally insane male patients.

Building 15, Wards 60-65, circa 1940s-1950s

Building 15, circa 1940s-1950s

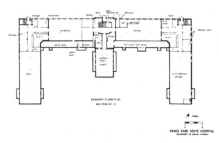

Building 15 floor plan (basement)

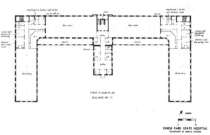

Building 15 floor plan (first floor)

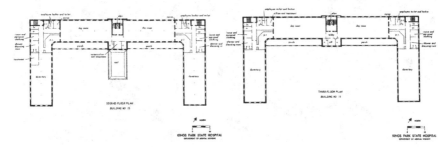

Building 15 floor plan (second floor)   Building 15 floor plan (third floor)

Barber chair in a basement recreation room on March 12, 2013

The patients of this building's six wards had their heads shaved regularly so they would stand out among the other patients of the hospital. This would prevent them from trying to blend in with other patients. There was a barbershop in the basement for this purpose. Their clothing was kept locked away at night, and they would be given pajamas to wear instead.

Access to the underground steam tunnels in the basement was sealed off long before the hospital actually ever closed. The pipes in that area were clustered very tightly together. It is possible this was done to prevent patient elopement, considering the dangers posed by some of these patients.

Basement tunnel access
on March 12, 2013

Looking into the partially blocked
tunnel on March 12, 2013

In the summertime, the employees would take the patients outside to the tree-shaded picnic area located behind the building, where they would have cookouts. There were brick barbecue grills near several of the buildings for these sorts of occasions.

BBQ behind Building 15

Eventually, the dangerous patients were all transferred to other facilities. The building was then utilized for the mentally ill residents of Nassau County. In 1958, a recreation room and movie room were set up in the basement of the south wing.

Theresa Ryan working in
Building 15 during the 1960s

Group of employees in
Building 15, circa 1978

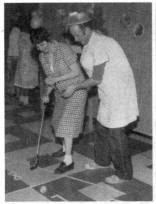

Taking time for a little fun

Betting on the horses

Building 15 day room, circa 1984

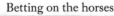

Employees Barbara Miller &
Tom Larkin on a porch, 1984

From 2002 to 2003, there were plans to gut the building and renovate it into a government office building for Suffolk County. Suffolk's Judiciary Facilities Authority was willing to bond $25 million for renovations and then lease it to the county. However, it remains abandoned.

It has been said that the tortured cries and agonizing screams of patients can still be heard coming from within its walls to this day. As spooky and haunting as that may sound, it is more likely the sound of trespassers making too much noise in the building.

Building 15 on July 30, 2013

Building 15 on March 9, 2015

Rear of Building 15 on Oct. 5, 2015

Rear entrance on Oct. 5, 2015

Porch on March 12, 2013

Pink Floyd The Wall graffiti
on March 11, 2010

Recreation room on March 12, 2013

Pool table in a recreation room on March 12, 2013

Horse head cutouts in the basement on April 29, 2010

Patient dormitory on March 12, 2013

Patient ward with blue dividers on March 12, 2013

Patient ward with white dividers on March 12, 2013

Ward kitchen on March 12, 2013   Serving area on March 12, 2013

This was actually the second building to use this number designation. The original Building 15 was a small square-shaped, wood-framed building with a basement and hip roof design. Built in approximately 1890–1892, it was located behind the male cottages on the east side of Industrial Road.

Originally, it served as the tailor shop until it was realized that a morgue was needed. In 1899, the building was converted into a laboratory and morgue, while the tailor shop was relocated to the newly built Building 28. A large refrigerating box with a capacity for nine bodies was installed in the basement of the

Original laboratory & morgue on Feb. 20, 1925

morgue. In 1915, a new refrigerating box was obtained to replace the old one. (*See Building 28.*)

In 1930, Building 82 replaced this morgue. The old morgue was abandoned and subsequently demolished sometime around 1928–1932. (*See Building 82.*)

Buildings 16 and 17

These two buildings were supposed to be large patient ward buildings that would have been used for the continued treatment of male and female patients. They would have been built on the site of Group 1 and replaced those buildings. At least that was the plan during the early 1950s. By that time, the

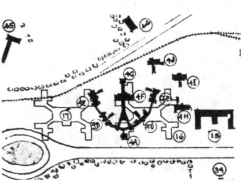

Close-up of 1954 Key Plot Plan, indicating outlines for Buildings 16 & 17

buildings of Group 1 were outdated and in need of major repairs and renovations.

Building 16 would have stood closer to Building 15 and housed both males and females, while Building 17 would have stood south of it and only housed female patients. Based on their X-shaped designs, they could have each housed four wards per floor. (*See Building 15.*)

However, these buildings were never constructed. It would have been more expensive to demolish the buildings of Group 1 and erect two new structures than to just repair Group 1.

There was an earlier Building 17, which was built in 1896 using lumber from the first temporary buildings. It was a toolhouse and mechanical repair shop that was located along Orchard Road, which leads from Old Dock Road to Industrial Road. This tool shed was demolished sometime around between 1925 and 1930.

Tool house on February 20, 1925

Buildings 18 and 19

The original Building 18 was a one-story wood-framed building with an attic and a gable roof constructed in 1896 using the wood from the six temporary buildings. It was located on the west side of Industrial Road near the male cottages and housed the paint and tinsmith shops. Originally, it only housed the tinsmith shop until the paint shop was moved here from Building 28 in 1906. A second two-story wood-framed building with an attic and basement was erected for this shop. It had a hip roof design. (*See Building 28.*)

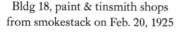

Bldg 18, paint & tinsmith shops from smokestack on Feb. 20, 1925

Building 18, paint & tinsmith shops

When the building was demolished from 1933 to 1934, two of these shops were relocated to Male Cottage 26, at which time, that cottage was renumbered as Building 20. (*See Male Cottage B and Building 20.*)

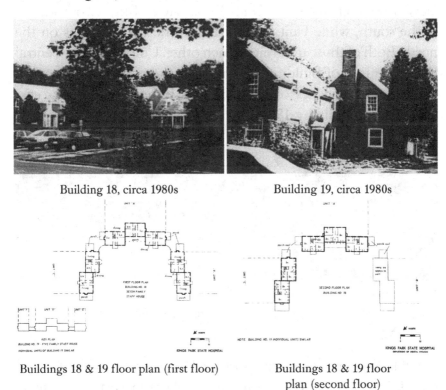

Building 18, circa 1980s   Building 19, circa 1980s

Buildings 18 & 19 floor plan (first floor)   Buildings 18 & 19 floor plan (second floor)

The next Building 18 was actually a series of cottages, as was Building 19. Because of the similarities of these two buildings, I have listed them together. They each consisted of a set of two-story brick veneer cottages complete with basements and attics, which were used by doctors and other medical staff as homes. They were located along East Fourth Street across from each other. Both were built from 1939 to 1940, which was one of the more notably productive eras for expansion at the hospital. The seven cottages of Building 18 form a U shape on the east side of the street, while the five cottages of Building 19 are around the bend up on a nearby hill at the south side of the street aligned in a linear pattern. The entrances of these cottages have copper pagoda roofs. These homes were occupied by 1941.

Each is divided into three units, ranging from Units A–F. Unit A consisted of the three central cottages of Building 18, which faced East Fourth Street. Unit B consisted of the two cottages at the south, while Unit C consisted of the two cottages on the north. Both of those units faced each other. Unit D was the central three cottages of Building 19. Unit E is the cottage on the west end closer to Student Road, while Unit F is the cottage on the east end closer to Building 18.

Aerial photo of Buildings 18, 19, & 37 from March 27, 1964

Building 18, HALI house, circa 2000s

In later years, the cottages of the Buildings 18 and 19 housed the Hands Across Long Island Inc. (HALI) Program, originally started by former patients of the hospital for the purpose of helping other former patients to reintegrate into society.

These cottages are currently abandoned and have fallen into a dreadful state of disrepair. Scavengers have stolen some of the copper from the pagoda roofs over the entrances. There are still personal belongings and furniture left behind. Camel crickets have taken over the basements, creating nesting areas where they could thrive undisturbed.

Aerial of Buildings 18, 19, 37, & 90 from March 5, 2005

Building 18, Units C & A
on May 11, 2011

Building 18, Unit C - Cottage
1 on May 11, 2011

Building 18, Unit C - Cottage
2 on May 11, 2011

Building 18, Unit A - Cottages
2 & 3 on Jan. 2, 2016

Building 18, Unit A - Cottage
3 on May 11, 2011

Building 18, Unit B - Cottages
1 & 2 on May 11, 2011

Building 18, Units A & B
on March 17, 2013

Building 18, Units C & A
on March 17, 2013

Open front door to Building
18, Unit B, on Aug. 2, 2011

Building 18 kitchen on Aug. 2, 2011

Camel cricket on the stairs
on Aug. 2, 2011

Second floor hallway of
Building 18 on Aug. 2, 2011

Bedroom filled with broken
furniture on Aug. 2, 2011

Stairs leading to the basement of
Building 18 on Aug. 2, 2011

Facing south from East Fourth Street
toward Building 19 on March 17, 2013

Building 19 facing east
on March 17, 2013

North side of Building 19 facing
east on March 17, 2013

South side of Building 19 facing
west on May 11, 2011

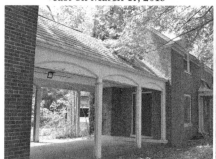

Porch on north side of Building
19 facing west on May 11, 2011

North side of Building 19 facing
west on May 11, 2011

Living room in Building
19 on May 11, 2011

Fireplace in Building 19 on May 11, 2011

Second floor hallway on Aug. 2, 2011

Looking up into the attic from the
second floor on Aug. 2, 2011

Concrete basement room of
Building 19 on Aug. 2, 2011

Camel crickets in the basement of
Building 19 on March 17, 2013

Sometime from 2001 to 2005, the northernmost cottage from Building 18, Unit A, was demolished. It would not be the only one destroyed. On New Year's Day of 2016, at around four o'clock in the morning, someone set fire to the easternmost cottage of Unit

B. The cottage was burned to the ground, leaving behind only its roof and a pile of rubble.

Building 18, Unit B - Cottage 1
burned to the ground on Jan. 1, 2016

A tree was cut down to make
battling the blaze easier

Building 18, Units A & B, after
the fire on Jan. 2, 2016

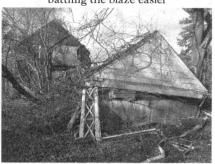

Building 18, Unit B - Cottages
1 & 2 on Jan. 2, 2016

Rubble from the fire blocks a
doorway on Jan. 2, 2016

The remaining cottages of
Building 18 on Jan. 2, 2016

Building 20

Building 20 was originally one of the early male cottages built from 1888 to 1889, which contained Ward 26. During the 1930s, it was converted into the new tinsmith shop and paint shop while also being used as a toolhouse. The previous building used for these shops was then demolished. (*See Male Cottage B and Building 18.*)

This cottage once stood exactly where the Building 94 currently stands. It was demolished by 1953, which was the year construction began on Building 94. By the mid-1950s, the shops within Building 20 were incorporated into Building 5, along with several other workshops formerly located within other buildings. (*See Buildings 5 and 94.*)

Building 21

Building 21 is a four-story brick building with a basement and a flat roof built from 1957 to 1965 to house patients for continued care. It had two elevators in the center of the building and enclosed fire escapes on the outside. Located on Roundtree Road between East First and East Second Streets, this building was mainly used as a geriatric infirmary in its early years but was later used for drug treatment. In 1960, a recreation room was added in the first wing of this building. On November 9, 1966, the Narcotics Addiction Unit opened, occupying the entire top floor. This building also housed disturbed patients. Inside were several units, which included Cumberland, Greenpoint, North Brooklyn, Brooklyn 3–4, and Ridgewood, along with Wards 201–214.

Building 21   Building 21 parking lot

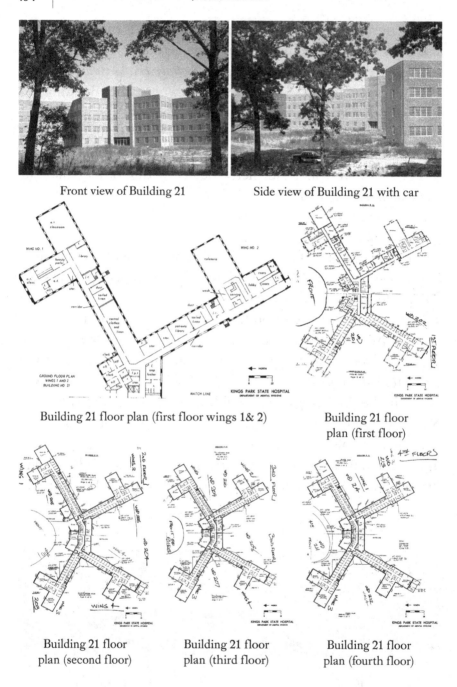

Front view of Building 21

Side view of Building 21 with car

Building 21 floor plan (first floor wings 1& 2)

Building 21 floor plan (first floor)

Building 21 floor plan (second floor)

Building 21 floor plan (third floor)

Building 21 floor plan (fourth floor)

A long corridor links Buildings 21 and 22 to each other on the first floor and in the basement. Another one-story brick corridor called a breezeway connects both buildings to the rear of Building 7. An enclosed courtyard is located between Buildings 21 and 22, which was used by the patients when weather permitted. The wall closing it in was added during the 1970s. (*See Buildings 7 and 22.*)

Young patient from the Children's Unit knocking down pins, circa 1970s

Handicapped patient also trying to knock down pins, circa 1970s

An elderly group seated in the courtyard, circa 1970s-1980s

Courtyard with Building 21 in background on March 12, 2013

Courtyard between Buildings 22 (L) & 21 (R) on March 12, 2013

Both Buildings 21 and 22 are very similar in design and were identical to the Corcoran Buildings at Central Islip, which consisted of Buildings 127 and 128. These Central Islip buildings have already been demolished.

Medical and patient libraries, classrooms, a beauty parlor, and distribution rooms for clothing, coats, and linen were located on the first floor. There was also an insulin shock therapy ward in this building. Dr. Irving Pinsley was in charge of it for a good many years.

Bird's eye view from the roof of
Building 7 on March 9, 2014

The front of Building 21 on July 11, 2011

Side view of Building 21 on July 11, 2011

Building 21's enclosed fire
escapes on July 11, 2011

Lobby of Building 21 on Dec. 7, 2011

Ground floor corridor bordering
the courtyard on Dec. 7, 2011

Ground floor kitchen and
serving area on Dec. 7, 2011

Dining room for Wards 209-
210 on March 9, 2014

Ward corridor on March 12, 2013

Hallway leading to the dormitory
on March 12, 2013

Patient dormitory on March 9, 2014

Day room on March 12, 2013

There was once a brick oil house that was built in 1906. It was the first Building 21 according to a map from 1912. This small building was located on the north side of West Fourth Street across from Male Cottage 26 (B). The hospital's electrical department used it to store oil. After the second storehouse (Building 44) was built during the 1930s, all of the oil houses had been removed by 1935. (*See Male Cottage B and Building 44.*)

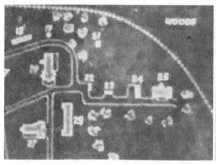 

Close-up of map from 1912 showing
location of original Building 21

Aerial photo of Buildings 21
& 22 from March 1962

Building 22

Building 22 is a four-story brick building with a basement and a flat roof, which was constructed from 1957 to 1965. It is located on Roundtree Road next to its reversed twin, Building 21. Both buildings were built at the same time. Like its sister building, it has two elevators, which are centrally located. Inside this building were the Smithtown and Huntington Units, along with Wards 215–228. Many of the wards were considered admissions wards because patients usually did not stay longer than forty days. (*See Building 21.*)

Building 22, circa 1983

Building 22 with Building 7 in
background, circa 1980s

Director Charles Buckman places
Building 22 cornerstone, 1957

Building 22 placing of the
cornerstone, circa 1957

This building housed the new Children's Unit when it first opened and had three hundred young patients right away. The Adolescent Unit had been transferred here from Group 2. Crisis Residency outpatient services were located on the first floor. The telephone switchboard operators and equipment that were formerly a part of Building A were also on the first floor. They were relocated here after Building A was abandoned and eventually demolished in 1976. (*See Building 8.*)

Telephone switchboard
room on March 9, 2014

Telephone switchboard room equipment
on the floor on March 9, 2014

In 1960, a recreation room was added to this building's third wing. The second and third floor housed the Extended Treatment Unit for long-term patients and the Intensive Treatment Unit, which was a secure unit. The top floors were used to house patients in the custody of the Sheriff's Department. These patients were remanded into psychiatric care by the court. Disruptive patients were also kept here on two wards that made up the Behavioral Treatment Unit. On the fourth floor, there was also a patient library that was open from Tuesday through Thursday, between the hours of 8:30 a.m. and 11:00 a.m., and 1:00 p.m. and 3:00 p.m. It also doubled as the music center.

Teachers sitting in a classroom
in Building 22, circa 1964

John Pruslow playing
piano in the library's
music center, circa 1974

Santa Claus visits
the Children's Unit
of Building 22

Building 22 dining room decorated
for Thanksgiving, circa 1980s

By 1977, the Children's Unit program was closed. These young patients were subsequently transferred to local centers near their homes. That area of the building was reused to house adult patients. Since many of the other buildings were being closed, more adult patients were being moved here.

After Building 2 closed and was abandoned during the early 1980s, this became the admissions building for all female and male patients. Newly admitted patients would be kept here until it could be decided what ward would suit them best, unless they were discharged.

In the later years of the hospital, there was also a room in this building that was used to conduct shock therapy treatments.

A long corridor connects Building 22 to Building 21 in the basement and on the first floor. Both buildings are also connected to a longer corridor called a breezeway that leads to the rear of their neighbor, Building 7. There is also an enclosed courtyard, once used for patients, situated between both Buildings 21 and 22. (*See Building 7.*)

Bird's eye view from the roof of Building 7 on March 9, 2014

The front of Building 22 on March 9, 2014

Building 22 on July 11, 2011

Side view of Building 22 on March 9, 2014

Rear view of Building 22 on Oct. 5, 2015

Courtyard access & picnic
tables on March 12, 2013

Lobby of Building 22 on March 9, 2014

Basement corridor linking Buildings
21 & 22 on Dec. 7, 2011

Kitchen area on the ground
floor on Dec. 7, 2011

Refrigeration rooms on the
ground floor on Dec. 7, 2011

Dining room/lounge area
on Dec. 7, 2011

Ward corridor on March 9, 2014

Patient dormitory on Dec. 7, 2011

Day room on March 9, 2014

Former classroom on Dec. 7, 2011

Sheriff's Department cellblock ward
entrance on March 12, 2013

The first Building 22 was a barn that was later used as a garage. It was built from 1890 to 1892 next to the Pest House and behind where Building 94 would later be built. This structure was demolished right before Building 94 was built sometime around 1950–1953. It can be found in the previous close-up section of the 1912 map. (*See Buildings 25 and 94.*)

Building 23

Building 23 was a two-story brick building with a flat roof called the Buckman Day Treatment Center. It was named after one of the last senior medical directors of the hospital, Dr. Charles Buckman, who ran the hospital from 1952 to 1972. Building 23 was built in 1970 and was located directly south from Building 7 on the east side of Kings Park Boulevard near the oval traffic circle that once was the lower reservoir.

Building 23, circa 1981

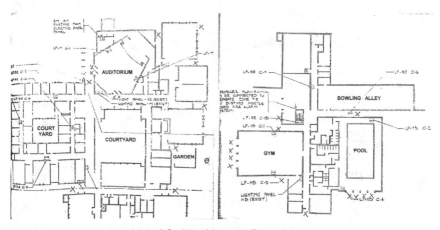

Modified Building 23 floor plans

Building 23 was used as a rehabilitation and recreational center for patients. It had its own bowling alley, a gymnasium, a movie room, a library, and an Olympic-sized indoor swimming pool. Annual blood drive donations were held here. This building also acted as a day care center for the children of the hospital employees. In addition to being the last recreation and day care center used, it also served as the last assembly hall. Its stage and auditorium replaced that of York Hall. (*See Building 80.*)

Donors sit and wait during
a 1976 Blood Drive

Dr. Neil Wallach & other employees
replenish during a 1978 Blood Drive

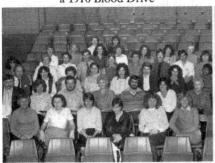

Daycare group, circa 1980

Employees installing a new light fixture
near the courtyard, circa 1980s

Outstanding employees
nominees, circa 1986

RNs Brenda Aith, Mary Jane Johnson,
& Bridget Blomberg, May 4, 1988

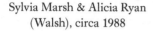

Sylvia Marsh & Alicia Ryan
(Walsh), circa 1988

Joe Fischetti (L) & Bob Birding (R)
in the garden, circa 1980s-1990s

A small pedestrian bridge was erected going over the parking lot in front of Building 7 and leading to Building 23. This made traveling by foot faster for those going from building to building without having to walk downhill through the parking lot and then back uphill. (*See Building 7.*)

The pedestrian bridge on July 11, 2011

Looking across the bridge from Building 7 to Building 23 on July 11, 2011

Prior to closing, there were parties held in this building. This gave the employees a chance to say their good-byes to each other. It was a sad occasion for all. When the hospital closed in 1996, this building remained open for another year as an outpatient clinic.

Nurses' farewell party audience applauding, May 1996

Nurses' farewell party, circa May 1996

Closing day party on November 15, 1996

Last CEOs, Alan Weinstock, Steve Goldstein, & Rob Hettenbach, Nov '96

In the early part of 1997, an elderly outpatient was abducted from the front of the building. He was later found murdered. In response, as of March of that year, security had been increased to six officers during the day and one during the evening and overnight shift.

Afterward, this building had practically become a security hub at Kings Park for the Office of Mental Health (OMH). There was almost always a security vehicle parked outside. Fencing was also put up around in certain areas of the grounds, while access to most of the roads was restricted. The local police also increased their presence in the area as a deterrent.

Oddly, the grounds were more secure after the hospital closed than when it housed thousands of patients.

The clinic was relocated to Pilgrim Psychiatric Center in October 1997. However, this building was not abandoned as intended. Instead, it became a security headquarters for the OMH. A couple of years later, they vacated the building, and it was finally closed.

As of 2003, there was still power surging through this and a few other buildings on the complex. This building also had an active alarm system for a while. OMH vans would often patrol the grounds keeping watch over the buildings. It is a never-ending losing battle.

Not long after this building was finally closed, it was offered to the Kings Park School District for use by the Kings Park High School. The Kings Park School District declined the offer because of the costs of maintaining and staffing the building. Instead, the building was abandoned. By 2006, it had fallen into a state of great disrepair. It was a waste of a good building, which has left some people in the community feeling bitter.

Building 23 from the boulevard
on June 22, 2010

Building 23 on March 26, 2011

Rear of Building 23 on March 26, 2011

Building 23 steps on March 26, 2011

Lobby of Building 23 on July 11, 2011   Corridor near courtyard on July 11, 2011

Missing windows on July 11, 2011   Courtyard seating & tables
on Nov. 7, 2011

Large recreation room on Nov. 7, 2011   Auditorium on Nov. 7, 2011

Kitchenette on June 15, 2007

Weights in gym on June 15, 2007

Locker room on July 11, 2011

Handicapped seating attachment
at pool on July 11, 2011

Bowling alley on July 11, 2011

Bowling alley lanes covered
by debris on July 11, 2011

Collapsed ceiling on July 11, 2011   Caved in roof from a different section
of the building on July 11, 2011

In its final years, it was quite dark inside, giving it a rather spooky appearance, especially near the empty swimming pool and bowling alley. Lockers in the locker rooms still held personal miscellaneous items that were left behind. The ceiling of the main corridor on the first floor was collapsing in on itself, making it extremely unsafe to roam around inside.

Demolition of this building began in November 2012 and continued into the beginning of 2013. I felt saddened to see it go, since it was the first building at the KPPC that I ever saw up close. It was one of the most interesting buildings. Today, nothing remains aside from a field of grass where it once stood.

Demolition of Building   Auditorium partially demolished
23 on Dec. 19, 2012   on Dec. 19, 2012

Remains of a corridor on Dec. 19, 2012

Building 23 large recreation room on Dec. 19, 2012

Partially demolished gymnasium & pool section on Jan. 23, 2013

Bulldozer on site, circa Jan. 23, 2013

Former site of Building 23 with Building 7 in background on July 30, 2013

Facing the boulevard from the former site of Building 23 on July 30, 2013

Bowling pins at Pilgrim Psychiatric Center Museum on Nov. 4, 2015

According to the map from 1912, this building number was originally used to identify a small storage shed. The shed had been constructed sometime during the early 1900s, probably around 1910. It was located near the Pest House on a small road that would have been behind the current laundry building (Building 94) east of the hike-and-bike trail. (*See Buildings 25 and 94.*)

It was demolished around 1950–1953.

Building 24

This was one of the original female cottages listed as Female Cottage 24 (I), which housed Ward 24. It was built from 1888 to 1889. Based on an old hospital map, it later became known as Building 24. It was removed in 1939. (*See Female Cottage I.*)

According to the 1912 map, there was an old garage that was built sometime around 1910 near the Pest House. It was also listed as Building 24. This garage was demolished sometime around 1950–1953. (*See Building 25.*)

Aerial photo showing Buildings 24 & 25 on Feb. 20, 1925

Building 25

The Pestilence House, or Pest House for short, was the hospital's first Isolation Cottage, as it was more commonly known. It was a small one-story wood-framed cottage with a basement and attic, which was built in 1905 at the mere cost of $1,606.77. It had a gable roof design. Patients were placed here generally to isolate them from the rest of the population, specifically in cases when the patients had infectious or contagious diseases, and quarantine was required for the safety of others.

According to one of the annual reports, in 1910, the Isolation Cottage was literally moved from its original location to a different location south of St. Johnland Road at the end of a small road near the male cottages north of West Fourth Street and behind the Tiffany Field. This

Brick foundation from a building in the woods on April 17, 2016

was done to clear the way for the construction of the Group 2 buildings. Afterward, a cement foundation and a basement were built underneath it to allow for a heater to be installed, since it did not have one at its previous location. (*See Building 54.*)

Once it was moved, it became an annex to Ward 28 of Male Cottage 28 (E), which was used to house male tuberculosis patients until the Group 4 TB wards were built. (*See Male Cottage E and Building 3.*)

It was demolished around 1950–1953. Building 140 (73P) of the Veterans' Memorial Hospital Unit took its place as the new isolation building. (*See Buildings 73 and 140.*)

Building 25.1

This was the small Pest House, or Quarantine Ward. It was actually a summerhouse built in 1906. It was located on the west side of Industrial Road near the main Pest House. It was also demolished around 1950–1953. (*See Buildings 25 and 94.*)

Small pest house on Feb. 20, 1925

Building 26

This was actually one of the original male cottages listed as Male Cottage 26 (B). Built from 1888 to 1889, it housed Ward 26 for male patients. The patients were eventually moved to larger patient wards, and during the 1930s, this cottage was converted into the new paint and tinsmith shop. It was also used as a toolhouse and renumbered as Building 20. (*See Male Cottage B and Building 20.*)

It was removed from 1950 to 1953 to clear the way for the construction of the new laundry building. (*See Building 94.*)

Building 27

This building number was the designation used for the hospital's last reservoir's valve box shed. It was a one-story hip-roofed, wood-framed shed built in 1921 and located in the wooded area beyond the water tower to the west of Old Dock Road just past Potter's Field Cemetery. An underground system of wells situated near the power plant was used to feed this underground reservoir, which opened two years later, with a water capacity of 1.5 million gallons. (*See Building 45.*)

In 1957, the water tower was built right next to it. The residents of the hospital used it until 1996, when the hospital closed.

The old box shed was removed sometime later, during the late 1960s, after the reservoir was abandoned. I have not been able to locate any photos of it. The wooded area, which currently covers the site, has left practically no signs of what used to be there so many years before. Only the abandoned water tower and a chain-link fence that once surrounded the reservoir remains. Water can still be heard through drainage openings running underground.

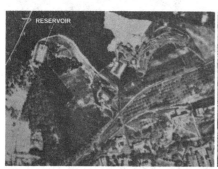
Aerial photo from 1931 showing area of final reservoir

Rusted chain link fence surrounding the old reservoir site on April 28, 2013

Hole near the gate at the former reservoir site on April 28, 2013

A water standpipe sticking out of the ground on April 28, 2013

Open manhole with running
water below on April 28, 2013

Concrete slab on April 28, 2013

Male Cottage 25 (A), which housed Ward 25, was also numbered as Building 27 at one time. It was built in 1888 and demolished by the late 1930s. (*See Male Cottage A.*)

Building 28

Built in 1896, mainly with reclaimed wood from the first temporary buildings, Building 28 was a one-story wood-framed building with a hip roof, basement, and attic. The tailor shop was moved here from its previous location at the original Building 15, while that building was converted into the hospital's first laboratory and morgue. (*See Building 15.*)

Tailor shop on Feb. 20, 1925

Tailor shop, circa 1920s

During the early 1900s, the paint shop was also located here. In 1906, that shop was moved to Building 18 with the tinsmith shop, at which time a sewing room workshop from Ward 8 was relocated to the tailor shop. (*See Buildings 9 and 18.*)

In 1915, there was a fire within this structure that caused some damage. This building once stood in the exact same spot where Building 94 now stands. It was demolished in 1953, prior to the construction of that building, which became the new laundry building. The tailor shop was relocated to Building 38. (*See Buildings 38 and 94.*)

Building 29

This was the final power plant built at the hospital. It was constructed from 1965 to 1966 at the cost of $1,220,794. Additions and improvements continued until December 1968. It is a brick building with a ground floor, basement, mezzanine level, conveyor loft floor, several metallic catwalks, penthouse, and brick smokestack. It has three separate flat rooftops at different levels. The elevator stopped at the basement, ground floor, mezzanine, and conveyor loft. Originally, it burned coal that was delivered via the railroad spur but was later modified to use oil and/or natural gas. It was capable of producing three to seven megawatts of power for the entire institution.

Building 29, the third power plant
built for the hospital, circa 1965

Power plant, circa 1960s-1970s

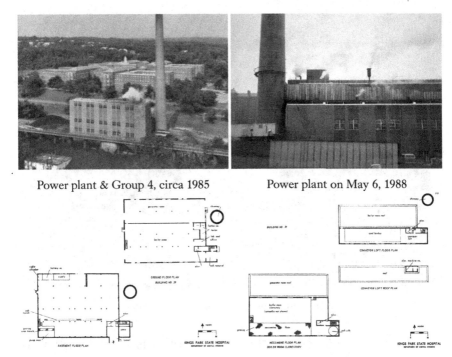

Power plant & Group 4, circa 1985   Power plant on May 6, 1988

Building 29 floor plans (lower floors)   Building 29 floor plans (upper floors)

Building 29 was erected on the east side of Old Dock Road on the opposite side of the railroad spur from its predecessor, Building 6. Once it was fully operational, Building 6 was shut down and later removed, leaving only a pump house in its place. (*See Building 6.*)

Aerial photo by Jerry Melvin, circa 1965

The ash produced by the incinerator was used as filler to pave some of the hospital's roads. Sometimes ash was also used as landfill for the unwanted swampy areas of the hospital. There were quite a few. Much of the ash was also dumped on the hill near the water tower.

Aerial photo of water tower & mounds of ash, circa 1986

Aerial photo of power plant & coalfield on April 1, 1980

Coal was delivered via the railroad and piled outside of the building in a coal chute. After a few years, the pile of coal became so large it covered more ground than the building itself. The power plant burned 110 tons of coal a day. Not long after the Bituminous Coal Strike of 1974, the price of coal totaled $2,952 per day. As if that were not bad enough, the Bituminous Coal Strike of 1977–1978 did nothing to help with the already increased prices. It became a national crisis that lasted 110 days.

By the 1980s, the Environmental Protection Agency strongly urged the hospital to make a switch from bituminous coal to the cleaner-burning anthracite coal.

As of 1987, the hospital began phasing out coal use in favor of a new oil-fired system. This gradual change was made to save money and improve the environment. At the time, the hospital had been using about thirty thousand tons of coal each year.

In 1988, an extension was added to the east side of the building at the ground level for the main control room and management office. A new coal shed and fuel tanks were also added just north of the building near Orchard Road. A fuel pumping station soon followed.

New oil tank was delivered by truck for the transition to oil, circa 1988

Oil tank near the power plant, prior to being buried in the ground, 1988

Construction was underway,
as of May 1988

A hole was cut into the power plant
wall to build a control room, May 1988

Work began on a cement
foundation, circa May 1988

The control room began to
take shape, circa May 1988

Foundation for the fuel tanks, circa 1988

Once the concrete hardened
work continued, circa 1988

A new coal storage chute, circa 1988

Looking down from the roof of
the power plant, circa May 1988

Work progressed with the construction
of the fuel tanks, circa 1988

A new trestle was erected near
the power plant, circa 1988

Coal storage chute near
completion, circa 1988

Fuel truck delivering oil to the
power plant, circa 1988

Scaffolding around the smokestack, circa 1988

The smokestack when the old twin smokestacks were still standing, 1960s

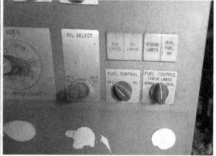

Interior of the power plant, circa 1988

Fuel control dials, circa 2007

By mid-February 1989, coal was completely phased out and replaced by an improved, environmentally safe, computerized oil and gasoline system. It took several months before the system was finally in place and functioning. After the conversion, the power plant had four burners. Two were used for oil and two for gas. Each morning, the supervisor would check the price of each fuel type and then use whichever was the cheapest.

The Long Island Lighting Company (LILCO), the power company used by the town, supplied gas as an alternative fuel source. It was provided on an "interruptible usage" plan. In the event of a power outage, the computerized oil-burning system would take over to keep the psychiatric center running.

At the end of the hospital's run, Building 29 was shut down at 2:22 p.m. on October 7, 1996. LILCO was to take over and switch on the power for the few remaining active buildings of the KPPC.

| Shutting down the power plant on Oct. 7, 1996 | Robert Ryan at the LILCO primary controls, Oct. 7, 1996 | Dan Stoffel, as power was turned off at 2:22 pm on Oct. 7, 1996 |

Although it closed down in 1996 for at least five years afterward, power still hummed through its large dust-covered transformers, indicating that it had not been turned off permanently. In fact, computer lights and other instruments were still blinking until around 2007–2008. All power is off now.

For many years, the old brick smokestack towered over the structure and could be seen from all around town. By the 2000s, it had become weakened and worn by weather corrosion, decay, and neglect. There were loose bricks that were out of place throughout the structure, making it a danger. Both the town of Smithtown and New York State conducted surveys, and it was deemed structurally sound. Some still believed it was on the verge of collapse.

Power plant & trestle on
September 9, 2011

Power plant with trestle & fuel
tanks on May 11, 2011

Power plant fuel tanks on May 11, 2011

Power plant broken windows
on Sept. 9, 2011

Power plant basement on Aug. 25, 2011

Ground floor on Aug. 25, 2011

Messy control room on Aug. 25, 2011

MicroSelect cleaning system & Zero Span calibrator on Aug. 25, 2011

Employee lounge area with graffiti-covered walls on Aug. 25, 2011

Looking down the metallic staircase on Aug. 25, 2011

Coal trough on Aug. 25, 2011

Mezzanine catwalk on Aug. 25, 2011

Building 29 from Old Dock
Road on Dec. 19, 2012

Ladder to smokestack coal
chute on Oct. 24, 2011

Smokestack coal chute
interior on Oct. 24, 2011

At the smokestack from within
the coal chute on Oct. 24, 2011

Looking down the smokestack
on Oct. 24, 2011

Looking up the smokestack
on Oct. 24, 2011

On the ground nearby, coal residue surrounded the outside and inside of the power plant. Over a period, a mountain of leftover coal gradually transformed into a grassy hill beside Building 6 and the old railroad trestle support pillars. Those structures were demolished in August 2012, and the hill was leveled. Also demolished were the fuel tanks and coal shed that stood nearby.

The smokestack was on the list of structures to be demolished by the end of that year. There was no reason to keep it around any longer. However, the demolition was postponed until the following year.

On March 27, 2013, at two o'clock in the afternoon, a controlled explosion was used to implode the smokestack at its base. A big production was made of the event with news teams, crowds of onlookers, and even a news helicopter flying overhead. I was lucky enough to be one of those onlookers.

After the oil tanks & trestle were removed, circa April 16, 2013

Spectators arrive to view the demolition on March 27, 2013

Smokestack demolition sequence on March 27, 2013

After the smokestack came down, the crowds dispersed fairly quickly. Only a few of us stuck around to see the aftermath and take photos of it. The rest were satisfied with what they saw, so for them, the show was over.

News helicopter captures the demolition from above

An aerial view of the demolition area on March 27, 2013

Only the base of the smokestack remained on March 27, 2013

Most of the rubble was removed over the next few weeks, April 16, 2013

The coal chute sealed with plywood, circa April 16, 2013

The spot where the smokestack stood on April 16, 2013

The demolition of the smokestack marked the end of an era for the hospital. It was the last smokestack to exist on the property. It will never be the same to look at Building 93 without seeing the smokestack in the background. The landscape and skyline have been forever changed.

It leaves me wondering how I will feel on the day Building 93 is finally demolished. I know that day will come. It is inevitable. It might be soon, or it might be years from now. Seeing the smokestack come down and watching it fall toward Building 93 from my angle, as if to say, "You're next," was a powerful image. (*See Building 93.*)

Current view of Building 29 on Sept. 15, 2014

On October 23, 2016, someone started a fire in the control room. The fire was extinguished before it could spread too far.

There was another structure numbered as Building 29 before this power plant was built–Male Cottage G, which was built in 1889. It served as the staff house for males. (*See Male Cottage G.*)

It was demolished around 1952–1953.

Building 30

Building 30 was a lumber storage house. It stood between Buildings

Lumber storage shed, circa 1912

44 and 57 on the east side of Orchard Road. It was moved here in 1914 from its original location near the electric heating plant. (*See Buildings 44, 57, and 59.*)

It was demolished in 1966.

Building 31

This was the hospital's main bowling alley for many years, not to be confused with Male Cottage 31 (I), which housed Ward 31. That cottage actually stood directly behind this building. It was demolished by 1939. (*See Male Cottage I.*)

By 1912, Male Cottage J, the male dining hall built from 1889 to 1890, was numbered as the first Building 31. It stood on the future site of Building 93 and was demolished from 1938 to 1939. (*See Male Cottage J and Building 93.*)

Bowling alley, circa 1970s   Recreation office sign, circa 1959

The next Building 31 was the bowling alley. It was a one-story rectangular, white, gable-roofed, wood-framed building located directly behind the Employees' Clubhouse. In fact, power was fed to this building from Building 32. It was built in 1926, although it was not ready to open until 1929. (*See Male Cottage K and Building 32.*)

Both patients and employees used this bowling alley, which had four bowling lanes. Employees paid a minimal fee to play, but all proceeds went toward building maintenance and for the salaries of patients that worked here as pinsetters. It was part of their occupational therapy.

Bowling team champions pose with their trophy, circa 1938

Bowling team holding bowling balls

After the bowling alley closed down and was eventually demolished in 1975, a new bowling alley replaced it when Building 23 was built to be the new recreational center. (*See Building 23.*)

Building 32

This was more popularly known as the Employees' Clubhouse, but before that, it was Male Cottage 32 (K). Initially, it was built as a residence for the male night attendants, who were previously crowded onto wards with patients. Ward 32 was located in this cottage, but there were never any patients here. It was a two-story wood-framed cottage with a basement, an attic, and a gable roof design. It was built from 1895 to 1896, using wood taken from the original temporary buildings. This cottage was located directly in front of the bowling alley on the west side of the boulevard north of Buildings C. (*See Male Cottage K and Buildings 11 and 31.*)

KINGS PARK STATE HOSPITAL, L. I.

Postcard of the Clubhouse, circa 1909

Clubhouse from across
the boulevard, circa 1924

Undated postcard showing the
Clubhouse, Buildings C& D, & Ward 31

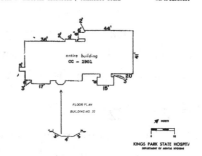

Building 32 floor plan

In the spring of 1899, the male night attendants were relocated to Ward 15 of Building D, and plans were set in motion to convert this cottage into an Employees' Clubhouse. Prior to this, the employees resorted to using one of the dayrooms from Building B during the evenings for the purpose of unwinding. The new clubhouse was opened to employees every day. On most nights, it closed at 10:00 p.m., except on Saturdays, when it stayed open until 11:00 p.m. (*See Buildings 9 and 10.*)

Establishing a lounge and recreational facility for the employees was very important, especially when employees were required to reside on the grounds. They needed somewhere to spend their time off, and this was it. It was conveniently situated and walking distance from all hospital buildings.

At the time, it was renovated and turned into the clubhouse. A new set of wooden stairs leading up from the boulevard was added. Longer-lasting cement stairs later replaced those stairs in 1911. There were many internal alterations made, which included a new paint job, carpentry work, plastering, electrical wiring, installation of electrical fixtures, and plumbing. New furniture was also brought in, along with a piano and pool table. By the time it was ready, the new clubhouse had a music room, card room, game room, reading room, and even smoking room. This cottage would serve as the clubhouse for the next few decades. A long-overdue refreshment room was added in 1928.

The janitor was allowed to sell tobacco and cigars. In the past, these purchases were mainly made at neighborhood hotels or bars. Employees would no longer have to be inconvenienced by leaving the premises for such purchases. A barbershop for employees was later established within, and there was an odontology room available for a dentist, who made weekly visits to the institution.

The second floor became the main gathering social center for the employees. Sometimes they would sit back and have casual conversations, and other times they might play a relaxing game of pool or pinochle.

The building was closed down for major renovations in 1954. New additions were made during this time.

By the mid-1960s, the clubhouse was moved into the new employees' lounge in Building 82, which had been the morgue. There were not many employees who were pleased by that thought. It is not a surprise the new lounge was not as popular as its predecessor. (*See Building 82.*)

Community Store with Buildings 31 & 93, circa 1973

Building 32 had been converted into a community store. It had everything a normal store would have, along with a few other necessities. Both employees and patients could come here to shop for goods.

Community Store staff at the entrance, circa May 1971

Community Store staff at the register, circa May 1971

This cottage only lasted as a store for about a decade. When Cafe 56 opened further down the boulevard as the new community store, this old cottage was abandoned. It was demolished in 1975, along with its neighbor, Building 31. (*See Building 56.*)

Building 33

P. J. Carlin was under contract to build the laundry building, which would later be numbered as Building 33, but what he created by the end of January in 1888 was a disappointment. The pavement within was not to term with the contract, which called for three inches of concrete. Instead, there was only one. Rather than a platform of blue stone for the washing machines of the washroom, there was plain concrete. The framing around the windows was botched too. The walls were only whitewashed one time when they should have been done twice. Obviously, this building was going to require a lot of repair work.

Building 32 demolition, circa 1975

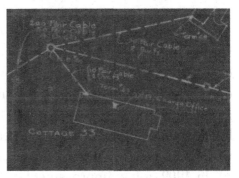

Blueprint showing Building 33 prior to the addition of its east wing

This one-story rectangular wood-framed building with a gable roof design was located north of St. Johnland Road on the east side of the boulevard across from the Group 2 buildings. In February of that year, a proposal was drawn up for someone to furnish and erect the machinery for the laundry building. This was the first laundry building built for the hospital and processed over one million items per year.

In 1899, the building had become so crowded a new wing had to be added behind it, giving the building an almost T shape. The hospital was in desperate need for a larger laundry facility because of the constantly increasing number of patients.

Building 33, the original laundry on Feb. 20, 1925

Aerial view of the laundry, 1927

At approximately nine o'clock in the morning on August 7, 1899, a small fire was discovered at the southwest end of the drying room. The fire alarm was sounded, and the fire companies quickly responded. By then, the laundry workers had managed to gain control of the fire by turning on the water. There was very little damage aside from some burned clothing. Apparently, the old woodwork caught fire from a pile of blankets in the room.

In 1902, a few improvements were made. There were thirty-one electric irons obtained as well as a twenty-thousand-watt transformer, a switchboard, and automatic reels to cut off the irons when not in use.

Four years later, another extension was added to the building. It had a special laundry area for the hospital staff. Four washers were installed in the extension, along with twelve washtubs and toilet fixtures for the staff. Nine six-pound electric flatirons were also installed at the staff laundry. Each was fitted with automatic take-ups and circuit breakers.

Also that year, three one-horse bobsleds were acquired for hauling laundry during snow days.

On the night of November 27, 1906, the entire building was badly damaged as a result of another fire. It was believed the fire began from sparks caused by the nearby railroad switch engine. A railroad siding went past the south end of this building and came to a stop between the original storehouse and main kitchen. It was an extremely windy night, and there was an abundance of dry leaves on the ground. At first, the fire was confined to the tar on the roof, but it soon spread quickly, leaving very little of the building standing. The loss, which included institutional clothing, patient clothing, uniforms, bed linens, laundry equipment, and machinery, was estimated at $86, 677.25. (*See Buildings 51 and 52.*)

Until Building 5 was built to take over as the new laundry building, the hospital's laundry was transported to a commercial laundromat via the railroad and also to Central Islip for a short time. As a temporary solution, small houses about eight-foot square in size were built near Wards 45 and 48 to store soiled clothing near Group 1, where temporary laundry facilities were set up. (*See Buildings 4, 5, 116, and 119.*)

In 1911, Building 33 was renovated to house up to three hundred working patients as Ward 33 with the first 150 patients being placed right away. It was only intended to be temporary patient accommodations until new buildings could be built. The wood walls had been covered with sheet iron, and the interior was lined with plaster. It consisted of two large dorms and a small dining room. There was no reception room or dayroom.

According to the map from 1912, this building number was changed to Building 53, although the ward number remained the same. It is very likely this supposed change on the map was made in error. In the annual report from 1913, this building is referred to as Cottage 33. However, Buildings 50–52 and 54 surrounded it, so it would make sense to number it as 53 on a map. (*See Buildings 50–52 and 54.*)

After a failed inspection on September 13, 1913, Deputy Marshal Peter P. Acritelli recommended to the State Fire Marshal that the use of this building be discontinued and it be removed.

The hospital continued using this building because of extensive overcrowding. It was not removed until around 1931. The sewage pump/screening house received the designation for Building 53, while Ward 33 was moved to Building 93 in 1939. (*See Buildings 53 and 93.*)

Once the old laundry building was gone, its original building number was reused for the steward's house, which stood in front of Building 93 on the west side of the boulevard next to the Employees' Clubhouse. The new Building 33 was originally Male Cottage H, which had been built from 1895 to 1896. (*See Male Cottage H, K, and Building 32.*)

This cottage was used as the first residence for superintendent Oliver M. Dewing until a more suitable home could be established for him on the current site of the senior director's mansion. The resident steward moved from Building 56 into the second Building 33, and it became the steward's house. (*See Buildings 56 and 67.*)

The second Building 33 was demolished sometime around 1940–1945.

Building 34

Building 34, also called Building H, was the nurses' residence, although it was more commonly referred to as the Employees' or Nurses' Home in its earlier years. This three-story U-shaped brick building stood on a hill across from the current location of Building 15 on the east side of the boulevard and was situated between Buildings 1 and the firehouse. It had a basement, an attic, and a hip roof design. The front porch had two balcony levels above it. A concrete staircase led down to the boulevard from the main entrance. The contract for this building was acquired at the end of 1901, but construction did not begin until 1903. A patient workforce excavated the land beforehand. The building was completed by 1906 at the cost of $60,000. Fire escapes were added during that final year. (*See Buildings 1, 15, and 83.*)

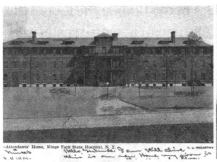

Postcard of the employees'
home, circa 1905

Postcard of Building 34, circa 1910

Dewing Home from across
the boulevard, circa 1912

Facing south toward Dewing Home

At the time of its completion, there were many defects in its construction. There were several complaints that it took longer to complete than expected. Furthermore, the workmanship of the interior was done haphazardly. The plaster would crumble at the slightest touch. The entire interior had to be redone to resolve this issue. Repairs over the next year cost an additional $11,473.46.

When the building opened on August 2, 1906, many of its residents were pleased with the result. It was the first large building built specifically to house employees. The males were housed in one wing, while females were in the other. There were three hundred rooms in total. Employees affectionately referred to it as the Riding Academy, as it gave off a rather impressive appearance atop its hill, overlooking the boulevard.

Over the next few years, pieces of plaster gradually kept falling off the walls. The cement on the basement floor began to bulge in areas. There were also large holes in the floor at the foot of the central stairs. By 1909, it became quite apparent more repairs were required, including replastering the walls and recementing the basement floor.

After the death of former superintendent Dewing on March 15, 1910, this building was named Dewing Home in his memory.

When Macy Home opened in 1918, most of the nursing activity was centralized to that building instead. In 1923,

Employees sitting on the steps of Dewing Home, circa 1928

an occupational therapy center opened in the basement of Dewing Home. During the early 1950s, part of the basement was renovated to provide a teaching center for in-service training classes. (*See Building 90.*)

By the early 1960s, only the south wing of Dewing Home remained open. According to a former employee, there were only about twenty-five African American employees working there at the time. The building closed in 1966.

Employees were given hammers and had to bang out the copper mesh from the old wooden screen windows to use as scrap. One employee, Paul Kelly, recalls how this process produced clouds of copper particles that were toxic to breathe. He said reflectively, "*I felt like a copper miner by the end of the day!*"

As the beginning of a demolition phase that lasted into the next year, this building was demolished in 1967, along with several other abandoned buildings. The demolition phase would also see the end of the former power plant and its boiler house. The rubble from Building 34 was buried within the basement, per the usual practice. Half of the area where it once stood was converted into a larger parking lot for Building 1. (*See Buildings 1, 6, and 84.*)

Building 35

Building 35 housed nursing students and was called Home V. It offered single-room occupancy not too different from a boarding house. It was a two-story rectangular brick building with an attic and basement. There was a tunnel in the basement that connected it to Building 36. It had a slate hip roof with a Georgian Revival design that was surmounted by two white louvered cupolas. The front entrance had a broken arch scrolled pediment design. Built from 1931 to 1932, it was located on the north side of East Third Street east of Building 3. It opened in 1934. (*See Buildings 3 and 36.*)

Home V under construction on Aug. 19, 1932

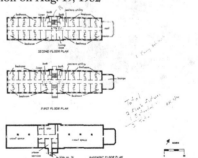

Home V east entrance, circa 1958   Building 35 floor plans

This building was vacant by the mid-1970s after the nursing school was closed. It remained abandoned for many years until it was finally demolished in April 2013, followed by Building 36.

Home V, circa Jan. 2008

Home V steps, circa Jan. 2008

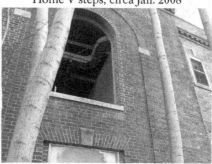

Home V lounge wing on July 11, 2011

Home V west entrance, circa Jan. 2008

Entrance steps on July 11, 2011

Looking up the stairwell to a hole in the roof on July 11, 2011

Main corridor on July 11, 2011   Basement of Building 35 on July 11, 2011

Building 35 between Buildings 3 & 36 on April 16, 2013   Fenced off demolition area for Buildings 35 & 36 on April 16, 2013

Building 35 on April 16, 2013   Former location of Building 35 on July 30, 2013

Building 36

Situated directly behind Building 35 on the north side of East Third Street, Building 36 was built from 1931 to 1932. Similar to Building 35, it was a two-story rectangular brick building with an attic and basement. It also had a slate hip roof with a Georgian Revival design that was surmounted by two white louvered cupolas. However, the front entrance differed from its neighbor. It had a segmental arch pediment design. Building 36 was better known as Home W. When it opened in 1934, it was utilized for housing nurses in single-room living quarters just like Building 35. Both buildings were connected via a tunnel in their basements. (*See Building 35.*)

Building 36 under construction
on Aug. 19, 1932

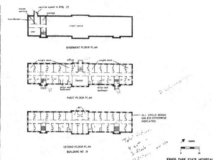

Building 36 floor plans

In the mid-1970s, this building was closed, along with its neighbor, Building 35, after the School of Nursing closed. Both buildings stood abandoned for decades afterward.

Home W, circa Jan. 2008

Home W steps on July 11, 2011

Facing south across the front of
Home W, circa Jan. 2008

Home W entrance,
circa Jan. 2008

Damage to roof of Home
W, circa Jan. 2008

Facing north toward Home W
in the woods on Jan. 23, 2013

Demolition of these buildings began in April 2013. Building 35 was razed first, followed by Building 36. The demolition of Building 36 was completed in May of the same year. I was able to take some photos of the event.

Building 36 on April 16, 2013

Demolition of Building
36 on May 1, 2013

Removal of rubble & wash down
of dust & debris on May 1, 2013

Former location of Building
36 on July 30, 2013

The first Building 36 was the third blacksmith and wheelwright shop that can be found on the 1912 map. It was located next to where Building 57 was later built to house several mechanical shops. (*See Building 57.*)

Here is where things may get confusing. This blacksmith and wheelwright shop was moved to this location and rebuilt in 1915, which means either the 1912 map was not drafted in 1912 or it was dated incorrectly. Based on known facts, it must have been created in 1915, if not later.

In 1924, a new blacksmith shop was built as a replacement, numbered as Building 86. (*See Building 86.*)

Building 37

Building 37 is an irregular two-story W-shaped brick building with a basement built from 1931 to 1932. It has a hip roof design and a metallic ladder in the basement leading down to a subbasement level connecting to the steam tunnels. This building has a single-story center wing with an octagon-shaped dining room that leads into a rectangular kitchen at the end of that wing, while its other two-story wings extend outward on either side to the west and to the north. The front entrance was done in a segmental arched design. This building was used as a nonmedical employee staff house.

Building 37 under construction
on Aug. 1931

Building 37

Building 37

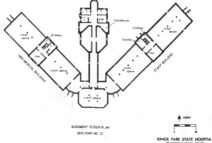

Building 37 floor plan (basement floor)

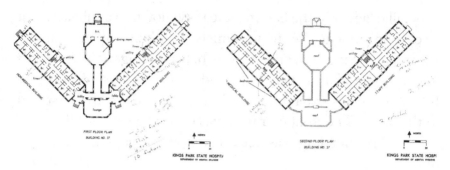

Building 37 floor plan (first floor)   Building 37 floor plan (second floor)

In 1934, once it opened, it had one of the coziest lounges on the grounds. There were psychiatric and neurological training films shown in this lounge on Tuesdays at seven o'clock in the evening every month. There were also many employee parties held here.

Class of 1968 Senior Dinner,
circa May 1968

Class of 1971 Senior
Dinner, circa 1971

Instructors & students at the
staff house, circa 1971

Class of '72 Senior Dinner, 1972,
Principal Anita Reyda with 2 employees

Kate Newcomb, Dr. Shepherd
Nathan, & Walter Lynch,
Sen Dinr May '72

Class of 1972 Senior Dinner students
help themselves to a meal, 1972

Student nurses seated in the
lounge, circa 1972

Employees in the staff
kitchen, circa 1974

The building was eventually closed sometime after 1980. It still stands behind Macy Home on the north side of East Fourth Street, although it is abandoned. (*See Building 90.*)

Building 37 on March 17, 2013

Rooftop of Building 37 on Sept. 15, 2014

Kitchen stoves & sinks on April 17, 2016

Kitchen on Sept. 15, 2014

Octagon-shaped room on April 17, 2016

Staff house lounge on April 17, 2016

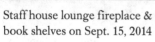

Staff house lounge fireplace &
book shelves on Sept. 15, 2014

Staircase on Sept. 15, 2014

First floor brick corridor
on Sept. 15, 2014

Second floor dormitory
corridor on Sept. 15, 2014

Building 38

This two-story brick building with a basement and attic was used as the kitchen for Buildings A and B. It was located behind these buildings and was built from 1896 to 1897 with a hip roof design. Its primary electrical source of power came from Building A. In 1909, the hydraulic elevator within was overhauled.

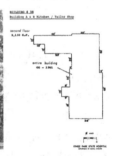

South side of
Building 38,
circa 1924

Rear of Building 38, circa 1913

Building 38
floor plan

For many years, this building was more commonly known as the cannery. The canning room of the building saw a lot of business during its early years. It was here where many vegetables and fruits collected on the farmlands and orchards of the grounds were canned and stored away for later use.

Safety Officers Patiky brothers, circa 1910s-1920s

Vaudeville Exchange posing at rear of Building 38 on Nov. 10, 1921

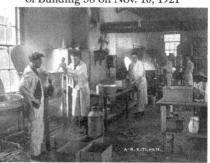

Kitchen staff, circa 1921

Kitchen staff, circa 1924

In 1911, a small storage shed was built next to this building to store coal, soiled clothing, and garbage. A small brick extension was added two years later, allowing for a dining room to be used by medical staff and clerical workers. During the same year, a new refrigeration machine was installed, and a concrete garbage vault was built outside. The large range stove was rebuilt in 1919–1920.

During the 1940s, the kitchen facilities within Building 93 became the main kitchen of the entire hospital, while the second storehouse acted as the bakery. Most of the other kitchen buildings were no longer needed. (*See Buildings 44 and 93.*)

In 1953 Building 38 was converted into a tailor shop, after the old shop was demolished to make room for a new laundry building. (*See Buildings 28 and 94.*)

This building shared the fate of the buildings it once served and was demolished from 1975 to 1976, after having been abandoned for several years.

Rear steps, after Building 38 was abandoned, circa 1970s

Bricks were gradually separating & falling out, circa 1970s

Building 39 (Building 73Q)

Building 39 was a two-story brick building with a basement, an attic, and a flat roof, built from 1931 to 1932. It was originally listed as Building 141 (73Q) but was renumbered as Building 39. In 1934, the building opened and was used for continued group care. Wards 87–92 and Brooklyn Unit 2 were located here. The building was located at the St. Johnland Road entrance to Sound View Road and stood on the west side of that road. It was the last building added to the Veterans' Memorial Hospital Unit. (*See Buildings 73 and 141.*)

Building 39 (73Q), circa 1970s

Creating an underground connection
between Buildings 39 & 139, 1928

Building 39 (73Q) from St.
Johnland Road, circa 1975

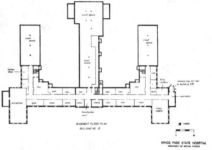

Building 39 floor plan (basement)

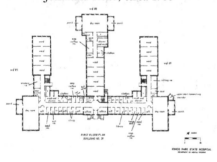

Building 39 floor plan

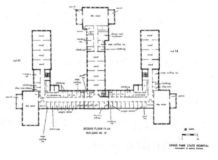

Building 39 floor plan (second floor)

The basement connected to the underground tunnel system. A staircase also led up to the first floor of its neighbor, Building 139 (73O), which served as the kitchen and dining hall for Buildings 39 and 138 (73N). (*See Buildings 138 and 139.*)

Constructing a handicapped accessible
ramp for Building 39 (73Q)

Rooftop solarium on April 28, 2013

Overturned laundry cart in the
solarium on April 28, 2013

Facing east toward the rest of the Vet
Grp from solarium on April 28, 2013

In 1956, a recreation area was set up in the brick solarium on the rooftop of the building. It had barred windows all around. Patients were able to read, play music, shuffleboard, and other quiet games while enjoying the fresh air. A ramp for the handicapped was added in front in the 1950s.

In the early part of 1983, Rehabilitation Services established a new program within this building. It was called the Pins N' Needles Sewing Program. Basically, the patients were paid to make repairs to the clothing of

Building 39 (73Q) employees

other patients and staff members under the close supervision of ward personnel.

Electroconvulsive therapy was conducted on Ward 88 of this building. Typically, there were twenty-two patients at a time taken to this ward for shock treatments.

Building 39 (73Q) on Dec. 22, 2011

Engraved 1932 stone near rooftop on July 3, 2009

Building 39 (73Q) from St. Johnland Road on Jan. 23, 2013

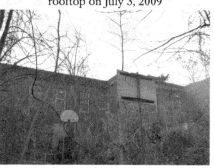

Rear courtyard with basketball hoops on Dec. 22, 2011

Building 39 (73Q) corridor with open doors on April 28, 2013

Another corridor on April 28, 2013

Looking into a patient ward
on April 28, 2013

Destroyed ward ceiling
on April 28, 2013

Patient shower stalls on April 28, 2013

Freight elevator on April 28, 2013

The original Building 39 was a small one-story wood-framed garage built in 1917, shortly after Macy Home was completed. It was used as the first garage for that building. In the mid-1920s, Building 91 replaced it around the same time new cottages were erected to house doctors. (*See Buildings 90, 91, and 95–99.*)

The original Building 39, circa Feb. 1925

Building 40

This was a one-story Y-shaped brick building with a basement built in 1932 as an annex for Group 2. It has a combined hip roof and flat roof design with a scrolled limestone cupola at the center. This building is located on the west side of Kings Park Boulevard north of St. Johnland Road, and it used to stand behind the older buildings of the group. This building housed Ward 50 and was the last building to be added to Group 2. (*See Buildings 54 and 122–124.*)

Building 40 with cars in parking lot, circa 1970s

Building 40, circa 1970s

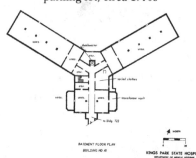

Building 40 floor plan (basement)

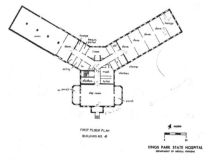

Building 40 floor plan (first floor)

It first opened as the female infirmary in 1935. A beauty parlor was later added to the first floor. Years later, it became a day care center for the employees' children. In 1953, a new Children's Unit was established, and soon the children were moved to this building. A library was set up for the new unit to be used by medical personnel. It consisted of basic books on psychiatry and child care. Many of the books were donated.

Toward its final years of use as a patient building during the 1970s, Ward 50 became Ward 851 as part of the Mental Retardation Unit (MRU).

During the summer of 1976, the front dayroom was divided in half. The west side was divided into two rooms separated by a hallway. The larger room on the east side was used as the nurses' station for the entire unit. The western side was divided into about four small offices. The shift supervisor's office was moved here from inside the ward.

After Group 2 was closed to patients, this building received the nickname the Playground by the Sound, which was very similar to Building 1's nickname, the Residence by the Sound. A playground was set up behind it, and the building served as a day care center for the employees' children. The building was vacant by 1983, along with the rest of Group 2. The day care center was moved to Building 23. (*See Buildings 1 and 23.*)

Building 40 entrance, circa 1981   Building 40 abandoned, circa 2008

The cupola, circa 2008   Building 40 on March 26, 2011

While it was a day care center, the walls inside were painted with various cartoon character murals, which are still there today. On the outside, the playground in the rear remains eerily silent. Many years after the building was closed, the painted hopscotch numbers are still visible on the ground. Rusted playground equipment still stand in a place that was once a lively area bursting with youthful energy. Over the years, nature has gradually swallowed this area up. However, if one listens closely, sometimes the sound of children can still be heard like a distant echo.

Playground swings on June 20, 2016   Playground slide on June 20, 2016

Faded hopscotch markings
on June 20, 2016

Tricycle, circa 2008

"Welcome to the Threes,"
circa Aug. 31, 2013

Sesame Street mural on Aug. 31, 2013

Fisher Price activity center
toys on Aug. 31, 2013

Kitchen on Aug. 31, 2013

Building 40 on Jan. 23, 2013, not
long after Group 2 demolitions

Building 40 on Sept. 15, 2014

Buildings 41, 42, and 43 (Group 4)

This group of buildings, often referred to as the Quad by urban explorers, is located on the west side of Old Dock Road across from the final power plant (Building 29). These three buildings are the second set of buildings known as Group 4. The original Group 4 was a cluster of one-story pavilions used to house tuberculosis wards. The newer Group 4 buildings formed a type of cross with the way they were connected. (*See Buildings 3 and 29.*)

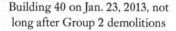

Buildings 41-43 (Group
4), Wards 101-128,
circa 1950s-1960s

Group 4 under construction,
circa 1933-1934

Old Dock Road
entrance to
Building 41, circa
1950s-1970s

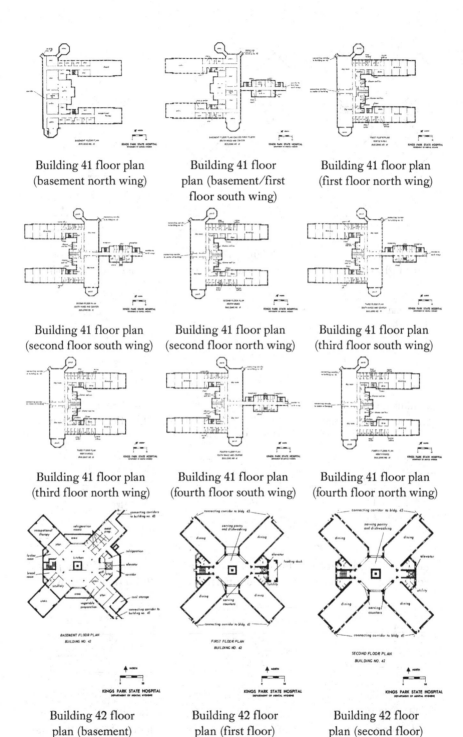

Building 41 floor plan
(basement north wing)

Building 41 floor
plan (basement/first
floor south wing)

Building 41 floor plan
(first floor north wing)

Building 41 floor plan
(second floor south wing)

Building 41 floor plan
(second floor north wing)

Building 41 floor plan
(third floor south wing)

Building 41 floor plan
(third floor north wing)

Building 41 floor plan
(fourth floor south wing)

Building 41 floor plan
(fourth floor north wing)

Building 42 floor
plan (basement)

Building 42 floor
plan (first floor)

Building 42 floor
plan (second floor)

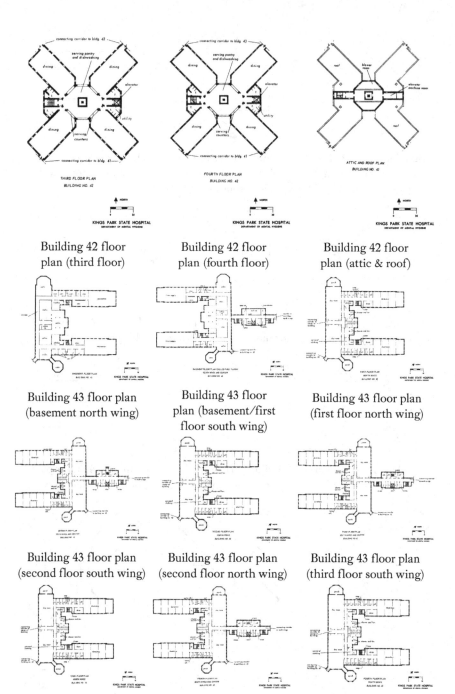

Building 42 floor plan (third floor)

Building 42 floor plan (fourth floor)

Building 42 floor plan (attic & roof)

Building 43 floor plan (basement north wing)

Building 43 floor plan (basement/first floor south wing)

Building 43 floor plan (first floor north wing)

Building 43 floor plan (second floor south wing)

Building 43 floor plan (second floor north wing)

Building 43 floor plan (third floor south wing)

Building 43 floor plan (third floor north wing)

Building 43 floor plan (fourth floor south wing)

Building 43 floor plan (fourth floor north wing)

Building 42 is situated at the center in the shape of an X. There was a loading dock on the ground level at the north side of the building. Buildings 41 and 43 are almost identical H-shaped buildings that are divided into north and south wings. They are on opposite ends of Building 42. Four octagonal towers flank the four wings of the building, although the two on the east are attached to Building 41, while the two on the west are part of Building 43. Buildings 41 and 42 were both built from 1932 to 1933, while Building 43 was completed a year later. All three are four-story brick buildings with basements and attics. Elevators are located at the central portions of all three. Each building has a part flat roof and part hip roof, while only Building 42 has a white Wren-style cupola at the center of its roof.

| Building 42 with turrets from Building 41 & 43, circa 1970s-1980s | Cupola atop Building 42 on Aug. 31, 2013 | East side of Building 41, circa 1980s |

While both Buildings 41 and 42 have basements, only Building 41 has a subbasement beneath the northeast wing that connects to the underground steam tunnels. Technically, Building 43 just has half of a basement at the south wings.

At their peak, these buildings once housed approximately two thousand patients and are among the most photographed buildings on the grounds because of their unique formation and

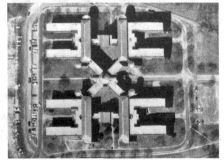

Aerial photo from April 10, 1976

close proximity to the road, making them more easily accessible. Building 41 is closest to the road, while Building 43 is the furthest situated closer to the woods. Maple Hill Road encircles this group of buildings and connects them to Old Dock Road.

When these buildings opened during the mid-1930s, the children's ward was moved here from the old cottages. In 1952, the ward was reorganized in the new Children's Unit to include boys and girls under the age of 16, thus dividing the wards into a ward for teens and another for adolescents and juveniles. There was a Boys' Unit and a Girls' Unit.

Recreational activities for children and adults generally took place in the basements of Buildings 41 and 43. During the early 1950s, a recreation room was added below Ward 109 for the females of the group. Another recreation room was set up below Ward 117 in 1954, also for female patients. In 1958, this recreation room was vacated and relocated to below Ward 113. Some of the recreational activities included bowling, music, ping-pong, pool, reading at the library, shuffleboard, and an occasional party. The children also had drama workshops, while the girls had home economics.

Elderly patients & swings, circa 1970s   St. Patrick's Day at Group 4, circa 1977

Building 41 housed the Female Unit and was home to Wards 101–108 and Wards 123–128. It was primarily used for geriatric and ambulatory care and referred to as Group 4 Front, because of its proximity to Old Dock Road. A chapel was set up in the basement of the north wing, as seen in a previous chapter.

Building 41 south wing on Dec. 19, 2012   Looking up at Building 41 from
Old Dock Road on Dec. 19, 2012

Building 42 was the kitchen and dining hall of Group 4. Therefore, it was conveniently situated between both other buildings. This X-shaped building was connected to the other two buildings at each wing of the group, allowing every ward access to the dining facilities. In the basement were cold storage rooms and a coal storage room.

Building 42 with turrets from   Cold storage rooms in the basement
Building 41 & 43 on Nov. 7, 2011   of Building 42 on Aug. 25, 2011

Building 43 housed the Male Unit and Juvenile Girls' Unit as well as geriatric female patients on Wards 109–122. It was referred to as Group 4 Back because it was the furthest of the group from Old Dock Road. Two wards were set aside for shock treatment in this building, which was used for all patients of the group, including the children. Convulsive therapy using insulin was mainly used on patients with schizophrenia. There was also a room on the ground floor in the rear of this building's south wing, where numbered stones for the cemetery were made.

Building 43 north wing on Nov. 7, 2011   Building 43 on Aug. 31, 2013

A recreation area was established outside of this building exclusively for female patients. There were benches, picnic tables, and swings set up here.

In 1953, a whole new Children's Unit was established, which divided the juveniles from the adolescents. The adolescents were all relocated to Group 2, while the children remained here. The buildings of Group 4 underwent rehabilitation for their rooftops during the same year. (*See Buildings 54 and 122–124.*)

In 1966, there was a fire at the top of Building 42, which had been caused by an accumulation of grease that left the cupola on the roof damaged. The cupola and ducts were rebuilt shortly afterward.

According to former hospital workers, the majority of patients in this group during the last decade or so were mainly ex-prostitutes from New York

Firefighters putting out fire at cupola, circa 1966

City who had grown too old and sick with no one else to care for them.

The buildings were closed in 1992 and abandoned. Today, they are among the most explored by urban explorers. In June 2017 there was a minor fire.

Group 4 on Jan. 11, 2009

South side of Building 42
on Jan. 11, 2009

Building 41 east entrance
on Aug. 21, 2013

Building 41 corridor on Aug. 21, 2013

Building 43 patient ward
on Aug. 25, 2011

Building 41 patient ward
on Aug. 31, 2013

Building 42 food service
area on Aug. 25, 2011

Hobart dishwasher in Building
42 on Aug. 25, 2011

Building 42 dining room
on Aug. 25, 2011

Attic of Building 41 on Aug. 31, 2013

Building 42 first floor corridor
on Aug. 21, 2013

Building 43 exit staircase
E on Oct. 23, 2011

Building 43 basement storage/
recreation room on Aug. 25, 2011

Stuffed rabbit on the floor
on Oct. 23, 2011

Building 44

Building 44 was a two-story brick storage warehouse with a basement and a flat roof. Built from 1934 to 1935, it replaced the first storehouse. The new storehouse contained general storage rooms on the second floor, a prefabricated freezer box installed in the basement in 1968, a refrigeration storage area on the first floor, seven cold storage rooms, an ice plant, a butcher shop, and a bakery in the basement that replaced the original bakery. It also had a freight elevator at the center of the building. It was located on the north side of Orchard Road behind Building 93. (*See Buildings 51, 52, and 93.*)

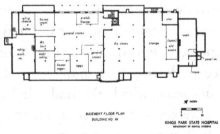

Storehouse, circa 1940s

Building 44 floor plan (basement)

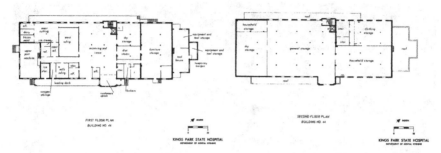

Building 44 floor plan (first floor)   Building 44 floor plan (second floor)

This building was used as a storage facility for goods delivered to the hospital, except for coal. It was the hospital's version of Home Depot and Costco rolled into one! Loading docks were at the front and rear of the building to make deliveries easier. A ramp was added to the railroad trestle near the power plant area leading down into a warehouse, making it easier for the deliveries by train.

Every week, the storehouse crew went through twenty-five thousand pounds of fresh fruits and vegetables, eighteen thousand quarts of milk, ten thousand hamburger buns and hotdog rolls, 5,600 loaves of baked bread, and thirteen thousand cakes and assorted pastries.

There were two different types of scales used to weigh items in the storehouse. One type had a dial, and the other had a triple beam. The scale in the butcher shop had a dial. When the doctors who lived on the grounds ordered food twice a week, there was a smaller table model scale. It was used for things like sugar, flour, etc., which came in one-hundred-pound bags. The kitchens received everything in full bags. There was a floor scale near the truck scale, which also had a dial. It was used whenever fruits and vegetables were delivered. There was one other scale with bars on it that was used at random.

The storehouse was also used for occupational therapy until that came to an end by the 1970s. Patients would work together with employees loading or unloading goods and storing them in the various rooms. The patients would also assist employees with other clerical and janitorial duties, as they did in many of the nonresidential hospital buildings.

Storehouse employees wrapping Christmas gifts, circa 1980s

Storehouse employees pose in front of Christmas tree, circa 1980s

Employees stacking boxes, circa 1980s

Storage room

During the 1980s–1990s, a separate storage room, only accessible from the outside, on the ground floor at the north end of the building was used as a temporary morgue to store deceased patients of the hospital who died over the weekend. Deceased patients from the Manhattan State Hospital and the Brooklyn State Hospital units were also stored here. The bodies would usually be buried on the next Monday morning.

Entrance to outer storage
room on April 17, 2016

Interior of outer storage
room on April 17, 2016

This area was also used as storage by the Grounds Department until they moved their tools and equipment over to Building 48 of the old dairy farm. After the hospital was closed, the equipment was relocated once more to the old firehouse, where they are currently stored and secured behind the doors of the garage. (*See Buildings 48 and 83.*)

In 2014, there was a fire that began on the second floor of the storehouse in an old records room, where old records had been left behind stored in boxes. It is believed to have been a case of arson set to deliberately destroy those old records, mainly consisting of census reports. The fire department created a large hole at the south side of the building to better put out the blaze. The hole remained in place with a wire mesh covering over it.

Building 44 fire damage
on Sept. 15, 2014

Visible damage to windows
on Sept. 15, 2014

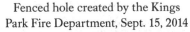

Fenced hole created by the Kings
Park Fire Department, Sept. 15, 2014

Pile of rubble on Sept. 15, 2014
left behind from the fire

Many old relics of the hospital could still be found inside for years, covered in dust and lost in time, such as the giant scales used to weigh food. The building could be seen through the trees across from Shanahan's bar on the south side of Old Dock Road with the eerie presence of Building 93 towering in the background, until it was demolished in 2017. (*See Building 93.*)

Building 44 on May 11, 2011

Building 44 east loading
dock on May 11, 2011

Forklift in the storehouse on May 11, 2011

Second floor general storage area on March 17, 2013

Boxes of census reports on March 17, 2013, before the fire

Large rolls of insulation material on March 17, 2013

Refrigeration rooms on March 17, 2013

Refrigeration machine room on March 17, 2013

Building 45

There were two buildings to use the number 45. The first was the piggery, built from 1897 to 1898. It was located just north from the current site of William T. Rogers Middle School near Flynn Road. It was a one-story L-shaped, wood-framed building with an attic and a gable roof. Both the interior and exterior pens were cemented to help keep the area clean, as it was connected to the water supply and sewage system. The piggery accommodated five hundred pigs.

Building 45, the piggery

Piggery on June 17, 1915   Piggery on Sept. 13, 1917

In 1907, there were twelve new hog troughs built. Another twenty were added two years later. Renovations were made from 1913 to 1915, which included the construction of approximately forty new colony houses to accommodate an additional ten pigs each, although it was desired that a new piggery be erected elsewhere.

A new one was eventually built in 1940, and the old one was abandoned. It was demolished sometime around 1965, and its number designation was reused for the water tower. (*See Building 87.*)

Water tower with ladder
hanging, circa 1970s

Worker walking around the
water tower, circa 1970s

Water tower, circa 1975

Water tower & truck dumping
ash from power plant, 1977

This aqua-colored water tower is located at the end of a long uphill road beyond Potter's Field Cemetery and west of Old Dock Road. It was built from 1957 to 1960 atop a hill largely made up of ash from the different power plants that existed. It overlooks the western part of the grounds.

According to the floor plan data sheet for this building, it was supposedly built from 1959 to 1960. However, this structure can be seen in aerial photography after March 1957, such as Vito Caponetto's photo shown in chapter 7 and this one from the New York State Archives. Built using welded steel plating, it had a water capacity of five hundred thousand gallons in its spheroid tank. Over a million gallons of water was used each day.

Aerial photo, circa 1957

When the tower was emptied after the hospital closed, the water flowed down the hill to Old Dock Road, dragging old bones with it. At first, residents of the town thought the bones were from the cemetery, which was a disparaging thought. The residents were quite relieved to learn the bones were actually pig bones from the old piggery.

Water tower visible from the
boulevard on June 22, 2010

View of the water tower from the
roof of Building 7 on March 9, 2014

The top of the water tower can be seen above the treetops from great distances around the hospital, but the constant tree growth surrounding that area is gradually making it impossible to view. It is now home to dozens of pigeons, which use the small porthole entrance located on the upper section to fly in and out.

Approaching the water
tower on May 11, 2011

Water tower on March 9, 2014

Water tower on April 28, 2013

Full spectrum photo of water tower on Sept. 15, 2014

Infrared photo of water tower on April 28, 2013

Sealed entrance to water tower on May 11, 2011

Open door on September 15, 2014

Looking toward the doorway from the inside on Sept. 15, 2014

Rusted pipe & water valve on Sept. 15, 2014

There is still water beneath the tower, as seen on Sept. 15, 2014

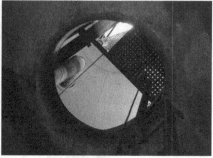

Looking up the first ladder to the second level on Sept. 15, 2014

Second level covered with bird droppings on Sept. 15, 2014

Looking up the ladder to the upper levels on Sept. 15, 2014

Another ladder leads to an open hatch at the top, circa 2000s

Pigeon perched at the port window on Sept. 15, 2014

Building 45.1

This was an eight-by-eight soiled clothing house erected in 1907 outside of Ward 45 soon after a fire destroyed the laundry building. It lasted until much of Group 1 was destroyed by fire in 1972. (*See Buildings 4, 6, and 116.*)

Building 46

Building 46 was a one-story concrete vegetable root cellar with a gable roof added to the dairy farm at the cost of $1,500. It was built in 1917 on the west side of Old Dock Road next to the original dairy barn with its back against the bank of the hill and its front facing north. (*See Building 2.*)

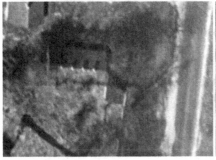

Aerial of root cellar with Old Dock Road on the right, circa 1964

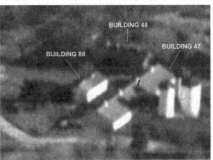

Aerial photo indicating farm buildings, from 1967

It was demolished from 1966 to 1967, although its foundation remained until the last of the farm buildings were demolished.

During the 1980s, Building 88, built in the 1940s, became confused with Building 46. This could have happened as the result of a survey that was done of the buildings in 1983. Both buildings were similar in size and shape and stood next to each other. This error has appeared on several maps and websites. (*See Building 88.*)

Foundation of Building 46 on Nov. 7, 2011

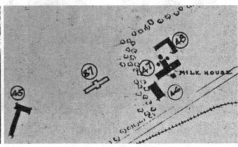

Close-up of 1941 map showing farm buildings

Building 88 was being used to store salt for the winter as of 1983. It continued in that capacity until the early 1990s, when a pyramid-type shed was added near the maintenance and engineering shop. Afterward, the second "Building 46" remained vacant and was eventually abandoned. (*See Buildings 5 and 5.1.*)

The hike-and-bike trail signs along the trail incorrectly refer to this building as Building 46. To maintain continuity, I will say Building 88 was renumbered as Building 46. It was demolished, along with Building 48 in December 2012.

Hike & Bike Trail sign on Nov. 7, 2011

Building 47

This was a long one-story wood-framed dairy barn made of white clapboards, built from 1940 to 1941 as a replacement for the previous dairy barn that was destroyed by fire. It had a gable roof and was built on a concrete foundation. Located on the west side of Old Dock Road, this barn had three silos on its west side. There were accommodations for about one hundred cattle inside.

Building 47 with silos

Demolition of the silos, circa 1970s

As of the late 1950s, the hospital phased out its farming operations. This building was used for storage during the final years of the hospital. The silos were demolished around 1972–1978. The building was abandoned by the mid-1990s.

Abandoned dairy barn, circa 1990s

Dairy barn close-up, circa 1990s

Crumbling foundation of the
dairy barn, circa 1990s

Dairy barn entrance, circa 1980s-1990s

By then, the building was in a terrible state of disrepair. It was demolished around 1998–1999. Only its foundation remained as of the 2010s.

Foundation of dairy barn
on September 9, 2011

Foundation of dairy barn with
tree branches on Sept. 9, 2011

Today, grass and overgrown weeds cover the entire area of the former dairy farm.

Building 48

The first Building 48 was the amusement hall. Built from 1888 to 1889, this cottage was located on the south side of East Fourth Street near Student Road. It originally served as the dining hall for female patients of the early cottages while doubling as an amusement hall and gymnasium for both male and female patients. (*See Female Cottage K.*)

Boys' physical culture class in the amusement hall, circa 1920s

Girls' physical culture class in the amusement hall, circa 1920s

Men's physical culture class in the amusement hall, circa 1920s

Women's physical culture class in the amusement hall, circa 1920s

Before St. Joseph's Church was built in 1898, its parish held religious services in the sunroom of this cottage. The building was not even complete at the time of the first mass in 1888. The parish was established at the hospital before later moving to the new church building. The hospital continued to hold religious services at the amusement hall for its patients and employees. (*See Building 121.*)

Major renovations were done over the next year, including the addition of a stage. A portion of the building was rebuilt to include a water closet (restroom). At this time, the building became a permanent amusement hall. Female patients began to eat their meals at their cottages instead. Dining rooms and pantries were set up at each cottage starting in 1897.

There were 250 lights installed on the stage in 1902. By 1910, a new improved stage was built to replace the old one. The entire building was repainted in 1920.

Some of the plays performed during the early 1900s were *The Arabian Nights, Box and Cox, Little Toddlekins, Married for Money, Miss Jerry, My Lord in Livery, My Turn Next, To Oblige Benson, What Happened to Jones,* and *Uncle, Turn Them Out.* There were also two minstrel shows and a Vaudeville performance by the end of 1900. Over the next year, the patients were also entertained by the Actors' Club of the Actors' Colony at St. James and members of the Methodist and Roman Catholic churches of Kings Park. There were also blackface minstrel shows, more Vaudeville shows, and various other plays ranging from the works of William Shakespeare to early American classics.

The Womanless Wedding, performed from Nov. 23-24, 1931

Gala St. Patrick's Celebration on March 17, 1932

The hall seated a maximum of 350–400 patients. However, there were more than two thousand patients to entertain, and the numbers kept climbing each year. The hospital was in great need for a new amusement hall, although one would not be provided for about another twenty years.

When the Kings Park State Hospital School of Nursing was established, all capping, chevron, and graduation ceremonies took place here until York Hall was built in the early 1930s. The old amusement hall was demolished to clear the way for new staff residences. (*See Buildings 19 and 80.*)

There were two rustic summerhouse gazebos located to the north of the amusement hall. Both were built in 1906 using cedar poles. They were demolished by the 1920s.

Building 48, circa 1960s-1970s   North side of Building 48, circa 1990s

Facing north toward Building 48, circa 1990s

Plow & closed garages, circa 1988

West side of Building 48, circa 1990s

The next Building 48 was a two-story L-shaped concrete horse barn and implement storage shed with a gable roof, built from 1940 to 1942, on the west side of Old Dock Road. The two levels of the building were like two separate buildings in that they were not connected on the inside by any staircase or elevator. Each had to be accessed from the outside through separate entrances at the front, rear, and north side of the building. There were garage bays at the ground level and one on the upper level in the rear of the building.

In later years, this structure became a grounds-keeping warehouse. As with the rest of the farm buildings, it was ultimately abandoned. During its final years, one could find scattered old tools and equipment inside that were once used to tend the grounds and farm.

Building 48 was demolished in December 2012, along with its neighboring former farm building. (*See Building 46 and 88.*)

North side of Building 48 on Sept. 9, 2011

Garages on Sept. 9, 2011

Garage & upper office space on Sept. 9, 2011

Facing north in front of the garages on Sept. 9, 2011

Facing south in the lower level on Sept. 9, 2011

Facing north in the lower level on Sept. 9, 2011

East garage on lower level
on Oct. 24, 2011

Upper office on Oct. 24, 2011

East side of Building 48 on Sept. 9, 2011

Demolition of Building
48 on Dec. 19, 2012

Building 48A

This house was built long before the hospital was established. It previously belonged to the Kelly family and was constructed sometime around 1837–1858. The state purchased this house from John Kelly in 1895 with the tract of land surrounding it to build the hospital's railroad spur. The house was located on the same spot where

Head Farmer's house,
circa 1900-1964

the Kings Park Library would be built on Church Street in what is now downtown Kings Park at the intersection of East Main Street/Route 25A, dividing Indian Head Road to the south from Church Street on the north.

For the first few years, this house was not used as a residence because it was too cold during the wintertime. By 1911, one of the employees was residing here, essentially to keep an eye on the house because it was so far from the rest of the buildings.

Once the house was made comfortable from 1913 to 1914, it was used as the residence of the assistant steward, who was the head farmer. It was widely known as the state hospital's farmer's house or the head farmer's house. The assistant steward lived here from the 1920s to 1960s.

Not long after it was abandoned, this old farmhouse was burned down as a part of a practice fire drill in 1964. It sat directly across from the Kings Park Fire Department's firehouse. The library was built soon afterward.

Building 48.1

This was a sixty-four-square-foot soiled clothing house erected in 1907 outside of Ward 48 (Building 119) at Group 1 after a fire destroyed the laundry building. (*See Buildings 4, 33, and 119.*)

It was demolished at the same time as the rest of Group 1 from 1972 to 1973.

Building 49

This was a two-story hip-and-gable-roofed, wood-framed, single-family cottage with a basement and an attic built in 1892, which served as the assistant medical director's house, also known as the first assistant physician or the clinical director. He was second in charge, after the superintendent or senior director. This cottage was constructed on the southeast corner of East Fourth Street and St. Johnland Road near the early female cottages in a design reminiscent of the Queen Anne Revival style with its pointed, southeast corner, octagon-shaped turret. Extensions were added in 1897 and from 1906 to 1908, including a two-story addition. (*See Female Cottage J.*)

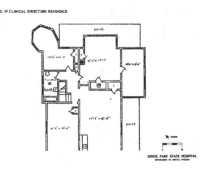

Facing south toward assistant
superintendent's residence,
circa 1910-1920s

Building 49 floor plan

From 1951 to 1953, the hospital's Maintenance Department remodeled the house and converted it into a two-family home. It was easily one of the most attractive homes on the grounds.

Building 49, circa 1976

This building stood abandoned for several years.

Sometime around late September or October 2000, it was practically burned to the ground, likely the result of arson. The smell of the burning wood reached as far as Kings Park High School. It was demolished a year later. Since then, trees have swallowed up the area where it once stood, leaving very little sign of it. Its unique staircase now leads to an old tree.

Building 49 abandoned,
circa 1990s-2000

Color photo, after fire in 2000

South side of house showing
fire damage, circa 2000

Distant view of south side
of house, circa 2000

Southeast corner of house, circa 2000

Northwest corner of
house, circa 2000

Interior of Building 49, after fire in 2000

Stone staircase to Building
49 on Jan. 2, 2016

South side foundation of
Building 49 on Jan. 2, 2016

Foundation of Building
49 on Jan. 2, 2016

Building 50

Building 50 consisted of two one-story square-shaped, wood-framed buildings with basements and hip roofs that were connected. The west wing was the employees' kitchen, called E Kitchen, and the east wing was the employees' dining room, or E Dining Room. While these structures catered to employees, patients occasionally dined here. Built in 1896 using wood from the original temporary buildings, they were located on the north side of St. Johnland Road next to the bakery and first storehouse on the west side of Garage Road.

Building 50, circa 1957   Building 50 with cars parked
in front, circa 1957

On August 11, 1899, at around six o'clock, the chimney in the kitchen caught fire. It is uncertain if this was during the morning or evening hours. An alarm was sounded, and the fire companies responded promptly. It was unnecessary to turn on the water, as the fire was extinguished without the need for it.

In 1906, the basement of the kitchen was sheathed so vegetables could be stored here as an alternative to the old nearby root cellar. A year later, the ceiling of the dining room was redone with wood because the old plaster from the ceiling was starting to fall apart. On February 2, 1908, strong winds blew the tin roof off of E Kitchen. It was immediately replaced. (*See Building 51.1.*)

Starting in 1909, any purchased vegetables were stored in the basement of E Kitchen. This had to be utilized as the temporary root cellar because the refrigerating pipes underneath the cold storage warehouse were heating up that basement, which had replaced the original root cellar a few years earlier. (*See Building 51.*)

Dining room, circa 1910s-1920s   Food service counter, circa 1910s-1920s

New equipment was acquired in 1911 to increase the capacity of the kitchen to account for the new patients that were placed in the old laundry building nearby. (*See Building 33.*)

When the state hospital purchased its first motor truck in 1912, E Kitchen was fitted to serve as a truck garage for the seven-ton vehicle. Items from within were stored nearby in the original storehouse. The employees now got their meals from the new kitchen of Group 2, while this portion of Building 50 was converted into a garage. In 1913, a small brick extension was added to E Dining Room, although this dining room was no longer used as often. (*See Buildings 54 and 123.*)

After Building 62 was built as a truck and maintenance garage in the late 1930s, the old E Kitchen truck garage was demolished, and the dining room was renamed Dining Room T. (*See Building 62.*)

It was abandoned and removed in 1967. It has been suggested that employees of the area dined within Building 123 of Group 2, until Group 2 became the MRU in the early 1970s.

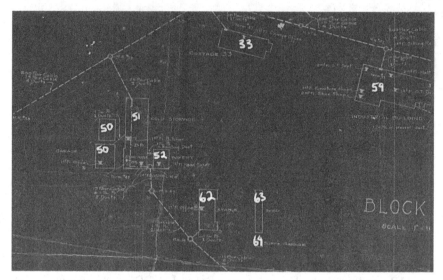

Blueprint showing Buildings 33, 50-52, 59, & 62-64, circa 1910s

Storehouse & kitchen, circa 1925

KPSH Plot Plan, circa 1970, indicating
Buildings 50-52, 62, & 80

Building 51

This was the hospital's first storage warehouse used for general and cold storage. Built in 1893, this two-story building with a basement had a hip roof and was located on the west side of Garage Road between the main kitchen/bakery and the employees' dining room. A butcher shop was located on the first floor. (*See Buildings 50 and 52.*)

Building 51, circa 1957   Buildings 50-53, circa 1957

An extension was added to the railroad spur in 1898, which came to a stop between this building and the bakery to make deliveries easier.

Although there was already an icehouse nearby, there was a great need for larger cold storage facilities. By 1901, a contract was made for a new cold storage building to be added as an extension to the storehouse. It would be built on the site of the root cellar, on the west side of the building. A year later, the root cellar was removed, and construction had begun on a long one-story rectangular brick building with a gable roof, an attic, and a basement. It was placed against the west side of the storehouse. (*See Buildings 51.1 and 58.*)

The cold storage building was completed only a few months later. It was also referred to as the refrigeration plant because of its several cooling rooms. The butcher shop was moved here to be closer to the new meat storage rooms. The former butcher shop at the storehouse was converted into a room for cleaning vegetables.

The basement of the cold storage building became the new root cellar. In 1903, a shed was built over the cellar entrance on the west side of the building, accessible from the outside.

A portion of the tin roof on the cold storage building was blown off during a powerful storm in 1905. It was subsequently replaced. During the same year, the windows were glazed and painted white on the outside of both buildings to deter theft. In addition, a new heavy coil was purchased and installed in the refrigeration plant.

More work was done during the next year. A vestibule was built for the meat room to prevent the warm air in the cutting room from reaching it. Considerable cork insulation was added to the structure, and more coils were replaced at the refrigerating plant. Work was done in 1908 to permit the storage of natural ice.

It was around this time that the original icehouse was abandoned.

During the same year, a track was built connecting the second floor of the storehouse to the second floor of the neighboring bakery to transport flour more easily. Storing flour at the storehouse had a tendency to attract rats, which was a major problem for many years.

Close-up showing rails between storehouse & bakery, circa 1957

By the spring of 1909, the old icehouse had been torn down, and the refrigeration plant officially became the new icehouse. A vestibule was built for the ice room to prevent warm air from melting the ice.

Unfortunately, the pipes in the basement that were connected to the refrigeration equipment were heating up the basement and making it impossible to store fresh vegetables. It became apparent the root cellar would have to be moved. Vegetables that were picked on the farm had to be kept in caches out on the field and brought in only as needed. This inconvenience resulted in a substantial loss in vegetables.

Sometimes, vegetables had to be purchased to make up for the lost crops. Purchased vegetables were stored in the basement underneath E Kitchen, which served as a temporary root cellar.

By 1910, there were plans to make room by building an addition to the refrigeration plant for an ice-making plant. This could help prevent possible typhoid contamination whenever using natural ice from Harned's Pond. During this year, a new icehouse was built on the site of the former one. It was believed the new icehouse could assist as the general cold storage building, while the refrigeration plant could serve as both an icehouse and ice-making plant.

A year later, the need for larger cold storage and refrigeration facilities became desperate. Meat was packed in so tightly there was barely enough room to move in the meat room. For the next few years, the hospital would make multiple requests to the state asking for the funds to build a larger storage facility, but relief would not come anytime soon.

In 1912, a roof was built over the rear porch of the storehouse, making deliveries easier during rainy days. Changes were also made in the cold storage house, allowing new ice-making machinery to be installed. At this point, the refrigeration plant had also become the ice plant.

By 1915, most of the hospital's kitchen buildings were equipped with their own refrigeration rooms, providing them with the means to make their own ice. The need for a general icehouse and ice-making plant became less important.

During the next year, there was a storage shed erected outside of this building for the purpose of covering the wagon scales, which had previously stood outside, unprotected from the weather. Prior to that, the scales would be affected each time they were covered by snow and ice, providing false readings. In addition, a refrigeration room was added on the second floor of the storehouse for cereal. A new asbestos roof was placed on the storehouse sometime around 1925.

In 1935, Building 44 was built as a new larger storehouse, which included a built-in refrigeration plant with improved ice rooms, meat rooms, and a butcher shop. Building 51 became obsolete and was closed. It was eventually abandoned between the 1940s and 1950s and then demolished in 1967. (*See Building 44.*)

Building 51.1

In 1890, a root cellar was built next to the original storehouse for storing vegetables. It was a one-story structure with a basement. Covers were added to the windows at some point to keep rodents from getting inside, as there was a constant rat problem in this area. As of 1899, additional covers were added to the windows. (*See Building 51.*)

There are no photos of this structure. It was demolished and replaced in 1902 after a cold storage extension was added to the storehouse.

Building 52

This two-story brick building with a gable roof, attic, and basement originally served as the hospital's main kitchen and bakery when it was built in 1892. A new roof was added in 1915. It was located on the west side of Garage Road north of St. Johnland Road. Supplies were received via the railroad spur, which had a special siding that stopped outside of the building.

Building 52 (bakery/ schoolhouse), circa 1950s-1970s

A new extension was added to the building from 1901 to 1902, and Duhrkop ovens were installed for baking bread, desserts, and other types of food for the entire hospital. At the time, these ovens were known for having the best capacity and baking the best breads. They were also cost effective in regard to fuel and labor.

For the first few years, all food would be cooked here and delivered to the male and female dining halls by wagon. By the time the food arrived at the dining halls, it was almost always cold. This changed in 1897, after Buildings A–D were constructed with new kitchens closer to the patient cottages. At last, patients could dine on hot meals! As new building groups were added with their own kitchens, these took over preparing meals for patients in the buildings nearer to them, including the cottages. (*See Female Cottage K, Male Cottage J, and Buildings 8–12, 31, and 38.*)

This building still served as the main bakery for many years. Bread, cakes, cookies, and pastries were baked here and delivered fresh to the kitchens.

In 1908, a track connecting the second floor of the storehouse to the second floor of the bakery was constructed for transporting flour. This made baking much easier without laborers going back and forth between both buildings, carrying the heavy bags upon their backs. Generally, it was the patients who did this labor in the name of occupational therapy.

During the same year, the hospital purchased a rolling dough trough made of steel, which was twenty-eight inches wide, twenty-two inches deep, and eight feet long. A second was obtained in 1911.

In 1909, Welch tiles were placed on the floor of the bakery, and an enclosure was built over the cement porch, improving the productivity space within.

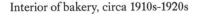

Interior of bakery, circa 1910s-1920s   Dishwasher, circa 1910s-1920s

As the hospital population grew, so did the demand for bread and other baked goods. The hospital was in need of a larger bakery, or larger ovens. Moving the bakery to the vacant old heating plant building was one option that was considered but was not done. (*See Building 59.*)

When Building 44 was completed in 1935, a new bakery was set up within to replace this outdated one. A new main kitchen was established in Building 93 during the early 1940s. (*See Buildings 44 and 93.*)

Building 52 was converted into a two-room schoolhouse for the child patients residing on the property. A school bell would ring in the mornings during school days to summon the children. It allowed the opportunity to teach the children, away from the distractions of adult patients. There was a significant improvement in the behavior of the children.

The school was affectionately known as the Little Red Schoolhouse. By 1939, this schoolhouse received high praise from the state for its good work with the hospital's children. This was noteworthy, since the hospital had only been admitting children for a little over ten years.

The younger patients were not the only ones to benefit from the hospital's new schoolhouse. Stenography and clerical training were also taught to hospital employees during nonschool hours.

The Children's Unit was relocated to Building 22 during the mid-1960s. It was too far away for the children to continue attending classes at the old schoolhouse. They were then taught at Building 22. By the 1970s, Building 52 had become obsolete. It was torn down sometime around 1976–1978. (*See Building 22.*)

Aerial photo from April 1, 1980 showing former site of Buildings 50-52

Building 53

This one-story brick building with a basement pit and flat roof was built in 1930 on the north side of the Nissequogue River boat basin along Canal Road. It was used as a sewage pump house, or lift station, and has a pump pit in its basement. Large sewage beds were set up in the rear of the building until the sewage disposal plant was built. (*See Building 66.*)

Building 53 on May 11, 2011

West side of Building 53
on May 11, 2011

Building 53 on April 16, 2013

East side of Building 53 on Dec. 22, 2011

Supposedly, it was originally used as a second boathouse when it was first built, but there is no information to corroborate that theory. However, it might have served as a second boathouse after it was no longer used as a pump house. It is located directly across from a small pier, where small boats and kayaks could be launched. The town continued to use this building after the hospital closed. It now belongs to the Nissequogue River State Park, although it is normally kept locked.

Sealed door in Building 53 on Jan. 1, 2016

Building 53 fuse boxes on Jan. 1, 2016

Building 53 basement access ladder on Jan. 1, 2016

Looking down into the basement of Building 53 on Jan. 1, 2016

This building number was originally used to identify the old laundry building for a short time. Built in 1890, it was previously Building 33. After a fire left it badly damaged in 1906, a new laundry was built elsewhere on the property. This building was later repaired and used to house Ward 33 until the 1930s. It was demolished sometime during that decade. (*See Buildings 5 and 33.*)

Building 54 (Group 2/Buildings 54A–C/Buildings 122–124)

Building 54 was the designation for the earlier buildings of Group 2, Buildings 122–124. They were constructed from 1910 to 1912. These cottages housed Wards 51–54 and were also known as Buildings 54A–C. Building 122 housed female patients, and Building 124 housed males. These two buildings were also referred to as Group 2 Cottage 1 and 2. The kitchen and dining hall were in Building 123, situated at their center. (*See Buildings 122–124.*)

Aerial photo of Group 2, circa Sept. 1927

These buildings were first home to chronic patients before housing the Adolescent Unit during the 1950s. A children's ward was also added. During the buildings' final decade in use, they were home to the Mental Retardation Unit (MRU).

By the early 1980s, these buildings were vacant. Building 124 was destroyed by fire during the mid-1990s and demolished soon after. The other two were demolished in 2012.

Building 55

The first Building 55 was a one-story white wood-framed building with a hip roof built from 1896 to 1897. It was constructed using recovered wood from the hospital's first temporary buildings and served as the firemen's cottage. A small one-story house addition was built in 1897, using spare bricks, to store the hospital's fire hose. It stood beside the firemen's cottage. In 1898, a new tin roof was added to the firemen's cottage. This was the first home base of the hospital's Volunteer Fire Department. Both structures were located behind Building B and next door to the kitchen of

Buildings A and B on the west side of Student Road. (*See Buildings 8, 9, and 38.*)

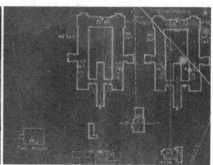

| Building 55, first firehouse, circa 1924 | Blueprint showing Building 55 with Buildings A & B, circa 1920s |

This primitive firehouse was demolished around 1925–1927 after the current firehouse replaced it. The new firehouse served as the home for the hospital's Safety Department for many years to follow. In 1928, construction began on a new laboratory and morgue on the site of the old firemen's cottage. (*See Buildings 82 and 83.*)

Although this next structure was never actually numbered, it stood near the future site of the next Building 55, along the south bank of the Nissequogue River on the north side of Mariner Road. It was slightly further west than its replacement. To identify it easier, I will use Building 55.

The original boathouse was a two-story wood-framed building with a gable roof built from 1896 to 1897, soon after the canal was constructed. It does not appear on any maps known to me, which probably accounts for why it did not have a number assigned to it. It can be seen quite clearly in a photo taken in 1912.

First boathouse & old pumping station at the canal, circa 1912

Second boathouse, circa 1910s-1930s   Boathouse, circa 1920s-1960s

The next boathouse was built in 1920. It was a two-story wood-framed building with a hip roof. The building was renovated from 1968 to 1969. It was expanded by the addition of an east wing and an upper-level porch. An improved marina was also built around the same time. A marina was added near the canal in approximately 1982–1984. It is still in use today but is closed by the end of October for the winter months, when the tide is at its lowest.

Aerial view of the canal & boathouse, circa 1967

Boathouse, circa 1990s

Boathouse cafe, circa 2000s

This building was still active for a few years after the hospital closed. It became part of the Nissequogue River State Park.

Eventually, it was closed and abandoned during the early 2000s. It had been scheduled for demolition, along with fourteen other structures in the later part of 2010. However, the demolition was postponed until the end of 2012. By January 2013, the boathouse had been razed.

| Boathouse & marina on May 11, 2011 | Boathouse & old pumping station on May 11, 2011 |

| Marina at canal on Oct. 5, 2015 | Foundation of boathouse on Oct. 5, 2015 |

Today, the marina is still in use. Yet there are no plans for a new boathouse. Hopefully, someday there will be a replacement boathouse for the townspeople, who make full use out of the marina each summer.

Building 55.1

This one-story brick shed with a gable roof has stood on the south bank of the canal since two years before the canal existed. Built in 1894, it originally served as a pumping station that drew water from the wells in the area, pumping them to the main pump house nearby. The first known dated photograph of this shed is from 1912, where it can be seen next to the original boathouse in a previous photo. (*See Buildings 55 and 60.*)

Former pumping station & annex to the boathouse on Oct. 5, 2015

Old pumping station with portable toilets on Oct. 5, 2015

When it was no longer needed as a pumping station, it was used for storage. Sometime after the mid-1900s, a bathroom was installed. After the second boathouse was demolished in 2013, this small structure was spared.

It is currently the oldest structure of the former state hospital. This frequently overlooked structure deserves a historic plaque to give it the proper recognition it deserves.

Marina without boathouse on Sept. 15, 2014

Frozen canal on Jan. 23, 2013

Building 56

This one-story prefabricated steel building with a gable roof was one of the last to be added. Built on the west side of Kings Park Boulevard in 1973, it resembled army barracks. Appropriately dubbed Cafe 56, it served as an eatery and community store to the patients, employees, and visitors. There was a dining area where customers could sit and enjoy a nice meal. Sometimes there were musical performances held at the cafe for the entertainment of patients and other customers. Profits of the community store went toward a luxury fund, which was used to provide items for the patients.

Building 56, the community store, circa 1970s

Community store, circa 1970s

Abandoned community store, circa 2011

Building 56 floor plan

The hospital's business officer, Walter J. Lynch, was in charge in the beginning, but it was Eugene E. Kuhne who managed it throughout most of the years it existed. Gene, as his friends affectionately called him, can be seen in some of the following photos taken at the community store.

Interior of community store, circa 1970s

Gene Kuhne adjusting the clothing
on a mannequin, circa 1970s-1980s

Steve Goldstein, Gene Kuhne, & Dr.
John Pitrelli at store, circa 1980s

Community store staff at
Christmas time, circa 1980

Former trustee of the Kings Park Heritage Museum, Stephen Weber, worked at Cafe 56 with Gene during his youth in the 1970s–1980s. It was one of the most memorable times of his life, which no doubt helped shape him into the caring man he is today.

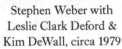

Stephen Weber with
Leslie Clark Deford &
Kim DeWall, circa 1979

Community store mobile cart, circa 1975

There was also a mobile store cart, constructed by the
Maintenance Department, which took goods to infirm patient
wards. This gave every patient the opportunity to shop.

Cafe 56 was closed and abandoned around the same time the
hospital closed. It was originally scheduled for demolition in the
fall of 2011, but the demolition was postponed. Demolitions began
on August 14, 2012.

They only ripped down the north side of the building on that
first day, leaving a gaping opening. A fence had been erected
around the site to prevent trespassing. The building was completely
gone by August 23 of the same year.

Building 56 on May 11, 2011

Building 56 on July 5, 2012

Rails where the customer
line began, circa 2000s

Looking across the counter, circa 2000s

Serving & dining area, circa 2000s

Support beam, circa 2000s

Sealed entrance, circa 2000s

Behind the counter, circa 2000s

Kitchen grill, circa 2000s

Community store hallway, circa 2000s

Demolition of Building
56 on Aug. 14, 2012

North side of Building 56 torn
open on Aug. 14, 2012

Behind the fence during demolition
of Building 56 on Aug. 14, 2012

Looking into Building 56
on Aug. 14, 2012

Pile of dirt remains, as of Sept. 5, 2012   Former site of Building
                                                   56 on Dec. 19, 2012

There was another Building 56 prior to Cafe 56. It stood across from Buildings 59 and 61 on the west side of the boulevard. This two-story wood-framed house with a basement, an attic, and a gable roof was part of the Sidney Smith farm when the property was purchased. It was built sometime around 1858–1873. In 1909, a new roof was installed, replacing the much older one.

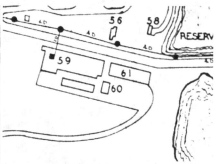

The original Building 56,   KPSH Plot Plan, circa 1970,
circa Sept. 1927   indicating Buildings 56-61

This house served as the steward's residence and then as the assistant steward's residence. The steward later moved into Building 33. (*See Male Cottage H and Building 33.*)

By the 1920s, the assistant steward moved into Building 48A, across from the village railroad station. The original Building 56 was razed a few years later in 1931. (*See Building 48A.*)

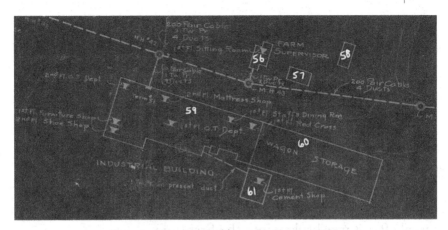

Blueprint showing Buildings 56-61, circa 1910s

Building 57

Building 57 was a one-hundred-foot-long-by-forty-foot-wide two-story building made of concrete and cement blocks. Built from 1912 to 1913 on the east side of Orchard Road across from the second storehouse, it had a half basement and a gable roof. As with Building 48, both floors were separate from one another and had to be accessed from the outside. There were no stairs within this structure, which served as workshops for electrical work, carpentry, masonry, and plumbing. It was also known as the machine shed during its earlier years. (*See Buildings 44 and 48.*)

Plumbing & maintenance shop, circa 1912

Maintenance personnel with Peter Hildenbrand (far left, back row), circa 1910-1912

Before this building was built, some of these shops were temporarily located in the basement of Building B. (*See Building 9.*)

A resaw machine was acquired for the carpentry shop in 1915. This helped prevent the wasting of lumber, which had been a problem in the past.

The building was closed by the early 1970s. In the 1980s, it was used to store maintenance equipment and supplies until it was abandoned during the 1990s. It was quite rundown by the 2000s. The wood from the doors and windows was rotted and falling apart. It was one of the few structures the park never bothered to reseal after it was broken into the first time.

Building 57 on May 11, 2011

Rear of Building 57 on May 11, 2011

Rear of Building 57 on Jan.15, 2008

Darkened doorway of Building
57 on Nov. 21, 2010

Interior ground floor of Building
57 on April 20, 2011

Tool storage room on April 20, 2011

Shelves on April 20, 2011

Oil drums & old lockers
on April 20, 2011

Toward the end of 2011, the second floor collapsed onto the first floor. Thankfully, no one was injured. This building was placed on the list of structures to be demolished in 2012. The job was finally done in March 2013, just in time for the implosion of the power plant smokestack.

Looking into a doorway at collapsed second level, Dec. 2011

Doors lying on collapsed second level in these 3 photos by Max Neukirch, Jr. taken in Dec. 2011

Collapsed second level of Building 57, circa Dec. 2011

Building 57 on Sept. 5, 2012

Building 57 behind fence on March 17, 2013

Demolition of Building 57 photographed by Sam Bartels in 2013

Rubble of Building 57 on March 27, 2013

There was another Building 57 before this one. Built in 1906, it was located on the west side of the boulevard between the original Buildings 56 and 58, across from Buildings 59 and 61. It served as the first lumber storage shed. While there are no photos, it can be seen on the map from 1912. (*See Buildings 56, 58, 59, and 61.*)

In 1914, it was moved to a new location further south to Orchard Road between Building 44 and the second Building 57, at which time it was renumbered as Building 30. (*See Buildings 30 and 44.*)

Building 58

This was a small one-story wood-framed cold storage warehouse with a basement. It was initially used as the first icehouse. Built from 1890 to 1892, it was located on the west side of the boulevard, south from the upper reservoir. It sat across from the heating plant and boat basin. (*See Building 59.*)

Aerial view of Building 58 on Nov. 6, 1951

In the earlier years of the hospital, tons of ice would be cut from both the upper reservoir and Harned's Pond during the winter and then stored here, so it would last until the summer.

By 1898, the hospital was in need of a larger icehouse. During the next year, the walls and ceiling were redone, and runs were constructed to make collecting ice from the upper reservoir easier.

Over the next few years, the icehouse began to fall apart, and soon the hospital was looking to replace it with a new icehouse. It became necessary to abandon this structure, at which time the cold storage warehouse of the original storehouse had to be used for ice. (*See Building 51.*)

During the spring of 1909, the old icehouse was condemned and demolished. The ground was excavated to build a new reinforced concrete structure with a basement in its place. Unskilled hospital employees and patients were called upon to do the job with the assistance of a few outside men employed for the task. Within a year, the new icehouse was completed at the cost of $2,154.97.

It was filled with natural ice from Harned's Pond at the first opportunity. This structure had a larger capacity for ice, and being made of sturdier material would allow the ice to last much longer. As the years went by, this icehouse was far too small for a hospital of this size. In 1912, an additional compartment had to be added outside for storing extra ice.

Soon after, Building 51 had taken over as the icehouse and ice plant. The former icehouse was converted into cold storage for vegetables. During the winter, cucumbers grown on the farm were stored here. They would be soaked in brine and turned into pickles. Eventually, this building became known as the Pickle House. Four wooden tanks with a 10,500-gallon capacity were installed on the ground level with their bottoms reaching down to the basement floor. Pickled beets were also made here. In time, the road that led from it and went alongside the reservoir became known as Pickle Road.

Sometime around the 1930s, the building became the Sauerkraut House, or the Sauerkraut Bunker. Every fall, the cooks would open it up, and truckloads of cabbage would arrive for them to process. By this time, Pickle Road had been conveniently renamed as Sauerkraut Road.

Pickle house, circa 1917

Trail, formerly known as Pickle Road, on July 5, 2012

The building finally saw its end around 1967–1969. The concrete foundation was still barely visible during the early 2000s but not any longer.

Building 59

By January 1888, Patrick J. Carlin built the first boiler house at the county farm to supply heat for the cottages. It is believed this structure stood on the future site of Building 93. As it turned out, the building was very poorly constructed and had nearly a dozen building violations.

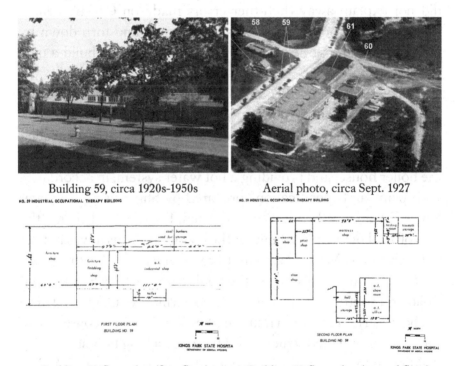

Building 59, circa 1920s-1950s   Aerial photo, circa Sept. 1927

Building 59 floor plan (first floor)   Building 59 floor plan (second floor)

The retaining wall for the coal room, constructed using rubble masonry, bulged out at the center and overhung by about five inches. There was frost in the mortar used between the bricks of the building. The floor in the boiler room had not been constructed, as agreed upon in the contract. Instead of two-and-a-half-inch-thick blue stone flagging, concrete was used. There was also supposed to be an eight-inch iron beam over the doorway, but it was not added, and neither was a rolled plate that was supposed to be on top of the beam to support the weight of the bricks. The window trimmings were not properly finished. The walls of the boiler room were not filled in to the roof, as they should have been. In addition, there was only one coating of whitewash on the walls rather than two.

Carlin blamed the appalling brickwork on a subcontractor, who would not listen when told he was doing the job wrong. That did not explain away the other errors made on Carlin's behalf. In the end, the boiler house was condemned and torn down by December of the same year. It became necessary to build a new one from scratch.

A new building was erected at a cost of $2,300 from 1890 to 1892. During the late summer of 1891, there were proposals for work to be done on the new boiler house. The work included supplying and setting six new boilers, repairing and extending the boiler house, and providing a hot water system, in accordance with plans and specifications prepared by Supervising Engineer James F. Carey. When it was completed, Building 59 became the first official power plant built for the county farm, as it was not yet a state hospital. More accurately, this was an electric heating plant.

It stood on the east side of the boulevard, north of St. Johnland Road and south from the entrance to Mariner Road, which led to the boathouse. This was a multibuilding combination consisting of three interconnected structures. There was a long two-story brick building with a basement and a combined gable and flat roof. This portion was referred to as the machine shop, and it housed the electric light plant. It was connected to the engine room building, where the dynamo was located. The engine room building had two floors and a gable roof. A smokestack was built directly behind these two buildings in the center atop a small one-story brick boiler house, containing six boilers at a cost of $4,122.66. These structures all counted as one building.

An elaborate system of steam tunnels was constructed underneath the buildings and connected to the heating plant so that it could provide heat to each building during the colder months.

The machine shop was enlarged from 1893 to 1894 to add space for coalbunkers on the first floor. When the state took over the hospital in 1895, six powerful new HT boilers were installed to replace the older, much smaller ones. The new ones generated a maximum of 150 horsepower. They would only be in use for about a decade. In 1897, a carpentry repair shop was added to the boiler house.

During the same year, a powerful fan was installed at the lower end of the main steam tunnel beneath the boulevard. The engine room at the heating plant was used to operate this new fan. The purpose of the fan was to make conditions in the tunnels more tolerable for workmen tending to the steam pipes, which emitted a great deal of heat.

For the first few years, coal deliveries were made via a man-made canal, which created a short cut from the Nissequogue River to the boat basin. During low tide, there was no more than six inches of water in the canal, making movement practically impossible, especially for a barge weighed down by a load of coal. A tugboat had to be used to tow the barge to the dock.

When the hospital's railroad spur was built not long afterward, a rail extension was built with a trestle to reach Building 59, which had been constructed on an incline. In 1899, four coal chutes were installed at the boiler house, and a new tin roof was added. Coal would then be delivered by train and dropped down the chutes into the new coal bunkers next door at Building 61. This was the northernmost point of the spur. (*See Building 61.*)

After the construction of ten additional buildings that made up Group 1, it was realized that the heating plant was not conveniently located for this group of buildings because it was too far away. It was too difficult for the heating plant to provide adequate heat to this group. Therefore, a temporary boiler house had to be erected next to the group. However, a permanent solution was necessary. (*See Buildings 4 and 4.1.*)

There was much work done at the heating plant to improve power distribution during 1902. A new 75-horsepower Westinghouse engine was installed. In addition, a new fifty-kilowatt Stanley-Kelly single-phase alternating current dynamo was installed. This installation included a two-kilowatt Northern Electric Company exciter, which is a component used to provide direct current for excitation. The main switch of the dynamo room was reconstructed to fit the new system. There were even extensive repairs done to the roof.

The Coal Strike of 1902, which was also known as the Anthracite Coal Strike, had lasting effects for the state hospital into 1903. It threatened to shut down the fuel supply to all major cities. The hospital had to cut down on its coal use to make it last because coal demand during the strike had increased the prices and decreased the quality of available supplies. Bituminous, buckwheat no. 3, pea, and stove coal were some of the types of coal used.

In 1905, all structures of the building were rewired, and the windows were painted white on the inside of the dynamo room and main boiler house. An extension was added to the carpentry shop a year later.

By 1908, construction began on a new power plant elsewhere on the hospital grounds, numbered as Building 6. It was fully operational two years later. Building 59 still served as the electric light plant. This was only for a brief time, as the new power plant would soon take on that responsibility as well. (*See Building 6.*)

The electric light plant was relocated to the new power plant in 1914. This building was then abandoned.

In 1921, plans were approved to convert this building into an occupational therapy center.   Two years later, this building underwent major renovations and was converted into several occupational therapy workshops and offices. The boiler house and smokestack were removed around 1924–1925, as was the portion of the railroad spur that ended here. An additional two-story concrete building was added in 1947, replacing the old dynamo and engine room structure. This new portion was used as the tin shop. A mattress shop was added in 1952. This section was renovated in 1958. There was a furniture shop on the first floor and several other shops on the second floor, which included a shoe repair shop, rattan and basket weaving shops, and a print shop.

Original engine room, after it was abandoned, circa 1940s

Building 59 hallway, circa 1970s

In later years, the hospital used to print its own newspaper. Prior to having its own print shop, most of the hospital's paperwork, calendars, cards, envelopes, labels, official handbooks, programs, vouchers, and all letterhead were printed at the Manhattan State Hospital.

The first floor of the old machine shop was used as the furniture finishing shop, cement shop, and industrial shop. The second floor was used as a mattress shop, hair-teasing room for mattress stuffing, mattress storage, and upholstery. The building also had a wood shop and a tin shop on the second floor.

Aerial photo, circa 1957

Facing north on the boulevard in front of Building 59, circa 1988

The main occupational therapy office was located on the second floor, along with an occupational therapy showroom. The occupational therapy of the patients became this building's main function for most of its existence, allowing patients to work in the many different workshops throughout the years.

In later years, this building was used as the medical records storage archive. The building was finally closed and abandoned in the 1970s. For a while, it was one of the oldest buildings on the property.

Facing south on the boulevard toward Building 59 on Dec. 22, 2011

Front of Building 59 on July 5, 2012

Rear of Building 59 on Dec. 22, 2011   Building 59 former engine room
addition on Dec. 22, 2011

Building 59 interior on Dec. 22, 2011   Building 59 interior on Dec. 22, 2011

As of 2012, Building 59 was scheduled for demolition. By the beginning of March 2013, it was gone, along with its neighbor, Building 60. Both had been two of the oldest buildings standing at the former hospital. These days, you cannot even tell they were there, but underneath the grass is a true part of this hospital's history. (*See Building 60.*)

Demolition of Building 59 photographed by Sam Bartels in 2013

Former site of Building 59 & 60 on March 17 2013

Foundation of Building 59 facing south on March 17 2013

Facing north toward where Buildings 59 & 60 once stood on July 30, 2013

Building 60

This one-story square brick building originally served as the water pumping station until the 1920s–1930s. Built from 1892 to 1893, this structure pumped water from wells dug near the Nissequogue River to the upper reservoir, allowing the rest of the buildings to have access to water. It was located on the south side of Mariner Road and stood behind Building 61. This building had a wonderfully detailed design on the interior brick wall and segmental arched bricks over each window. The roof had a hip roof design with a steel skylight at the center. (*See Building 61.*)

Building 60, circa 1920   Building 60, circa June 1978

Aerial photo showing Buildings 59-61, circa 1967

The fire pump was connected to the lower reservoir in 1907. Suction pipes could then draw water from the reservoir in the event of a fire, if the wells ran dry.

In 1940 the building was rehabilitated and later used for occupational therapy as a cement shop and a metal shop. It was turned into a printing shop, and for a time, it was also a shoe repair shop. It has sometimes been mistaken as part of the old power plant, but it was never part of that building.

While it was abandoned, old cement and printing press equipment could still be found inside, along with piles of furniture and rusted iron gates.

Building 60 on Dec. 22, 2011

Building 60 entrance on Dec. 22, 2011

Pile of furniture in Building
60 on Dec. 22, 2011

Building 60 sealed rear
entrance on Dec. 22, 2011

Chair & handmade wooden
toolboxes on Aug. 2, 2011

Building 60 skylight on Dec. 22, 2011

It was one of the oldest buildings standing on the hospital grounds. Unfortunately, it was demolished in the early part of 2013, at the same time as Building 59. Demolition began at the end of February, and by March, both were gone. (*See Building 59.*)

Building 61

Built in 1892, this one-story wood-framed brick building first served as a coal storage shed for the heating plant's boiler house. It did not have a roof during its first few years. A trestle was built for the railroad spur, and coal was delivered down chutes into the bunkers. In 1899, a partial roof was built over the coal shed to cover an area for storing iron pipes. (*See Buildings 59 and 61.1.*)

In 1910, the building was extended, although it was abandoned only four years later. During the 1920s, this building was converted into a wagon storage barn and continued as such until the late 1930s.

Aerial view of Building 61, Nov. 6, 1951

KPSH siding map from 1934 indicating Building 61 as ice plant

In 1939, it was extended again and converted into an ice-making plant. Ice would be cut down to smaller sizes, cleaned, and stored for the winter. As needed, ice was transported to the kitchens and dining halls of the hospital.

This building was also used for occupational therapy, along with Buildings 59 and 60, until it burned down around 1978–1979, along with Building 61.1. It was later demolished. (*See Buildings 59, 60, and 61.1.*)

Building 61.1

Originally, this was a covered portion of Building 61, but over the years, it practically became a separate building. In 1899, a roof was added so that iron pipes could be stored here. The structure was eventually modified into a one-story brick building with a basement, attic, and gable roof sometime in the mid-1920s. It was used as office space for the US Veterans' Bureau and for the Knights of Columbus. The front, which faced the boulevard, looked more like two separate buildings, while the rear looked more like a residential home. (*See Building 61.*)

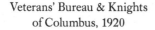

Veterans' Bureau & Knights   Rear of the building from the
of Columbus, 1920   boat basin, circa 1940s-1950s

The old boiler house for the heating plant stood directly behind this structure until it was removed. (*See Building 59.*)

These offices were badly damaged by fire in 1949. Four years later, plans were made to establish a library on this spot for the patients. By 1956, those plans were fully realized when the new library was completed. It became a great place for the patients to go where they could read in peace. The library's collection of books was quite extensive for its small size.

After being decimated by fire, the library was demolished in the late 1970s. According to a former hospital employee, this fire took place either during the latter half of 1978 or in 1979. There were no injuries, but many books were lost. (*See Building 54.*)

Fortunately, there were other buildings at the hospital that had their own libraries.

These photos show the fire damage to the library building

Foundation on Sept. 5, 2012   Library sign at the Kings Park
Heritage Museum on Jan. 22, 2016

Building 62

The original Building 62 was a large one-story wood-framed stable and coach barn with a gable roof. Built from 1896 to 1897 using wood from the original temporary buildings, it was located north of St. Johnland Road between the boulevard and what would later be Garage Road. It accommodated twenty-eight horses. In 1905, an additional room was added where the horses could be rubbed down. There were at least nine carriages owned by the hospital as of 1906, which filled the barn. A concrete foundation was placed under the coach barn in 1910.

There was a call bell connected to a device at the nearby superintendent's driveway. It allowed the superintendent to signal the coach barn whenever he required a ride. A driver would then take a horse-drawn carriage to pick him up. First, one or two horses from the stable would

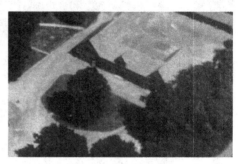

Aerial view of original Building 62, circa Sept. 1927

be harnessed to the carriage. This was not a quick process. It usually took several minutes before the carriage arrived at the superintendent's house, which was only about a five-minute walk away. (*See Building 67.*)

In 1916, the hospital purchased two Studebaker motor trucks, which were kept here. These trucks relieved the horses of much work previously saved for them. When there was no longer a need for horses, this stable was used as a truck garage.

By 1939, it was demolished and replaced by the current Building 62, built at the same location from 1939 to 1940. It is a one-story rectangular brick truck garage with a gable roof. It also served as a mechanic's shop.

Second Building 62, circa 1950s-1960s   Bus parked in front of Building 62

Building 62 supervisor
at desk, circa 1950s

Building 62
employee lockers,
circa 1950s

Building 62 employees posing
in front of garage, circa 1950s

Building 62 employees
squatting on grass,
circa 1950s

Building 62 employees
sitting on grass, circa 1950s

Building 62 employees
posing with hospital
truck, circa 1950s

Building 62 employees, circa 1959

Building 62 employees' names
on rear of photo, circa 1959

During the time of occupational therapy, the mechanic's shop was a good place for patients with a knack for mechanics to lend a hand. This garage was later used to store the buses and maintenance vehicles of the hospital.

It is now used by the Nissequogue River State Park to store and maintain their trucks. Sometime during the late 2000s, two small storage sheds were added behind it. (*See Buildings 62.1 and 62.2.*)

Facing north toward Building
62 on July 30, 2013

Building 62 on July 30, 2013

West side of Building 62
on Aug. 14, 2012

Building 62 at night on Aug. 2, 2011

Building 62.1 and 62.2

In 2009, the New York State Office of Parks, Recreation and Historic Preservation built two white metallic, prefabricated storage sheds behind Building 62 on land belonging to the Nissequogue River State Park. These structures were never used by the state hospital and are still in use today. They are not accessible to the public.

Storage sheds behind Building
62 on Aug. 2, 2011

Building 63

Building 63 was a one-story rectangular, wood-framed wagon barn with a gable roof that stood behind the main stable next to Building 64. The wagon barn was one of the first barns built on the grounds in 1889. (*See Buildings 62 and 64.*)

The hospital had several wagons to store here. There

Aerial view of Building
63, circa Sept. 1927

was a bread wagon, a swill wagon, two delivery wagons, an express wagon, one laundry wagon, and a heavy mail cart. During the winter, two horse-drawn snowplows, built in 1907, were used to clear the roads and paths until trucks could be used for that purpose.

In 1906, a new sixty-foot-long addition to the wagon shed was built, along with an improved roof, providing better protection of the stored wagons. Two years later, the rear was extended and enclosed. It was still not large enough to fit all of the wagons securely. It was extended once again in 1910, but it still was not large enough.

A new one-story rectangular, wood-framed wagon shed with a gable roof was built as a replacement from 1912 to 1915. It stood at the same location. This building remained in place until 1953–1955, before being demolished.

Building 64

There were two Building 64s. The original was a corrugated iron wagon shed, added near the main stable in 1901. It was demolished by 1912 to make room for the next Building 64, which became the garage supervisor's personal garage. It was built around 1912–1915 and demolished by 1966–1967. (*See Building 62.*)

Supervisor's garage, circa 1957

Building 65

This was the main propagation house. Built from 1939 to 1940, it was the last greenhouse erected on the hospital grounds. This one-story steel-framed glass structure has a gable roof design and adjoins a one-story gable-roofed, wood-framed center workroom with a basement. It is located along the east side of Garage Road north of St. Johnland Road.

Greenhouse, 1990s

Facing north toward the greenhouse, 1990s

Looking at the greenhouse from the nearby gazebo, circa 1999

In its earlier years, the greenhouse was used for the occupational therapy. Patients would help care for the plants and flowers, or make floral arrangements that could be sold at the community store. The plants and flowers displayed in building wards, offices, and dining halls came from the greenhouse, as did the plants and flowers, transplanted into the flowerbeds outside of the buildings.

Employees painting the
greenhouse interior, circa 1980

Krystina Crimi & Rose
Hughes, circa Oct. 1996

Tim Olsen & King Pedlar,
circa Oct. 1998

Employees & volunteers behind
greenhouse, circa Oct. 1998

Employees & volunteers in front
of greenhouse on Dec. 21, 1998

Greenhouse interior, circa 1999

Krystina Crimi gives a tour of the greenhouse in Jan.1999

Krystina Crimi & Daniel Boone in greenhouse, circa 1999

The greenhouse stayed open a few years after the closing of the hospital. It finally closed in April 1999. It was a sad day for the former hospital employees who visited frequently. It eventually reopened and is now part of the Nissequogue River State Park. Botanical research is conducted here. A cozy white wood-framed gazebo stands behind it. (*See Building 65.1.*)

Approaching greenhouse on May 11, 2011

Greenhouse north wing on May 11, 2011

Greenhouse south wing on May 11, 2011   Greenhouse entrance on May 11, 2011

There was an earlier structure identified as Building 65, which can be found on the 1912 map. It was a small corrugated iron building built in 1901 behind the heating plant. This was one of the several oil houses erected on the grounds. It was enlarged in 1905. (*See Building 59.*)

Additional oil houses were typically located near the power plants or storage houses. These oil houses were all demolished by 1935 once Building 44 was constructed as the new storehouse. However, this particular oil house was demolished by 1915, if not sooner, after Building 59 was no longer used as a heating plant. (*See Building 44.*)

Building 65.1

There was a white gazebo, built around the year 1996, behind the greenhouse in the Nissequogue River State Park. It is situated on the north side of St. Johnland Road and is the private property of the park. (*See Building 65.*)

Gazebo, circa 2003   Gazebo interior with fisheye
lens, circa 1990s

Building 66

A breakout of typhoid fever in 1905 brought about the need for a sewage disposal plant at the hospital. Until that time, the hospital used to empty its sewage into the Nissequogue River. The people of Smithtown protested against this daily pollution of their harbor and river and with very good reason. It was having a tragic effect on the wildlife and ecosystem, not to mention poisoning popular food sources of fish and shellfish. Typhoid fever and diphtheria were threatening the health and lives of the community because of constant pollution.

Sewage disposal plant pump house, 1916   Blueprint of early sewage disposal
plant structures near the canal

In that year alone, there were nineteen cases of typhoid fever at the hospital.

Unfortunately, a sufficient amount of money would not be provided by the state until 1909, when the hospital received an appropriation of $30,000 to build its first sewage disposal plant. Construction began immediately. This project included the addition of a screen house and large settling tanks. It was located at the eastern edge of Jones Point in a wooded area, along the canal, near where the barge would later be situated.

Contracting disputes prevented its timely completion, which should have been at the end of 1909. It was not completed until 1910. After it was put into operation, garbage was sometimes used as fertilizer or dumped into trenches as landfill. Inside the screen house was an incinerator, used to dispose of accumulations that built up on the screen. In 1912, sludge trenches were added. A year later, the capacity of the plant was doubled to accommodate the additions of building Groups 2–4.

Aerial view of sewage disposal   Aerial view of sewage
plant (R), circa Sept. 1927   disposal plant, circa 1947

Over the years, it became necessary for a modernized sewage disposal facility. An additional settling tank was built in 1920. Work on the improved disposal plant was completed and fully operational by 1921.

As of the late 1930s, a new location was chosen for the sewage disposal plant. It was placed on the banks of the river to the east of the superintendent's residence, not far from Harned's Pond. A one-story brick building with a basement was built in 1939 at a cost of $37,900. In time, this became a small complex of buildings.

During a six-month period, starting in the spring and ending in the summer of 1953, weekly cultures and chlorine content tests were conducted to test the new plant's efficiency. In 1960, the plant was rehabilitated.

Aerial view of sewage disposal plant near director's mansion, 1957

Aerial photo of old sewage hotbeds on April 10, 1976

Aerial photo of new sewage disposal plant on April 10, 1976

Sewage disposal plant, circa 2000s   Entrance to sewage disposal
plant on July 11, 2011

The old screening house was demolished around the time the new plant was built, although the old sewage hotbeds were abandoned. As the decades went by, the woods gradually swallowed them up. By 1976, the trees were cleared out, and the area was converted into a storage lot.

After the hospital closed, Kings Park continued to use the hospital's sewage disposal plant, which was now under the control of Suffolk County. In 2004, a sophisticated sewage treatment plant, completed by 2010, replaced it. It is still in use today by the residents of Kings Park as Sewer District 6. The abandoned hotbeds are still standing in the woods nearby and have sometimes been mistaken for greenhouses.

Abandoned sewage hotbeds   Sewage hotbeds photographed by
photographed by Sam Bartels in 2016   Edward Johnson on April 20, 2014

Entrance to old sewage hotbeds
near the canal on May 11, 2016

Old sewage hotbeds near the
canal on May 11, 2016

Long ago, there was another Building 66. The original was a large storage shed for coal, located behind Building 59. It was erected in 1899. It was demolished once Building 6 took over as the new power plant. (*See Buildings 6 and 59.*)

Map from 1912 indicating
Buildings 50-66

Blueprints indicating Buildings 67-72

Building 67

This house was once a beautiful two-story brick mansion with a basement, attic, and hip roof. Built from 1939 to 1940, it served as the residence of the superintendent and then of the senior director. The house is located on a desolate part of the property north of St. Johnland Road on the side of the former hospital that is now the Nissequogue River State Park. A long driveway once led directly to it from St. Johnland Road.

Aerial view of Building 67, circa 1957   Building 67 photographed by
                                                King Pedlar, circa 1990s-2000s

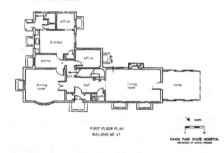 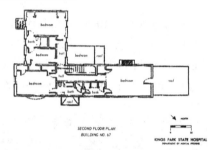

Building 67 floor plan (first floor)   Building 67 floor plan (second floor)

This building was rehabilitated in 1960, and its west wing was extended from 1969 to 1972. The last senior director to reside here was Dr. Charles Buckman during the 1970s. Not all of his predecessors lived in this house. Superintendent Charles Parker, some twenty years prior, chose to live in the "White House." (*See Building 78.*)

In the final years of the hospital, the former director's mansion was utilized as a group home. A few other senior directors also chose to reside in the White House. Some of the last senior directors, who were not medical doctors, resided off the grounds, such as senior directors Stephen Goldstein and Alan Weinstock.

Like so many other buildings on the grounds, it is now abandoned, boarded up, and in a state of disrepair. Animals leave feces and urine scattered throughout the once grand home, creating a mighty fine odor within. The driveway that once led to it was closed in 1996.

Building 67 on Jan. 1, 2016

Building 67 on Jan. 1, 2016

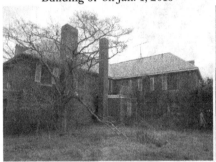
Building 67 chimneys &
balcony on Jan. 1, 2016

Building 67 entrance on Jan. 14, 2008

Destroyed patio on Jan. 1, 2016

Living room & fireplace on Jan. 1, 2016

Kitchen on Jan. 1, 2016   Staircase to the second
floor on Jan. 1, 2016

Upstairs bedroom on Jan. 1, 2016   Bathroom on Jan. 1, 2016

Animal droppings on Jan. 1, 2016   Basement pool table on Jan. 1, 2016

Prior to its construction, there was another two-story wood-framed house with an attic and basement that stood just a few feet away. This was one of the original farmhouses in existence before the hospital was established. This pre-1837 home previously belonged to Noel Joseph Bécar. Prior to the Bécar family, the Blydenburgh family owned it. It was one of the oldest houses in Kings Park. According to the hospital's annual report from 1899, several rooms were papered and painted at the Bécar House, as it was known for a few years.

In 1900–1901, it became the residence of the superintendent Dewing. Streetlights were added to the driveway for his convenience. An extension was added to the house in 1905, which greatly improved its comfort value and appearance. A lot of work was also done in regard to the electrical and lighting fixtures. There was a library on the first floor, a study on the second, and a maid's hall on the third, which was actually the attic. This house was so large many referred to it as the Bécar Mansion.

In 1906, a call bell was installed on the driveway, connected to the coach barn, which enabled the superintendent to signal whenever he needed a ride. (*See Building 62.*)

A few repairs to the house became necessary in 1909 after a small fire caused minor damage. Several superintendents used this home as a residence over the next few decades until it was replaced by the current structure. The same building number was used to identify both homes.

Postcard of superintendent's residence, circa 1900s-1920s

Building 68

The original Building 68 was a one-and-a-half-story white clapboard, wood-framed building with a gable roof and a basement built out of ground on two sides. Built in 1906, it was later converted into a coach barn for the superintendent.

An open carport garage was built between 1969 and 1972 as

Aerial view of original Building 68, circa 1967

the new Building 68, although the original structure remained in place until 1988–1989. The abandoned carport is still standing next to the former senior director's mansion. (*See Building 67.*)

Building 68 on Jan. 1, 2016   Building 68 on Dec. 22, 2011

Building 69

This was the building number used for the greenhouse near the superintendent's residence. There were actually two greenhouses at this location. The first was a small one built in 1905. It was the third greenhouse to be erected on the grounds. There are no photos of it.

It was demolished by 1922.

The next greenhouse was the replacement for the previous one. It was a one-story steel-framed glass structure with a gable roof adjoined by a one-story hip-roofed, stucco-finished, wood-framed workroom that had a boiler room basement. Its electrical power was fed from the superintendent's residence. Built in 1922, it was located in a wooded area south of the house. It was referred to as the superintendent's greenhouse or as the upper greenhouse, since there was once another greenhouse at the lower end of the hospital and another in between both. (*See Buildings 4.3, 12, and 67.*)

Aerial photo from 1969 shows
greenhouse covered with glass

Aerial photo from April 1, 1980
shows the structure is open

This greenhouse has been mistaken for the lower greenhouse in the past. The lower greenhouse was in the lower garden near Group 1 at the lower end of the property, while this greenhouse was more toward the upper northeastern end of the property, hence the names for each. (*See Buildings 4 and 4.3.*)

After being badly damaged by fire in 1980, it was demolished. Only an old white doorway and a foundation remain, surrounded by thorn bushes.

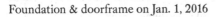

Foundation & doorframe on Jan. 1, 2016

Nearby spigot on Jan. 1, 2016

Building 70

This was not a building but rather a series of ground level hotbeds for growing plants, which had glass wood-framed covers. There were about four rows of hotbeds set closely to one another. Added in 1922, it was adjacent to Building 67, northeast from the upper greenhouse. (*See Buildings 67 and 69.*)

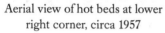

Aerial view of hot beds at lower right corner, circa 1957	Aerial view of hot beds (center), circa 1969

In 1972, it was destroyed by fire and removed. By 1980, the entire area was covered with grass, leaving behind no indication of the old hotbeds.

Aerial view from April 1, 1980 identifying structures

Building 71

The first Building 71 was a small one-story white wood-framed hennery with a gable roof, built between 1911 and 1912, east of Building 67. It consisted of a laying house, a brooder house, and an incubator house. (*See Building 67.*)

Hennery (center), circa 1957

This structure was demolished between 1960 and 1961, after farming operations ceased at the hospital.

The second Building 71 was a one-story wood-framed, six-car garage with a gable roof located behind Building 135. It was built in 1928 on the east side of Upper Dock Road. (*See Building 135.*)

It burned down during a fire sometime between 1994 and 1999.

| Aerial photo showing Building 71, Nov. 6 1951 | Aerial photo over Building 71, circa 1964 | Former location of Building 71 on Dec. 22, 2011 |

Building 72

This was a one-story white brick building with a gable roof, located east of Building 67, along the road that leads to the sewage disposal plant. It was built in 1925 as a toolhouse.

Aerial view of Building 72 (upper left corner), circa 1968

Aerial photo of Building 72 on April 1, 1980

It was demolished sometime between 1988 and 1989, at the same time as the original Building 68. (*See Buildings 66–68.*)

Building 73 (Veterans' Group/Buildings 73A–W/Buildings 125–147)

This was not a single building but a series of twenty-one buildings consisting of the Veterans' Memorial Hospital Unit, more casually known as the Veterans' Group. These buildings were built north of St. Johnland Road at the end of Kings Park Boulevard. On July 4, 1923, the group made its spectacular historic debut with a publicized groundbreaking ceremony performed by Gov. Alfred E. Smith. A dedication ceremony followed several years later on September 24, 1927, when the buildings were ready for use. The last to open was Building 39 (73Q), completed in 1932.

Group 3, future site of Veterans' Group, Feb. 16, 1925

Aerial view of Veterans' Group, circa March 1962

Building 125 (73A) with Building 144 (73T) aka Home T behind it

Home T & staff residences behind it, circa March 1979

This large group initially consisted of buildings with both number and letter designations, ranging from 73A–W. This numbering was based on the original number designation of Group 3, Building 73. Built from 1910 to 1912, the three buildings of Group 3 were originally known as Buildings 73A–C. They became a part of the Veterans' Group, by default, and were later numbered as Buildings 143 (73), 147 (73W), and 137 (73M). In 1926, two breezeway corridors connecting Building 136 (73L) to Building 137 (73M) were added, along with an extension to Building 137 (73M). (*See Buildings 125–147.*)

By the 1960s, the Veterans' Group was renumbered as Buildings 125 (73A)–147 (73W). However, most of the employees preferred to use the number 73-letter designations. Not many former employees even know the building numbers, ranging from 125 to 147.

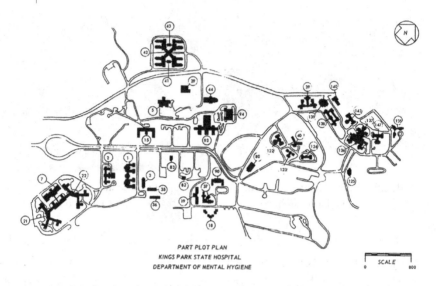

PART PLOT PLAN
KINGS PARK STATE HOSPITAL
DEPARTMENT OF MENTAL HYGIENE

SCALE

KPSH Part Plot Plan with alternate building numbers, circa 1960s

An original plan for this unit included twenty-two buildings, later increased to twenty-three. Two buildings were supposed to be added to this group but were never built. They would have been numbered as Buildings 145 (73U) and 146 (73V).

This entire section of the hospital became the bulk of what is now the Nissequogue River State Park, a popular recreation spot for local families, nature enthusiasts, former hospital employees, photographers, urban explorers, and historians. Most of the buildings and cottages in this area are still standing but are abandoned and closed to the public.

Sunset over the Veterans' Group panoramic view on Dec. 22, 2011

Building 74

Building 74 was originally the chief engineer's house. Built in 1890, it is a two-story Federal Revival-style, wood-framed, single-family house with a basement, attic, and hip roof. It is located on Upper Dock Road behind Building 143 of Group 3. (*See Building 143.*)

Aerial view of Building 74 from 1964

Bird's eye view of Building 74, circa 2007

It has been said, when this house was first built, it served as the original superintendent's home, but based on my research, that is incorrect. When the superintendent moved to the grounds from Brooklyn in the mid-1880s, he resided in one of the cottages on the west side of the boulevard near the male cottages. That cottage was later numbered as Building 33. It eventually became the home of the resident steward after the superintendent moved into the old Bécar Mansion. The Bécar Mansion served as the superintendent's residence for nearly forty years. (*See Buildings 33 and 67.*)

In the final years of the hospital, a volunteer group called Voluntary LIFE used Building 74 before it was turned over to the town as a residential plot. The house is now a private residence. The current owners wish not to be disturbed.

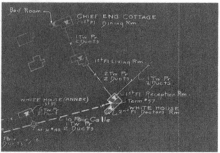

The former Building 74
on April 28, 2013

Blueprint showing cottages
on Upper Dock Road

Buildings 75 and 76

These were both one-story wood-framed staff garages with gable roofs that were built in 1938, although they were initially used as barns. Building 75 was a two-car garage built directly behind Building 74, while Building 76 was a one-car garage built specifically for Building 77, which is now gone. (*See Buildings 74 and 77.*)

Building 75 with car in
front on April 28, 2014

Rear of Building 75 on April 28, 2014

Building 76 on April 28, 2014

A day program called the FOD later utilized Building 76 as its garage.

Both structures still stand today but are no longer a part of the hospital grounds. They are now garages for residential homes.

There was a small barn on the same spot as Building 75, built in 1890. In 1910, a new foundation was placed beneath it. The barn was demolished in 1938 so the current garage could replace it.

Building 77

This two-story Federal-style, wood-framed house was built in 1890 as a two-family residence. It had a brick foundation and flaring eaves with a flat roof addition. Located at 12 Upper Dock Road, it served as the master mechanic's house. It was later used for the FOD day program.

Building 77, from the Richard H. Handley Collection, LI Americana, courtesy of the Smithtown Library

It was demolished around 1995–1996.

Building 78

According to the floor plan data sheet available for this building, known as the White House, it was built in 1890. That information is incorrect. While there were houses on the bluff belonging to the hospital built in that year, this was not one of them. In the annual report from 1912, it clearly states a new house was built that year on the bluff near Group 3 to be used by a physician for that group. The report goes on to mention how the "White House" on the bluff had been wired for electricity and connected to the water, heating, and power lines. A bathroom was also installed, and the house was painted. Furthermore, there is never any mention of the White House until 1912. (*See Building 73.*)

Building 78 driveway, circa 1910s-1930s   Building 78, circa 1910s-1930s

Building 78 floor plan (first floor)   Building 78 floor plan (second floor)

The one(s) responsible for gathering the information on those floor plans likely estimated the year of construction based on when the surrounding houses were erected.

The White House was a two-story Federal Revival-style, wood-framed house with a flat roof. It was built in 1912 as a two-family staff residence. It was located at 14 Upper Dock Road. A porch and stoop were added sometime later. This residence was originally intended for doctors of the "new" chronic buildings of Group 2 and 3 that were completed during the same year this house was constructed. In 1958, it was converted into a two-family home. (*See Buildings 54 and 73.*)

In later years, there were a few superintendents and directors, such as Dr. Charles Parker, who resided here. He was the superintendent from 1931 to 1941. Some of the directors also resided here until the 1980s.

The house stood abandoned for a few years before being demolished sometime around 1986–1988.

Back door of Building 78, after being abandoned, circa 1980s

Building 78 staircase, after being abandoned, circa 1980s

Window screen leaning against abandoned house, circa 1980s

Building 78, circa 1910s-1930s

Looking towards small
windows from the
inside, circa 1980s

Former site of Building 78, circa 1988-1990s

Building 79

This structure appears
on undated blueprints of the
property listed as the "White
House Annex." It can only barely
be seen as a blurred object in
photos from 1913 to 1940 taken
from a great distance. It was
referenced as a garage in the
key of a map from 1954, but the
actual structure was never added

Staff cottages, circa 1913

to the map because of an error on the part of the mapmaker. Proof of
its existence can be found in annual reports from 1913 to 1914.

This was originally a two-story wood-framed barn with a
gable roof built in 1912 as an annex to Building 78. A year after it
was built, the second floor was converted into a one-family staff
residence that could house additional employees from Groups 2
and 3. In 1914, a bathroom was added on the ground floor for their
convenience. The ground floor was later used as a garage for the
White House. (*See Buildings 54, 73, and 78.*)

This structure was removed sometime around 1940–1947.

Building 80

Building 80 is a two-story brick building with a half basement and a partial second-floor gallery at the east end of the building overlooking the first floor. There is also a ladder leading up to a projector room. It has a hip roof design and was situated on the northwest corner of St. Johnland Road and Kings Park Boulevard across from Tiffany Field. The three front entrances facing the boulevard have brick arches over them with alternating Beaux Arts pilasters, which are rectangular columns protruding from the wall. Constructed in 1932, it served as an assembly building called York Hall.

York Hall construction, circa 1932

York Hall, circa 1930s

Employee walking near York Hall, circa 1930s

York Hall on opening day, Sept. 7, 1932

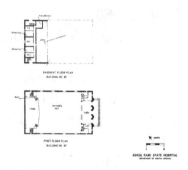

York Hall, circa 1980s-1990s   Building 80 floor plans

York Hall was named after Rev. Msgr. John C. York, who served as reverend for twenty years at the hospital as well as secretary of the board of managers and member of the State Charities Aid Association. Reverend York was instrumental in securing the funds to build this desperately needed building. For more than three decades, the different superintendents of the hospital each pleaded with the state to supply funding for a new amusement hall. The original amusement hall only seated about four hundred patients, while there were well over five thousand. It was thanks to the efforts of Reverend York that this building was made possible. The building was dedicated in his honor during a ceremony held at the hall's opening day on September 7, 1932. (*See Female Cottage K and Building 48*)

Opening Ceremony Dedication   Rev. York in doorway at Opening
on Sept. 7, 1932   Ceremony on Sept. 7, 1932

Auditorium stage on opening
day, Sept. 7, 1932

Auditorium seating on
opening day, Sept. 7, 1932

Opening Ceremony in York
Hall, Sept. 7, 1932

Opening Ceremony Dedication
program cover, circa Sept. 7, 1932

Many plays, shows, concerts, and parties were held here to entertain the patients and give them a taste of culture. There was singing and dancing here on a weekly basis. The nursing school held their graduation ceremonies here for many decades. Sometimes graduation ceremonies from local Kings Park schools were also held here. There was a fallout shelter located within the basement, and a community store was later set up near the entrance on the main floor, where patients could purchase items using tokens they earned.

In 1933, a recreation center was added at York Hall. The hospital's recreation office was located here for a while. The main chamber also acted as a gymnasium. During the winter season, soccer was played here. In 1953, the recreation office was relocated to the former occupational therapy headquarters at the old heating plant. (*See Building 59.*)

Employees seated in the audience at York Hall, circa 1964

Nurses' conference at York Hall, circa 1968

Rabbi Wachtfogel (L) with fellow employee during Chanukah, circa 1970s

Employees celebrating Chanukah in York Hall, circa 1970s

Employees' children playing music at York Hall, circa 1974

Passover Seder at York Hall, circa 1980s

Religious ceremonies and services were held here too. Jewish services took place on Saturdays. Catholic mass was held every Sunday at 8:30 a.m. Protestant services followed at 10:00 a.m. Christian science readings were done each Sunday afternoon from 2:30 to 3:30 p.m. The hall was also utilized as a synagogue during Jewish holidays. It was one of the largest synagogues on Long Island. Sometime around 1953–1954, the members of the Metropolitan Council of B'nai B'rith donated a scroll, prayer shawls, and Jewish prayer books.

From the 1950s to 1960s, 35 mm movies were shown weekly to 1,600–1,800 patients. Sometimes local kids from Kings Park would sneak in while a movie was being shown. Most of the time, the Safety Department would just throw them out with a stern warning and a slap on the wrist.

The building was closed and abandoned during the 1990s. It remains so today. These days, there are mainly pigeons living in here.

North side of York Hall on July 5, 2012

York Hall from the boulevard on July 5, 2012

York Hall handicapped accessible ramp on July 30, 2013

Front of York Hall on July 30, 2013

The following interior photos of York Hall provided by Max Neukirch, Jr.

York Hall stage on April 10, 2007

York Hall auditorium on April 10, 2007

Looking down from the
balcony on April 10, 2007

Balcony seating at York
Hall on April 10, 2007

Projector room at York
Hall on April 10, 2007

Projector room controls
on April 10, 2007

Main lobby of York Hall
on April 10, 2007

Pigeons in York Hall on April 10, 2007

In 2008, there were plans to possibly renovate York Hall, but those plans fell through. It would be great to see this building put to use for the benefit of the town before it becomes too decrepit to save like with what happened to Buckman Center. There is a lot of history tied to this building, and it is not too late to preserve it. (*See Building 23.*)

Building 81

This small one-story white wood-framed building with a gable roof was the chemical feed and milk house for the second dairy barn. Animal feed was cooked and prepared here. It stood right beside the dairy barn on the exact spot Building 88 would be built a few years later. It was built in 1940 but only lasted until 1943. The milking facilities were then moved into the barn. (*See Buildings 47 and 88.*)

Aerial photo from 1940,
indicating farm structures

According to a 1970 plot plan map, Buildings 95–99, the doctors cottages behind Macy Home, were listed as Building 81A–E for the sake of indicating their location on the map. (*See Buildings 90 and 95–99.*)

Building 82

Building 82 was a two-story flat-roofed brick building with a basement, constructed from 1928 to 1929. It was located behind Building B on the west side of Student Road. It had been erected on the exact site of the former firemen's cottage, which was demolished after a new firehouse was built. Building 82 served as the laboratory and mortuary. It replaced the original building used for that purpose, which stood near the early male cottages. The Photography Department had a photography room in this building as well. The building was opened for business in 1930. (*See Buildings 9, 15, 55, and 83.*)

Building 82   Building 82 floor plans

In 1953–1954, the Photography Department prepared a series of more than 250 Kodachrome lantern slides based on different neurological case material in the collection of the Armed Forces Institute of Pathology at Washington DC. This added to the hospital's collection, which consisted of more than eight hundred Kodachromes.

Kodachrome was an early version of Kodak brand color film used in old-fashioned cameras. There was no such thing as digital cameras at the time.

In 1954, a new entrance leading to the basement mortuary was added, along with a separate mortuary driveway. Bodies no longer had to be carried downstairs from the main entrance. At this point, the upper level became the second floor, while the basement was now the first floor. There was also a subbasement that connected to the steam tunnels, which became the basement. New replacement equipment acquired this year included a modern autopsy table and a binocular microscope.

When Building 7 was built in 1966, it had a modernized morgue with a larger-capacity freezer for more bodies. It replaced the much smaller one at Building 82. (*See Building 7.*)

That same year, Building 82 was renovated and converted into a nurses' lounge, although there were not many nurses who wanted to spend time in the former morgue. This new lounge was meant to replace the former Employees' Clubhouse, which had become the first community store of the hospital. (*See Building 32.*)

Recreation Employees on upper floor
of Building 82, circa 1960s-1970s

Same room on July 5, 2012

After Building 82 was abandoned, the basement connecting to the tunnels had become completely flooded by years of polluted rainwater, making it virtually impossible to enter.

Building 82 viewed from Student
Road on July 11, 2011

Building 82 west entrance
on July 5, 2012

Former upper level game
room on March 26, 2011

Chairs & table in game
room on July 5, 2012

Building 82 upper level
hallway on July 5, 2012

Roof access ladder in front of
TV room on July 5, 2012

Staircase between upper &
lower levels on July 5, 2012

Building 82 lower level
hallway on July 5, 2012

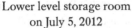

Lower level storage room on July 5, 2012   Stairs leading to the flooded basement on July 5, 2012

Since the early 2000s, there had been talk of demolishing some of the structures on the former hospital grounds. The project was always delayed for financial reasons. It was not until 2012 that a contract was finally secured, which would result in a vast demolition project.

By the second week of July 2012, this building was the first structure that would undergo the demolition process. The trees around it were cleared away, and a fence was erected around the building. Within weeks, the old furniture was removed, and the asbestos removal process had begun. This mandatory procedure known as abatement would have to take place with practically every building scheduled for demolition. It is a necessary and expensive process used to clean out toxic materials.

Another major task was to drain the flooded basement. This would take a lot of time, but it marked the beginning of the phase 1 demolitions for 2012.

Abatement process of Building 82 on Aug. 3, 2012

Abatement Building 82 & discarded furniture on Aug. 3, 2012

Former site of Building 82 on Dec. 19, 2012

On Student Road facing former site of Building 82, March 17, 2013

By the end of September, the actual demolition of the building took place, leaving only the basement behind, as hundreds of gallons of old polluted rainwater still had to be drained. Once that was completed, the rest of the building was demolished, and the basement and tunnel nearby filled with the rubble. The land over it was flattened, and the grass has since grown over it.

Building 83

Building 83 was the firehouse, constructed from 1925 to 1926. It is a two-story brick building with a four-story hose-drying tower, a half basement, and a garage for storing the hospital's fire apparatus. The copper roof of the tower has a pyramidal shape, while the rest of the building has a flat roof.

Safety vehicle parked in front
of Building 83, circa 1970s

Building 83, circa 1992

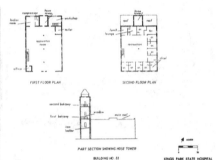

Apparatus garage, circa 1925

Building 83 floor plans

When it opened in 1927, it replaced its predecessor, a simple wood-framed firemen's cottage that stood nearby behind Building B. The new firehouse was placed on the east side of the boulevard for easier access to the other buildings. (*See Buildings 9 and 55.*)

After the 1930s, the firehouse became the hospital's fire and police safety station for the combined Safety Department. A flagpole stood outside with the American flag waving proudly over the boulevard.

Building 83, circa 1970s-1980s

Vehicles parked in front of
Building 83, circa 1988

KPPC fire truck near the power
plant, circa 1980s-1990s

Building 83, circa 1980s-1990s

When the Safety Department was phased out, this building was utilized for the storage of grounds maintenance equipment. It still stands across from Buildings 15 and 93 next to the abandoned tennis courts. The garage was used to store lawnmowers and backhoes.

Building 83 on Dec.19, 2012

Park vehicles in front of Building 83 on March 17, 2013

North side of Building 83 on April 16, 2013

Rear of Building 83, circa Jan. 2008

Police office, circa Jan. 2008

Police office TV, circa Jan. 2008

Garage, circa Jan. 2008

Chief's office on second
floor, circa Jan. 2008

Recreation room & staircase,
circa Jan. 2008

Recreation room support
beam, circa Jan. 2008

Basement, circa Jan. 2008

Hose drying tower, circa Jan. 2008

All interior photos of the firehouse were provided by Max Neukirch, Jr.

In mid-September 2016, an unknown person broke down the north garage door of the firehouse. A fire was started inside, causing minimal damage. A cinderblock wall was erected to seal the open garage door. A week later, on September 28, at approximately two o'clock in the morning, another fire was set, this time resulting in more damage and leaving people to wonder if this building would soon be added to the list of buildings to demolish.

My photo of Building 83, showing
fire damage on Sept. 28, 2016

Bird's eye view provided by
Edward Johnson showing the
fire damage on Sept. 28, 2016

Building 83.1

There was a small white wood-framed storage shed that was built behind the firehouse in 1954. The Recreation Department built it to store recreational athletic equipment. It was used in connection with an outdoor recreational center established that year, which included games like badminton, basketball, handball, horseshoe throwing, miniature golf, tennis, and volleyball. Sound equipment was also stored inside for listening to music.

Recreation shed behind
firehouse, circa 1970s

Recreation shed, circa 1980s

| Aerial photo from 1965, indicating recreational structures | Recreation shed & tennis courts, circa 1980 |

By the 1980s, the shed had been extended.

The shed was taken down during the early part of 1990, after being abandoned. The tennis courts had already been abandoned by this time.

Building 84

Built from 1924 to 1925, this three-story brick building was added as an annex to the second power plant. It was a boiler house and incinerator extension with twin smokestacks that stood at about 225 feet tall. It was located next to Building 6 on the west side of Industrial Road. (*See Building 6.*)

Aerial photo from 1965 of
power plant & boiler house

Looking at the boiler house from
Group 4, circa 1940s-1960s

Boiler house on Nov. 3, 1925

Boiler house conveyors pit
on March 30, 1926

It became necessary to build a new boiler house with additional smokestacks to keep up with the increasing size of the hospital and the growing distance between the power plant and other new buildings that were added around this time. The smokestack was removed from Building 6 a few years later during the 1930s.

After Building 29 was built in the mid-1960s, to serve as the new and final power plant, the former boiler house remained abandoned for a few years. It was demolished in the early part of November 1968, along with the old power plant. The twin smokestacks were knocked down near the end of the month. (*See Building 29.*)

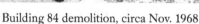

| Building 84 demolition, circa Nov. 1968 | Building 84 smokestack demolition on Nov.21, 1968 |

The number designation used by the boiler house was reused for a series of one-story brick water wells with flat roofs that had been placed around the power plant. Four wells were built from 1957 to 1958, but two more were soon added. These wells were designated as Building 84A–F. They still exist today but are no longer active.

Well house on May 11, 2011   Well house near Building 93 on May 11, 2011

Well house near Group 4 overlooking
Old Dock Road, Nov. 7, 2011

Well house near Group
4 on Nov. 7, 2011

Rooftop view from Building 42 at
explorers taking photos, Aug. 31, 2013

Well house at dusk on Sept. 9, 2011

Well house in the woods south
of Building 5 on Nov.7, 2011

Well house west of Building
15 on April 17, 2016

Northwest wall & entrance of
well house # 8, circa 1980s

Pump controls on in well
house # 8, circa 1980s

Pipe access ladder in well
house # 2, circa 1980s

Well house interior on Sept. 9, 2011

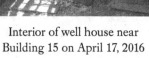

Interior of well house near
Building 15 on April 17, 2016

Pipe access ladder on Nov. 7, 2011

Two can be found on the west side of Old Dock Road near
Group 4. There is a third behind the final power plant on the
other side of the road. Another two are in the wooded hills south

of Building 5. The last is behind Building 93 on Industrial Road. They each have access hatches with ladders that lead down into maintenance tunnels. These tunnels do not connect to the steam tunnels. (*See Buildings 5, 41–43, and 93.*)

Building 85

Building 85 was a one-story brick building with a flat roof. It was built in 1939 on the west side of Industrial Road next to the second power plant and served as a steam pipe junction house. (*See Buildings 6.*)

Facing north toward steam pipe junction house on May 11, 2011

Steam pipe junction house with power plant on May 11, 2011

Steam pipe junction house entrance on May 11, 2011

North side of steam pipe junction house on May 11, 2011

After Buildings 6 and 84 were demolished in 1968, this building had to be partially rebuilt. It was then renumbered as the next Building 6, taking on the number of its former neighbor. For many years, it stood surrounded by piles of coal in the shadow of the new power plant. (*See Buildings 29 and 84.*)

As soon as you entered this building, a metallic staircase led you down into a large basement room. There was no first floor level. Once at the bottom, a large array of steam pipes could be accessed with several tunnels that led to other buildings.

Looking up to the east
entrance on Oct. 24, 2011

Looking down the staircase
on Oct. 24, 2011

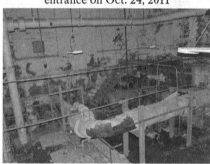

Steam pipe junction house
interior on Oct. 24, 2011

Steam pipes on Oct. 24, 2011

Like most of the other buildings, this structure was abandoned when the hospital closed. When it was demolished at the end of August in 2012, a gaping hole in the ground filled this portion of darkened steam tunnels with sunlight for the first time since they were excavated during the early 1900s. The hole was later filled in, and these sections of the tunnels were sealed.

Abatement process, circa 2012

Demolition phase, Sept. 2012

Demolition on Sept. 5, 2012

Demolished steam pipe junction
house on Sept. 5, 2012

Building 86

The fourth blacksmith and wheelwright shop was built sometime around 1917. It was a one-story rectangular wood-framed building with a gable roof, built as a replacement for the previous shop numbered as Building 36. It was located on the east side of Old Dock Road to the north of Orchard Road and from where the second storehouse was later built. (*See Buildings 36 and 44.*)

Blacksmith shop near pile of coal
at end of trestle, Nov. 3, 1925

Blacksmith & wheelwright
shop, Nov. 3, 1925

Another blacksmith shop was built in 1924 to replace the first Building 86. This one was a one-story concrete building with a hip roof. It was located on the north side of Orchard Road behind Building C. By this time, a wheelwright shop was no longer required. The new Building 62 was built as a truck and maintenance garage at around the same time. (*See Buildings 11 and 62.*)

Replacement blacksmith
shop, Nov. 3, 1925

Building 86 was demolished around 1954–1957.

Building 87

Building 87 was an additional piggery that was built from 1940 to 1941, closer to the rest of the dairy farm buildings. It was actually two structures. The first was a one-story square-shaped, wood-framed building with a gable roof. The second was a one-story cinder block building with a slanted roof. Fenced-in pigpens surrounded the first building on the east and south side.

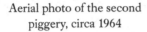

Aerial photo of the second piggery, circa 1964

Aerial view facing south showing the second piggery near dairy farm, 1967

After the pigs were gone by the 1960s–1970s, one of the small structures was utilized for making the cemetery grave markers for a few years. Eventually, these structures were abandoned.

Ever since being abandoned, the former piggery has fallen into ruin. It is well hidden by the woods upon a hill on the west side of Old Dock Road, south from the old dairy farm location. All that remains are four cinderblock walls with two open doorways of the second structure. The roof is nonexistent, and a tree is growing through the floor. It is a mere shell of what it once was but is in better shape than its neighbor. There are only fragments of wood remaining of the first structure. A partial fence from an old pigpen can be found in the area near some barbed wiring. There are also mounds of discarded broken furniture.

Building 87 on Nov. 7, 2011

Destroyed wooden portion of Building 87 on Nov. 7, 2011

Building 87 concrete structure
on Nov. 7, 2011

Interior of concrete structure
on Nov. 7, 2011

Building 88

This building was used
as a slaughterhouse for the
dairy farm. It was a one-story
concrete building with a gable
roof built in 1943. Inside, there
were large vats connected to
the water and sewage pipes.
A rail stretched across the
ceiling above, where animals
were hung by hooks. The

Slaughterhouse, circa 1990s

walls inside were made of tiles, so it would be easier to clean the
spattered blood.

Slaughterhouse on March 27, 2012

East entrance of slaughterhouse
on March 27, 2012

West entrance of slaughterhouse
on Sept. 9, 2011

Rusted chair & shelves in
slaughterhouse room on Sept. 9, 2011

Slaughterhouse tubs on Sept. 9, 2011

Slaughterhouse tubs on Oct. 24, 2011

Slaughterhouse interior on Sept. 9, 2011

Slaughterhouse steps & east
entrance on Sept. 9, 2011

After the farming operations were shut down between the 1950s and 1960s, this building was used for storage. It was abandoned in the 1990s.

Ever since the 1980s, this building has been mistaken quite often for the farm's root cellar. The sign on the hike-and-bike trail also listed this structure as Building 46. Both buildings were the same shape and situated close to one another. This building was not a root cellar, and it was never used as such. (*See Building 46.*) The building was demolished by December 2012.

Slaughterhouse from Old Dock Road on Sept. 5, 2012	Demolition company trailer parked near slaughterhouse, Aug. 3, 2012

Building 89

This one-story brick building with a gable roof was built in 1955 as a comfort station for Tiffany Field. In simpler terms, it was a public bathroom. It is located along the southern path around the field, closer to Building 93, and drew its electrical power from that building. (*See Building 93.*)

East side of comfort station on May 1, 2013	West side of comfort station on May 1, 2013

| Rear of comfort station on April 16, 2013 | Damaged roof on south side of building, circa March 17, 2013 |

This building was abandoned when the hospital closed and is now on the list of buildings to be demolished from 2016 to 2017. Portable toilets, added after 2005, have since replaced it.

| Portable toilets at entrance to Tiffany Field on June 20, 2016 | Portable toilets at Tiffany Field on May 11, 2016 |

Building 90

Building 90 is a three-story brick building with a basement and an attic that was built from 1917 to 1919. It has a flat parapet roof and four two-story white pillars centered at the front entrance with a flat roof covering the second-floor balcony and ground-floor porch. This building is located on the east side of Kings Park Boulevard, just south of St. Johnland Road. Originally known as the Employees' Home, it was officially named Macy Home following the sudden death of then hospital superintendent, Dr.

William Austin Macy, on May 21, 1918. Together with the staff cottages located behind it, Macy Home cost $733,830 to build.

Macy Home in 1920, prior to the extension of its north & south wings

Macy Home, circa 1920s-1950s

Rear of Macy Home from St. Johnland Road, circa 1923

Macy Home, circa 1980s-1990s

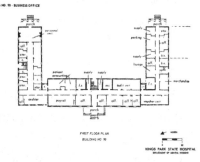

Building 90 floor plan (basement)

Building 90 floor plan (first floor)

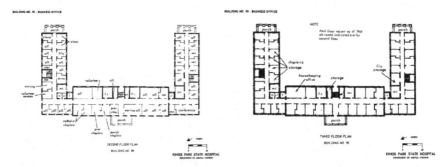

Building 90 floor plan (second floor)   Building 90 floor plan (third floor)

The building was opened and occupied by the spring of 1919, serving mainly as a business and clerical building. Employees were housed on upper levels, while nurses were trained on lower levels. There were fifteen single rooms and forty-five double rooms. It was used as an additional home for nurses, particularly the nursing students.

The nursing school moved from its original location at Building C to this building, where it remained for many years. The main classrooms were in the basement. (*See Building 11.*)

Several offices were located within this building, including a cashier, credit union, payroll office, personnel office, chaplains' offices, and numerous other clerical offices. The hospital newspaper had an office on the second floor until it was relocated to Building 7 during the late 1960s. (*See Building 7.*)

In the later part of 1923, additional north and south wings were added on either side of the original rectangular portion of the building. This allowed for an additional 250 residents. Balconies were added to the second floor at each new wing facing the rear with flat roofs and four two-story white support columns at each wing.

Power washing Macy Home in 1968

Painting the rear south wing
porch, circa 1960s-1970s

Anita Reyda (white dress) with other
employees on rear porch, circa 1970

Main office awards, circa 1970

Business Office staff with Ken
Meyer (far right), circa 1970s

Business Officer Ken Meyer (seated)
& Business Office staff, circa 1980

Chandler Bliss, Marie Clark, Phil S. Stasuk, & other employees, circa 1981

Office personnel, circa 1987

One of the former apartments was converted into a badly needed library in 1953. A few partitions had to be removed during the construction to expand the size of the room. The hospital's Maintenance Department installed bookshelves and storage cabinets, making research much easier for the teaching staff and nursing students.

The nursing school was later relocated to Building 7 in 1967. By April 1968, the third floor was emptied and no longer used because of a large destructive fire, which left that area badly damaged. (*See Building 7.*)

After the hospital closed in 1996, this building was sealed up. It remains abandoned and is one of the oldest buildings on the grounds. In 2013, someone started a fire in an old records room in the basement. At the time, the rusty cabinets in the room were still filled with useful information.

Fire damaged file storage room in basement, circa 2013

Despite being abandoned, this building still has a special appeal. Its exterior resembles a mansion. However, the interior is very much like an office building with its white halls and dark-colored doors and window frames.

The nicest-looking area is the rear room of the north wing, where a grand fireplace must have made for a cozy atmosphere when this building was occupied.

Macy Home on Dec. 19, 2012

Macy Home, circa 2013

Main entrance on Oct. 5, 2015

Rear of Macy Home on May 11, 2011

Inside rear entrance of north wing on March 17, 2013

Opened north wing rear entrance on Jan. 2, 2016

North fireplace on March 17, 2013

South fireplace on March 17, 2013

North entrance near payroll
office on March 17, 2013

Support columns on March 17, 2013

North wing rear balcony facing
south on March 17, 2013

Front balcony looking toward
Building 93 on March 17, 2013

Upper level corridor, circa 2013   Basement classroom, circa 2013

First floor room on March 17, 2013   Same room decorated for
                                            Christmas when Macy Home
                                            was still operational

Building 91

This is a one-story wood-framed, six-car staff garage with a gable roof that was erected directly behind Macy Home. It was built in 1931, after the addition of the doctors' cottages, numbered from 95 to 99. Staff members that worked at Macy Home and resided in the nearby cottages used this garage until Building 90 was closed. There was additional parking in a parking lot on the north side of the garage. (*See Buildings 90 and 95–99.*)

West side of Building 91
on May 11, 2011

Building 91 from the balcony
of Macy Home, circa 2013

West side of Building 91 on Jan. 2, 2016

East side of Building 91 with
open garages on Jan. 2, 2016

Garage interior on Jan. 2, 2016

Garage interior with closed
gate on March 17, 2013

This garage replaced a smaller wooden garage numbered as the original Building 39. (*See Building 39.*)

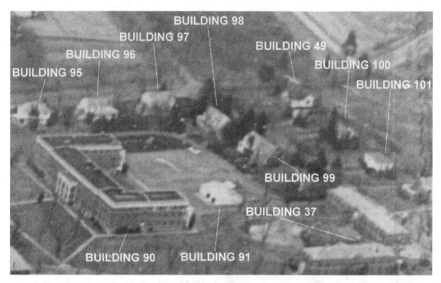

BUILDING 98
BUILDING 97
BUILDING 96
BUILDING 95
BUILDING 49
BUILDING 100
BUILDING 101
BUILDING 99
BUILDING 37
BUILDING 90   BUILDING 91

Aerial photo of Macy Home, garage, & cottages, circa 1965

Building 92

The grandstand was located at the southeastern end of Tiffany Field, north of Building 93 and across from Building 90. Construction began in 1924 and was completed by April 1925. Built of concrete and steel, it seated 114 people comfortably. It had electrical service and an announcer's booth at the top. For many years, it was used to seat spectators for sporting events, ceremonies, and shows. (*See Buildings 90 and 93.*)

Grandstand at Tiffany Field with
Building 93, circa 1930s-1950s

Seated in front of the grandstand during
the 1985 Centennial Celebration

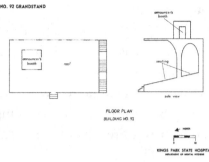

Ready to throw out the first ball at
a baseball game, circa 1920s-1930s

Building 92 floor plans created
by Jason Medina in 2016

This structure was torn down between 1999 and 2001, a few years after the hospital closed.

Grandstand & Building 93, circa 1979

Grandstand, circa 1990s

Close-up of grandstand, circa 1990s

Front steps of grandstand, circa 1990s

The previous 3 photos of the grandstand were provided by Robert Saal

Building 93

Building 93 is probably the most recognized building of all Long Island asylums, despite being abandoned. It is a magnificent relic of asylum architecture that was designed by state architect William E. Haugaard, who was better known for designing Attica State Prison. The building cost $1,912,311 to build, using money from President Roosevelt's Work Projects Administration (WPA). The Turner Construction Company began construction in January 1939 on this massive, eleven-story brick building on the southwest corner of Kings Park Boulevard and West Fourth Street on the site of the early male cottages. The building has a basement, subbasement, two-story unfinished attic, hip roof design, and concrete framing. There is also a Georgian Revival influence. There are scrolled decorative designs on the facade gables and a one-story front entrance pavilion with a half gable and half flat roof. There is another one-story extension at the rear of the building with a flat roof. The elevator bank is centrally located with two freight elevators and two passenger elevators. This building housed Wards 17–38, also known as the Brooklyn Unit.

Rear of Building 93, while under construction, circa 1939

Roof over kitchen at rear of Building 93, circa 1939

Building 93 from the "Brooklyn Daily Eagle" by Lyman W.T, circa Oct. 1939

Building 93, as seen from Building B   Building 93 main entrance

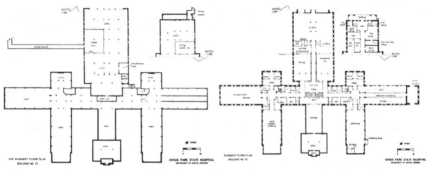

Building 93 floor plan (sub-basement)   Building 93 floor plan (basement)

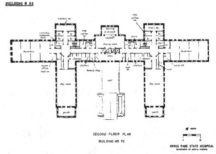

Building 93 floor plan (first floor)   Building 93 floor plan (second floor)

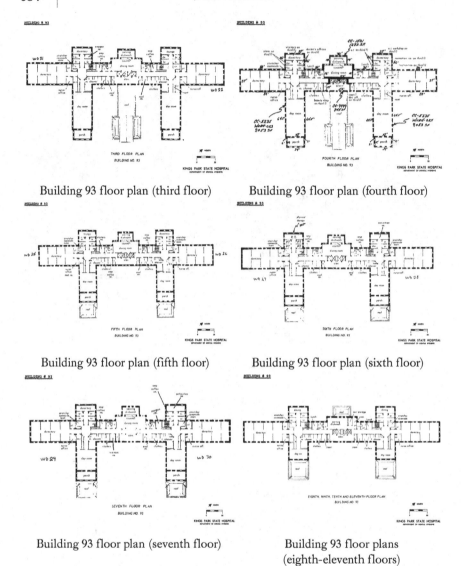

Building 93 floor plan (third floor)

Building 93 floor plan (fourth floor)

Building 93 floor plan (fifth floor)

Building 93 floor plan (sixth floor)

Building 93 floor plan (seventh floor)

Building 93 floor plans
(eighth-eleventh floors)

At the time it was completed in 1941, Building 93 was the largest hospital building on Long Island, constructed during a time when state hospitals wanted to build upward rather than outward. Despite its height, the structure has a very small footprint, totaling 262,879 square feet in size. It is very slender in design. This was to allow almost every room and hallway the maximum amount of sunlight possible. You can actually see right through the windows to the other side, if standing at the right angle.

Building 93 main entrance by
King Pedlar, circa 1970s-1990s

Looking south toward entrance

Looking up at Building 93 by
King Pedlar, circa 1970s

Building 93 from Tiffany
Field, circa 1970

Building 93 at dawn by David
M. Flynn, circa January 1978

The year Building 93 closed
during the summer of 1992

Building 93, after it closed, by   Building 93 by King Pedlar, circa 1993
Robert Saal, circa early 1990s

Building 93 was originally intended for the US Navy, but the military decided not to use it. Instead, it was used as a geriatric infirmary and for drug treatment. A pharmacy was established in the basement, relocated from Building A. There was also a large kitchen in the basement within the rear extension of the building. On the first floor were the dentist's office and an x-ray room. (*See Building 8.*)

By 1948, the Shock Therapy Department occupied the third floor. Many patients dreaded being taken to this building because of it. During that first year, there were 638 patients treated with shock therapy here. There were 439 who were treated using electroshock and 118 with insulin shock, and 111 unlucky patients got a combination of both.

There was a one-story ambulance bay with an arched entrance and a flat roof, which accessed the north side of the building. It led into a long corridor, which sloped upward to the first floor. This bay was removed soon after the building was closed.

Aerial photo showing
ambulance bay from 1957

Employees conducting an emergency
drill using the ambulance, circa 1966

Ambulance bay on Oct. 6, 2013

Entrance ramp leading to the
ambulance bay on Oct. 6, 2013

In 1958, a recreation area was established in the basement for both male and female patients. It was located in the south wing of the building.

During the late 1970s and into the 1980s, Building 93 became the main kitchen for the entire hospital. Food would be delivered to the other dining halls in food trucks. There was a loading dock at the rear of the building. The trucks would also pick up food supplies from the nearby storehouse. (*See Building 44.*)

Hospital dietician, Chris Barrier
(center), poses with cooks, circa 1972

Kitchen staff, circa 1978

Hospital cooks, circa 1980s-1990s

A patient dining room near the elevators

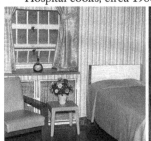

Single patient dorm room

Several single patient dorm rooms on Oct. 6, 2013

Dr. Robert D'Annibale (center) poses
with employees & patients, 1976

Employees are distracted, while
bringing mattresses out, circa 1977

Employees pose near Christmas tree, circa 1977

Employees pose near
Christmas tree, circa 1980

The bedridden patients were placed on the top floors, and the more physically able lived on the lower floors. The building is stepped outward on the bottom floors, creating dayrooms for able-bodied patients. As you go higher, the dayrooms get smaller. The patients on the upper floors did not require such large dayrooms. There were open porches with barred windows outside of the dayrooms of the first eight floors, where patients could take in the fresh air or have a cigarette break. Sometime around the early 1970s, screens were installed over these windows. Pigeon droppings became a hassle, and this was one way to put an end to it.

When the hospital began its mass release of patients in the 1970s–1980s, the upper floors were closed starting with the top three floors. The abandonment slowly worked its way down until everyone was gone by the early 1990s. The building closed during the summer of 1992.

For a while, there were concerns that the building might be sinking because of the amount of grading done on the land before it was built. It could have made for an unstable ground in some places. At one time, there was a lot of marshland, which was filled using dirt or ashes from the boiler house. The building is still standing tall, so there does not seem to be any truth to the rumors of it sinking. Otherwise, it would be halfway into the ground by now. Even if it were sinking, it is only a matter of time before the building is demolished.

Because of its vast popularity, Building 93 is the most vandalized building on the property. Immediately after closing, the power lines were cut. A tall chain-link fence eventually had to be put up around the building in 2001 to keep trespassers out. That has not done much to deter anyone from cutting holes in the fence all around the building to gain access.

Once inside, it is quite common to come across the various artifacts left behind by the patients and staff members on the many floors. Assorted clothing can still be found hanging in the closets or scattered along the floor. Chairs hang from the windows and ceilings in a strange manner on the upper levels of the building. Rusted metal beds fill the large rooms of the basement. Old medieval-looking cages once used to lock away patients like animals lie hidden away down in the basement. There are even a few patient dorm rooms that still have curtains on the windows and bedsheets on the beds.

Building 93 on Oct. 25, 2011

Building 93 sign from the Hike
& Bike Trail on June 22, 2010

Rear of Building 93 on Sept. 5, 2012

Looking up at Building
93 on Oct. 6, 2013

Building 93 main entrance
on April 16, 2013

Building 93 front lobby on April 17, 2016

Food service area on Oct. 6, 2013

Elevators on Oct. 6, 2013

Dormitory beds & knocked down
partitions on Oct. 6, 2013

Upper level dormitory on April 17, 2016

Day room on Oct. 6, 2013

Television set, circa
2000s, courtesy of
Max Neukirch, Jr.

Clothing in closet on July 31, 2009

Cage on wheels on April 11, 2011

Chairs in the hallway on
railing on July 31, 2009

Chairs on the ceiling pipes
on Oct. 6, 2013

Attic & ladder on Oct. 6, 2013

Attic floorboards leading to
roof access on Oct. 6, 2013

Rear roof walkway on Oct. 6, 2013

Looking down to the roof of
the kitchen on Oct. 6, 2013

Front roof walkway on Oct. 6, 2013

Looking across the top of the
building on Oct. 6, 2013

Looking down to the front
entrance rooftop on Oct. 6, 2013

Roof over front entrance on Oct. 6, 2013

Looking up elevator shaft at
stopped elevator on Oct. 6, 2013

Ladder in elevator shaft leading to
the sub-basement on Oct. 6, 2013

Building 93 sub-basement
on Oct. 6, 2013

Building 93 sub-basement
on April 17, 2016

One of the most popular attractions of this building can be found in a basement recreation room of the south wing. A series of beautifully done murals span across the walls of this large room, which depict the way the patients lived at the time. It is widely believed that a patient, who was a well-known cartoonist named Percy Crosby, painted the murals during the 1970s after being committed for a suicide attempt. There are also those who believe a female doctor created the murals. This is a much-debated matter.

Basement mural room on Oct. 6, 2013

During the summer of 2014, there was a fire within this building, which was supposedly accidental, according to my sources. On June 30, 2015, there was another fire on the sixth floor shortly before one in the morning, while on September 23, there was another fire. Someone also started a fire in the elevator shaft on March 5, 2016. There was another fire at around four o'clock in the afternoon on the very next day, and yet another fire the next day!

There is a gaping hole in the roof caused by recent harsh winters and a large crack going up the north side of the building. The bricks at every other floor are slowly starting to cave in on that side. It is very easy for rain and snow to enter through the hole in the roof and pass through the poor flooring in the attic and down to the top floor creating rotting conditions.

| Visible hole in roof of Building 93 on March 9, 2014 | Collapsed brickwork on north face of building on Oct. 6, 2013 |

Dangerous floors of attic, circa April 2011 & Oct. 6, 2013   Recent fire damage on April 17, 2016

Considering all of these factors, it is only a matter of time before this building begins to collapse one floor at a time. While I do have a special affection for this building as a photographer and urban explorer, I highly advise keeping out for your own safety. You do not want to be trapped in here when someone else starts another fire or when it collapses.

Building 94

Building 94 replaced Building 5 as the laundry building. Designed by Hart, Jerman & Associates, it was built in 1953, although improvements were added until 1956. This three-story flat-roofed brick building complete with a basement and penthouse level cost $1,137,508 to build. It had a loading platform and a freight elevator on the west side of the building that was used for the transportation of large laundry loads between levels.

There was also a loading dock on the east side of the building for laundry deliveries. The main workroom was on the first floor, the main washing room and lint removal room were located on the second floor, and the main sorting room was on the third. Soap mixing was also done on the third floor. Located on the north side of West Fourth Street in the shadow of the ominous Building 93, it was the third building to be used as a laundry building on the property. (*See Buildings 5 and 93.*)

Building 94, hospital laundry, circa 1970s-1980s

Checking the washer, circa 1970s-1980s

Using the laundry chutes, circa 1970s-1980s

Removing laundry from the dryer, circa 1970s-1980s

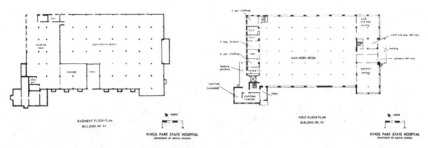

Building 94 floor plan (basement)   Building 94 floor plan (first floor)

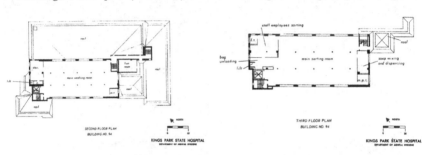

Building 94 floor plan (second floor)   Building 94 floor plan (third floor)

The tailor shop was removed to make room for this building. That shop was relocated to Building 38, which had formerly served as the kitchen for Buildings A and B. (*See Buildings 8, 9, 28, and 38.*)

While it was operational, this laundry building processed over 170,000 pounds of laundry per week. The laundry was moved easily between floors via chutes, and it would be caught in large baskets, which had wheels for easy mobility.

This building was also used for storage, but there is not much to see in here now. It has been abandoned since the hospital closed. Most of the equipment was removed, leaving behind large empty rooms.

View of Building 94 from Building
93 on March 27, 2013

Building 94 on March 27, 2013

Building 94 east loading
dock on March 17, 2013

Building 94 west loading
dock on March 17, 2013

Laundry chute openings on
third floor, March 2013

Laundry chutes on second
floor, March 2013

Second floor sorting tables & chutes on March 17, 2013

Chutes emptying out to the first floor on March 17, 2013

Toiletries on the floor on March 17, 2013

Paper & plastic cups, March 2013

On November 24, 2005, there was a fire set by arsonists. One firefighter was injured battling the blaze.

Buildings 95–99

These were small two-story wood-framed, single-family cottages with basements and attics built by the hospital mechanics in 1925. Most of them had gable/gambrel roofs, except for Building 95, which had a hip roof. They were also known as the Staff Doctor's Cottages 1–5. The roofs were all redone in 1967.

Doctor's cottages under construction
with Macy Home on May 4, 1925

Facing north on E. Fourth Street
toward doctor's cottages

These cottages were used as housing for the senior assistant physicians of the hospital. They are all located behind Macy Home in the area north from where the early female cottages existed. Buildings 95–97 are on the south side of St. Johnland Road, while Buildings 98 and 99 are on the west side of East Fourth Street. At one time, there was a small tennis court located next to them, used by employees.

All of these cottages are currently abandoned. Some of them are in pretty bad shape. There was talk of turning them over to the Kings Park Fire Department, but nothing has been done.

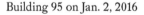

Building 95 on Jan. 2, 2016

West side of Building 95 on Jan. 2, 2016

Building 96 on Jan. 2, 2016

Sunset over Building 96 on Jan. 2, 2016

Building 97 on Jan. 2, 2016

Building 97 back door on May 11, 2011

Sunroom on May 11, 2011

Living room graffiti &
doorway on Jan. 2, 2016

Fireplace on Jan. 2, 2016

Kitchen counters & sink on Jan. 2, 2016

Building 98 on Jan. 2, 2016

Collapsed front porch of
Building 98 on Jan. 2, 2016

Building 99 on Jan. 2, 2016

North side of Building 99
on May 11, 2011

Staircase to the basement
on May 11, 2011

Looking into the kitchen
on May 11, 2011

Buildings 100 and 101

These were additional two-story hip-roofed, wood-framed, single-family homes built for doctors in 1950. They were completed and occupied by 1953. These houses were located along the east side of East Fourth Street across from Buildings 98 and 99. They remain abandoned today. (*See Buildings 98 and 99.*)

Building 100 on Jan. 2, 2016

South side of Building
100 on Jan. 2, 2016

Building 100 back door on Jan. 2, 2016

Sunlight creeping in through
the back door on Jan. 2, 2016

Fireplace in living room on Jan. 2, 2016

Kitchen on May 11, 2011

Staircase looking down to the
first floor on Aug. 2, 2011

Upstairs bedroom on Aug. 2, 2011

Basement shelves on Aug. 2, 2011

Chair & tub in the basement
on Aug. 2, 2011

Building 101 on Jan. 2, 2016

Building 101 garage on Jan. 2, 2016

Living room, similar to Building
100, on Jan. 2, 2016

Looking towards front
door on May 11, 2011

Open back door on May 11, 2011   Garage interior on Aug. 2, 2011

Building 102

Building 102 would have been another residential cottage for doctors, built near Buildings 100 and 101, but it was never built. (*See Buildings 100 and 101.*)

Buildings 103–110

Based on maps dating back to the late 1800s, photography going back as far as 1909, annual reports from 1889 to 1925, and a vast collection of aerial photography of the entire grounds from the mid-1920s to the present, these numbers were never assigned to any buildings.

Maybe these numbers were used to identify buildings that already existed. It definitely does not make any sense for these numbers to be skipped deliberately, so they must have been used at one time.

Considering the typical patterns used when numbering structures on maps, I can only speculate these numbers represented a series of structures that were either near the staff cottages behind Macy Home or next to Group 1. This presumption is based on the numbers, which continue after the staff cottages and come before the building numbers used for Group 1. (*See Buildings 4, 18, 19. 90, 95–99, 100, 101, and 111–120.*)

I tried multiple theories using groups of buildings that added up to eight to match these numbers, but the one that made the most sense to me includes Buildings 18, 19, 37, and 49. First, you have the staff cottages numbered as Buildings 95–101. There was never a 102, since it was not built, although it was intended. Of course, that might be the key to this mystery, but we will probably never know. If you take the cottages that were in that area and use these numbers, it fits. Building 49, which was the oldest of these dating back to the 1800s, would have been 103. Building 18 is broken up into three units, which could be 104–106. Building 19 also consists of three units, which could be 107–109. Last, you have the staff house (Building 37). That could have been listed as 110.

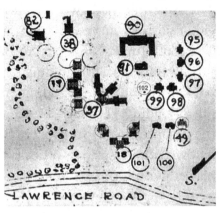

Modified key plot plan from 1954, showing possible Buildings 102-110

Buildings 111–120 (Group 1/Buildings 4A–J)

These were the buildings of Group 1 built from 1897 to 1898. They consisted of a kitchen, a dining area, and both male and female wards. Most of them were connected in a sort of semicircle shape along the west side of the boulevard. Most of these structures were two-story brick buildings with basements, attics, and hip roofs.

Aerial view facing south over Group 1, circa February 1968

Only Building 115 (4E) had three floors. Some of the buildings were equipped with elevators. These buildings were also known as Buildings 4A–J collectively and housed Wards 41–49. (*See Building 4.*)

Building 111 (4A) stood at the front and center of the group facing the main boulevard. The front half was almost like a detached cottage, except it was connected at the rear on the ground floor. The back half had two turrets with conical roofs that stood at either side of a curved solarium sun parlor, which had a gable roof. The south turret connected to Building 112 (4B), while the north turret connected to Building 114 (4D). Two corridors extended outward from the rear, connecting the building to Building 116 (4F). Building 111 (4A) served as the administration building of the group. Being a group of ten buildings, it was necessary to have its own administrative offices. The staff members of the group resided within this building.

Building 111, circa 1910

Building 111, "Group" office, circa 1910

South side of Building 111 with cars in lot, circa Aug. 1966

Playground at north side of Building 111, circa Aug. 1966

Laundry on rear porch of
Building 111, circa Aug. 1966

Bathhouse windows, circa Aug. 1966

NYS Hospitals Quarterly
Conference on June 12, 1926

NYS Hospitals Quarterly Conference
in solarium, June 12, 1926

The solarium sun parlor was, by far, the most attractive part of the group. Dinners, parties, and other events were held here. In 1907, this area was repaired extensively. The glass across the ceiling was reset, and six large ventilators were inserted.

Buildings 112 (4B) and 113 (4C) were at the south end of the group. They consisted of Wards 41 and 42. Building 112 (4B) was connected to Building 111 (A) on its east side and connected to Building 113 (4) on its west side.

Road leading to Buildings 112 & 113
from boulevard, circa Aug. 1966

Building 112 with cars in lot &
Building 113 on the left, Aug. 1966

Building 113, circa Aug. 1966

Barred windows at Building 113

Opposite of those buildings were Buildings 114 (4D) and 115 (4E), which faced the north side and consisted of Wards 43 and 44. Building 114 (4D) was connected to Building 111 (4A) on its east side and Building 115 (4E) on its west side.

After years of requests, by 1920, a Kirker-Bender fire escape was finally installed at the rear of Building 115 (E), as it was the tallest building of the group. In 1958, a recreation room was established for female patients in the alcove of Ward 43 in Building 114 (4D).

Building 114 with Building
111 on the left, circa 1913

Building 114, circa Aug. 1966

Building 115, circa 1913

Building 115, circa Aug. 1966

Ward 45, which was the women's infirmary, and the dining hall were located in Building 116 (4F), while Ward 46 and the kitchen were in Building 117 (4G). Both were connected to each other. Building 117 (4G) was directly behind Building 116 (4F), which was behind Building 111 (4A). Buildings 116 (4F) and 117 (4G) were situated at the center of the attached buildings of the group. Male and female patients of the group shared the kitchen and dining hall, which could hold up to 1,200 people. Building 117 (4G) had an elevator.

Building 115, circa Aug. 1966

Building 117, circa 1910

Building 117, circa Aug. 1966

Group 1 kitchen, circa 1915-1916

Group 1 kitchen, circa 1920s

Kitchen improvements, circa 1920s

Kitchen improvements &
back door, circa 1920s

Group 1 dining hall, circa 1920s

Kitchen & housekeeping staff
near Building 117, circa 1920s

Kitchen staff outside of
kitchen, circa 1920s

Kitchen staff sitting on a
fence, circa 1920s

Kitchen & housekeeping staff &
patient with a carriage, circa 1920s

There were several occupational therapy workshops in the various wards of this group. In 1900, the shoe shop and other manufacturing patient workshops were relocated to a large basement room underneath the dining hall. At the same time, new additions were made to the shoe manufacturing appliances, allowing a wider range of shoes to be created. In 1907, two Kirker-Bender fire escapes were installed outside of Building 116 (4F). Two years later, a cement garbage vault was constructed and placed outside of the kitchen. In 1913, a new refrigeration machine was installed in the kitchen.

Buildings 118 (4J), 119 (4I), and 120 (4H) were all built as detached cottages from the main part of the group. These three detached cottages were located across a small road called West Third Street, which was north of the other buildings from the group. Males were kept in these cottages on Wards 47, 48, and 49, while the females were kept in the attached section of cottages. Ward 47 was located in Building 120 (4H), and Ward 49 was inside of Building 118 (4J), which can be a bit confusing. A room on the first floor of Ward 48 in Building 119 (4I) was used as a drug room. This ward also housed the men's infirmary. In 1903, a dumbwaiter was added to this ward.

Heading westbound on West Third Street toward Building 120, 1920s

Facing east toward Buildings 118-120, circa 1913

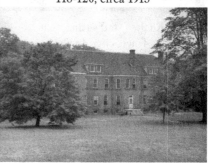

Building 118, circa 1920s

Building 118, circa Aug. 1966

Building 119, circa 1915   Aerial view of Building 119, circa 1965

Building 119, circa Aug. 1966   Building 120, circa 1915

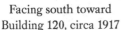

Facing south toward   Building 120,   Rear of Building 120,
Building 120, circa 1917   circa Aug. 1966   circa Aug. 1966

By the 1960s, the buildings of this group had become severely outdated. They were constantly in need of repairs and upgrades. Toward the middle of the decade, these buildings were finally closed, and the patients were moved to other buildings as space began to open up with the gradual decrease in population.

Soon after Group 1 was abandoned, there were a series of fires caused by vandals during the early 1970s. The first occurred at Building 115 (4E). The next fire in 1972 destroyed nearly half of the attached buildings of the group. By end of that year, the three detached structures, Buildings 118 (4J), 119 (4I), and 120 (4H), had already been demolished. The rest of the buildings followed about a year later as Building 56 was built nearby. (*See Building 56.*)

Building 111 main office & staff quarters abandoned, circa 1970s

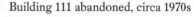

Building 111 abandoned, circa 1970s

Building 113 abandoned, circa 1970s

Building 113 demolished, circa 1970s

Building 114 abandoned, circa 1970s

Building 115 abandoned, circa 1970s

The field where this group of buildings once stood is now a flying field for remote control planes, but a permit is required.

Flying permit sign at former site of Group 1 on Oct. 5, 2015	Back of former Group 1 location on Oct. 5, 2015	Facing east toward boulevard at former site of Building 120, Oct. 5, 2015

Building 121

Building 121 was the unofficial designated number for the original St. Joseph's Church, built in 1898 on former hospital property at the same time as the previously mentioned Group 1 buildings. The church was not part of the group, nor was it part of the hospital. It was likely never referred to by this number. However, the church and rectory did share the same power lines as the Group 1 buildings and the head farmer's house at East Main Street/Route 25A. (*See Buildings 48A and 111–120.*)

St. Joseph's Church, circa 1926

A ceremony in front of the church, circa 1920s

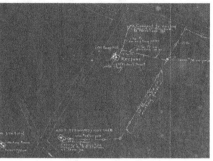

St. Joseph's Church interior, circa 1926

Blueprint showing power lines connecting Asst Steward's house & church

The effort to raise money for building the church was begun by the town in 1894. The result was a wood-framed building built at a cost of $17,000, located on the east side of Kohr Road, aptly renamed Church Street. The church had seating for three hundred people. A rectory was added next to the church in 1919 at a cost of $27,000. A school was added as well.

Old convent, circa 1933

St. Joseph's School, circa 1920s

While it is true the church did not belong to the hospital, no one can deny its roots originated there. Before an actual church building was ever built for the parish, St. Joseph's held its first mass in the sunroom of one of the hospital's first cottages in 1886, the amusement hall. The first parish was officially established two years later in 1888. During its first ten years, it celebrated its masses in the hospital's amusement hall until the church on Kohr Road was constructed. (*See Building 48.*)

After the church was built, every Sunday, the priest would go to the hospital with a nun, an altar boy, and members of the choir for a separate mass, which was held for hospital patients and employees first in the amusement hall and then at York Hall as of 1932. (*See Building 80.*)

Construction of the new church, designed by Eggers & Higgins, 1957

Builders from W.L. Oestreicher Co., Inc. on scaffolding, circa 1957

Rear of new St. Joseph's Church under construction, circa 1957

Construction of the bell tower, circa 1957

Scaffolding inside the new church, circa 1957

Most of the scaffolding removed from the inside, circa 1957

The nearly completed St. Joseph's Church, circa 1957

Aerial photo of the church area, circa 1970s

In 1957, the church purchased additional property from the hospital, and construction began on a new church building. Designed by architects Eggers and Higgins, the new building was built by W. L. Oestreicher Co. Inc. and completed in 1958. The original church was demolished a year later once the new church opened.

The church and the hospital still remain connected in spirit.

St. Joseph's Church on June 22, 2010

Side view of St. Joseph's
Church on June 22, 2010

Building 122

Built from 1910 to 1912, this two-story brick building with
a basement, unfinished attic, and flaring hip roof was home to
female patients of Wards 51 and 52. This building originally
housed chronic bedridden females. It was later used for adolescent
females. It was part of Group 2, located on a hill west of Kings
Park Boulevard, overlooking St. Johnland Road from the north.

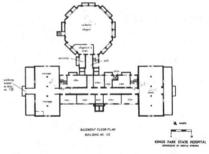

Building 122, circa 1913

Building 122 floor plan (basement)

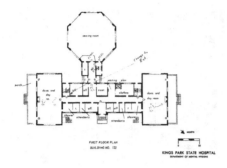 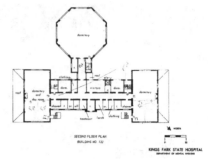

Building 122 floor plan (first floor)   Building 122 floor plan (second floor)

A small section of the central portion of the building's first floor was designated for the attendants that worked here. The second floor ward was a high-security ward used for high-risk patients. The porches were caged in, and the patients almost never left their ward. They were only allowed to leave once a week, after dinnertime, when movies were shown on the first floor.

New additions were made in 1915–1916. A two-story octagon-shaped wing with a basement and flat roof was added, which gave it a similar appearance to Buildings 143 and 147 of Group 3. The basement of the octagon wing was used as a chapel. Other recreational activities were also made available in the basement. A sewing room was on the first floor of that wing. The second-floor section was used as a dorm/dayroom. (*See Buildings 143 and 147.*)

Construction of new addition with   Aerial photo from 1957
Patiky brothers, circa 1915   showing new addition

Building 122, circa 1947   Building 122, Wards 51 & 52, with octagon-shaped extension, 1960s-1970s

At the time the building was designed and built, it was supposed to have an elevator at its central portion. Instead, an elevator shaft was built, but no elevator was installed because the state had not provided sufficient funding. Stairs had to be added into the elevator well to avoid possible injuries. By 1916, an elevator was installed, although it operated poorly and was constantly out of order. This building also had two steel fire escapes on the north side of the building.

The dormitories were located at the far ends of the building with direct access to the wooden porches. When the buildings were renovated, each dormitory was split by a wall to add new dayrooms that took up one-third of what was once part of the dormitories. There were doors in these dayrooms that accessed the porches. The porches were rebuilt in 1957.

Building 122 new porch design, circa 1960s-1970s   The addition of a handicapped accessible ramp is clearly visible, 1960s-70s

In 1966, this building was rehabilitated more extensively. During this time, the patients were relocated to a new Adolescent Unit in Building 22. As part of the renovations, the ceilings were all redone and lowered. Handicap accessible ramps were installed, and by the early 1970s, it was used to house females of the Mental Retardation Unit (MRU). This building also housed the worst of the MRU patients. Wards 51 and 52 were renumbered as Wards 852 and 853.

By the early 1980s, the building was vacant, and the unit was moved to another facility in Melville. Over the years, this building had slowly fallen apart, making it an extremely unsafe structure to enter. One could easily have fallen through the old decayed wooden floors of the main corridors, as they were so weak from decay. When I stepped onto the first floor hallway, my foot began to sink through the floor. I decided to leave rather than risk injury.

Building 122, circa Jan. 2008

Building 122 on March 26, 2011

Collapsed porch on March 26, 2011

Octagon-shaped extension on March 26, 2011

Building 122 entrance, circa Jan. 2008

First floor collapsing into
basement on Aug. 2, 2011

First floor hallway on Aug. 2, 2011

Second floor hallway, circa March 2009

Dangerously weak second floor
beams on Aug. 2, 2011

Looking into a second floor
room on Aug. 2, 2011

| Basement of Building 122, circa 2012, by Max Neukirch, Jr. | Building 122 octagon addition interior provided by Ray Staten, circa 2000s |

Building 122 with octagon addition, circa 2012, by Max Neukirch, Jr.

This building was scheduled to be demolished in the fall of 2010, along with thirteen other structures on the property. Demolitions were postponed for two years because of a lack of funding. After the abatement process was completed, the building was demolished by the end of September 2012, together with its neighbor, Building 123. (*See Building 123.*)

Building 122 during the first week of
Aug. 2012, when it was demolished

Dumpster outside of Building
122 on Aug. 3, 2012

Building 122.1

This was a small wooden
gazebo located to the north of
Building 122. Built in 1916, it
was gone by the early 1940s, a
few years after the boys' ward
was moved to Group 2. (*See
Buildings 54 and 122.*)

Aerial view of gazebo behind
Building 122, circa Sept. 1927

Building 123

Building 123was a one-story brick building with a basement
and a hip roof. It was built between 1911 and 1912 to serve as a
kitchen and dining area for Group 2. The scullery and two dining
rooms had wood floors, while the kitchen had a concrete floor.
A new refrigeration machine was installed in the basement a year
after construction was completed. The kitchen and dishwashing
area were located on the first floor. This building had a freight
elevator added in 1916, at its center. The porches of the building
were rebuilt in 1957, and the building was later rehabilitated in
1966, along with Buildings 122 and 124. (*See Buildings 54, 122,
and 124.*)

Building 123 with first power
plant's smokestack in the
background, circa 1917

Aerial view of Building 123, circa 1957

Building 123, circa 1960s-1970s

Group 2 dining hall staff with Mary
Hildenbrand (R), circa 1916

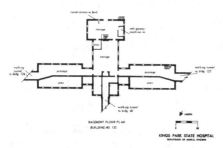

Building 123 floor plan (basement)

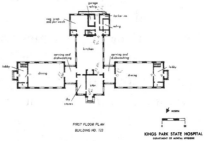

Building 123 floor plan (first floor)

Nurses pose together at a Group 2 retirement party, circa 1970-1972

This building was abandoned, along with the rest of Group 2, in the early 1980s. Over the next few decades, the floors and ceilings collapsed in different areas because of weather erosion and vandalism, creating hazardous conditions. Along with its neighbor, Building 122, these were the most structurally unsafe buildings at the KPPC for many years.

Building 123 on Dec. 22, 2011   Building 123 side view, circa Jan. 2008

Building 123 side entrance, Jan. 2008

Looking into through a doorway, Jan. 2008

Destroyed dining room, circa Jan. 2008

Basement storage intake & refrigerator room on April 11, 2011

Double images showing rear damages to Building 123 on March 26, 2011

They were both scheduled for demolition sometime in the fall of 2010, but the process was postponed to August 13, 2012. It was completely gone by September.

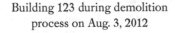

Building 123 during demolition
process on Aug. 3, 2012

Construction excavator was used
for most of the 2012 demolitions

Building 124

Built from 1910 to 1912, this building was almost identical to its neighbor, Building 122, except it did not have the octagon-shaped extension. It was a two-story brick building with a basement, attic, and flaring hip roof. It was used to house chronic bedridden male patients of Group 2 and was home to Wards 53 and 54. There was a section on the first floor for attendants who worked here, just as in Building 122. Building 124 stood on the west side of the boulevard upon the edge of a hill that overlooked the heating plant. (*See Buildings 59 and 122.*)

Building 124, circa 1910s

Aerial view of Building 124, circa 1967

Building 124 with new porch &
Building 123 on right, circa 1960s-1970s

Building 124 with new
lamppost, circa 1960s-1970s

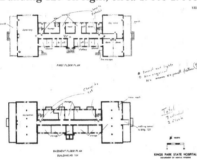

Building 124 floor plans
(basement & first floor)

Building 124 floor plan (second floor)

When this building was designed, it was intended to have an elevator. Its elevator shaft was located at a different part of the building than the one in Building 122. Because of insufficient state funding, an elevator was never supplied. Instead, a wooden staircase was built within the empty elevator well, accessible from the lounge. There were two fire escapes on the west side of the building.

This building never had an octagon extension because of its position on the edge of the hill, where it stood, which bordered a steep incline on its east side. It would have been very difficult to add one without having to bring in mounds of dirt to use as landfill for support and then rerouting the boulevard around it.

In the 1930s, a Boys' Unit was established here. In the 1950s, it became the Adolescent Male Unit. The recreation area was located in the basement. Here, the boys would read, learn to play musical instruments, and play ping-pong, pool, shuffleboard, and other games. They could also box, wrestle, and practice gymnastics. As in Building 122, the second floor was a high-security ward used for high-risk patients. The second-story porches were enclosed to prevent escape. They were rebuilt in 1957, and the building later received extensive renovations in 1966, after the Adolescent Unit was moved to Building 22. Dividers were added to the dayrooms, creating two separate dorm rooms with one large dayroom. (*See Building 22.*)

In the beginning of 1974, this building became home to the male wards for the newly established Mental Retardation Unit (MRU) and Transitional Living Unit (TLU). It was at this time when Wards 53 and 54 were renumbered as Wards 854 and 855.

The basement recreation room was used for Boy Scout activities during this time. The Boy Scout contingent was responsible for raising and lowering the flag every day.

There were murals depicting cartoon characters done in this building using latex paint. The employees assigned to this building created these beautifully designed murals, pictured in a later chapter of this book.

The building stood vacant by the early 1980s, once the patients were relocated to another facility. It was demolished in mid-1996, after being badly damaged because of fire caused by vandals in 1995. The only physical evidence that remained of the building was in the underground tunnels in the form of rubble. Now, even that has been buried.

Building 124 with handicapped
access ramp, 1981

Rear porch of Building 124, circa
1981, by Barry Charletta

Former site of Building 124, south
walkway, March 26, 2011

Rubble from Building 124 in tunnels
of Group 2 on Aug. 2, 2011

Building 125 (Building 73A)

Building 125 (73A) is a two-story steel-and-concrete-framed brick building with a basement, which was built in 1925 by Chas. G. Armstrong and Son. The hip roof is a varied peaked, flat, and gambrel design. A large, open, octagonal cupola built upon a square base rests atop the center of the building. Brick pilasters divide the three recessed brick arched bays of the main facade in a Beaux Arts style. The front entrance has a segmental arch with a broken pediment over it. This building was first used as the admissions center and administration offices for the Veterans' Memorial Hospital Unit. It is located to the north of St. Johnland Road at the traffic circle near the end of Kings Park Boulevard just north of the former upper reservoir. (*See Building 73.*)

Building 125 (73A), administration building, circa 1920s-1930s

Building 125 (73A), circa 1940s-1960s

Building 125 (73A), circa 1981

Building 125 (73A) floor plans

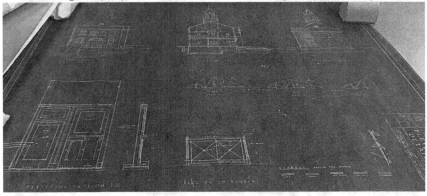

Blueprints of Building 125 (73A)

Two years after its construction, this building became the main administration building of the entire hospital, replacing Building A. Medical records were stored on the first floor, while the senior director's office was on the second floor in the southeast corner.

There was also a conference room on the second floor near the staircase facing the central rear of the building. (*See Building 8.*)

The laboratory was helpful with modernizing the medical library in this building. The best of the older books and journals were transferred to the medical boardroom. New bookshelves and magazine racks were installed. The books were organized based on the Dewey Decimal System, the common system used at libraries.

In the 1960s, the medical records had been relocated to Building 59. That building was abandoned by the 1970s, but the records would remain there until the hospital closed. Most of the records were taken to Pilgrim Psychiatric Center before being sent to the state archives in the early 2000s. (*See Building 59.*)

Employees hard at work behind the information desk, circa 1969

Director Dr. Buckman seated at head of the table during meeting in 1969

Dr. Shepherd Nathan looks over chart with patient resources staff, 1971

Building 93 employee recognition awards, circa 1972

Building 93 employee recognition
awards, circa 1973

Dr. Nathan & Bus Off Morris Keller
swear in Affirm Action reps, 1973

Main office employees, circa 1970s

Dr. Shepherd Nathan shakes
hands with Stephen Goldstein

Building 93 employee recognition awards, circa 1978

Dr. John Bellia in
front of Building 125
(73A), circa 1993

Building 125 (73A) remained the administration building until a few years before the hospital closed. By that time, Building 7 had taken over administrative duties. Building 125 (73A) was abandoned for a short time.

It was renovated in 1999 and converted into the main offices for the Nissequogue River State Park and the New York State Office of Parks, Recreation and Historic Preservation. The park opened to the public a year later.

Because of the connection of electrical wiring to the old underground tunnel system, accessible from most of the other abandoned buildings, new phone and electric lines had to be installed. The access to the tunnels from this building was sealed, and an alarm was installed to prevent trespassers from breaking in.

In addition to park offices and restrooms, a museum now exists within this building. There are both historical and nature exhibits on display. The exhibits within the museum have been changed from time to time, as is the case with most museums. More exhibits from the park have been added, replacing information about the hospital. Information and photos about the hospital have been gradually removed. The second floor is mainly used for storage now.

Building 125 (73A) & traffic circle on Oct. 5, 2015

Park bench in front of Building 125 (73A) on May 1, 2013

Handicapped entrance
ramp on west side of
building on July 13, 2015

Main entrance on Sept. 15, 2014

West side of museum exhibit room
& entrance on Aug. 3, 2012

East side of museum exhibit
room on Aug. 3, 2012

Red fox in museum exhibit
room on March 26, 2011

Entrance to the Children's
Room on Jan. 2, 2016

Nissequogue River mural in
Children's Room on Sept. 15, 2014

Forest mural in Children's
Room on Sept. 15, 2014

Gallery on Sept. 15, 2014

Main hallway leading to park office,
restrooms, & exit on Dec. 19, 2012

During the early 2000s, this building was considered as a location for the Kings Park Heritage Museum. RJO Intermediate School was chosen instead.

In 2006, an outdoor playground for visiting children was added on the west side of the building. In the late summer of 2015, the building was closed for about two months because of electrical issues. It reopened in time for the New Year.

Buildings 126–129 (Building 73B–E)

These were four identical two-story steel-and-concrete framed brick buildings with basements, attics, and hip roofs that served as four-family staff residences with two apartments on each floor. Built in 1925 as part of the Veterans' Memorial Hospital Unit, they were also numbered as Buildings 73B–E and were located on the northern side of the property near the bluff on the east side of Sound View Road at Grandview Circle behind Home T. The entrances that face the center of the quadrangle have three bricked arches in the front and one at each side with the doorway recessed beneath a flat roof. Each has a set of stairs beneath these decks that lead down to alleys, which can access the basements. (*See Buildings 73 and 144.*)

Aerial view of Buildings 126 (73B)-129 (73E), circa 1967

Typical view of one of these staff houses, circa 1980s-1990s

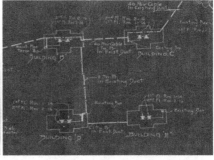

Blueprints indicating Buildings 126 (73B)-129 (73E)

Hospital employees rehabilitated Building 129 (73E) in 1948. In 1963, an outside contractor was hired to rehabilitate Buildings 126 (73B)–128 (73D). The windows and roofs were redone in 1967.

In the winter of 1993, there were plans to use Building 126 (73B) and one other similar building near it as alternative housing for the hospital's Brooklyn patients that were ready to be discharged but were unable to return to city living. This proposal would have included bringing in the Federation Employment and Guidance Services (FEGS) to operate the residences. This never happened partially because of overwhelming protests by the community, who did not want former criminals or drug addicts living in their community, possibly causing an increase to the crime rate.

These buildings are abandoned and scheduled for demolition around 2016–2017.

Buildings 126 (73B) & 127 (73C) on Jan. 1, 2016

Buildings 128 (73D) & 129 (73E) on Jan. 1, 2016

Building 126 (73B) on May 11, 2011

Building 126 (73B) rear porch on April 19, 2016

Building 127 (73C) on May 11, 2011

Building 128 (73D) on April 19, 2016

North side of Building 128 (73D) on May 11, 2011

Building 129 (73E) on March 26, 2011

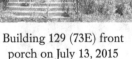

Building 129 (73E) front porch on July 13, 2015

Building 129 (73E) basement stairs on May 11, 2011

Buildings 130–134 (Building 73F–J)

These were five two-story single-family, Georgian Revival-style brick houses with basements and attics, built by hospital work crews in 1925 for use as doctors' residences. They were also known as Buildings 73F–J. Buildings 130 (73F) and 134 (73J) were built with gable roofs, while the others had hip roof designs.

Buildings 132 (73H) and 133 (73I) have pagoda roofs over bricked arch doorways. These homes were all located around Seaview Court on the far northern side of the property as part of the Veterans' Memorial Hospital Unit. For several years, Building 130 (73F) was the residence of the senior business officer of the hospital. (*See Building 73.*)

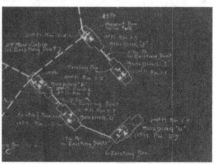

Aerial photo from 1986 of Buildings 130 (73F)-134 (73J)

Blueprints indicating Buildings 130 (73F)-134 (73J)

During the 1940s, modifications were made, including the additions of single wood-framed rooms to house patient servants. A second-story room and porch were added to Building 130 (73F).

Building 130 (73F) showing room on second floor porch, May 11, 2011

Building 130 (73F) behind a fence on April 19, 2016

Building 131 (73G) on May 11, 2011

Building 131 (73G) prepared for abatement on April 19, 2016

Building 132 (73H) on July 13, 2015

South side of Building 132 (73H) on April 19, 2016

North side of Building 132 (73H) on April 19, 2016

Porch of Building 132 (73H) on July 13, 2015

Building 133 (73I) on April 19, 2016

Basement door of Building 133
(73I) on March 26, 2011

Building 134 (73J) on May 11, 2011

Building 134 (73J) with wooden board
knocked down on July 13, 2015

Building 134 (73J) entrance with
open door on July 13, 2015

Staircase leading to second
floor on July 13, 2015

Living room fireplace on July 13, 2015   Sealed porch on July 13, 2015

Kitchen on July 13, 2015   Basement staircase on July 13, 2015

Second floor hallway on July 13, 2015   Second floor bedroom on July 13, 2015

These homes were abandoned a few years before the hospital closed. During their final years in operation, they were no longer used as doctors' residences. A few were used by an organization called Hands Across Long Island Inc. (HALI), which helps former psychiatric patients to integrate into society.

Buildings 133 (I) and 134 (J) were demolished in June 2016. Building 131 (G) was demolished a month later. The park has plans to renovate Buildings 130 (73F) and 132 (73H).

Doctors' cottages during
demolition on June 20, 2016

Doctors' cottages after
demolition on Sept. 17, 2016

Building 135 (Building 73K)

Building 135 (73K) is the closest building to the Long Island Sound located at the end of Sound View Road at Soundview Court on Kings Park Bluff. It is a two-story Y-shaped, Georgian Revival brick building with a basement, attics above its two extended wings, and a hip roof design. Both wings are connected at their center by a beautifully designed, arcaded, covered brick walkway. Built from 1925 to 1929 as part of the Veterans' Memorial Hospital Unit, it housed Wards 85 and 86, part of New York City Unit 1. (*See Building 73.*)

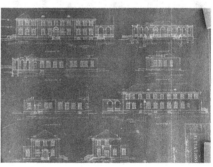

Building 135 (73K), circa 1940s-1970s

Building 135 (73K) blueprints

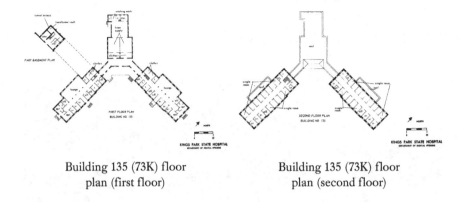

Building 135 (73K) floor
plan (first floor)

Building 135 (73K) floor
plan (second floor)

In 1947, the first recreation departments were established in New York State hospitals. As a result, the first television for the patients of this hospital was placed here on Ward 85.

This building originally housed convalescent patients, but it was later used for patients with honor card privileges and as self-support patient housing. When patients were discharged and had no place else to go, they were sometimes allowed to stay here. The one-story center wing had its own laundry room.

Before Building 135 (73K) existed, there was a hotel, which stood on the same location. It was called the Sound View Hotel. It was quite a popular hangout for the employees of the hospital because of its convenient location near the Kings Park Bluff and the beach. The hotel acted as a vacation resort for the employees, who only had five days off after working twelve-hour shifts for twenty-five days straight.

The hotel closed down in 1924. Building 135 (73K) was built in its place a year later. Directly behind it are residential houses.

Building 135 (73K) was demolished from mid-September to late October 2016.

Building 135 (73K) on May 11, 2011

Building 135 (73K) entrance
on May 11, 2011

Building 135 (73K) brick
arches on May 11, 2011

Sealed door on March 26, 2011

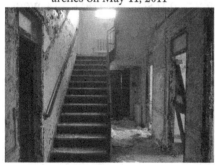

Staircase to second floor on Feb. 7, 2015

Lounge on February 7, 2015

Second floor corridor, circa 2015

Stairway to the basement on Feb. 7, 2015

Building 135 with open
windows on Sept. 9, 2016

Building 135 brick arches
on Sept. 9, 2016

Building 135 demolition
on Sept. 17, 2016

Building 135 demolition
site on Sept. 17, 2016

Building 136 (Building 73L)

The Medical Diagnostic Clinic and Surgical Center was built from 1925 to 1929. This three-story brick building with a basement was a Georgian Revival-style structure with a part hip roof and part flat roof. It has brick pilasters with a recessed two-story arch and a broken pediment design over the front entrance. The building has one elevator located at its center. A tall flagpole was situated in front of the building, located north of St. Johnland Road at the intersection of Soundview Court and Canal Road. This building was added to Group 3 and connected to the kitchen and dining hall through brick breezeway corridors. Fire escapes are located at the front and rear wings.

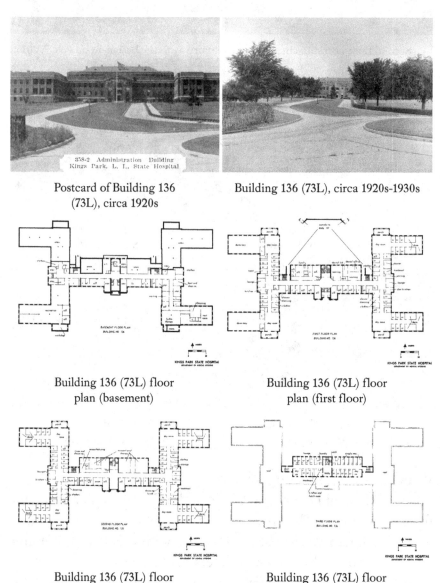

Postcard of Building 136
(73L), circa 1920s

Building 136 (73L), circa 1920s-1930s

Building 136 (73L) floor
plan (basement)

Building 136 (73L) floor
plan (first floor)

Building 136 (73L) floor
plan (second floor)

Building 136 (73L) floor
plan (third floor)

Building 136 (73L) did not officially open until the fall of 1934. When it opened, it became the main medical center for the Veterans' Memorial Hospital Unit. It housed Wards 72–80. Prior to the construction of this building, Building B had the only other surgical unit at the hospital. That building was mainly used to house patients, while this was not. Building 136 (73L) became the first main medical building of the hospital, although it belonged to the Veterans' Memorial Hospital Unit. (*See Buildings 9 and 73.*)

Both patients and sick employees were treated here. Ward 80, on the top floor, was used for treating employees. This ward had beautifully designed arched windows that provided a nice view of the grounds. Hydrotherapy was conducted in the east wing of the basement. There was a weaving shop located in the basement as well. Other occupational therapy workshops were located on the second floor. There were two dental offices and a dental lab on the first floor. The anaesthetizing room was located on the second floor with the operating room. The diagnostic clinic and shock units were also located within this building. There was even a beauty salon for the residents of the hospital.

In October 1953, a physical therapy room was established in the basement. This department was responsible for electroencephalography, electrocardiography, and basal metabolic testing. There were over one thousand various treatments given here monthly.

It was around this time when this building was divorced from the Veterans' Group and made into an independent medical and surgical building for the entire hospital. By 1954, all acute cases were being treated here. The records of all antiluetic patients were stored in this building, and quarterly reports were sent to Albany. In 1955, the roof received some rehabilitation work.

Dr. Shepherd Nathan talks with
employees on the third floor, 1971-1972

Dr. Shepherd Nathan talks with
employees on the third floor, 1971-1972

Building 136 (73L), circa 1980s-1990s

East side of Building 136
(73L), circa 1980s-1990s

When the more modern Building 7 replaced this building as the main medical and surgical center for the hospital, Building 136 (73L) became a typical patient building. It mainly housed geriatric patients. A quarantine ward was located on the upper floor.

This building was abandoned by the early 1990s. During the mid-2000s, local schoolchildren painted picture boards to place on the outside of the front lower-level windows, making this abandoned building look less forgotten and more artistic. It still stands prominently today looking over its old parking lot, which is now used by visitors of the Nissequogue River State Park. (*See Building 7.*)

Building 136 (73L) hallway,
after being abandoned

Building 136 (L) basement
by King Pedlar

Building 136 (73L) on Dec. 22, 2011

Fire escape on Dec. 22, 2011

Fire escape entrance on Dec. 22, 2011

Porch with chair on Dec. 22, 2011

First floor day room on Dec. 22, 2011

Third floor day room on Dec. 22, 2011

Building 136 (73L) rooftop
on Dec. 22, 2011

Attic of Building 136 (73L)
on Dec. 22, 2011

First floor hallway on Dec. 22, 2011

Main entrance on Dec. 22, 2011

Building 137 (Building 73M)

Built from 1911 to 1912, this one-story brick building with a basement, partial attic, and hip roof was the kitchen and dining area for Group 3. A new refrigeration machine was installed a year after this building was built. Building 137 (73M) served Buildings 136 (73L), 143 (73S), and 147 (73W). In 1925, it was added to the Veterans' Memorial Hospital Unit, along with the rest of the original Group 3 buildings. It is located directly behind Building 136 (73L). There was a loading dock on the east side of the building for deliveries. (*See Buildings 73, 136, 143, and 147.*)

Building 137 (73M) with car parked in front, circa 1980s-1990s

Side view of Building 137 (73M), circa 1980s-1990s

Building 137 (73M) loading dock, circa 1980s-1990s

Building 137 (73M) back door, circa 1980s-1990s

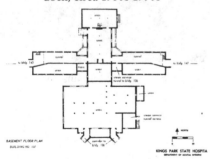

Building 137 (73M) floor plan (basement)

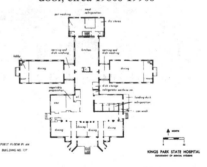

Building 137 (73M) floor plan (first floor)

A one-story addition was built in 1926, connecting this kitchen to the newer Building 136 (73L) via two identical brick breezeway corridors. The roof was rehabilitated in 1959. In 1964, the entire building underwent major renovations, including the roof again.

Employees holding up award certificates, circa 1970s

Employees demonstrate recycling for Earth Day, circa 1970s

Ever since being abandoned, this building became home to numerous stray cats. It is currently one of the oldest buildings left over from the state hospital, second only to the old shed near the boat basin. (*See Building 55.1.*)

Building 137 (73M) on March 26, 2011

Side view of Building 137 (73M) on Dec. 22, 2011

Breezeway corridor to Building 137 (73M) from Building 136 (73L), 12/11

Breezeway corridor on March 26, 2011

Food serving area on Dec. 22, 2011

Dishwashing room on Jan. 5, 2014

Sinks on Jan. 5, 2014

Blodgett baking ovens on Jan. 5, 2014

Refrigeration rooms on Nov. 15, 2010   Darkened corridor on Jan. 5, 2014

Dining room on Dec. 22, 2011   Small dining room on Jan. 5, 2014

Building 138 (Building 73N)

Building 138(73N) was part of the Veterans' Memorial Hospital Unit. It was built in 1925 and housed Wards 81–84 and the North Brooklyn Unit 1. This two-story brick building had two separate basements in its west and east wings. There was also a brick solarium with barred windows on the roof.

A one-story brick breezeway corridor extended from the west wing and connected to Building 139 (73O). South of the breezeway was an enclosed courtyard for the patients. Building 138(73N) is located on the north side of Sound View Road and was accessible from St. Johnland Road.

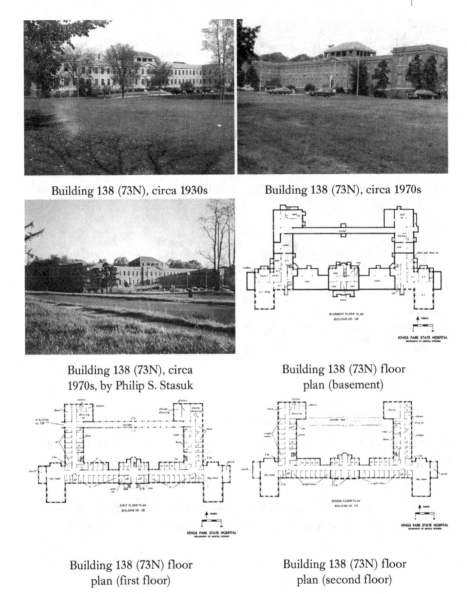

Building 138 (73N), circa 1930s

Building 138 (73N), circa 1970s

Building 138 (73N), circa 1970s, by Philip S. Stasuk

Building 138 (73N) floor plan (basement)

Building 138 (73N) floor plan (first floor)

Building 138 (73N) floor plan (second floor)

Sometime around the early 1950s, the front entrance steps were rebuilt, and a long handicapped accessible ramp was added. The roof was rehabilitated in 1955. (*See Buildings 73 and 139.*)

Roof rehabilitation, circa 1970s-1980s   Building 138 (73N), circa 1980s-1990s

Building 138 (73N)   CPR class, circa 1979
employees, circa 1978

There were several occupational therapy shops in the basement. A drug room was located on the second floor. This building had a beauty parlor, which was painted in lilac and pink. It prided itself on being the best-looking parlor of the hospital.

Before the building was vacated, the underground steam tunnels that connect to the rest of the hospital were sealed.

Building 138 (73N) on Dec. 22, 2011

Rear of Building 138 (73N)
on April 28, 2013

Breezeway at rear of Building
138 (73N) on April 28, 2013

Looking down into the
courtyard on April 28, 2013

Rooftop solarium on April 28, 2013

Solarium exit onto roof
on April 28, 2013

First floor day room on April 28, 2013   Sofas on porch on April 28, 2013

Ashtrays on windowsill of porch
window on April 28, 2013

Basement occupational therapy
room on April 28, 2013

Building 139 (Building 73O)

Known as Kitchen O, this one-story brick building with a basement was part of the Veterans' Memorial Hospital Unit and was located on Sound View Road. Built in 1925, it served Brooklyn Units 1 and 2 as a kitchen and dining hall. Deliveries were made at the rear loading dock. (*See Building 73.*)

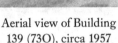

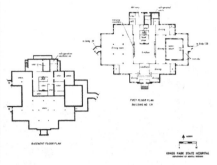

Aerial view of Building
139 (73O), circa 1957

Building 139 (73O) floor plans

From 1928 to 1932, it was rehabilitated because of the construction of Building 141 (73Q), or 39. An underground connection was made between these two buildings from the basement of the newer building, leading up a staircase to the first floor of the kitchen and dining hall. There was also a breezeway corridor that connected Building 139 (75O) to Building 138 (73N). (*See Buildings 39, 138, and 141.*)

In 1957, the roof was redone and built up using gravel.

The cooking services of Kitchen O were shut down in the summer of 1978. Group 3's Building 137 (73M) took over the responsibilities of cooking for Buildings 39 and 138. Building 139 (73O) is currently abandoned. (*See Building 137.*)

Building 139 (73O) on Dec. 22, 2011

Loading dock at the rear of Building
139 (73O) on April 28, 2013

Loading dock storage room
on April 28, 2013

Dining room on April 28, 2013

Food serving area on April 28, 2013

Dishwasher on April 28, 2013

Breezeway connecting Buildings 138
(73N) & 139 (73O) on April 28, 2013

Staircase leading down to Building 39
(73Q) basement on April 28, 2013

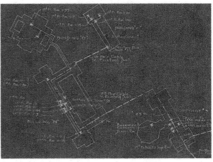

Aerial view of Buildings 138 (73N)-
141 (73Q) facing south, circa 2007

Blueprint of Buildings 138 (73N)-140
(73P) & Building 143 of Group 3

Building 140 (Building 73P)

Building 140 (73P) was built in 1925. It replaced the Isolation Cottage and was originally used as an isolation building for patients who were banned from contact with other patients. It was kindly referred to as the Crisis Residence and consisted of Ward 140 and Brooklyn Unit 2. This one-story brick building with a partial basement and hip roof can be found on the north side of Cotton Wood Drive near Old Dock Road shortly before Upper Dock Road begins. It was deliberately placed in an isolated corner of the Veterans' Memorial Hospital Unit. (*See Buildings 25 and 73.*)

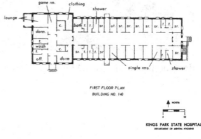

Building 140 (73P), circa 1947

Building 140 (73P) floor plan (first floor)

This was the only building of this group where the patient dormitories were entirely single-room units, similar to a boarding house. The patients that were here usually remained confined until their doctors deemed them capable enough to be placed on other wards.

In later years, it was used as an office building for the Civil Service Employees Association (CSEA). However, these days, it can be quite dark within its lonely walls making it a little creepy inside. Who knows for sure what kind of tortured souls were confined to this building and whether they are truly gone?

Building 140 (73P) on Dec. 22, 2011

Building 140 (73P) main
entrance on March 26, 2011

Basement entrance on March 26, 2011

Basement on March 26, 2011

Lounge on Jan. 23, 2013

Kitchen on Jan. 23, 2013, at one
time served as a dorm room

Day room on April 28, 2013

Main hallway on April 28, 2013

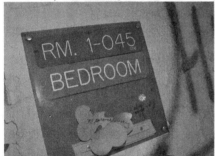

Patient bedroom sign on Jan. 23, 2013

Most bathrooms in this building were
narrow as seen here, Jan. 23, 2013

Building 141 (Building 73Q)

This was actually the old number designation for Building 39 (73Q) built from 1931 to 1932. It was renumbered shortly after it was built for the Veterans' Memorial Hospital Unit. It

Building 141 (73Q)
on April 28, 2013

was the last building to be added to the group. This two-story brick building has a rooftop solarium and was home to Wards 87–92. The basement led to a staircase that connected to Building 139, which served as its kitchen and dining hall. (*See Buildings 39, 73, and 139.*)

Building 142 (Building 73R)

Building 142 (73R) is a one-story brick building with a partial basement, recessed entrance, and hip roof design. It was built in 1925 on the west side of Sound View Road just north of Shore Road. It originally contained two one-family apartments but was later converted into an employee dining hall.

Aerial photo of Building 142 (73R), circa 1967

The employees' dining room, circa 1920s-1930s.

In later years, the building was converted again and utilized for the transition between long-term care and independent living for elderly patients. This building was part of the Veterans' Memorial Hospital Unit. It was one of the last buildings to close in 1996. (*See Building 73.*)

It was demolished from the end of August through September in 2016.

Building 142 (73R) on Dec. 22, 2011

Facing west toward Building 142 (73R) on April 19, 2016

North entrance on Nov.4, 2015

Rear entrance & stairs to basement on April 19, 2016

Daylight shining in through an old screen door on Nov. 4, 2015

Entrance lobby on Nov. 4, 2015

Old hallway, once part of the
dining room, on Nov. 4, 2015

Significantly smaller old dining
room on Nov. 4, 2015

Demolition of Building 142
(73R) on Sept. 9, 2016

Demolition of Building 142 (73R)
from Grandview Circle, Sept. 9, 2016

Destruction of the basement
on Sept. 17, 2016

A pile of rubble on Sept. 17, 2016

Building 143 (Building 73S)

Building 143 (73S) was a two-story brick building with a basement, an attic, and a flaring hip roof. It housed male patients of Wards 55 and 56 and New York City Unit 1 of the Veterans'

Memorial Hospital Unit. It was originally part of Group 3 and was built from 1910 to 1912. (*See Building 73.*)

Building 143 (73S) Wards
55 & 56, circa 1910s

Aerial photo of Building 143 (73S)
showing octagon addition, Sept. 1927

Building 143 (73S) showing renovated
porches, circa 1960s-1970s

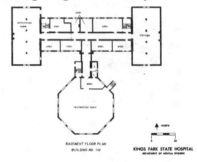

Building 143 (73S) floor plan (basement)

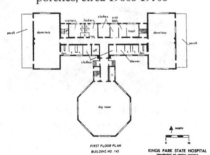

Building 143 (73S) floor plan (first floor)

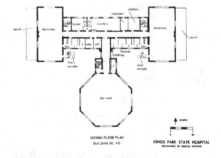

Building 143 (73S) floor
plan (second floor)

The octagon-shaped section of the building was added from 1915 to 1916. There was a craft shop in the basement, and on the main and upper floors were a dining room and a dayroom. In 1957, a recreation area was set up below Ward 55. The porches were rebuilt the same year, and the building later underwent a complete rehabilitation from 1964 to 1965. There were two fire escapes on the south side of the building.

Male patients in the day room with Red Cross volunteers, circa 1920

Patients playing pool in the day room, circa 1920

Several male patients playing cards with a Red Cross volunteer, circa 1920

The building was abandoned by the 1970s. It was demolished around 1982–1984. An empty field remains in its place that will likely be converted into an athletic field for the Nissequogue River State Park by 2017. The underground tunnel that once led to it from Building 137 (73M) is now a dead end. (*See Building 137.*)

Building 144 (Building 73T)

Built in 1928, this three-story rectangular, steel-and-concrete-framed, multifamily brick building with a basement and an unfinished attic was one of the last buildings constructed for the Veterans' Memorial Hospital Unit. It has a hip roof design, and two louvered cupolas evenly situated near the center of the building. There are no elevators. Located to the east of Sound View Road between Canal Road and Grandview Circle, it was designated as Building 144 (73T), but most people knew it as Home T. A long concrete stairway leads from the west side of Building 125 (73A) up the hill, toward the front entrance of Home T. (*See Buildings 73 and 125.*)

Home T, circa 1930s-1960s   Home T, circa March 1979

Home T housed the hospital's many dedicated attendants. The state charged them a small rental fee. Both the second and third floors had thirty-three single-room apartments, one two-room apartment, a lounge, two bathrooms, and a linen room. The first floor mainly consisted of clerical offices.

In December 1953, the occupational therapy office was moved to the basement of this building. This provided a more suitable location for finished articles that could be displayed.

In spring of 1974, one resident caused a fire in his room by having a hot plate that was left on too long. The damage was limited to his room. He received a fair warning for the violation. The use of hot plates was not allowed in the rooms, and breaking the rules could lead to eviction from the premises. Permission was required before installing any electrical appliance in a room.

Local historian and former employee King Pedlar resided in this building for most of his career at the hospital. Many of the photos I have of this building from its glory days came from his personal collection.

Employee Andy DiChiara touches up the outside of Home T in 1980

Room 330 was home to King Pedlar for many years, circa 1985

Clothes hanging to dry, circa 1985

Open closet door, circa 1985

The building was closed down and abandoned by 1992. King Pedlar was the last resident of room 330. During the early 2000s, King was able to return to his former residence one last time with his fellow historian and friend Leo Polaski. While he was there, he took photos of his former room and his neighbor's old room for old time's sake.

Abandoned Home T, circa 1996

West side of Home
T, circa 1996

King Pedlar's old room

King Pedlar's old bed

Another room on the third floor

One of the only double
occupancy rooms

By 2005, all of the windows were boarded up barring any sunlight from breaching the interior. In 2005–2007, local schoolchildren painted beautiful murals on each of the white sheets of wood used to board up the windows, giving this building a certain artistic beauty. This was most likely done around the same time as the windows of Building 136 (73L). (*See Building 136.*)

For quite some time, this building was home to dozens of pigeons that roosted in the attic. These new residents provided a unique odor that could be smelled from the ground floor on a hot summer's day. Since being abandoned, fire and water damage has destroyed much of the interior, especially on the upper floors.

There are still some personal belongings and clothing belonging to former employees that were left behind, which now lay scattered throughout the partially furnished rooms.

Home T on Dec. 22, 2011

West side of Home T on July 13, 2015

Rear of Home T on May 1, 2013

Rear entrance to Home T on Nov. 4, 2015

Entrance on Jan. 1, 2016

Hallway inside of Home
T on Jan. 1, 2016

An office on the first
floor on Jan. 1, 2016

Staircase on Jan. 1, 2016

Room 330, King
Pedlar's old room,
on Jan. 1, 2016

Former location of the mirror
in room 330 on Jan. 1, 2016

Hangers in the
closet of room 330
on Jan. 1, 2016

Third floor lounge on Jan. 1, 2016

Employees' belongings left behind in the lounge, Jan. 2016

Buildings 145 and 146 (Building 73U–V)

These two buildings were intended for the Veterans' Memorial Hospital Unit but were never built. They would have been numbered as 73U and 73V had they been added. Building 145 (73U) would have served as an assembly hall for the group, but York Hall was built instead. (*See Buildings 73 and 80.*)

Building 147 (Building 73W)

Building 147 (73W) was a two-story brick building with a basement, an attic, and a flaring hip roof, built from 1910 to 1912. It was part of Group 3, and it housed female patients of Wards 57 and 58, along with New York City Unit 2. In 1925, it was added to the Veterans' Memorial Hospital Unit. (*See Building 73.*)

Building 147 (73W), circa 1912

Aerial photo showing octagon-shaped addition, circa 1967

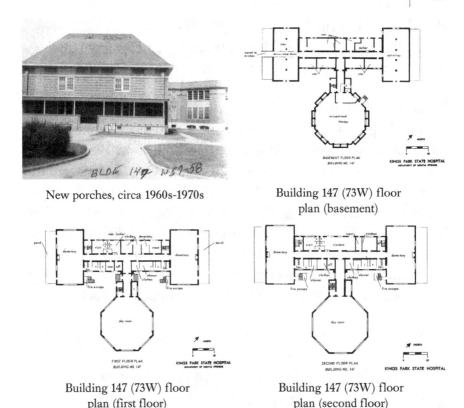

New porches, circa 1960s-1970s

Building 147 (73W) floor
plan (basement)

Building 147 (73W) floor
plan (first floor)

Building 147 (73W) floor
plan (second floor)

An octagon-shaped wing was added to the east side of the building from 1915 to 1916. The basement room of this new wing was used as a craft shop. There was a linen room on the first floor above it. The second floor of that wing was used as a dayroom. There was also a barbershop in the basement of this building.

There were two fire escapes located on the east side of this building. The porches were rebuilt in 1957. The building underwent a complete rehabilitation from 1964 to 1965. This was a tremendous waste of time and money because the building was abandoned by the 1970s.

It was demolished together with its neighbor, Building 143 (73S), sometime around 1982–1984. As with Building 143 (73S), the underground tunnel that led to it from Building 137 (73M) now leads to a dead end. (*See Buildings 137 and 143.*)

Buildings 148 and 149

To the best of my knowledge, there were never any buildings with these numbers assigned to them.

Buildings 150 and 151

Buildings 150 and 151 are a pair of two-story white houses with basements, attics, and gable roofs, built from 1987 to 1988. Each has a covered car shelter at the south wing. These were the very last buildings to be added to the hospital before it closed. They are located on Kings Park Boulevard north of the East Main Street/Route 25A entrance onto the grounds. Building 151, on the west side of the boulevard, is known as Community Residence West. Building 150, across from it on the east side, is Community Residence East. Both are identical mirror images of each other.

Aerial photo of south boulevard entrance on April 10, 1976	Same location on March 3, 1988 showing new Buildings 150 & 151	Aerial view of Buildings 150 & 151 on March 4, 1990

These buildings are still in use today as state-operated community residences for former patients mainly from Pilgrim Psychiatric Center. Residents remain here for several months to be integrated into society and placed in public housing.

Facing north on the boulevard toward
Buildings 150 & 151, March 8, 2016

Facing north on the boulevard toward
Building 150 on March 8, 2016

Building 150 on March 9, 2015

Facing south on the boulevard toward
Building 150 on March 9, 2015

North side of Building 150
on March 9, 2015

Facing north on the boulevard toward
Building 151 on March 8, 2016

Building 151 on March 9, 2015

Facing south on the boulevard toward
Building 151 on March 9, 2015

Facing south on the boulevard toward
Buildings 150 & 151, March 9, 2015

Papallo Gardens sign, next to
Building 151, on June 22, 2010

ADDENDUM III

Kings Park Psychiatric Center Building Chart

Kings Park Psychiatric Center Building Chart				
Building Number	Year Built	Building Name	Building Details	Year Demolished
PRE-EXISTING FARMHOUSES				
(67)	Pre-1837	Temp Admin Bldg / Superintendent's Home	Refurbished Noel J. Bécar Mansion (Bldg 67)	1939
N/A	Pre-1870	Unknown Farmhouse	Refurbished farmhouse across from the LIRR station	1923-1924

		Warren W. Conklin House	Situated near the canal	1898
N/A	1858-1873			
N/A	Pre-1837	Capt. John H. Smith House	Located on Dairy Rd	1899
(56)	1858-1873	Assist Steward's House	Refurbished Sidney Smith Farmhouse (Bldg 56)	1930
(48A)	1837-1858	Assist Steward's House / Head Farmer's Residence	Refurbished John Kelly House on Route 25A (Bldg 48A)	1964
FIRST TEMPORARY BUILDINGS				
(1)	1886	Temporary Wooden Pavilions	1st Female Ward	1895-1896
(2)			1st Male Ward	
(3)			Dining Hall	
(4)	1887		2nd Female Ward	
(5)			2nd Male Ward	
(6)			3rd Female Ward	
FIRST 16 PATIENT COTTAGES				
1	1888-1889	Female Cottage A	Female Staff House	1939
17	1888	Female Cottage B	Ward 17	1939
18	1888-1889	Female Cottage C	Ward 18	1927-1931
19	1888-1889	Female Cottage D	Ward 19	1927-1931
20	1888-1889	Female Cottage E	Ward 20 / Additions added in 1897	1939

21	1888-1889	Female Cottage F	Ward 21	1927-1931
22	1888-1889	Female Cottage G	Ward 22 / Additions added in 1897 / TB Cottage	1939
23	1888-1889	Female Cottage H	Ward 23 / Additions added in 1897 / TB Cottage	1939
24	1888-1889	Female Cottage I	Hospital Ward 24 / TB Cottage	1939
25	1888	Male Cottage A	Ward 25 / Renumbered as Bldg 27	1938-1939
26	1888-1889	Male Cottage B	Ward 26 / Renumbered as Bldg 20	1952-1953
27	1888-1889	Male Cottage C	Ward 27	1932-1934
28	1888-1889	Male Cottage D	Hospital Ward 28 / TB Cottage	1938-1939
29	1888-1889	Male Cottage E	Ward 29 / Renumbered as Bldg 14	1939
30	1888-1889	Male Cottage F / Employee Dining Hall	Ward 30 / TB Cottage / Extended in 1897 / Renumbered as Bldg 13	1939
31	1888-1889	Male Cottage I	Ward 31 / Cottage I	1939

ADDITIONAL UNNUMBERED STRUCTURES				
N/A	1906	Bandstand (Female)	Near the Female Cottages	1917
		Bandstand (Male)	Near the Male Cottages	1932-1939
N/A	1966-1967	Barge Clubhouse	Yacht Club near the Canal	2013
N/A	2005	Bird Watching Shelter	Near Upper Reservoir/Pond	**Active**
N/A	1896	Blacksmith & Wheelwright Shop	1st Blacksmith / Replaced by new Blacksmith Shop	1901
N/A	1901	Blacksmith & Wheelwright Shop	Relocated & Replaced by Bldg 36	1915
N/A	1913	Cottage 24 Linen Shed	Behind Female Cottage 24 (I)	1939
N/A	1901	Garbage Burning House	Replaced by Sewage Disposal Plant	1910
N/A	1923-1931	Garbage Storage Shed	Storage / Greenbelt Trail	Abandoned
N/A	1890-1892	Locksmith	Future site of Building 93	1938-1939
N/A	1908	Male Cottage I Gazebo	Next to Male Cottage I	1922-1924
N/A	1897	Music Pavilion	Next to the Amusement Hall	1925
N/A	2000	Guardhouse	Nissequogue River State Park	**Active**

N/A	1908-1909	Oil House	Located near 2nd Power Plant & Soap Factory House	1935
N/A	2017	Picnic Pavilion	Former site of Bldg 134	**Active**
N/A	1907	Reservoir Valve Box Shed	Lower Reservoir	1931-1939
N/A	1897	Reservoir Valve Box Shed	Upper Reservoir	Abandoned
N/A	1905	Steamroller Shed	Garage	1939
N/A	1890	Stenographer's House	1-Family Staff House	1938
N/A	1896	Superintendent's Greenhouse	1st Propagating House / Behind Superintendent's Home	1898
N/A	1907	Temporary Laundry	2nd Laundry / Replaced by Bldg 5	1910
N/A	1897	Watchman's Gatehouse	Boulevard Guardhouse	1930
BUILDINGS 1-151				
1 (Original)	1897-1898	1st Piggery	OT / Additional pig colonies added in 1914 / Renumbered as Bldg 45	1965

1	1930-1931	Male Reception / RCCA	Group 5, Wards 93-100 / Residence by the Sound / Pilgrim State Bldg 700	Abandoned
2 (Original)	1889	Cow Barn	The Dairy Farm / OT / Replaced by Bldgs 47 & 48	1940
	1896	Cistern		
	1897	Stable / Shed		
	1897-1898	1st Slaughterhouse		
	1895-1901	3 Silos		
2	1919-1923	Female Reception / RCCA / Kitchen & Dining Hall	Group 5, Kitchen & Wards 66-71 / Extended in 1930	1984-1985
3A	1912-1913	Group 4, TB Wards Cottage 60	Original Group 4, TB Wards 60-61	1932
3B	1912-1913	Group 4, TB Wards Cottage 62	Original Group 4, TB Wards 62-63	1932
3C	1912-1913	Group 4, TB Wards Cottage 64	Original Group 4, TB Wards 64-65	1932
3D	1922-1923	Group 4, TB Wards Kitchen & Dining Hall	Original Group 4, Kitchen	1932
3E		Group 4 Shed	Storage House	
3	1931-1934	NNPH Administrative Staff Residence	Group 5, Admin Bldg / Home U	Abandoned

4A	1897-1898	Group 1, Building A, Administrative Offices	Group 1, Main Offices / Staff Residences / Renumbered as Bldg 111	1972-1973
4B	1897-1898	Group 1, Building B / Cottage 41	Group 1, Ward 41 / Renumbered as Bldg 112	1972
4C	1897-1898	Group 1, Building C / Cottage 42	Group 1, Ward 42 / Renumbered as Bldg 113	1972-1973
4D	1897-1898	Group 1, Building D / Cottage 43	Group 1, Ward 43 / Renumbered as Bldg 114	1972-1973
4E	1897-1898	Group 1, Building E / Cottage 44	Group 1, Ward 44 / Renumbered as Bldg 115	1972-1973
4F	1897-1898	Group 1, Building F / Cottage 45	Group 1, Ward 45 / Renumbered as Bldg 116	1972-1973
4G	1897-1898	Group 1, Building G / Cottage 46 / Kitchen & Dining Hall	Group 1, Ward 46 / Kitchen G / Renumbered as Bldg 117	1972-1973
4H	1897-1898	Group 1, Building H / Cottage 47	Group 1, Ward 47 / Renumbered as Bldg 118	1972

4I	1897-1898	Group 1, Building I / Cottage 48	Group 1, Ward 48 / Renumbered as Bldg 119	1972
4J	1897-1898	Group 1, Building J / Cottage 49	Group 1, Ward 49 / Renumbered as Bldg 120	1972
4K	1901	Group 1, Summer Houses	Group 1, Gazebos	1935-1938
4L	1908			
4.1	1900-1901	"The Group" Auxiliary Boiler House	Group 1, Temp. Boiler House / Enlarged from 1904-1905	1912
4.2	1901	Group 1, Fire Hose House	Group 1, Fire Hose Storage	1925
4.3	1906	Lower Greenhouse	4th Greenhouse / OT / Located in Lower Garden	1947-1950
4.4	1898	Tool House	Lower Garden	1908-1909
4.5	1909	Tool House	Replaced previous one in Lower Garden	1947-1950
5	1909-1910	Laundry / Lock Shop / Work Control	Building Planning / OT / Extended from 1988-1992	Abandoned
5.1	1990-1992	Sand Pyramid	Storage hut near Bldg. 5 / Built for Grounds Maintenance	2012

6 (Original)	1908-1910	2nd Power Plant	Boiler House / Electric Light Plant / Replaced Heating Plant / Extended in 1913	1968
6	1939-1940 & 1968	Pump Room	Steam Pipe Junction House / Formerly Bldg. 85	2012
7 (Original)	1902	Soap Factory House	Soap Manufacturing / Storage	1932-1934
7	1966-1967	Medical & Surgical / Morgue	Wards 229-238 / Admin. Offices	Abandoned
8	1891-1897	Building A	Wards 1-4 / Main Offices / Telephone Switchboard	1977
9	1891-1897	Building B	Wards 5-8 / Medical & Surgical	1975-1976
10	1891-1897	Building D	Wards 13-16	1975-1976
11	1891-1897	Building C	Wards 9-12 / Nursing School / Photography Rm	1975-1976
12 (Original)	1897	Mist House / Hothouse	2nd Greenhouse / OT	1938-1939
12	1896-1897	Kitchen for Bldgs. C & D	Behind Buildings C & D	1957

12.1	1908-1914	Storage Shed	Annex to Building 12	Abandoned
13	1888-1889	Male Cottage 30	Ward 30 / Formerly Male Cottage F	1939
14	1888-1889	Male Cottage 29	Ward 29 / Formerly Male Cottage E	1939
15 (Original)	1890-1892	Laboratory & Morgue	Former Tailor Shop, until it moved to Bldg 28	1928-1932
15	1939-1941	Maximum Security Wards	Wards 60-65 / Wisteria House / Continued Care	Abandoned
16	N/A	Continued Treatment (Male & Female Patients)	Meant to replace Group 1 / Never built	N/A
17 (Original)	1896	Tool House	Mechanical Repair Shop / Storage	1925-1930
17	N/A	Continued Treatment (Female Patients)	Meant to replace Group 1 / Never built	N/A
18 (Original)	1896	Paint Shop / Tinsmith	OT / Relocated to Ward 26 & renumbered as Bldg 20	1933-1934

18	1939-1940	7 Doctors' Residences / HALI Care	Center Unit A (3 Cottages)	Abandoned
			South Unit B (2 Cottages)	Abandoned
			North Unit C (2 Cottages)	Abandoned
19	1939-1940	5 Doctors' Residences / HALI Program	Center Unit D (3 Cottages)	Abandoned
			West Unit E (1 Cottage)	Abandoned
			East Unit F (1 Cottage)	Abandoned
20	1888-1889	Tinsmith / Paint Shop	OT / Relocated from Bldg 18 / Formerly Male Cottage 26, Ward 26	1952-1953
21 (Original)	1906	Oil House	Near Old Dock Road	1935
21	1957-1965	Geriatric / Infirmary	Wards 201-214 / Geriatric Care & Drug Treatment	Abandoned
22 (Original)	1890-1892	Barn / Garage	Storage / Site of Bldg 94	1950-1953
22	1957-1965	Continued Care / Admissions Bldg	Wards 215-228 / Temp placement for patients	Abandoned
23 (Original)	1910	Small Shed	Storage / Garage / Near Pest House	1950-1953
23	1970	Buckman Day Treatment / Rehab Center / Recreation	Bowling Alley / Gym / Library / Swimming Pool / Theater	2012-2013

24	1888-1889	Female Cottage 24	Ward 24 / Formerly Female Cottage I	1925
24 (Original)	1910	Garage	Pest House Garage / Storage	1950-1953
25	1905	Pest House / Isolation Cottage	Quarantine Ward / Annex to Ward 28 / Moved in 1910 / Replaced by Bldg 140	1950-1953
25.1	1906	Little Pest House	Isolation Summer House	1950-1953
26	1888-1889	Male Cottage 26	Ward 26 / Formerly Male Cottage B	1952-1953
27 (Original)	1888	Male Cottage 25	Ward 25 / Formerly Male Cottage A	1935-1938
27	1921	Reservoir Valve Box Shed	Near Reservoir, which had a 1,500,000 gal capacity	1964-1969
28	1896	Tailor Shop / Paint Shop	Formerly used to house night attendants / OT / Relocated here from Bldg 15 / Moved to Bldg 38	1953

29 (Original)	1889	Male Cottage G / Doctor's House	Male Staff House / Cottage G / Extended in 1906	1952-1953
29	1965-1966	3rd Power Plant	Extended in 1988 / Coal Shed & Fuel Tanks razed in 2012 / Smokestack razed in 2013	Abandoned
	1988	Coal Shed & Fuel Tanks		2012
30	1914	Lumber Storage Shed	OT / Carpentry Dept	1966
31 (Original)	1889	Male Cottage J / Male Dining Hall	Medical Officers' Laundry / Future site of Bldg 93	1938-1939
31	1926	Bowling Alley	Recreation Center	1975
32	1895-1896	Male Cottage K / Employee Clubhouse	Community Store / Formerly Ward 32 / Extended in 1954	1975
33 (Original)	1888	Laundry	Ward 33 / New wing in 1899 / Renumbered as Bldg 53	1931
33	1895-1896	Male Cottage H / Steward's House	Former Superintendent's Home	1940-1945

34	1903-1906	Building H / Nurses' Residences	Employees' Home / Dewing Home	1967
35	1931-1932	Nursing Students' Homes	Single Employees' Home V	2013
36 (Original)	1915	Blacksmith & Wheelwright Shop	Moved from original site / Replaced by Bldg 86	1924
36	1931-1932	Nursing Students' Homes	Nurses' Home W	2013
37	1931-1932	Staff House	Non-Medical Employee Home	Abandoned
38	1896-1897	Kitchen for Bldgs A & B / Tailor Shop	Behind Bldgs C & D / The Cannery / Extended in 1913 / Tailor Shop relocated here from Bldg 28	1975-1976
39 (Original)	1917	Doctor's Garage	Replaced by Building 91	1930
39	1931-1932	Building 73Q / Continued Care	VMHU, Wards 87-92 / Formerly Bldg 141	Abandoned
40	1932	Infirmary / Children's Ward	Group 2, Ward 50 / Daycare / Playground by the Sound	Abandoned

41	1932-1933	Group 4, Geriatric & Ambulatory Care	Group 4, Wards 101-108 & 123-128	Abandoned
42	1932-1933	Group 4, Kitchen & Dining Hall	Group 4, Kitchen	Abandoned
43	1933-1934	Group 4, Geriatric Care	Group 4, Wards 109-122	Abandoned
44	1934-1935	Storehouse / Bakery / Refrigeration Plant	Temporary Morgue / OT	2017
45	1897-1898	1st Piggery	Dairy Farm / OT /Formerly Farm Bldg 1 / Additional colonies added in 1914	1965
45	1957-1960	Water Tower	Replaced Bldg 27 & Reservoir / Located near Potter's Field Cemetery	Abandoned
45.1	1907	Soiled Clothing House	Outside of Ward 45	1972
46 (Original)	1917	Root Cellar	Dairy Farm / OT	1966-1967
46	1943	Slaughterhouse	Dairy Farm / OT / Formerly Bldg 88	2012
47	1940-1941	Dairy Barn	Dairy Farm / Replaced original Bldg 2 / OT	1998-1999

48 (Original)	1889	Female Cottage K / Amusement or Assembly Hall	Gym / OT / Formerly Female Dining Hall / Extended in 1899	1932
48A & B	1906	Summer Houses	Gazebos near the Amusement Hall	1924-1925
48	1940-1942	Horse Barns / Grounds Dept Storage	Dairy Farm / Implement Storage / OT	2012
48A	1837-1858	Assist Steward's House	Former John Kelly Farmhouse / Head Farmer's Residence	1964
48.1	1907	Soiled Clothing House	Outside of Ward 48	1972
49	1892	Female Cottage J / First Assist Physician's / Assist Medical Director's House	Cottage J / Extended in 1897 & from 1906-1908	2001
50	1896	Employees' Kitchen / Garage	E Kitchen / Converted into a Truck Garage in 1912	1939
		Employees' Dining Rm / Storage House	E Dining Rm / Dining Rm T / Extended in 1913 / Storage	1967

	1893	Storehouse	General Storage	
51	1902	Refrigeration Plant	Cold Storage / Ice Plant	1967
	1916	Shed	Wagon Scales Storage	
51.1	1890	Root Cellar	Vegetable Storage / Replaced by Bldg 51 Addition	1902
52	1892	Main Kitchen & Bakery / School House	Main Kitchen & Bakery / "Little Red Schoolhouse"	1976-1978
53 (Original)	1888	Former Laundry Building	Renovated in 1911 / Ward 33 / Formerly Bldg 33	1931
53	1930	Sewage Pump House	Screen House	Abandoned
54A	1910-1912	Group 2, Cottage 1	Group 2, Wards 51 & 52 / Renumbered as Bldg 122 / Extended from 1915-1916	2012
54B	1911-1912	Group 2, Cottage 3 / Kitchen & Dining Hall	Group 2, Kitchen / Renumbered as Bldg 123	2012
54C	1910-1912	Group 2, Cottage 2	Group 2, Wards 53 & 54 / Renumbered as Bldg 124	1996

55 (Original)	1896-1897	Firemen's Cottage	Behind Bldg B / Replaced by Bldg 83	1925-1927
	1897	Hose House		
55	1896-1897	1st Boat House	Boating Supplies / Storage	1919-1920
55	1920	2nd Boat House	Marina Office	2012-2013
55.1	1894	Pumping Station / Boat House Shed	Storage Shed / Restrooms	**Active**
56 (Original)	1837-1858	Assist Steward's House	Former Sidney Smith Farmhouse / Farm Supervisor	1931
56	1973	W.J. Lynch Community Store	Cafe 56 / Community Store	2012
57 (Original)	1906	Lumber Storage Shed	Across from Bldg 59 / Replaced by Bldg 30	1914
57	1912-1913	Carpentry, Electrical, Masonry, & Plumbing Shops	Machine Shed / Maintenance Stores / OT	2013
58 (Original)	1890-1892	Icehouse	Cold Storage	1910
58	1910	Icehouse / Pickle House / Sauerkraut House	Cold Storage / Extended in 1912 / Vegetable Storage	1967-1969
59 (Original)	1888	Original Boiler House	Located on site of Bldg 93	1888

59	1890-1894	Machine Shop / Electric Light Plant / Medical Archive	1st Power Plant / OT Workshops / Later used as Medical Records Archives	2013
	1890-1892	Heating Plant	Boiler House / Smokestack / Carpenter's Repair Shop	1915-1923
		Dynamo Plant	Original Engine Rm	1947
	1947	Mattress & Tin Shop	OT Workshops / Furniture & Weaving / Print Shop	2013
60	1892-1893	Main Pump House	Water Pumping Station /OT Workshops	2013
61	1892	Coal Bunkers / Wagon Barn / Ice Plant	Storage / OT / Extended in 1910 & 1939	1978-1979
61.1	1899	US Veterans Bureau & Knights of Columbus / Main Library	Originally part of Bldg 61 / Renovated in 1956	1978-1979
62 (Original)	1896-1897	Main Stables / Coach Barn	Storage / Truck Garage / OT / Replaced by 2nd Bldg 62	1939
62	1939-1940	Truck Garage	Storage / OT / Replaced original Bldg 62	**Active**

62.1	2009	Storage Sheds	Behind	**Active**
62.2			Building 62	**Active**
63 (Original)	1889	Wagon Shed	Storage / OT / Extended in 1906 & 1908	1912
63	1912-1915	Wagon Shed	Storage / OT / Replaced original Bldg 63	1953-1955
64 (Original)	1901	Wagon Shed	Storage	1912
64	1912-1915	Supervisor's Garage	Storage	1966-1967
65 (Original)	1901	Oil House	Behind Bldgs 59 & 60 / Enlarged in 1905	1908-1915
65	1939-1940	Propagation House	6th Greenhouse / OT	**Active**
65.1	2000	Gazebo	Next to 6th Greenhouse	**Active**
66 (Original)	1899	Coal Shed	Storage / Behind Bldgs 59-61	1920s
66	1909-1910	1st Sewage Disposal Plant	Screening House & Settling Tanks / Extended in 1913 / Replaced by new Bldg 66	1972-1976
66	1939	2nd Sewage Disposal Plant	Replaced by current one used by Kings Park	2004

67 (Original)	Pre-1837	Superintendent's Residence	Former Noel J. Bécar Mansion / Replaced by new Bldg 67 / Extended in 1905	1939
67	1939-1940	Senior Director's Mansion	Residence / Replaced original Bldg 67 / Extended from 1969-1972	Abandoned
68 (Original)	1906	Shed / Small Coach Barn	Storage	1988-1989
68	1969-1972	Covered Outdoor Carport	Garage / Replaced original Bldg 68	Abandoned
69 (Original)	1905	East Greenhouse	3rd Greenhouse / Superintendent's Greenhouse	1922
69	1922	Upper Greenhouse	5th Greenhouse / Superintendent's Greenhouse	1980
70	1922	Hotbeds	Garden near Building 69	1972
71 (Original)	1911-1912	Hennery	Near Building 67	1960-1961
71	1928	6-Car Staff Garage	Storage / Behind Bldg 135	1994-1999
72	1925	Tool House	Tool Storage / Near Senior Director's Mansion	1988-1989

73A (Original)	1910-1912	Group 3, Cottage 1	Group 3, Wards 55 & 56 / Extended from 1915-1916 / Renumbered as Bldg 143	1982-1984
73B (Original)	1910-1912	Group 3, Cottage 2	Group 3, Wards 57 & 58 / Extended from 1915-1916 / Renumbered as Bldg 147	1982-1984
73C (Original)	1911-1912	Group 3, Cottage 3 / Kitchen & Dining Hall	Group 3, Kitchen / Extensions added in 1926 / Renumbered as Bldg 137	Abandoned
73A-W	1910-1932	Veterans' Group (Bldgs 39 & 125-147)	VMHU (Including Group 3)	Abandoned
74	1890	Chief Engineer's House	Voluntary LIFE / Currently used as private residence	**Active - Rezoned**
75 (Original)	1890	Barn	Storage behind Bldg 74 / Replaced by new Bldg 75	1938
75	1938	Staff Residence Garage	Storage / Replaced original Bldg 75 / Currently used as residential garage	**Active - Rezoned**

			FOD Program /	Active -
76	1938	Staff Garage for Bldg 74	Currently used as residential garage	**Rezoned**
77	1890	Master Mechanic's House	FOD Program	1995-1996
78	1912	The White House	2-Family Staff House	1986-1988
79	1912	Barn / Garage / White House Annex	Storage / 1-Family Staff House	1940-1947
80	1932	Assembly Hall / Community Store	York Hall / Synagogue	Abandoned
81A-E (Alternate)	1925	Doctor's Cottages 1-5 / See Bldgs 95-99	Replaced original Female Cottages / Numbered as Bldgs 95-99	Abandoned
81	1940	Chemical Feed House / Milk House	Dairy Farm / Near Dairy Barn	1943
82	1928-1929	Laboratory & Morgue	Converted to Nurses' Lounge	2012
83	1925-1926	Firehouse & OMH Police / Grounds Keeping Storage	Storage for Nissequogue River State Park	Abandoned
83.1	1954	Recreation Equipment Storage Shed	Storage / Behind Firehouse	1990

84 (Original)	1924-1925	Boiler House	Incinerator for 2nd Power Plant	1968
84A-F	1958	Water Wells 1-2, 4-5, 7-8	Replaced Bldg 84 / Located near Power Plant	Abandoned
85	1939-1940	Steam Pipe Junction Hse	Renumbered as Building 6	2012
86 (Original)	1924	Blacksmith & Wheelwright Shop	Replaced Bldg 36 / OT / Replaced by new Bldg 86	1927-1931
86	1927-1931	Blacksmith Shop	OT / Replaced original Bldg 86	1954-1957
87	1940-1941	2nd Piggery	Replaced the 1st Piggery / OT	Abandoned
88	1943	2nd Slaughterhouse	Dairy Farm / OT / Renumbered as Bldg 46	2012
89	1955	Comfort Station	Restrooms for Tiffany Field	Abandoned
90	1917-1919	Business & Clerical Offices / Nursing School	Macy Home / Wings Extended in 1923	Abandoned
91	1931	6-Car Staff Garage for Bldg 90	Storage / Replaced original Bldg 39	Abandoned
92	1924-1925	Grandstand	Located in Tiffany Field	1999-2001

93	1939-1941	Ambulatory Geriatric Infirmary / Shock Therapy / Drug Treatment	Wards 17-38 / Replaced original Male Cottages	Abandoned
94	1953	Laundry Bldg / Storage	OT / Replaced Building 5	Abandoned
95	1925	Staff Dr's Cottage #1 (Senior Assist Physician)	Near St. Johnland Rd / Alternate Bldg 81A	Abandoned
96	1925	Staff Dr's Cottage #2 (Senior Assist Physician)	Near St. Johnland Rd / Alternate Bldg 81B	Abandoned
97	1925	Staff Dr's Cottage #3 (Senior Assist Physician)	Near St. Johnland Rd / Alternate Bldg 81C	Abandoned
98	1925	Staff Dr's Cottage #4 (Senior Assist Physician)	Located on E. 4th St / Alternate Bldg 81D	Abandoned
99	1925	Staff Dr's Cottage #5 (Senior Assist Physician)	Located on E. 4th St / Alternate Bldg 81E	Abandoned
100	1950-1953	Staff Cottage #18	Located on E. 4th St	Abandoned
101	1950-1953	Staff Cottage #19	Located on E. 4th St	Abandoned

102	N/A	Staff Cottage #20	Never built	N/A
103	*1892*	*Staff Cottage / Bldg 49*	*Medical Director's House*	*2001*
104	*1939*	*Staff Cottage / Bldg 18*	*Center Unit A (3 Cottages)*	*Abandoned*
105	*1939*	*Staff Cottage / Bldg 18*	*South Unit B (2 Cottages)*	*Abandoned*
106	*1939*	*Staff Cottage / Bldg 18*	*North Unit C (2 Cottages)*	*Abandoned*
107	*1939*	*Staff Cottage / Bldg 19*	*Center Unit D (3 Cottages)*	*Abandoned*
108	*1939*	*Staff Cottage / Bldg 19*	*West Unit E (1 Cottage)*	*Abandoned*
109	*1939*	*Staff Cottage / Bldg 19*	*East Unit F (1 Cottage)*	*Abandoned*
110	*1931-1932*	*Staff House / Bldg 37*	*Non-Medical Staff House*	*Abandoned*
111	1897-1898	Bldg 4A / Group Admin Offices	Group 1, Main Offices / Staff Residences	1972-1973
112	1897-1898	Building 4B	Group 1, Ward 41	1972
113	1897-1898	Building 4C	Group 1, Ward 42	1972-1973
114	1897-1898	Building 4D	Group 1, Ward 43	1972-1973
115	1897-1898	Building 4E	Group 1, Ward 44	1972-1973
116	1897-1898	Building 4F / Dining Hall	Group 1, Ward 45 / Temp Laundry	1972-1973

117	1897-1898	Building 4G / Kitchen	Group 1, Ward 46 / Group Kitchen	1972-1973
118	1897-1898	Building 4H	Group 1, Ward 47	1972
119	1897-1898	Building 4I	Group 1, Ward 48 / Temp Laundry	1972
120	1897-1898	Building 4J	Group 1, Ward 49	1972
121	1897-1898	St. Joseph's Church	Not part of hospital / Prayer Mass	1959
122	1910-1912	MRU Female Wards	Group 2, Cottage 1, Wards 51 & 52 / Formerly Bldg 54A / Extended from 1915-1916	2012
122.1	1916	Gazebo	Located behind Bldg 122	1940-1945
123	1911-1912	MRU Kitchen & Dining Hall	Group 2, Kitchen / Formerly Bldg 54B	2012
124	1910-1912	MRU Male Wards	Group 2, Cottage 2, Wards 53 & 54 / Formerly Bldg 54C	1996
125	1925	Bldg 73A / Admin Office	VMHU / Nissequogue River State Park Offices / Museum	**Active**

126	1925	Bldg 73B / 4-Family Staff Residence	VMHU / Residence	Abandoned
127	1925	Bldg 73C / 4-Family Staff Residences	VMHU / Residence	Abandoned
128	1925	Building 73D	VMHU / Residence	Abandoned
129	1925	Building 73E	VMHU / Residence	Abandoned
130	1925	Bldg 73F / Staff Cottage F	VMHU / Doctor's Home / Future Comfort Station	Renovated
131	1925	Bldg 73G / Staff Cottage G	VMHU / Doctor's Home	2016
132	1925	Bldg 73H / Staff Cottage H	VMHU / Doctor's Home / Future KPPC Museum	Renovated
133	1925	Bldg 73I / Staff Cottage I	VMHU / Doctor's Home	2016
134	1925	Bldg 73J / Staff Cottage J	VMHU / Doctor's Home	2016
135	1925-1929	Bldg 73K / Convalescence Bldg	VMHU, Wards 85 & 86 / Self Support / Honors Patients	2016
136	1925-1929	Bldg 73L / Medical & Surgical Support	VMHU, Wards 72-80	Abandoned

137	1911-1912	Bldg 73M / Group 3 Kitchen & Dining Hall	VMHU / Group 3, Kitchen M / Extended in 1926	Abandoned
138	1925	Bldg 73N / Continued Care	VMHU, Wards 81-84	Abandoned
139	1925	Bldg 73O / Kitchen O & Dining Hall	VMHU / Kitchen O	Abandoned
140	1925	Bldg 73P / Isolation Bldg	VMHU, Ward 140 / Crisis Residence / CSEA Office	Abandoned
141	1931-1932	Building 73Q	VMHU, Wards 87-92 / Renumbered as Bldg 39	Abandoned
142	1925	Bldg 73R / Staff Residence / Dining Hall	VMHU Dining Hall / Elderly Care	2016
143	1910-1912	Bldg 73S / Patient Wards	VMHU / Group 3, Wards 55 & 56 / Extended from 1915-1916	1982-1984
144	1928	Bldg 73T / Staff Residence	VMHU / Home T for Attendants	Abandoned
145	N/A	Bldg 73U / Assembly Hall	VMHU / Never built	N/A
146	N/A	Building 73V	VMHU / Never built	N/A
147	1910-1912	Bldg 73W / Patient Wards	VMHU / Group 3, Wards 57 & 58 / Extended from 1915-1916	1982-1984

148	N/A	N/A	VMHU / Never built	N/A
149	N/A	N/A	VMHU / Never built	N/A
150	1987-1988	Community Residence East	SOCR	Active
151		Community Residence West	SOCR	Active

Chart Abbreviation Key

CSEA – Civil Service Employees Association
FOD – ???
HALI – Hands Across Long Island
LIFE – Life and Health Insurance Foundation for Education
LIRR – Long Island Rail Road
MRU – Mental Retardation Unit
NNPH – National Network of Public Health
OMH – Office of Mental Health
OT – Occupational Therapy
RCCA – Residential Care Center for Adults
SOCR – State-Operated Community Residence
VHMU – Veterans' Hospital Memorial Unit

* *NOTE: Buildings 103-110 are based on an educated guess due to a lack of available information.*

CHAPTER 12

Patient Wards

The Hospital Wards

There is a place, like no place on earth. A land full of wonder, mystery, and danger. Some say, to survive it, you need to be as mad as a hatter. Which, luckily, I am.

–Lewis Carroll (author), *Alice in Wonderland*, 1865

WARDS ARE THE patient living quarters in patient buildings. Most of the patient buildings at state hospitals were divided into separate wards for females and males. In some cases, entire buildings were used for all females or all males. Each ward consisted of a bedroom dormitory, smaller seclusion rooms, a day hall or dayroom, the visiting area, offices for the doctors, the nurses' medicine room, a nurses' station, bathrooms, showers, and a room for the ward attendants. In earlier times, there were dorm rooms for staff members. The wards usually had a kitchen and dining area as well. It might be located in a separate building. Most of the time, the dining rooms were shared by both sexes.

There were several types of wards that existed such as the common ward, the octagon ward, the isolating block ward, and the detached ward.

In the mid-1800s, Florence Nightingale created a system where the main area of a medical ward was long and narrow with beds situated against the walls, opposite from each other. Each bed should be placed between windows to allow for proper ventilation. Enough space had to be left between the beds for the nurses to tend to each patient. A nurse should be able to watch over all patients on a ward from the nurses' station so the ward could operate efficiently. Nightingale preferred wards to house anywhere between twenty and fifty patients.

In 1863, she wrote *Notes on Hospitals*, which established the importance of utilizing natural ventilation at hospitals. Keeping the windows on a ward open was part of the nurse's job, even if it meant making the room a bit chilly. This practice helped let in fresh air while ridding the ward of infected air. It defeated the purpose for a patient to be treated for one illness only to catch something else from bacteria lingering in bad air. Many doctors of the time agreed ventilation was a very important aspect of patient care. They felt the best pavilions were those that let in rural air from their windows rather than polluted city air, which is one reason hospitals were built in rural open fields.

The first wards at Kings Park were only meant to be temporary, built in the hospital's earliest conception, as part of a county farm. These were located in temporary wood-framed pavilions that were bunched together near the marshlands, which was not very ideal. Within the first couple of years, there were permanent wards established in the early cottages. One side of the boulevard was used for males and the other for females. Patients were crowded into these small cottages for several years until the first large brick ward structures were built. All ward buildings constructed afterward were made of brick, since they were considered fireproof.

An innovation of 1900 was female attendants assigned to male wards. This had a very positive effect on disgruntled male patients. Violence and profanity decreased significantly on wards that were now brightened by the presence of flowers from the greenhouse and gardens.

Plenty of rocking chairs were set up for patients, both in the early cottages and the later brick structures. It was very therapeutic for patients to relax in these chairs.

Patients sitting on porch rocking chairs, circa 1910s-1920s

Rocking chairs in hallway of Building C, circa 1910s-1920s

By the 1930s, many of the wards were constructed with partitions to give the patients some form of privacy, as opposed to having the beds side by side, the norm in the average overcrowded ward. Some partitions were concrete, while others were simply made of wood.

No matter how crowded the dorm might have gotten, they were always kept clean, especially at Kings Park. The floors were swept and mopped. The patients' belongings were neatly stored somewhere near their beds or in compartments under their beds. Some beds had built-in drawers either underneath or at the foot of the bed. Sometimes cabinets or closets were used.

Most wards had at least one isolation or seclusion room used for the patients that misbehaved. These rooms would generally consist of only one mattress for the patient to sleep upon. No other furniture was placed inside of these rooms for fear that the patient would use it as a weapon. It was not unusual for a patient to be locked in a closet as punishment as well, although that was generally frowned upon. Such treatment was against hospital policy, and from what I have been told, the state hospital at Kings Park adhered to the rules more strictly than most other Long Island hospitals.

Still, it does not mean rules were not broken from time to time. There are always those who feel the need to make their own rules as they go.

As a general rule, patients were kept in isolation for no more than a few hours. That was more than long enough to teach the patient a lesson in manners. However, according to more than one former patient source, there were times when the rules were broken and a patient was left in isolation overnight.

Most hospitals for the mentally ill had what were known as back wards. They were very similar to isolation wards but not necessarily the same. These wards were used for the more-violent or misbehaved patients. These wards were usually hidden away from the prying judgmental eyes of the public.

Patients were required to shower at least once a week to maintain a tolerable personal hygiene level, although they were encouraged to shower more often. Clean towels and fresh soap were provided daily, especially at places like Kings Park, where they made their own soap and did laundry every day. It was not a fun experience for the attendant or nurse who had the duty of getting the patients to bathe when they refused. The hospital employees usually ended up soaking wet or covered in soap by the end of the day.

Patients were given haircuts in a barbershop on the premises, which was usually located in one of the patient ward buildings. Beauticians were also on staff for the female patients. Wigs were sometimes made from the leftover hair. There were several barbershops at Kings Park, so the patients were always well groomed.

Patient barbershop, circa 1972   Wig making, circa 1970s

Each ward had a dayroom, which is very similar to family rooms, dens, living rooms, and lounges. This is where the patients could watch television, play games, read, or enjoy arts and crafts. Ward nurses and attendants were in charge of establishing recreational activities for their patients. Most patients enjoyed these social interactions with the staff and other patients. It gave them the opportunity to practice their self-control while helping to build friendships.

The dayrooms of each building differed. The solarium sun parlor of the Group 1 was without a doubt one of the best at Kings Park. Buildings 39 (73Q) and 138 (73N) of the Veterans' Group had their solariums set up on the rooftops, which provided the patients with plenty of fresh air. Over the years, the dayrooms became more and more unpleasant with patients in chairs lined up in front of the televisions while drugged up with tranquilizing medications to keep them docile. It was a far cry from the early 1900s, when patients would pass the time enjoying some form of occupational therapy craft.

Patients that were more capable could sometimes visit the community store to purchase snacks, books, newspapers, and cigarettes. Kings Park had a few structures that served in this capacity over the years. However, for those patients incapable of making such a trek, there was a mobile community store cart. It was basically a large cabinet on wheels, which the Maintenance Department built. The mobile store would visit the wards on occasion providing the patients with some of life's normal pleasures. It carried candy, gum, cigarettes, books, comic books, puzzles, games, and other such treats.

During the mid-1950s, 16 mm movies were shown on the wards weekly. By this time, patient life on the wards was taking a turn for the worse. Overcrowding made it too difficult to properly care for the increasing number of patients. There just were not enough employees. State funding was an issue at most facilities, often leading to less food, clothing, supplies, and activities. When combined with the new drug treatment methods of that era, most the patients were being overmedicated to keep them docile for the shorthanded staff.

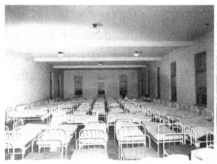 

| Central Islip ward with too many beds, circa 1950s | Central Islip ward with patients in beds, circa 1950s |

At Kings Park, ward journals were kept on each ward. Employees entered daily routines of the ward using entries that were kept very brief, only about two or three lines of the page. Any significant incidents were noted. It is unknown how long this practice was done, but it definitely went on during the 1980s, as there are ward journals from 1982 to 1983.

Some interesting examples of life on a patient ward at a state mental institution during the late twentieth century can be seen in the classic Warner Brothers film *One Flew Over the Cuckoo's Nest* (1975), starring Jack Nicholson, or Columbia Pictures' *Girl, Interrupted* (2004), starring Winona Ryder and Angelina Jolie. Of course, many of the scenes involving mental health facilities in films are greatly exaggerated for dramatic effect, but the facility layouts and treatments are based on actual methods used at such places like the one at Kings Park.

Another film that merits mentioning is the Premiere Films independent movie *Eyes Beyond Seeing* (1995), starring Keith Hamilton Cobb as a mental patient claiming to be Jesus Christ. The film features a cameo appearance by actor/comedian Henny Youngman as a mentally ill patient claiming to be Henny Youngman! This was to be his final movie role before his death.

Henny Youngman actually performed his comedy act for the patients of the Kings Park Psychiatric Center, so it was a nice homage for him to portray a patient.

The bulk of the hospital scenes in *Eyes Beyond Seeing* were filmed at the KPPC in Building 136 (73L) of the Veterans' Group. Filming took place shortly after the building officially closed. The film also contains several exterior shots of the renowned Building 93. The name of the hospital was changed to a fictional location.

On an interesting side note, the film also features a cameo by Kings Park historian and former hospital employee King Pedlar. He plays the part of a patient in a couple of scenes where patients are gathered together in a dayroom.

Wards 1–855 and More

You gain a deep sense of perspective when you look out at the busy world you came from, while peeking through the barred windows of a psych ward.
   —John Leita (urban explorer, photographer, founder of *Long Island Oddities*, and author), *L. I. Asylums Revealed: Kings Park Psychiatric Center*, 2007

Wards 17–31 were the first wards established at the Kings County Farm and Asylum. The ward numbers were a continuation from Wards 1–16 at the Kings County Lunatic Asylum. After the state took over, things changed. The first new buildings to be completed at Kings Park would now house a new set of wards numbered as Wards 1–16.

Aside from the first cottages, the wards of the many different buildings at Kings Park were not numbered in any particular order. Instead, much like the building numbers of the hospital, they were scattered all across the property. Nevertheless, the wards within each building and building group were numbered in sequential order.

The following list mentions the buildings in which the wards were located and, if known, the types of patients housed on each. The lower ward numbers began on the lower floors of the buildings and increased as they went to higher floors in the building. A few wards that did not have any particular numbers have also been included.

Over the years, some ward numbers were changed. A few were relocated to different buildings. Some ward numbers were reused after buildings were demolished. Several numbers are repeated, while others are missing. Those that are missing remain a mystery to me.

I apologize this could not be a more complete and thorough list. It was quite difficult to obtain this information. It took a lot of research, patience, and time. It is far more complete than I ever thought it would be.

Wards 1–4

Wards 1–4 were located in Building A (8). Established in 1894, when the building opened, they housed female patients. There were two wards on each of the two floors located on opposite sides of the building from each other. In these wards, the patients slept in individual rooms, unlike the typical ward, where they all slept together in a large dormitory. These wards were the first of their kind at Kings Park. There were very few wards with single-room units throughout the history of this hospital.

In 1909, Ward 3, on the second floor, was equipped with a hydrotherapeutic apparatus, while the partitions on Wards 3 and 4 were torn down to create small dormitories rather than keeping the single rooms. Eventually, it was realized having single-room units was not practical for the general treatment of patients.

By the early 1970s, these wards were cleared out, and the patients relocated to other buildings. Buildings A–D had gotten too old to continue using for patient treatment.

Wards 5–8

Wards 5–8 were in Building B (9). Also established in 1894, there were two wards on each floor, located on opposite sides of the building, as with Building A. The patients in this building also slept in single-room units.

In 1899, the corridors of Ward 8, on the second floor, were cleared of patients and set aside for night attendants after these attendants were relocated from Ward 32. This provided them with single rooms to sleep in during the daytime without being disturbed. A year later, Ward 7, also on the second floor, was changed into an acute convalescent ward, and the dayroom of Ward 5 was used as a dormitory for depressed and suicidal patients. Wards 5–7 were later all used for acute services.

In 1901, a new therapeutic bath was installed on Ward 6 to be used for hydrotherapy. An electric diet kitchen was installed on Ward 5 in 1904. For a short time, Ward 8 had a sewing room, but in 1906, it was relocated to a more suitable location at the tailor shop. Three years later, the partitions at Wards 6 and 8 were eliminated to create small dormitories, doing away with the single rooms, as in Building A.

Also in 1909, a patient day school was established on Ward 7. It took place during the afternoons and had a daily average attendance of twenty-four patients. The curriculum included basic education, callisthenic exercises, drawing, paper folding, parquetry, singing, and stenciling.

According to the annual report from 1912, song service was conducted every Sunday evening for a half hour after dinner in the large sitting room of Ward 7. Usually, a list of songs was selected. A patient would play the piano, while other patients sang along.

A certified teacher conducted the patient school until she resigned in the summer of 1915. By that time, the daily average attendance of patients had increased to 176.

The wards in Building B were closed by the early 1970s, and the building was abandoned.

Wards 9–12

These wards were established in 1894 within Building C (11). There were two on each floor, located on opposite sides of the building. Wards 9 and 10, on the first floor, were combined early on to allow for the entire acute service of male patients in one building. Most convalescent patients were moved to these wards. Just as in Buildings A and B, the patients slept in single-room units.

In 1904, an electric diet kitchen was installed on Ward 10. Five years later, the partition on Ward 10 was removed to create a small dormitory.

These wards were closed by the early 1970s.

Wards 13–16

Located in Building D (10), these wards were also established in 1894. There were two on each floor, located on opposite sides of the building. Ward 16, on the second floor, was used for violent patients. The wards consisted of single-room units, as in Buildings A–C.

Much like in Building B, the corridors of Ward 15 were cleared of patients in 1899 and set aside for the night attendants, previously housed in Building 32. They were relocated after Building 32 was converted into the Employees' Clubhouse.

An electric diet kitchen was installed at Ward 13, on the first floor, sometime around 1904–1905. In 1906, a shower bath was placed on the same ward, while Ward 16 was equipped with a hydrotherapeutic apparatus in 1909. In the same year, a small dormitory was created after the partition on Ward 15 was taken down.

These wards were also cleared out by the early 1970s, when the building was abandoned.

Wards 17–24 (Original Female Wards)

These wards were located in the early female cottages on the east side of Kings Park Boulevard, across from the male cottages. Only one ward was assigned to each cottage. That ward number generally became the number used to identify that particular cottage. Therefore, these wards were located in Cottages 17–24. These wards were first occupied in 1889.

Ward 20 was used as a convalescent ward for patients with a delayed recovery. During the early 1900s, Wards 22–24 were converted into tuberculosis wards until the Group 4 cottages were built in 1913.

The early female cottages were all condemned and demolished during the 1930s. The ward numbers were reused after the construction of Building 93.

Wards 25–32 (Original Male Wards)

Wards 25–32 were located inside of Cottages 25–32. One ward was assigned to each cottage. These were the early male cottages, located on the opposite side of the boulevard from the female cottages. Most of these wards were established in 1889, except for Ward 32, which was not established until 1895.

Ward 32 was removed only four years later in 1899 so that Building 32 could be converted into an Employees' Clubhouse. There were no patients residing at Ward 32. It had been used to house the hospital's night attendants, who were relocated to Building B.

During the early 1900s, Wards 28 and 30 were used as tuberculosis wards until 1913, when the Group 4 cottages were established. A Pestilence House was built as an annex to Ward 28 and used solely for patients carrying other contagious viruses. It was the first official isolation ward to be established at Kings Park.

Ward 27 was removed sometime around 1932–1934, when the cottage that housed it was removed for the construction of a new storehouse (Building 44). Also, during the 1930s, Ward 26 was closed, and the cottage that housed it was renumbered as Building 20. That building was to be used as a tinsmith and paint shop. Most of these other wards were gone by 1939 with the construction of Building 93, including Wards 25 and 28–31. The patients from these wards were moved into Buildings A–D.

These ward numbers were all reused in Building 93 after it opened.

Ward 33

This ward was established in the original laundry building (Building 33) after it was converted into a patient building in 1911. It did not have a reception room or a dayroom, since it was intended to be temporary. However, patients were housed here for more than a decade. The building had a capacity of up to three hundred patients, and it was almost always filled despite being deemed unsafe by the state fire marshal.

The building was eventually abandoned by the late 1920s, and the ward number was later reused in Building 93.

Wards 17–38

The new Wards 17–38 replaced their predecessors. They were located in Building 93 and opened in 1941. There were two wards per floor from the first floor to the eleventh floor. These wards were part of the hospital's Brooklyn Unit.

Electroconvulsive therapy was conducted on Wards 21 and 22 of the third floor. Wards 17–24 had the largest dayrooms, since they were on the lower floors. Wards 31–38 had the smallest, since they were closer to the top. Ward 38 on the eleventh floor faced the Long Island Sound and was used for male diabetic patients. The upper floors were not really used and were the first part of the building to be closed before the building was abandoned in the early 1990s.

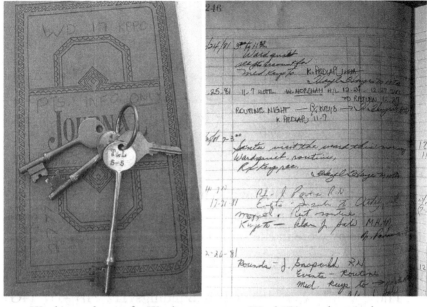

Ward journal cover for Ward
17 & King Pedlar's keys

Ward 17 journal entries by
King Pedlar, circa 1981

Ward 17 journal entries by
King Pedlar, circa 1981

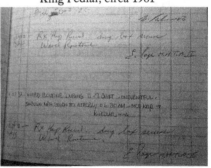

Ward 17 journal entries by
King Pedlar, circa 1982

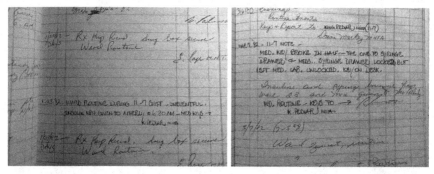

Ward 17 journal entries by   Ward 17 journal entries by
King Pedlar, circa 1982   King Pedlar, circa 1982

Wards 39–40

These wards are unknown to me. It is unlikely these numbers were skipped. I could not figure out where they might have been. It is likely they were in the same building.

Wards 41–46

These wards were located in Buildings 112 (4B)–117 (4G) of Group 1. Established in 1898, these buildings were classic examples of the Kirkbride Plan. Wards 41–46 were located in the portion of the group where the buildings were connected forming a semicircle with the dining hall and kitchen extending back from the center. One ward was assigned to each two-story building, and they only housed female patients. Ward 41 was in Building 112 (4B), Ward 42 was in Building 113 (4C), and so on. Ward 44 of Building 115 (4E) was the only three-story ward of the group. There was an office and drug room on the first floor of each ward, while the dorms were on the upper floors.

The women's infirmary was located at Ward 45 of Building 116 (4F). This ward housed nearly two hundred "*feeble, filthy and bed-ridden patients,*" according to one of the hospital's annual reports. In 1906, two rain baths and six lavatories were installed on this ward.

After the first laundry building burned down at the end of 1906, laundry had to be shipped elsewhere for a while. It was beginning to pile up fast. In 1907, a small eight-foot squared wood-framed house was built outside of Ward 45 for storing soiled clothing.

In 1910, dayrooms were created at Wards 41 and 43 by using part of the solarium sun parlor of Building 111 (4A) and the two turrets at either end. This allowed for additional beds to be placed at the old dayrooms to help ease overcrowding at Group 1.

In November 1912, the sewing room used for occupational therapy on Ward 48 in Building 119 (4I) was moved to the much brighter Ward 43. In the same year, spray baths were installed on the second floors of Wards 42 and 44.

Wards 47–49

Wards 47–49 were located in Buildings 118 (4J), 119 (4I), and 120 (4H) of Group 1, which were the separate buildings of the group. However, it is a bit confusing because Ward 47 was in Building 120 (4H), while Ward 49 was in Building 118 (4J). This was only because of the order in which the buildings were numbered. Established in 1898, these wards were home to male patients. As with the other wards of Group 1, there was an office and drug room on the first floor of each ward, while dorms were on the second floors.

After a dietary study was conducted, a new electric diet kitchen was installed on Ward 48 in 1902. This ward housed the men's infirmary. The new kitchen consisted of two thirteen-by-twenty-inch ovens, a ten-inch stove, one six-inch stove, and an eighteen-by-thirteen-inch broiler.

As with Ward 45, a small eight-foot squared wood-framed house was erected in 1907 outside of Ward 48 to store soiled clothing.

In November 1912, the sewing room from Ward 48 was relocated to Ward 43 of Building 114 (4D).

Sitting room from a male ward at Group 1, circa 1910s-1920s

Ward 50

This ward was established in 1932 and originally used as an infirmary for acute female patients at Group 2. It was located in Building 40, an annex added to the group. Within a few years, it became the children's ward. Ward 50 was the only ward located in this one-story building.

There was a model train set room in the basement recreation room of this building.

Model train set in the basement recreation room of Ward 50, circa 1954

The same room captured by Sam Bartels on Aug. 31, 2013

As of 1974, the building became part of the Mental Retardation Unit (MRU). During this time, it housed low-functioning adult male patients of the unit and then ambulatory female patients of the unit. This ward was renumbered as Ward 851.

By the early 1980s, this building was abandoned, and the patients were relocated to another facility in Melville. This building then served as a day care center, but the ward number was no longer utilized.

Wards 51 and 52

These two wards could be found within Building 122 of Group 2. They were established

Ward 51 of Group 2, circa 1915

in 1912. This building was originally used to house acute female patients.

In 1953, it became the Female Adolescent Unit. During the 1960s, it was renovated, and the adolescent patients were moved to the newer Building 22.

As of 1974, these wards became part of the Mental Retardation Unit (MRU). Ward 51 on the second floor was used as the children's ward for the MRU. Ward 52 was used for older female patients, since it would have been difficult for them to go use the stairs.

Wards 53 and 54

Wards 53 and 54 were established in 1912 and located in Building 124 of Group 2. Originally, they were utilized for acute male patients. Ward 54, on the second floor, offered a braided rug class as part of the occupational therapy program.

Ward 53 of Group 2, circa 1916

During the 1930s, the patients in this building were moved to other wards, while these wards became home to the new Boys' Unit. By 1953, it became the Male Adolescent Unit until it was renovated during the 1960s. The adolescents were all moved to Building 22.

As of 1974, this building became part of the Mental Retardation Unit (MRU). Ward 53 was used for male patients of the unit, while Ward 54 was referred to as the Transitional Living Unit (TLU).

Patient dorm from Ward 55 or 56
at Group 3, circa 1960s-1970s

Wards 55 and 56

These two male wards were established in 1912 inside of Building 143 (73S) of Group 3. In 1925, they became part of the Veterans' Memorial Hospital Unit. New York City Unit 1 was located in this building.

Wards 57 and 58

These two female wards, established in 1912, were located in Building 147 (73W) of Group 3. They also became part of the Veterans' Memorial Hospital Unit and were known as New York City Unit 2.

Ward 59

This ward number might have been reserved for the old heating plant (Building 59) after it was abandoned. There were a few ideas of what to do with the building from 1910 to 1920. If it were converted into a new patient building, having Ward 59 inside would have been convenient.

Wards 60–65

These wards originally belonged to the old Group 4 tuberculosis buildings, also known as the tuberculosis wards or TB wards. Established in 1913, these long one-story pavilions primarily housed female patients. Wards 60 and 61 were located within the smaller Building 4A, Wards 62 and 63 were in Building 4B, and Wards 64 and 65 were in Building 4C. Each of these wards had electric diet kitchens installed.

During the 1920s, the patients of these wards were relocated to Central Islip State Hospital, which was equipped with better accommodations. The old TB wards of Group 4 were demolished, while a new Group 4 was built nearby.

As of 1941, these ward numbers were reused and assigned to Building 15, which housed disturbed patients. There were two wards on each floor of this three-story building. These were maximum-security wards for the hospital's more-dangerous patients. Ward 65 was used for criminally insane male patients. That ward alone held about eighty-five patients. The patients of this building were all kept with their heads shaven to distinguish them from other patients at the hospital.

By the mid-1960s, this building was no longer used for the hospital's worst patients. They were sent to Building 21. However, these wards still housed patients until the building closed sometime in the 1980s–1990s.

Building 15 sign for Wards 60-65 at PPC Museum on Nov. 4, 2015

Wards 66–71

These wards were in Building 2 of Group 5, the female reception building. Established in 1923, there were two wards per floor.

During the 1960s, these wards made up the Northeast Nassau Unit, which was under a separate administration from the rest of the hospital. It even had a separate director and staff.

The building was closed, and its wards abandoned by the 1980s.

Wards 72–80

These wards, located in Building 136 (73L), were part of the Veterans' Memorial Hospital Unit. They were established in 1929, although the building did not open until 1934. There were four wards on the first floor, four on the second, and one on the third. Shock Units were located on Wards 74 and 75, on the first floor. During the 1940s, experiments were conducted for the treatment of syphilis using malaria on Ward 78, on the second floor. Sick hospital employees were treated on Ward 80, the only ward on the third floor, also used as a quarantine ward.

Laundry basket for Wards 72 & 73, circa April 28, 2013

Single-patient dorm room   Day room for Ward 80
from Ward 80

Wards 81–84

These four wards were established in 1925 within Building 138 (73N) as part of the Veterans' Memorial Hospital Unit. There were dorms and single rooms. These wards were also known as Brooklyn Unit 1. There was an enclosed solarium on the rooftop with barred windows, which served as a recreation area for the patients of these wards.

Wards 85 and 86

These two wards were in Building 135 (73K) and were part of the Veterans' Memorial Hospital Unit. They were established in 1929. There was one ward inside of each extended wing of this Y-shaped building. These wards were also known as New York City Unit 1.

After 1947, when the first televisions were allowed on patient wards of state hospitals, the first television was placed on Ward 85 at Kings Park.

Convalescent patients were kept on these wards. These wards also housed honor patients, who were patients with special honor card privileges. They were allowed to come and go unescorted as long as they returned when they were supposed to return.

Wards 87–92

Wards 87–92 were established in 1932 inside of Building 39, formerly Building 141 (73Q), and were part of the Veterans' Memorial Hospital Unit. There were three wards on each floor, one per wing. At one point, Ward 88, in the first floor's central wing, was used to administer electroconvulsive therapy to twenty-two patients a day. These wards were also known as Brooklyn Unit 2. This building also had an enclosed solarium on the rooftop, which served as a recreation area for the patients.

Wards 93–100

Established in 1931, these eight wards were located in Building 1 of Group 5, which was the male reception building. This two-story building has four wings, and each floor had four wards, one per wing.

After the hospital closed, this building was reopened and under the control of Pilgrim Psychiatric Center. I am uncertain if the ward numbers remained the same, but the building number was changed to 700.

This building was closed by November 2012, and its patients were sent to Pilgrim.

Rear of Building 1 on April 16, 2013   Snow-covered rear of Building 1 on Feb. 7, 2015

Wards 101–108

These wards were located in the north wing of Building 41, one of the buildings of the second Group 4. Wards 123–128 were also in this building, but they were located in the opposite wing. Established in 1934, there were a total of fourteen wards in this building with an average of four wards per floor, except for the first floor, which only had two wards. Ward 108, on the fourth floor, was used to house criminally insane female patients until around the 1960s, when they were moved to Building 21. These wards were also known as Group 4-A.

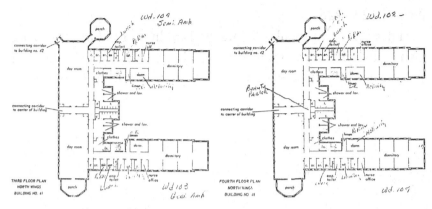

Building 41 floor plan showing
Wards 103 & 107

Building 41 floor plan showing
Wards 104 & 108

Wards 109–122

Also established in 1934, these wards were in Building 43 of Group 4. There were fourteen wards in this building with an average of four wards per floor, with the exception of the first floor, which only had two wards. Wards 109–116 were in the north wing of the building and known as Group 4-B, while Wards 117–122 were in the south wing and known as Group 4-C.

Laundry basket for Ward
110 on Sept. 3, 2011

On February 1, 1953, the Juvenile Girls' Unit was separated from the Female Adolescent Unit, which was moved to Wards 51 and 52 of Group 2. Afterward, there was an average of sixty patients on Wards 115 and 118, which housed the remaining juvenile females. Some of the beds were removed to make room, since they were no longer needed.

Wards 123–128

These wards were also located in Building 41 of Group 4, along with Wards 101–108. They were established in 1934. Located in the south wing, these wards were also referred to as Group 4-D.

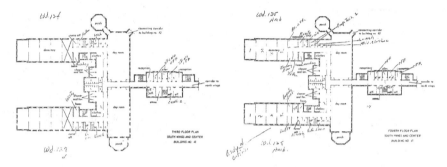

Building 41 floor plan showing
Wards 124 & 127

Building 41 floor plan showing
Wards 125 & 128

Wards 129–139

The location of these wards is unknown to me. Perhaps they were intended for Buildings 16 and 17, which were never built as replacements for Group 1. Each building could have had at least four wards or more, depending on the number of floors added.

Ward 140

This was the only ward inside of Building 140 (73P) that housed part of Brooklyn Unit 2. It was part of the Veterans' Memorial Hospital Unit. The ward was divided into multiple single rooms rather than the typical patient ward layout. It was established in 1925 and replaced the hospital's original isolation ward (Pestilence House).

In the beginning, most of the patients here carried contagious viruses such as typhoid. Sometime around the 1980s, this building was used as an office building for the Civil Service Employees Association (CSEA). By then, there were no patients kept here.

Wards 141–200

It is likely these wards were intended for the buildings of the Veterans' Group that were planned but never built. Of course, these wards could have been intended for Buildings 16 and 17 instead.

Aerial photo of Buildings 7, 21 & 22, listing Wards 202-238, circa 1967

Wards 201–214

These wards were established in Building 21 in 1965. There were four wards on each floor. The following units were located among these wards: North Brooklyn, Brooklyn 3–4, Greenpoint, Cumberland, and Ridgewood Unit. Ward 210, on the third floor, was used for violent female patients. The Narcotics

Sign for Wards 206, 210, & 212, circa 2008, by Max Neukirch, Jr.

Addiction Unit occupied the four wards on the top floor, Wards 211–214. In later years, when Building 93 was closed, Ward 212 housed geriatric patients.

The first patients admitted to this unit were four men sent from the Manhattan House of Detention. They chose to face commitment rather than criminal charges. Upon being admitted, a team of psychiatrists screened these men to make certain they were not aggressively violent. Furthermore, the men had to be serious about wanting to be cured of their dependencies before being allowed entry into the unit.

Wards 215–228

These wards were established inside of Building 22 in 1965. Just like in Building 21, there were four wards on each floor. One of them originally served as a Children's Unit. These wards were part of the Huntington-Smithtown Unit.

Soon after the building opened, a section on the top floor where Wards 225–228 were located was used to house patient-prisoners who were in the Sheriff's Department's custody. Disruptive patients were kept here as well.

The Huntington-Smithtown Unit began their own edition of the *Times* newspaper in the early part of 1977, complete with news articles, cartoons, puzzles, and poetry.

Sign for Ward 216, circa March 9, 2014

Wards 229–238

These were medical wards established in 1967. They were located inside of Building 7, which was the medical and surgical building. There were two wards on each floor, from the fourth to eighth floor. In later years, most of these wards housed geriatric patients.

Laundry basket for Ward   Laundry basket for Ward
235 on March 12, 2013   236 on March 17, 2013

Wards 239–850

These wards did not exist.

Wards 851–855

These were the new ward designations for the wards of the three patient buildings of Group 2 before the unit closed in 1980. During the late 1970s, administrative control of the Mental Retardation Unit (MRU) at Group 2 was transferred over to the Suffolk Developmental Center (SDC) in Melville. The original ward numbers 50–54 were increased by one number and preceded by the number 8.

Building 40's Ward 50 became Ward 851 and so on with the wards in Buildings 122 and 124, changing from Wards 51–54 to Wards 852–855. Wards 852 and 853 were in Building 122, while Wards 854 and 855 were in Building 124.

Other Wards

Live, then, and be happy, beloved children of my heart, and never forget that until the day when God shall deign to reveal the future to man, all human wisdom is summed up in these two words,–"Wait and hope."
–Alexandre Dumas (author), *The Count of Monte Cristo*,
1844

There were a few wards that were not numbered. They existed during the hospital's earlier days, when there were mainly cottages and only a few large buildings. These wards were the children's ward and the isolation ward, which no doubt housed some of the most sensitive cases of the hospital.

It was necessary to separate certain patients from the rest of the population for safety and health reasons. The children and patients in isolation were better suited by being separated from other adult patients, if they were ever to be cured. Most wards for children tended to have educational facilities and play areas, while

patients in isolation are generally in a position to get the attention they require, usually the bare minimum. There were times when the patients locked in isolation tended to be overlooked, which sadly took place at Kings Park in at least one case.

Most wards provided the same amenities. There were usually a dorm, dayroom, shower facility, dining area, nurses' station, and drug room. The significant thing about these wards is the unique type of patients that were treated.

The children's ward and isolation ward at Kings Park existed at several different locations throughout the years. They were moved to newer and better facilities as the years went by. Eventually, both of these wards were phased out by the 1970s.

Children's Ward

While this ward was not confined to one particular number or building, I thought it was necessary to include it separately from the numbered wards.

The original children's ward was established in February 1924 within two of the original male cottages. These cottages were situated next to one another. Originally, only one was used for boys under the age of twelve, but soon, another ward was added in a second cottage for girls, creating a Children's Unit.

It is not known exactly which specific cottages were used, but it is believed they were located on the male side of the boulevard. The unit started out as boys only, which would have been placed near the males. Another reason for this belief can be seen in a 1925 photo of Male Cottage 28 (D), showing what appears to be a swing set, as seen in the previous chapter.

At first, all of the children admitted were under the age of sixteen, but by 1930, the children of these wards included all ages under seventeen. While on

Boy in gazebo, circa 1920s-1930s

these wards, the children learned proper personal hygiene habits, table manners, and how to care about their general appearance. In the mornings, they were taught standard schoolwork and given the opportunity for exercising, which is very important for growing children. In the afternoon, they learned craftwork, games, and more to provide them with an educational outlet for fun.

These early cottage wards did not have bars on the windows or guards at the doors. They were made to look and feel as close as possible to regular houses for the sake of the children. It was hard enough for them to be away from their families. At least the wards could feel like home. These wards were chiefly used as encephalitis wards because many of the children at the time were suffering from this illness.

Encephalitis is an inflammation of the brain that causes flu-like symptoms such as fever and headaches, and is also known to cause seizures and mobility issues.

At some point, an Adolescent Unit was established in Building B. When the new Group 4 opened in 1936, the Children's Unit was split up. The girls were moved to this new group of buildings, while the boys were all relocated to Building 124 of Group 2.

During the early 1950s, Group 2 became the new Adolescent Unit for females and males. In 1953, a new Children's Unit was established at Group 4. After a new children's ward was set up at Building 40 of Group 2, all children were moved there to Ward 50. This way, all children and adolescents could be kept together in one building group.

When Building 22 was completed and opened in 1966, a new Children's Unit was established there. It was a newer building with improved facilities for the children. A large playground was established behind it in an enclosed courtyard. The Children's Unit would remain there until being closed permanently in 1977, after fifty-three years.

The Mental Retardation Unit, established in 1974, also had a children's ward on the second floor of Building 122. These children had been relocated to Melville with the rest of the unit by 1983.

From then on, there were no more patients admitted to the Kings Park Psychiatric Center who were under the age of eighteen. At that point, the hospital was about twenty years away from closing anyway, so it was gradually phasing out buildings.

Isolation Ward

The hospital's first official isolation ward was located in the Pestilence House, or Pest House, which was later numbered as Building 25. It was also known as the Isolation Cottage. Established in 1905, it was located where Group 2 was later built.

Prior to its existence, the hospital personnel would set up tents in the nearby woods to house their quarantined patients.

As mentioned earlier, the isolation ward was primarily used for patients that had contagious and infectious diseases who were in need of being quarantined from the rest of the patient population. For a brief time, there were hospital attendants residing on this ward because there was nowhere else for them to sleep.

In 1910, the Isolation Cottage was moved from its original location and placed at the end of Industrial Road. It became an annex to Male Cottage 28, which was being used to house male patients with tuberculosis.

A summerhouse that was erected nearby in 1906 was used for the patients of this ward. It became known as the Little Pest House. The patients were allowed to sit out there to get their share of fresh air and sunshine while still being separate from the other patients.

There was also a second isolation ward established when the Veterans' Memorial Hospital Unit was built in the mid-1920s. It was located within Building 140 and numbered as Ward 140. Once it took over as the new isolation ward, the previous one was ultimately abandoned. The building was finally demolished by the early 1950s, when a new laundry building was built in that area.

CHAPTER 13

Building Artwork

Building Murals

I would bounce around and paint on one section or another almost nightly. The patients got a kick out of seeing the dragon being painted. I added red pupils and shading to the dragon's eyeballs and shading to the horns and fingernails. I also added a handful of Hobbits to the right holding a spear.

You can see that the psychedelic woodland scene is also a work in progress with the lizard on the mushroom painted in outline. The picture of the B-24 and the geometric pattern were in the hallway. You can see that the B-24 was only roughed in at that point and the geometric picture was only started.

The first mural I did was the one with the woman holding the grapes. We decided to spruce up the ward by painting some murals in the dayroom. Craig W. took charge of getting some gallon cans of acrylic paint. We sat around one night trying to figure out what we wanted to do. Someone brought in a wine bottle with that picture on it, so we decided to start from there. I went crazy after that.

Notice the wall with the rainbow and clouds. That was to be a scene reminiscent of "Pepperland" from the Beatles' movie. Maintenance had come in to do some work on the walls. You can see plaster marring the painted surface in some locations.

–Barry Charletta (former employee of the Kings Park Psychiatric Center's Mental Retardation Unit [MRU] of Group 2, Building 124)

Building 124 mural
by Barry Charletta

Building 124 mural
by Barry Charletta

Building 124 mural
by Barry Charletta

Building 124 mural by
Barry Charletta

Building 124 mural by
Barry Charletta

Building
124 mural
by Barry
Charletta

B ARRY CHARLETTA'S BROTHER, Dale, took these fantastic photos of some wall murals done by Barry and his coworkers on the first floor of Group 2's Building 124. The paintings were started sometime during the autumn or winter of 1977–1978.

Dale had been home on a college break when he went to visit his brother at the MRU in Building 124. It was a good thing Dale brought along his camera; otherwise, these murals would never have been captured.

Building 124 no longer stands. It was demolished in the mid-1990s. The actual murals are forever lost with it, since the building was demolished prior to the huge influx of urban explorers that go through the buildings. Only these extremely rare photos remain to show what once existed. In the photos, it is apparent how the murals are in various stages of completion.

Looking at the photos recently brought back a string of memories for Barry, who had forgotten all about them. Until recently, it had been approximately thirty years since he had seen them.

Building 40 was the last building to be added to Group 2. There were a lot of murals painted in here as well. Most of them were done to make the ward more welcoming to children on the children's ward and then as a day care center for the employees' children.

The Lion King mural,
March 26, 2011

Disney mural,
Aug. 31, 2013

Sesame Street mural,
March 26, 2011

Another set of murals painted at the state hospital is the most well known. These are the murals that were painted on the walls of an entire recreational room in the basement of Building 93. Popular belief has always been that Percy Leo Crosby, the author and illustrator of an old comic strip titled *Skippy*, which was

The Clancy Kids, March 30, 1919, by Percy Crosby

published from 1923 to 1945, was the artist that painted these nearly legendary murals.

Crosby spent his last years as a patient of the Kings Park Veterans' Unit from 1949 to 1964, after a failed suicide attempt. He was diagnosed as a paranoid schizophrenic. At the time, his wife's uncle, Dr. Arthur E. Soper, was superintendent of the hospital. After a heart attack left him in a coma for months, Crosby died on December 8, 1964. It was his seventy-third birthday.

Dr. Arthur E. Soper   A page from Percy Crosby's sketchbook

Research conducted by the Kings Park Heritage Museum revealed some very interesting clues, suggesting he was the artist or that another artist painted the murals in his style, perhaps as a tribute to him. However, according to those at Pilgrim Psychiatric Center Museum, the art does not match Percy Crosby's style. Al Cibelli, who works in the museum at Pilgrim, said he looked at original artwork by Crosby during Crosby's time as a patient. In his opinion, the style is different from that of the murals in Building 93.

Based on sketches made by Crosby, there is a resemblance, although it is different from his *Skippy* comic strip. Speaking as an artist, I do not always draw or paint in the same style. My mood plays a big role in the result. Therefore, the sketchbook is insufficient evidence to say whether Crosby created the mural.

Depicted here are several photos of the elaborate mural that spans across three walls of this very large rectangular room. According to some employees who knew Crosby while he was a patient, the man painting at the easel in the mural is identical to Crosby.

He was a tall thin man who always dressed neatly, which explains the dress shoes and cuffed pants on the artist. The same employees also mentioned that Crosby always wore an ascot, which the artist in the mural is clearly wearing. This could have easily been a self-portrait or a tribute to him by a fan of his work.

Another interesting fact is that Crosby often used cats and dogs in his comic strips to help tell the story. Sometimes they were part of the story, or they were used to point out ironic or surreal aspects of what was going on in the story. The cat balancing a mouse on its nose in one part of the mural is a good example of that.

Mural of a patient playing ping-pong, circa 2008

Mural of patients playing checkers, circa 2008

Mural of an elderly female patient, circa 2008

Mural of a patient enjoying music, circa 2008

Mural of cat & mouse & patients at desks, 2008

Mural of what appears to be Percy Crosby painting, circa 2008

There is another theory regarding the creation of this mural. It is possible a female doctor who worked in Building 93 could have done it. This information came from a reliable source. It would have been helpful if the artist could have at least signed the work. Alas, there is no signature and no known date for when these murals were created. There is only speculation and hearsay.

I like to think it was done for Percy Crosby, a man who truly got the short end of the stick in life.

There was an employee, Matt Werkheiser, who painted murals of fish on the walls of Ward 32, on the eighth floor of Building 93. These murals were done in the 1960s. There are no known photos of this artwork. It was likely painted over during the 1970s.

According to a source of mine who worked at the hospital, there were murals painted on the top floor of Building 7. The murals were caricatures of the employees that worked in the building. The murals were created while she was pregnant, so she was made to look like a tugboat. She said the murals were quite amusing.

Unfortunately, they were painted over before the building was closed. I was unable to acquire any photos of them. It is odd how the state insisted on painting the buildings before closing them. It is not as if they were planning to lease or rent them out to anyone.

Fortunately, some great murals survived the closing of the hospital. There are quite a few in the basements of Buildings 21 and 41. These rooms were used as recreation rooms for the patients. The murals helped create pleasant environments in otherwise isolated areas of the buildings.

Basement mural in Bldg 21 of a
Castle in the Sky on Dec. 7, 2011

Group 4 - basement mural of an
arch & trees from Aug. 25, 2011

Group 4 - basement mural of an
Oriental sculpture from Aug. 25, 2011

Group 4 - basement mural of a person
on a bridge from Aug. 25, 2011

Group 4 - basement mural of women
in a wheat field from Aug. 25, 2011

Group 4 - basement mural of cart
pulled by oxen from Aug. 25, 2011

Group 4 - basement mural of a
forest & field from Aug. 25, 2011

Group 4 - basement mural of a
chapel from Aug. 25, 2011

There were murals painted in many of the buildings throughout the years. Some were more noteworthy than others, but all were of equal significance because they were created to help the patients feel like they were in comforting surroundings. There is no doubt these murals made a difference for many patients. I applaud all of the employees who took the time to beautify the buildings with these fantastic works of art.

Employee Terri Davin painting a mural
in Building 21 of a clown in 1975

Terri painting a Disney mural on the
third floor of Building 21 in 1975

Mural of the Nissequogue River in
Building 15 on March 11, 2010

Mural of a playground in Building
15 on March 11, 2010

There was a time when the patients used to learn how to draw and paint in art classes that were taught to them. It was one of the most peaceful times they experienced while at the hospital. Perhaps they forgot where they were as they focused on their creations.

A few murals were painted on the outside of buildings rather than on the inside. The most notable ones are outside of Buildings 136 (73L) and 144 (73T). These colorful murals created by children of the nearby schools were placed on the many windows of these two buildings as window covers. In fact, every window of Building 144 (73T) was covered by one of these mural boards at one time. Some have fallen off or have been pulled off by trespassers. This was also done at Building 136 (73L).

Front view of Building
144 on May 11, 2016

Murals on the front windows
on May 11, 2016

Murals on the west side of
Building 144 on April 19, 2016

The rear of Building 144
on Sept. 17, 2016

Mural on a rear door on April 19, 2016

Mural on a rear window
on April 19, 2016

Murals on the front of Building
136 on Dec. 22, 2011

Two front windows of Building
136 on April 19, 2016

Mural of raccoons on a basement window of Building 136, April 19, 2016

Mural of birds on a basement window of Building 136 on April 19, 2016

Currently, the only kind of artwork done at the hospital would be the graffiti sprawled all over the interiors and exteriors of the buildings. Most of it is a montage of messages, "tag" names, unnecessary curse words, insults, and claims of victory for having gained access to certain areas of the buildings.

The only useful graffiti is the warnings and directional messages pointing to the exits, which can be quite helpful to a lost or uncertain urban explorer.

Message in the stairwell of Building 93 on July 31, 2009

Graffiti in Bldg 93 indicating the location of the nearest exit, Oct. 27, 2007

Leftover evidence in Building
44 on March 17, 2013

A mural in Building 44
on March 17, 2013

The graffiti covered lobby of
Building 7 on Oct. 5, 2015

Someone painting graffiti from the
roof of Building 7, March 9, 2014

The solarium of Building
138 on April 28, 2013

An American flag on the roof of
Building 93 on April 17, 2016

Painting the KPPC

All you need to paint is a few tools, a little instruction, and a vision in your mind.

–Bob Ross (artist)

The architectural style of the buildings at the Kings Park Psychiatric Center or most any of the old state hospitals can be inspiring even to an average artist. One look at Building 93 from just the right angle, or at the buildings of Group 4, is enough to make anyone want to capture those images in some artistic way. The beautiful parklike surroundings and proximity to the Long Island Sound and Nissequogue River only add to that urge to be creative when seeing the hospital grounds. Seeing these old-style brick buildings surrounded by trees and near the ocean water provides a great backdrop for an artist or a photographer.

Like so many others, I have spent hours using different photo programs to tweak photos I have taken of Building 93 and some of the other prominent structures to give the image a feeling of unforgettable intensity. It is almost like painting a photo with special effects. As an artist and lover of photography, I can see the beauty in almost any structure, whether it is brand new or falling apart.

Building 93 on March 26, 2011   Edited version of Building
                                        93 from March 26, 2011

Building 93 on March 9, 2015   Edited version of Building
93 from March 9, 2015

Not long after I started working on this book, I recruited my father, who is an excellent artist, to paint a portrait of Building 93 for me. After about a week, he was able to complete the following painting without having seen the building in person yet. His inspiration was based solely on photos I provided. He managed to give it an eerie look, making it seem almost more like a haunted hotel on a dark and stormy road.

My father's initial sketch of
Building 93 on April 8, 2011   The completed painting
on April 17, 2011, by
Waldemar Medina

Upon seeing the great work of art he created, I knew I was going to have to take him to Kings Park so he could see the building with his own eyes. In fact, I took both of my parents and showed them this fascinating place that has captured my imagination for the past decade. They were rightfully impressed by what they saw during their tour. Of course, I did not take them inside of any buildings. Seeing them from the outside was enough to make an impression.

I was inspired by my father to paint a building myself. After about a year of practice, I felt confident enough to attempt painting the water tower from the hospital. I always found that structure to have an interesting look.

On November 17, 2015, I painted the structure listed as Building 45 on a sixteen-by-twenty-inch canvas based on a photo I had taken a few years back. I chose to leave out the graffiti at the base of the tower because I wanted it to look more how it did around the time when it was first abandoned.

Another painting I did can be seen at the beginning of chapter 1. The painting depicts Alice from *Alice in Wonderland* when she meets with the Cheshire Cat. I actually did that painting right before the one of the water tower on the same night. I felt inspired that night.

My painting of the water tower, Building 45, on Nov. 17, 2015

There was another artist I know about who loved to venture onto the hospital grounds for her inspiration. Her name was Morgan Mauro. She was an elderly Long Island woman, born in 1937. One day, she happened to drive through the boulevard, and she instantly fell in love with the architecture of its buildings.

She soon returned and set out to create several paintings of the buildings, which included Building 15, the greenhouse, the firehouse, the grandstand, and more. Each painting was done on location.

According to former hospital employee Stephen Weber, she could be found at all hours of the day or night with her watercolors, easel, and brushes interpreting the area in her own way. She is remembered as a kind, fun lady who often wore a baseball cap and would step back and forth in front of her easel as she created her paintings.

Unfortunately, she passed away sometime in 1997. Depicted here are some of her works of art from the Kings Park Heritage Museum.

Painting of Buildings 93 & 83 by Morgan Mauro   Painting of Buildings 123 & 40 by Morgan Mauro   Painting of Building 40

There are countless other unsung artists out there who have successfully captured the totality of some of Kings Park's buildings on canvas or in sketches. It is a shame I could not include more work by other artists.

Buildings 29 & 93, from the water tower hill, by Kelly Lindner, 2005   Blurred graffiti sketch of Building 93 in the power plant, Aug. 25, 2011

A cake of Building 45 baked by my wife, Jo-Ann, on April 23, 2016

I included an architect's concept art painting of Building 7. The architect was Carl W. Larson, but a fellow architect, Harry M. Prince, was responsible for the concept artwork.

Architect's concept art of Building 7, circa 1960s

SECTION VI

Getting Around The Hospital

CHAPTER 14

Waterways and Waterworks

The Nissequogue River

I thought how lovely and how strange a river is. A river is a river, always there, and yet the water flowing through it is never the same water and is never still. It's always changing and is always on the move. And over time the river itself changes too. It widens and deepens as it rubs and scours, gnaws and kneads, eats and bores its way through the land. Even the greatest rivers–the Nile and the Ganges, the Yangtze and the Mississippi, the Amazon and the great grey-green greasy Limpopo all set about with fever trees–must have been no more than trickles and flickering streams before they grew into mighty rivers.

–Aidan Chambers (author), *This is All: The Pillow Book of Cordelia Kenn,* 2005

DURING KINGS PARK'S earliest years as a small village, it relied quite heavily on the Long Island Sound and nearby rivers for many things. At one time, the rivers were the major means of trade for the Smithtown villages, built along the northern shores of Long Island. One such river is the Nissequogue River.

The Nissequogue River is just over eight miles long, extending from Caleb Smith Park, at the heart of Smithtown, through the Nissequogue River State Park and out to the Long Island Sound. Most of the river is an estuary, which means the tide moves in both directions. The water does not originate from a lake. Instead, it is a freshwater river derived from groundwater. It got its name from the Nesequake Native Americans that once lived around it and fished its waters.

Mouth of the Nissequogue
River on July 21, 2016

Nissequogue River on May 1, 2013

The river is home to many forms of wildlife. In the waters are numerous species of fish, crabs, and shellfish. There are alewives, bluefish, brook trout, brown trout, eels, herring, largemouth bass, porgies, rainbow trout, shad, striped bass, summer flounder, winter flounder, and yellow perch. On the banks of the river, one can find turtles as well. Mallard ducks, Canadian geese, heron, and the great egret feed on fish and insects in the river and on the sound.

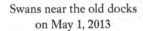

| Swans near the old docks on May 1, 2013 | Black Brant geese at Short Beach on May 11, 2016 |

Prior to the arrival of the Long Island Railroad in 1872, the people of Long Island relied heavily on horses and wagons and the surrounding waterways to get around. It was the Nissequogue River that supplied the fastest transportation and trade route for Kings Park to the main area of Smithtown and other places like New York City and Connecticut. The river was largely responsible for connecting the small rural community that eventually became Kings Park to the outside world.

It took days to travel by horse and wagon if one wished to go beyond Long Island. There were only dirt roads, trails, forests, and open plains to ride across. There were also many risk factors to consider such as hostile Native American tribes, dangerous wildlife, and rough terrain.

That is essentially what made the waterways so much more inviting. Although there is more than one river flowing through Smithtown, it is the Nissequogue River that is the closest to Kings Park, making it ideal because it connects the Long Island Sound to the heart of Smithtown.

This is what made it so significant to the growth of the Kings Park Psychiatric Center when it was still a county farm. It allowed a faster means for the transportation of various products, food supplies, construction materials, and even people to the small growing hospital community. However, it was not until the canal was built that the hospital made full use of the river. The canal made it quicker and easier to reach the northern part of the property at the most convenient location near the first power plant and storehouse.

The Canal and Boat Basin

Hospital workers would moor their boats in the basin and row out through the canal to the bluff and out into the Long Island Sound. The problem was, and still is, that at low tide, there is only six inches of water in the canal.

–George Washington Tiernan (author, dentist, and historian), *Kings Park: A Pictorial History, 1870–1960*, 2007

Considering the Nissequogue River's importance to Kings Park, it made a great deal of sense for the hospital to build an easier connection to the waterways. An old dock already existed in the cove when the county farm was established. It was located on the east side of the dam, which had been built to create a reservoir. This dam was rebuilt and extended in November 1886 at a cost of $1,800. This expense had not been previously authorized, although it was necessary to allow deliveries by barge and for creating a road to pass over that could reach the northern part of the property at Jones Point. Apparently, the old dam had fallen victim to weather erosion from the freezing of the water during the winter.

As of the spring of 1887, all work would continue under the distant but watchful eye of the new medical superintendent, Dr. Daniel A. Harrison, who was based in Kings County. By this time, former Charities commissioner Joseph Reeve was no longer residing at the county farm to watch over operations, as he had done during the first year or so.

In January 1888, when the County Farm Committee paid a visit to the grounds to inspect the progress, they were not very pleased. The dam that was built by Charles Hart had caved in so badly that the overflow pipes broke. It was the same with the sewer. Both were in need of major repairs. It was going to cost additional money for labor and supplies.

According to a newspaper article, both the upper and lower reservoirs already existed in November 1891, but they would still require a great deal of work. The storage reservoir had a capacity of at least seven million gallons of pure spring water, while the distributing reservoir had an additional two million gallons.

In 1892, near the end of November, a proposal was made for the improvement and extension of the sewers to accommodate the new buildings being added in accordance with plans and specifications prepared by supervising engineer James F. Carey.

In 1896, a small canal was dug out near a small cove at the Nissequogue River through the surrounding wetlands, cutting a path from the mouth of the river straight into the hospital property. Construction continued into the next year at a cost of $11,800.50.

Not long after, the canal was greatly improved and widened, making deliveries by barge much easier, cutting down travel time, and lessening the amount of turns required to reach the dock at the cove. Barges would come from Manhattan across the Long Island Sound and bring in supplies, mainly coal for the boiler house, only a few yards from the dock. Low tide was a problematic issue when it came time for a barge to make a coal delivery. After passing through the canal, a tugboat would be required to tow the barges through the cove toward the dock. In the beginning, an employee named Edward Clark piloted the tugboat.

Kings Park Bluff, circa 1920

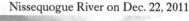

Nissequogue River on Dec. 22, 2011

Entrance to the canal on May 11, 2016

Looking down the canal from
the beach on May 11, 2016

Facing north through the
canal on Sept. 15, 2014

The canal heading into the marina
& boathouse on May 11, 2011

Considering construction on the canal began at the same time the hospital's railroad spur was completed, it is likely coal was only delivered by barge for a couple of years at the most. Once the spur was extended to the heating plant, it became much faster to receive coal deliveries by train. That did not mean use of the canal had to be discontinued, although it was no longer used for regular deliveries by barge.

It did not stop the hospital from constructing an additional forty-foot dock near the original coal dock, forming a T-shaped pier, after much of the dock was carried away by storms in 1897. Also, one hundred feet of the sewer that emptied into the river near this dock was overhauled to avoid clogging, and one thousand feet of new sewage piping was installed. At some point, probably during the 1890s, a boathouse was built on the south bank of the cove.

KPPC sewer tunnels map, circa 2002

In 1898, trenches were dug alongside the canal to prevent surface water from running into it or washing sand and other materials into it. Another measure taken to prevent this was implemented at a nearby outlet creek, where wooden pegs were driven in at the sides, and barrels filled with sand or stone were then placed there to block the washing in of sand.

As use of the canal lessened, it gradually became abandoned. By 1915, it was being referred to as the old canal on the hospital's annual report. Still, this would not be the end of the canal. It would have other uses in the near future.

In 1920, a new boathouse (Building 55) was erected to replace the old one, and a small marina was established with new docks replacing the older T-shaped dock. Of course, only small boats were allowed to dock at the marina because of the shallow waters of the canal. This renewal of the area brought new life to the cove and old canal.

Unfortunately, it came with a price. Whenever the tide receded, it was virtually impossible for most boats to travel along the canal. In a few areas of the canal, the water was no more than three inches deep, which was worse than before. The canal was obviously in need of dredging to clear out buildup at the bottom of the river.

All boats had to be removed and relocated during certain times of the year when the tide was at its lowest to prevent the boats from becoming beached. It is still common practice today. Boats must regularly be removed from the canal by mid-October of each year.

During the mid-1960s, a private yacht club for hospital employees purchased an old abandoned barge that had been beached along the south bank of the cove for several years from a private company named Grumman. The barge was relocated closer to the marina on the west bank of the canal, and a clubhouse was built on the deck.

An improved marina was constructed at the boat basin between the years 1968 and 1972. By 1976, the marina was extended beyond the canal across the river where the water was not as shallow.

Aerial photo of canal from March 1962   Aerial photo of canal
                                               from April 10, 1976

Soon after the hospital closed, the abandoned barge became a part of the Nissequogue River State Park. Over the years, the barge and the neighboring boathouse had fallen into disrepair like so many other structures on the former state hospital grounds.

By the fall of 2012, both were heavily damaged by Hurricane Sandy, which tore up a great deal of coastal areas of both New York and New Jersey. The boathouse and barge were demolished by the end of January 2013 in an attempt to improve the appearance of the boat basin. Only a small structure remains along the shores from the old hospital days, serving as a restroom for visitors.

For many years, seafaring people have used the marina at this cove to set sail for the Long Island Sound. Today, the marina is still in use by the people of Kings Park. The docks are typically full of life by late spring and during the summertime. However, in the winter months, the waters lie empty because of the low tide. It is a never-ending cycle for the boat owners who dock their boats here.

Tide schedules are regularly available to all boaters on pamphlets in the lobby of Building 125 (73A), the main office building of the park. They are also available online.

| Marina showing low tide on Dec. 22, 2011 | The marina a year later on July 5, 2012 |

Hospital Reservoirs and Water Supply

Owing to the present condition of the reservoir the water pressure in the cottages, and particularly in the four brick buildings (Buildings A–D), is extremely light and generally insufficient, even for sanitary purposes.

—William Paul Gerhard (consulting engineer for sanitary work), *2nd Annual Report of the Long Island State Hospital to the State Commission in Lunacy for the Year 1897*, February 23, 1897

As of May 1886, the board of supervisors at Kings County was shopping around for a Kings County contractor to build sewers and lay down water pipes at the newly established Kings County Farm at St. Johnland. At the time, no structures had been added yet. During the summer, a company named Wilson and Baillie of East New York was hired to do the job. The company normally dealt in concrete paving construction but occasionally worked on sewer pipes and steel sidewalk curbs. The job was well under way by September of the same year.

Pipes that were said to be the very best quality for sewer purposes were shipped out of Kings County by barge to the county farm property. Every once in a while, some of the pipes had broken at the collars during transport, but cement would be used to fill those broken sections once they were placed in the ground.

In November 1886, construction began on a dam made of sand under the supervision of Charities commissioner Joseph Reeve, creating a pond about one acre in size with a depth of five feet that could serve as a reservoir. It was supplied with a waste weir and overflow pipe to prevent it from getting too deep.

For many years, the hospital mainly used to gather its water supply from wells that were drilled near the shores of the Nissequogue River. The first wells were drilled during the early 1890s. These early wells only went down about forty-five feet, but the depth was gradually increased to about 50–120 feet. There were a few that were not too far from the medical superintendent's residence.

The water was then pumped out through pipes using a pump at a small pumping station, which ran continuously for about twelve hours each day. Two distributing main water pipes, a six-inch and a twelve-inch, connected this pumping station to a nearby pump house (Building 60) via an underground steam tunnel. The pump house, located behind the electric heating plant, was equipped with two larger condensing, direct-acting pumps and a noncondensing pump. Water was pumped to the other buildings of the hospital from here through water pipes that were installed in the underground tunnels.

Steam pipes near the main
junction area on Oct. 24, 2011

Sewage pipe crossing steam
tunnel on April 17, 2016

During the early 1890s, there were two reservoirs established on the hospital grounds. As of September 1892, they were both already in use. Improvements were made starting in 1893, but work would not be completed until 1897. The delay was due to the takeover by the state in 1895. New wells were dug to replace several of the old ones that had to be abandoned. The old wells were filled in with dirt and ash.

The dam between the cove and the reservoir was rebuilt from 1896 to 1897. It was much wider at the base and sturdy enough to support a road, which was about ten feet wide. The road connected to the new boulevard and extended it into the area of Kings Park Bluff and Jones Point. It is still in place today.

Dam separating the reservoir & canal, circa 1920s

The road over the old dam facing Building 125 (73A) on May 11, 2011

The first of the reservoirs to be completed was the current duck pond that exists near the boat basin at the Nissequogue River State Park. It was fed by natural springs. In *The City That Was Kings Park* by Leo Polaski, he described it as an "earthen reservoir." It can be found on several old maps listed as a reservoir. This reservoir became known as the upper reservoir, since it was located on the northern part of the property. It is only about six feet deep, although it was intended to act as a storage reservoir with a depth of twenty feet. Water would be pumped into it and kept for when it was needed.

The second reservoir, also an earthen reservoir, became the lower reservoir. It was located at the highest point of the main boulevard between East First Street and Flynn Road, across from the future site of Buckman Center. Wagonloads of dirt had to be removed to dig a hole large enough that could be filled with water. The dirt was then used to form an embankment around it.

Facing south on the boulevard toward the lower reservoir, 1910s-1920s

Facing south over the lower reservoir, circa 1932

There were a few concerns created by these reservoirs. Both the upper and lower reservoirs were soon found to have several challenging issues, preventing them from remaining in use for too long. Shortly after being constructed, the lower reservoir suffered from surface drainage. This led to it being abandoned early on. The upper reservoir had leaking problems that prevented it from ever reaching its intended depth of twenty feet. Anytime the water rose higher than six feet, it began to leak. Without a sufficient amount of water, there was no way the hospital could ever supply all of its widely spread buildings adequately. A new solution had to be found.

Between 1897 and 1898, the hospital turned to the nearby pond on the Harned farm. The hospital made an

Harned's Pond, circa 1910s-1930s

agreement with Henry Harned and rented his pond for several decades to follow. A platform was installed to support a pump that was connected to new wells dug in the vicinity of this pond. In addition, the hospital constructed another dam at the nearby cove to prevent injury to their waterline while making sure the pond did not drain. Over the following years, they constantly had to maintain this dam, but it was worth the effort to keep their water supply intact.

Unfortunately, the water being drawn from Harned's Pond contained too much debris, making it virtually undrinkable. To make matters worse, the water pressure in the wells was diminishing, and salt water had started to seep in from the river. The salt water caused extensive rust and corrosion to the pipes and boilers throughout the hospital's property, which eventually had to be replaced at high cost. As a result, the hospital continued using the lower reservoir while making improvements to Harned's Pond.

In 1899, the dam at Harned's Pond was raised three feet. Also, the dam for laying water pipes across the swamp near the Nissequogue River was washed out until it was raised by four feet and made eight feet wider. This dam was sometimes used as a road as well.

During the same year, the Bacon Air Lift Company agreed to install a new water supply for the hospital. This new system would allow the water to be easily pumped from the wells near Harned's Pond rather than being hauled by patients, as it had been in the past. By the next year, this improvement helped with increasing the water pressure, although it was still weak. Plus, there was still the matter of pollution in the system that needed to be addressed.

A few standpipes were added and scattered around the grounds near and inside of some buildings for the purpose of increasing water pressure to the taller buildings such as the ones at Group 1. At the time, this group had one of the tallest buildings on the grounds (Building 115). A standpipe essentially acts as a cushion for the pumping engines preventing "water hammer" or shock to the pipes while also providing steam for heating. However, hard or fast lines could not be drawn from a standpipe. Fire hydrants are actually a type of standpipe, and the hospital had quite a few. Some of the older ones were replaced in 1900. New fire hydrants and standpipes were added in 1908 around the home of the superintendent, the main stable, and the storehouse.

| Fire hydrant near Building 3 on April 16, 2013 | Fire hydrant in front of Building 93 on April 16, 2013 | An open hydrant |

During the winter months, ice would be cut away out of the upper reservoir and from Harned's Pond. The ice was transported to the icehouse for storage. It was processed at a nearby ice plant.

It was essential for the hospital to manufacture and store its own ice because it would have been too costly to purchase ice from elsewhere. Ice cutting was a huge industry until the mid-1900s. In 1908 alone, 1,200 tons of ice was harvested from Harned's Pond. At least a third of whatever was collected could not be consumed because of pollutants.

In 1900, superintendent Oliver M. Dewing made a request to the state for funding so repairs could be made to the lower reservoir and to increase its capacity to a depth of seventeen feet. This request was denied, and the reservoir remained abandoned. In 1905, the lower reservoir was emptied of its stagnant water and cleaned out. A lot of grading was done to make it higher rather than deeper. It was then refilled with water, and a valve box shed was built to control it.

By 1910, it was still leaking, and large amounts of water were being wasted. To make matters worse, work had to be done at Harned's Pond because the dam had collapsed.

During the same year, the upper reservoir was temporarily drained and cleaned in the summertime in hopes of improving the water quality. Once it was refilled, it continued to have leaking issues. In time, it also became far too polluted. It was deemed unwise and unsanitary to continue using these reservoirs as water supplies. However, until money could be provided for a better solution, there was very little choice.

In the meantime, new wells were continuously drilled, while old ones were abandoned. They dug them deeper in search of cleaner water. Some of these new wells had a depth of five hundred feet. The water supply had to be made to reach the new groups of buildings that were added during the early 1910s. As was the case previously, wells had to be abandoned at times because of the excess of salt in the water and the corrosion it was causing to the water pipes.

In 1911, a test well was dug near the new power plant (Building 6) to see if the water in that area could be designated as drinkable, so it would be possible to drill more to increase the hospital's water supply. At one time, before Group 4 was built in the field across from the power plant area, there were natural springs. The springs were drained long ago, but it was believed the land there had potential for supplying water for the thousands of people at the hospital. The test was a success.

Within the next year, four more wells were drilled. Two additional wells were sunk in 1913, and another two were added two years later. Each of these new wells had an average depth of 450–500 feet and an average flow of 140 gallons per minute.

Kings Park Heritage Museum - www.KingsParkMuseum.com

Drilling a well near the TB cottages with a donkey engine nearby

In 1914, funds were allowed for the construction of a cistern with an eighty-thousand-gallon capacity in connection with the water supply. I believe the plan was to build it near the pump house or perhaps on higher ground somewhere along the west side of Old Dock Road. Funds were also allowed for connecting the reciprocating pumps to the cistern to act as an emergency pump, if needed. However, there is no evidence that this was ever done, and it was not mentioned again in the annual reports that followed. This particular year was one of great financial difficulty for the hospital, so these plans might have been put off indefinitely and ultimately scrapped.

Between 1917 and 1918, the Department of Health conducted a survey for the construction of a new underground concrete reservoir, along with underground connections from the present water supply system. The State Engineer's Department also did a survey for a proposed site to build this new reservoir.

By 1921, construction began up high on a hill beyond the dairy farm and piggery, near where the abandoned water tower now stands. At the time, the water tower did not exist. The reservoir was fed by well water using no treatment or additives. A small shed was erected to protect the water valves from harsh weather.

When the reservoir was completed two years later, it had a water capacity of 1.5 million gallons, the combined capacity of the three previous reservoirs. Because of its elevated location, water pressure would no longer be an issue.

At long last, the water situation was finally resolved. The other reservoirs were all abandoned. By the early 1920s, the lower reservoir was emptied. It was filled in with dirt and flattened out by the 1930s. The upper reservoir became a pond, a wrought iron fence was erected around it, and it was basically left in the hands of Mother Nature. Meanwhile, Harned's Pond was left to its owner.

The former upper reservoir on May 11, 2011

Duck pond through the iron fence on May 11, 2011

Old signposts at the former lower reservoir site on July 11, 2011

Flagpole at the former lower reservoir site on July 11, 2011

After the construction of the new reservoir, the old pump house became inadequate to supply water to the entire hospital, especially from its distant location from the new reservoir. In 1939, a new pumping station and steam pipe junction house, Building 85, was created next to the new power plant.

By the late 1950s, a water tower was built near the new reservoir. The main purpose of the water tower was to apply hydrostatic pressure to the waterline system, while the reservoir stored the bulk of the water. The water tower had a capacity of five hundred thousand gallons and was less susceptible to pollution or freezing. This became the ideal solution for the hospital. In 1958, six new brick well houses were drilled in the vicinity of the power plant to increase the water supply. An underground receiving basin was added beneath the one on Industrial Road behind Building 57.

KPPC waterlines map, circa 2002

The water tower and wells would continue to supply water to the hospital until it closed. Use of the reservoir was discontinued by the early 1960s.

Today, the water tower is just an empty shell. Water can still be heard flowing underground at the old reservoir. The abandoned well houses still stand scattered on both sides of Old Dock Road like small monoliths of the past.

Water tower on
Sept. 15, 2014

Looking up at the water
tower on May 11, 2011

An old well house
near Old Dock Road
on April 28, 2013

By the 2000s, Harned's Pond had been renamed Harrison's Pond. Since 2004, the pond has been drying up after a terrible storm caused major damage to what was left of the old dam. Many years had gone by since it was maintained, so it was easily destroyed. It looks nothing like it once did. It is a far cry from the salvation it once represented for a growing hospital at the turn of the century. Time and Mother Nature can be deadly enemies even to the most beautiful landscapes and landmarks.

The area is currently a park for local residents.

Harrison's Pond Park sign on Jan. 22, 2016

Harrison's Pond drain into the Nissequogue River on Jan. 22, 2016

Harrison's Pond on Jan. 22, 2016

Shallow water at Harrison's Pond on Jan. 22, 2016

CHAPTER 15

The Railroad Spur

The Kings Park State Hospital Railroad Spur

The trains roared in on iron rails, bringing people from places he had never seen, taking them away to places he had only heard about.
    –Victoria Wilcox (author), *Inheritance*, 2013

T HE LONG ISLAND Railroad was established in the 1830s, but it did not reach the village now known as Kings Park until 1872, when a branch was extended further out to Eastern Long Island. In those earlier days, the area where the station was established was better known as Indian Head. However, the station was named the St. Johnland Station to identify the location as being related to the Society of St. Johnland.

When the hospital was established as a farm colony in 1885, most of its buildings were far from the railroad station. Therefore, anyone visiting the hospital by train would most likely pay for a livery coach to take them from the railroad station onto the hospital grounds. Otherwise, it was quite a long walk.

One such company was the J. J. Cusick Livery Stable, whose horse-drawn wagons carried passengers and supplies from one point of the village to another, including to the county farm. There were also livery services owned by other local families such as the Clayton and Carlson families.

In the fall of 1889, the Department of Charities and Corrections was seeking a company to build a 1.3-mile railroad spur at the Kings County Farm to connect to the railroad for the transportation of coal and other things. The selected contractor would also be required to supply the various building materials needed. A proposal was drawn up, and an advertisement was placed in the newspapers. One such ad appeared in the *Brooklyn Daily Eagle* on September 29, 1889.

By 1893, the Kings Park Station served as the county farm's railway and telegraph station as well as its post office. The railroad station had its own Western Union office, which the county farm made full use of to stay in touch with the main asylum at Kings County. It was around this time when steps were taken to

Original Kings Park Station, circa 1910s-1920s

make its use more convenient for the county farm. It was decided that a railroad spur extending onto the county farm property would serve the asylum well.

Construction began in 1895 during the same year the county farm became a state-owned hospital. This new railroad spur would become the second largest in the state, spanning two miles in length and descending from 175 feet to thirty feet above sea level. By the completion of this project about a year later, the station would have three rail lines. Two passed in front of the station heading to eastern Long Island, while the third passed along the rear of the station on its way to the hospital.

Laying down the railroad during the mid-1890s was no easy task. It required the use of picks, shovels, and sledgehammers.

Railroad track sample diagram
on Oct. 28, 2013

It was a very laborious job, and it often took a whole team of men to get the job done. First, the land had to be cleared of trees, brush, and rocks. Hundreds of railroad ties were placed an equal distance apart from each other as the foundation of the iron road with ballast laid out for the track bed.

Next came the laying of heavy iron rails over the ties that had to be evenly parallel to one another. Large spikes had to be driven into place to hold it all together.

This work all had to be done in a very specific manner. The railroad ties had to be eight feet by six inches in size with twenty-four ties per thirty-nine feet of rail, twenty ties per thirty-three feet of rail, and eighteen ties per thirty feet of rail. Each joint had to be supported on three ties, which all had to be creosoted and made of white oak, yellow pine, or some other kind of wood agreed upon by the Long Island Railroad. Two steel or wrought iron tie plates were used on each tie. The track spikes were either made from soft steel or wrought iron. Either chisel type or Goldie type was acceptable. Two staggered spikes were used to fasten each rail to each tie while avoiding splitting the ties accidentally. The rails were the standard type adopted by the railroad company. Cinders from the power plant's boiler house were normally used as ballast for the tracks, but rocks could be used as well.

However, to build the railroad spur along the route most convenient for the hospital, the state had to make a few necessary land purchases. One in particular was an eleven-acre parcel of land that went right through the middle of the Kelly farm. This parcel of land included the area where his home stood. Once the land was purchased, John Kelly built a new house further north on Church Street on a parcel of land that still belonged to him.

The former Kelly house was not demolished. Instead, it was used as a home for the hospital's farm supervisor until the 1960s.

After the railroad spur was completed, it instantly undermined passenger service and the freight wagon business for local livery services. People could now take the train straight onto the state hospital grounds. The state hospital's railroad spur was used for the transportation of patients, coal, construction materials, and other goods.

In 1900, the Long Island Railroad provided the hospital with specially designed railcars for the transportation of the mentally insane. Special compartments were set up in two of their passenger coach railcars, where the patients would have privacy without the curious annoyance of other passengers, or vice versa. Patients could now be transferred directly onto hospital grounds from Kings County and Manhattan more safely.

The train took an interesting route through the hospital grounds. The railroad spur began a few feet east of Mile Post 43 on the Port Jefferson branch, where it broke off from the main line just west of the Kings Park Station. After passing the rear of the station, it continued east and crossed over Indian Head Road before making a sharp curve to the north and crossing East Main Street/Route 25A onto the former Kelly property. It passed over a small gorge shortly before entering the hospital grounds right around where Building 151 currently stands.

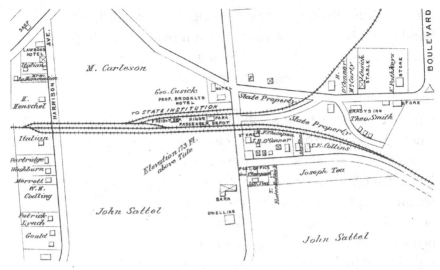

Belcher Hyde map from 1909, showing the Kings Park Station

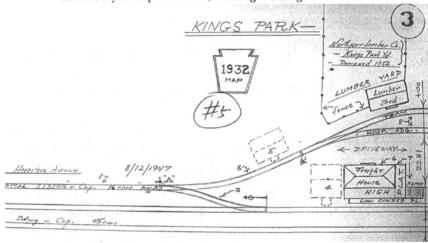

Diagram of the Kings Park Station, as it was in 1932

Once on the grounds, it traveled north on the west of the boulevard. The first siding was the passenger platform, which was located just south of the Flynn Road crossing, before the Group 1 buildings. It ran parallel to the west side of the boulevard. The platform consisted of concrete-lined soil and could only fit up to three cars.

Prior to the construction of the platform, passengers stepped on and off the train at the ground level. The platform was built in 1910 for the convenience of the passengers boarding and disembarking the train. The passenger trains always arrived on Sundays with three passenger cars at most. Some referred to it as the Kings Park State Hospital Sunday excursion.

Whenever the train stopped at the platform, the passenger cars were unhooked from the engine and left here. The engine would then carefully back out of the hospital grounds until it reached the Kings Park Station. With only the crew aboard, it continued on to Port Jefferson to get serviced. The crew would take a break, and sometime later, the engine returned to the hospital to pick up the passenger cars. It would back up the spur until it could be reattached to the passenger cars.

Diagram of the KPSH spur & hospital platform near the boulevard in 1934

Freight trains carrying coal bypassed this stop at the passenger platform. Throughout the years, coal was the principal commodity delivered by train. These trains would continue on over Flynn Road past the back of Group 1 on its way toward the power plant area. That is where it got scary. The grade dropped considerably to a 3.3 percent downgrade. Slippage was always a major concern when backing a loaded coal train down through that area. What made it more dangerous was that this area was completely covered by trees.

The track continued north along the east side of Old Dock Road crossing over Third Street and dipped down, passing through where the final power plant (Building 29) would eventually be built. From there, it continued to follow the route of the current hike-and-bike trail going behind Tiffany Field toward St. Johnland Road. At that point, it crossed over a wooden trestle.

Once on the other side, it passed adjacent to the buildings of Group 2 before the tracks split into three directions on the broad lawn, thanks to a switch that was added in 1898. One track continued northbound on the east side of the boulevard to the heating plant (Building 59), where it came to a stop on another wooden trestle. Coal chutes where installed in that area so coal could be dropped into the coalbunker. In later years, this building was converted into an ice plant. The newer track went east and stopped across the boulevard between the original storehouse and bakery, where it delivered supplies to those buildings. A third siding went to the original laundry building until the early 1900s.

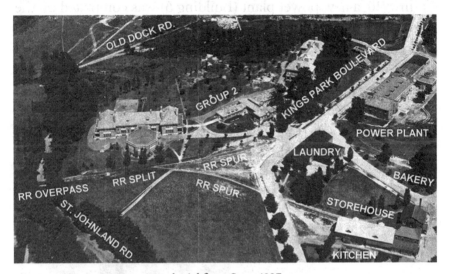

Aerial from Sept. 1927

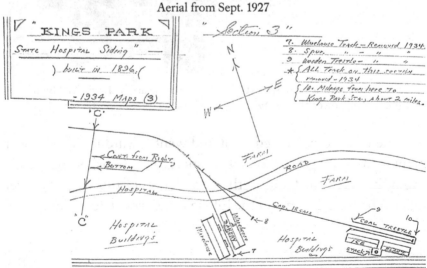

Diagram showing the hospital spur splitting in 1934

In the spring of 1906, the entire wooden trestle near the heating plant and coal shed had to be removed and rebuilt. The railroad company had condemned the old one and refused to allow trains onto it. There was a delay in replacing it because the railroad company failed to deliver the promised supplies in a timely manner. By the time it was rebuilt several months later, the coal scales had also been replaced.

In 1910, a new power plant (Building 6) was completed on the site near the new laundry. It became necessary to add a new siding to the spur. After crossing over Third Street and heading north along Old Dock Road, the spur would split in two. The original track still went north past St. Johnland Road to make deliveries to the storehouse and bakery, but by the mid-1930s, it would stop at the new storehouse (Building 44) instead. There would no longer be a need to cross over St. Johnland Road.

Diagram of the hospital spur at
the second power plant in 1934

Graphic art, by David M. Flynn,
showing train on power plant trestle

The new siding veered right and went toward the new power plant area, leading to a wooden trestle. Excavations for this trestle began in 1911, shortly after the completion of the second power plant. The trestle came off the hill near the west side of Building 5.

Train passing behind
Group 1, circa 1969

Train crossing W. Third St.
behind Group 1, circa 1969

Train with Building 93 in the
background, circa 1969

Train passing Building 5 &
backing onto trestle, circa 1969

After the ten buildings of Group 1 were built in 1898, an auxiliary boiler house had to be added nearby at the turn of the century. In 1901, the railroad spur was extended once more to reach this boiler house, which would only last until 1912. A trestle was added by 1902.

Modified Belcher Hyde map,
showing the Group 1 spur in 1909

Map from 1912, showing the
railroad spur at Group 1

Railroad spur near Group 1, circa 1913

In 1912, a path was cut from Kings Park Boulevard to Old
Dock Road right next to the hospital's passenger platform, making
getting to the train much easier from both sides. It shortened the
distance considerably for those approaching from Old Dock Road.
This path would later become known as Flynn Road, named for
the family that often crossed through there to work at the hospital.

During the same year, another switch was added for a new
section of the spur that turned toward the piggery. This new siding
was called the manure fork. It split out westward just north of
Flynn Road, after the passenger platform, and crossed Old Dock
Road stopping at the piggery. The railroad delivered loads of horse

manure all the way from New York City. The manure would then be used as fertilizer for the farm.

One can only imagine the combination of odors that came from the piggery and the manure pile on a hot summer's day.

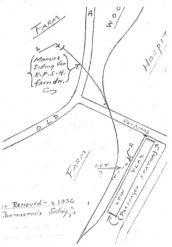

The railroad bridge that crossed over St. Johnland Road was repaired and repainted between 1919 and 1920. After the last power plant was built, the section of the spur that led to it was the last section to ever be used in later years. The portions that stretched beyond the power plant were all removed by the 1930s, including the trestle over St. Johnland Road.

Diagram showing the manure siding in 1934

When the hospital railroad was first put into service, it used steam engines. During the 1930s, the railway systems of the world had already begun phasing out steam engines in favor of electric trains. The use of electrical power was obviously more practical than coal, although it was an expensive changeover. Fortunately, the steam engines of old still had a few good years left in them. The hospital railroad would continue using steam engines until the 1940s.

Steam engine leaving the power plant area, circa 1910s-1930s

Steam engine passing behind Group 1, circa 1910s-1930s

Whenever the train delivering coal reached the power plant area, the loaded coal cars would have to be detached and reattached to its other side. This required a bit of ingenuity, since there was no way for the locomotive to turn around on the hospital grounds.

First, the locomotive partially pulled into the power plant siding. The loaded coal cars behind it would be unhooked. Workers would then push these cars down the storehouse fork on the left and leave them there temporarily. At this time, the engineer would operate the locomotive facing the opposite direction. Next, the locomotive backed down the power plant siding and picked up the empty coal cars that were left there from the previous delivery. It would then pull these cars up the hill past Building 5 and travel back down Old Dock Road to the siding along the west side of the boulevard near the passenger platform at Flynn Road. Afterward, the train would go back to the storehouse fork to pick up the full coal cars.

Once they were attached, the engineer had to switch sides again. The loaded coal cars were hauled up to the switch for the power plant siding, and then the entire train had to carefully back up onto the trestle to drop off the coal cars, which would be unloaded by hospital workers and patients. The locomotive was detached from the coal cars, and then it traveled back up the hill all the way to the passenger platform to retrieve the empty cars from the siding. Its next destination was the coalmines in the south. Upon its return, the process was repeated.

Train 229 backing up on the trestle
to the power plant, circa 1970s

Train backing up on the trestle
over piles of coal, circa 1970s

Coal cars on power plant trestle, circa 1970s

Train 223 at the passenger platform on Kings Park Boulevard, circa 1970s

During harsh weather or other unforeseen conditions, sometimes a coal car would slide off the end of the trestle while the train was backing up. It did not happen often, only when the conditions were bad enough. Still, there were quite a few accidents during the history of the hospital spur. Thankfully, they were not fatal.

One accident that occurred as a result of backing up onto the trestle took place on August 25, 1913. As the coal cars were backing onto the trestle near the second power plant, the railroad engineer approached too fast and bumped the last car, knocking it off the trestle and forty feet down to the ground, along with a trainman on the car. The trainman was seriously injured when he was thrown, but he did not die. Considering there were numerous other workers and patients in the area at the time, it is a miracle no one was crushed by the coal car.

A similar incident happened on August 31, 1917. This time, Peter Hildenbrand was there to photograph the accident.

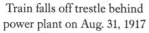

| Train falls off trestle behind power plant on Aug. 31, 1917 | Aerial from 1940 showing power plant trestle |

The wooden trestle near the second power plant was replaced with steel and concrete in 1934. The replacement trestle was eight railcar lengths long and was elevated by approximately twenty sturdy concrete pillars that stood nearly twenty-five feet tall. The tracks were set on steel beams situated atop the pillars.

On each side of the trestle was a catwalk, so the crews could empty the coal cars and dump the coal for the power plant and its boiler house.

For many years, patients were transported to the hospital via the railroad in special railroad cars. However, this practice was gradually discontinued after the hospital acquired a fleet of buses in 1936. The buses were less costly and provided more privacy.

In 1939, there was a contract to demolish and reconstruct the approaching railroad tracks on the east side of Old Dock Road near the power plant area. This work included necessary excavations, grading of the land, and removal of the old coal bin roof. All pieces removed had to be disposed of by the company that agreed to take on the contract.

As of the 1940s, most railroad companies in the United States had finally begun to use diesel locomotives instead of steam engines. It was not until the 1950s that most railroad companies discontinued the use of steam engines, once and for all. Diesel engines were far easier to maintain and only required one person to operate them. This reduced operating costs significantly while increasing reliability and speed.

In 1947–1948, the old Kings Park Station was torn down, and a new station was built in its place.

Kings Park Station, circa 1950s   The switch on the tracks west of the station, circa 1940s-1950s   An old railroad switch

For the train to go toward the hospital from the main line, a switch had to be opened. It would have to be closed right after the train passed. Failing to do so usually ended in disaster. This occurred in 1947, when an eastbound train crossed First Avenue, called Harrison Avenue at the time. The train went off the tracks only one hundred yards away from the Kings Park Station as a result of the switch accidentally being left in the open position. There were fifty-five people injured, but none were critical. However, the train was virtually turned into a thirteen-car accordion.

Train derailment near water tower from 1947   A worker assesses the damage   Passengers & onlookers gather near the 1947 wreckage

Later that night, crews of workers removed the rail cars to the side of the tracks. They then worked feverishly to repair the three hundred feet of track that was torn up during the derailment. They wanted to make sure the tracks would be ready for use the next day.

On September 24, 1966, a coal hopper rolled off the coal trestle and fell toward the second storehouse. It did no damage to the building, and no one was hurt. However, the accident temporarily disrupted the hospital's coal service. By this time, Building 29 had just been completed as the new power plant, taking over for both Buildings 6 and 84.

Coal car falls from trestle near
storehouse on Sept. 24, 1966

Looking at it from the other
side on Sept. 24, 1966

Looking up at the trestle
on Sept. 24, 1966

Axle & wheels from train
car on Sept. 24, 1966

Front end of coal car on the
ground on Sept. 24, 1966

Coal cars from Pennsylvania falls off
the trestle near the storehouse

While railroad electrification in the United States began shortly after the start of the twentieth century, it did not reach Long Island for many years. As of 1970, the electrification of tracks only extended from Mineola to Huntington, which was just west of Kings Park. For the next fifteen years, it was only a single track from Amott Interlocking, east of Syosset Station to west of Huntington. In 1985, the LIRR finally constructed a second electrified track to avoid bottlenecking of trains. For years, there was anticipation of extending the electrified line to Port Jefferson.

A train riding up the boulevard, circa 1960s   The same area on April 19, 2016

However, in lieu of electrification, the railroad turned to using dual-mode locomotives, or electro-diesel locomotives, which could switch between diesel power and electrical power. The LIRR began using these locomotives during the late 1990s, which did very little to help the hospital, since it was ready to close by then.

A typical train to the hospital included three ALCO RS-1 four-axle diesel-electric locomotives. These models were built from 1941 to 1953 and used until the 1960s. Afterward, the trains normally consisted of eight cars of coal with two C420s, ALCO Century 420 diesel-electric, 2,000-horsepower, four-axle locomotives. These were used until the final days of the spur. The American Locomotive Company (ALCO) manufactured both models.

An ALCO RS-1 engine at the passenger platform, circa 1964

ALCO C-420 on spur approaching Main St. on July 28 1984

In the 1980s, the LIRR brought coal in either eight or sixteen-car trains. Only about eight cars fit on the coal trestle at a time. Generally, two C420 engines would be used for sixteen cars to compensate for the added weight, while only one engine would be used for eight cars.

If there were sixteen cars on a train, then eight would be dropped off at the passenger siding on Kings Park Boulevard. They would be removed, and then the other eight would be pulled forward to clear the switch. They would then be backed all the way to the coal trestle.

The coal was usually dumped into large piles between the final power plant and second storehouse. Someone from the storehouse would log in the deliveries of coal, and then it would be brought over to the power plant using wheelbarrows, or wheel barrels, which is actually the original name.

The use of coal was gradually phased out during the late 1980s in favor of oil. Trains were no longer used by the hospital afterward.

Train 224 traveling on the spur beside the boulevard, circa April 1984

Train 224 traveling on the spur beside the boulevard, circa April 1984

Train 224 traveling on the spur beside the boulevard, circa April 1984

Train 224 leaving hospital grounds on July 19 1984

As an interesting footnote, today, the line that extends west of Huntington finally runs on double electrified tracks.

Kings Park Station & tracks on Oct. 20, 2013

Removal of the Spur

Mental wounds still screaming . . . Driving me insane . . . I'm goin'
off the rails on a crazy train.
          –Ozzy Osbourne (singer and songwriter), *Crazy Train*,
                                                                1980

As time went on, the need for the railroad spur became less
necessary. Sections of it were abandoned and forgotten, much like
the buildings. Of course, removing the railroad was far simpler
than building it. The unnecessary portions of the railroad spur
were demolished one section at a time, while any remaining tracks
were paved over until there was almost nothing left.

One portion of the railroad spur that did not last very long was
the extension to Group 1, added in 1901. When the temporary
boiler house there was no longer needed in 1912, it was demolished.
The railroad siding and wooden trestle that led to it were also
removed. This was the first major section of the spur to be taken

out. Building 15 was later built on the spot of the temporary boiler house, erasing any trace of this railroad spur extension.

The wooden trestle that crossed over St. Johnland Road was the next major section to be removed in 1934. All sidings north of St. Johnland Road, which included the forks that split out to the old heating plant, the former storehouse, and the old bakery, had to be removed. By this time, there were replacements for all of these structures to the south of St. Johnland Road in the vicinity of the second power plant.

For many years, hints of this portion of the railroad spur's existence could still be found behind Tiffany Field and near Group 2.

Another section of the railroad spur to be removed was the manure fork. It was removed in 1936, long before the abandonment of the piggery and dairy farm buildings. No signs of its existence remain, and there are practically no known photographs of these old sections of the spur.

The last passenger train came onto the hospital grounds on a Sunday of 1968, although it might have been in 1970. There is conflicting information regarding the correct year. The last coal train arrived in 1988, and then the spur was permanently shut down at the end of that year. Next came the task of using up the last of the coal.

One of the last passenger trains to visit
the hospital grounds, 1968-1970

A sign warning about
coal, circa 1970s

Some employees tried to help with this task by stealing coal and taking it home. It got so bad the safety officers had to patrol the coal piles at night. Signs were also put up warning people that the coal was not safe for home use.

In 1976, when Barry Charletta worked at Group 2, he saw a leftover railroad bulkhead hidden away by brush and trees in the southeast corner of the parking lot across the boulevard from Group 2. It was also covered with poison ivy. A bulkhead is basically a flatbed railcar. Barry recalls it was made of wood and iron.

The parking lot was actually the former site of the original laundry building. At the time, there were also some rails visible at the boulevard that belonged to the old laundry siding. The bulkhead was removed not long after.

By the late 1980s, Kings Park was the last major coal burning facility on Long Island. Since 1987, it had slowly been making its transition into a more efficient oil-fired system for environmental reasons while using up much of the huge pile of coal near the final power plant. The switch was expected to improve the air quality of the area that was constantly polluted by smoke from the power plant's smokestack.

Facing west toward the trestle near the power plant & Group 4, circa 1960s

The trestle in 1988, when coal deliveries came to an end

In mid-February 1989, the last bits of coal it would ever use were burned up. It had been using an average of approximately thirty thousand tons of coal per year. Aside from environmental benefits, switching to oil would be more economical. The Long Island Lighting Company (LILCO) supplied gas to the hospital as an alternative fuel source.

When the hospital was closed in 1996, the railroad spur had virtually been forgotten. For many years, it sat abandoned, along with the hospital buildings. By 2003, some portions of the track still remained, although the ties were gradually being removed. They were stacked in piles alongside the former spur's track route.

Later that year, the old route was converted into a hike-and-bike trail for the public. Most of the tracks had been removed or covered by pavement. The old concrete support pillars of the trestle were left in place near the abandoned power plant as stoic reminders of the hospital's once viable connection to the railroad.

In late 2007, informational signs were created and later set up along the trail, thanks to the Kings Park Chamber of Commerce and a grant partly funded by Suffolk County. Each of these signs provides a brief history of the nearest building or hospital section along the trail.

Originally, there were vintage photographs placed on each of these signs, but, unfortunately, vandals have managed to steal every last one of these photographs, as they were only held in place by glue because it would have been too expensive to have them engraved. The pictureless signs can still be seen today along the trail.

Hike & Bike Trail sign for Group 1 on Nov. 7, 2011

Hike & Bike Trail crossing Flynn Road on April 19, 2016.

The coal trestle's concrete support pillars were scheduled for removal during the fall of 2010, but the demolition project was delayed until 2012. Another piece of Kings Park history had come to a close. These days, there is very little evidence of the old railroad spur aside from old photographs and documentation.

Old trestle supports facing south toward Building 5 on Sept. 9, 2011

Old trestle supports facing north toward Building 44 on Sept. 9, 2011

However, if one looks hard enough, part of the railroad tracks along Flynn Road can still be found, and there is still a portion of the old concrete platform remaining as well as a few splintered ties. It is only a matter of time before the roads are repaved and these tracks disappear forever.

Before Flynn Rd was repaved, a rail could still be seen on July 11, 2011

This small portion is all that can be seen as of April 19, 2016

The former site of the passenger platform on April 19, 2016

Left over ties could still be found under the dirt on April 19, 2016

Facing south on the boulevard with ties on the ground on April 19, 2016

CHAPTER 16

Roads of the Hospital

Hospital Access Roads

Roads are no place for naive chickens dreaming of nirvana.
    –Shalom Auslander (author), *Hope: A Tragedy*, 2012

THE STREET NAMES of Kings Park are fascinating in that they reflect the growth and changes of the village. There are streets named for famous historic figures of the area, early settlers, Native American tribes or tribal language, politicians, and even a few of the village's early families that helped build this close-knit community.

There is no doubt the state hospital played a significant role in helping to shape the community. It brought in many individuals and families who migrated to Kings Park in search of work at the hospital. Some of these people became the backbone of the community. New businesses were established, and more people came.

Throughout these earlier times, some of the roads that exist today were not yet built. There are several roads that would later be established, leading onto the state hospital grounds. These very roads helped guide these aspiring new residents to their future paths.

In one of superintendent William A. Macy's annual reports, he expressed regret that the hospital roads were open to the people of the village. He felt there was no privacy for the patients while traffic constantly passed through hospital grounds to get from one end of the village to another. He also felt it was unwise to have schools built near hospital grounds because it posed a potential danger to the children to be so close to the mentally ill.

Had someone heeded his words back then, perhaps the students from the several schools that surround the abandoned psych center property would not be venturing into the abandoned buildings as often as they do today. The property is practically a stone's toss away from almost every school in Kings Park.

If Dr. Macy were alive today, he would not be pleased, considering the former hospital grounds still pose a danger to children. However, these days, it is no longer due to the proximity of the mentally ill but rather because of the dangers posed by the abandoned hospital buildings that seem to draw the children to the property in search of adventure.

In the beginning, the roads were all dirt or covered with gravel. Dirt roads tended to get quite muddy, so gravel was preferred. Every once in a while, the roads had to be covered with a special road oil to keep traffic from dragging the gravel and to prevent gravel from being blown away by wind. The oil also helped preserve the road, keeping it from wearing out too fast.

In time, the roads were paved over. Oftentimes when a road was made, there would be gutters added along the sides to prevent flooding. These were usually made of granite stone. Loam, which is a mixture of sand, clay, and silt, was sometimes placed around the roads to be used as topsoil.

Because of the poor construction methods used in the past, many of the roads, especially the main boulevard, required constant repairs. Squads of able-bodied patients were often employed for such work. Repairs were usually made using a combination of crushed stone, clay, and cinders.

Some of these roads that connect the hospital to the community have been around for a very long time. According to a map from 1865, Old Dock Road was simply known as Dock Road. Lawrence Avenue was known as both Rye Lot Road and Hog Pond Road. Sunken Meadow Road was the Old Northside Road, which connected to St. Johnland Road. East Main Street/Route 25A still had not been established. Instead, there was a road called Crooked Tree Road, cutting across the south end of the hospital property, near where Flynn Road would later be established. This portion of the road no longer existed by the 1890s.

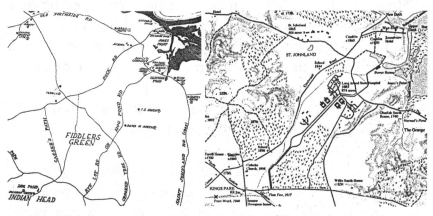

Map of Smithtown, circa 1865   Map of Kings Park, circa 1898

According to the property purchase map from 1885, which appeared in chapter 6 of this book, East Main Street/Route 25A was being referred to as the New Highway during its earliest years. It is also listed as such in a map from 1902. At first, it was numbered as Route 35. By 1909, it was called the Smithtown Road. It would later become East Main Street/Route 25A.

The first road created by the hospital while it was still a county farm would become its main boulevard. It was later named Kings Park Boulevard. This road for the most part has been the main artery of the hospital's roads. Work first began on the boulevard in November 1886, starting from St. Johnland Road and working its way south. It was decided the first permanent cottages would be built around it. At first, the boulevard did not extend to the new highway, although it was intended to reach it soon to provide quicker access to the railroad. Within the first month, work had progressed significantly. Of course, it was still far from being the wide thoroughfare it would someday become.

Belcher Hyde map from 1909, focusing on Smithtown Rd

In 1892, the Charities Commissioners drew up plans and specifications for a new improved boulevard. At the end of November of that year, a proposal was made for the improvement and macadamizing, or paving, of the roads. By this time, the work had progressed all the way through to the new highway. By 1893, most of the current boulevard was completed.

Once it was finished, it immediately became the main road of the hospital. It travels in a north-south direction, starting from East Main Street/Route 25A. It bends to the right and continues in a northeast direction around the lower reservoir, just past where Flynn Road now exists. It essentially divides the hospital into east and west halves, intersecting several of its streets in the process. The intersecting streets, added later, were also divided into east and west, creating an East and West Second Street, Third Street, and Fourth Street. First Street only existed on the east side.

Kings Park Boulevard,
circa Aug. 31, 1920s

Clearing the gravel from
the road, circa 1920s

Workers & equipment on
the road, circa 1920s

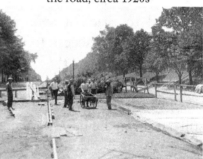

Widening the road, circa 1920s

Laying down the asphalt, circa 1920s

Starting in 1897, there was significant road building on the hospital grounds in connection with Buildings A–D and the buildings of Group 1. Roadwork continued here for the next couple of years. By this time, the hospital had a road roller for such purposes.

When the boulevard reaches St. Johnland Road, it also becomes R. Mastrocinque Avenue. After crossing St. Johnland Road, it enters into the northern section of the hospital currently known as the main section of the Nissequogue River State Park. At one time, it traveled past York Hall and between the buildings of Group 2 and where the original laundry and electric heating plant used to be. Now, there is only the abandoned York Hall and Building 40 of Group 2, which is hidden by trees, on the west side and the park's maintenance garage (Building 62) on the east side.

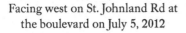

| Facing west on St. Johnland Rd at the boulevard on July 5, 2012 | Building 125 at the traffic circle on March 26, 2011 |

Shortly after passing that area, the boulevard crosses over the dam that separates the former upper reservoir from the boat basin. It then came to an end in front of Building 136 (73L). However, these days, it comes to an end at the traffic circle in front of Building 125 (73A), which is now the main office of the park.

In 1904, a footpath that ran parallel to the boulevard, leading from the cottages to the main entrance at East Main Street/Route 25A, was added. A portion of the boulevard was resurfaced in 1912 using Peekskill gravel, which made for a fine top dressing. In addition, the road next to the newly built Group 2 was adjusted from its original position slightly to the west, and the boulevard was extended leading to Group 3. There was another slight adjustment done sometime prior to 1915. This was before the boulevard ended in front of Building 136 (73L), beyond the traffic circle. That traffic circle was created when the Veterans' Memorial Hospital Unit was established in the mid-1920s.

Prior to the existence of Groups 2 and 3, the boulevard crossed over St. Johnland Road, around the east side of the employees' kitchen and dining hall, the original storehouse, and the main kitchen/bakery, banking westward to its current position, and continued over the dam. This can be seen in a few maps prior to 1912. The older portion of the boulevard remained in use and became a separate road called Garage Road. It leads to the maintenance garage and greenhouse. It is still used by the park personnel.

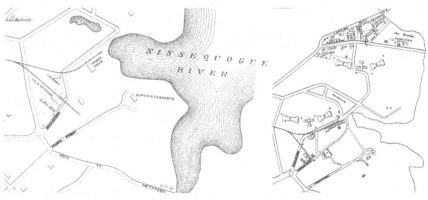

Belcher Hyde map from 1909, showing original route of the boulevard

Belcher Hyde map from 1917, showing how boulevard was adjusted

In 1920, there were eighteen cast-iron light poles installed along the length of the boulevard, which made traveling the road at night much easier and safer for all. For many years afterward, the boulevard would be well lit at night. Only now is it mostly darkened as a way of discouraging travelers from passing through at night when the park is closed.

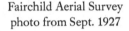

Fairchild Aerial Survey
photo from Sept. 1927

Map from 1865, showing site of St.
Johnland still owned by Abram Smith

St. Johnland Road cuts across the boulevard, dividing it into its north and south portions. This road was named after Dr. William A. Muhlenberg's Society of St. Johnland, which was established at Kings County during the 1860s. Dr. Muhlenberg did not purchase the land until 1870. Yet the 1865 map shows the road was named St. Johnland Road in 1865, which is not possible. The 1865 map must have been drafted at a later time and does not even show the Society of St. Johnland, as it was not built yet. The property is still listed as Abram Smith's. Therefore, the accuracy of this particular map is questionable.

St. Johnland Road extends east from Old Dock Road traveling through the former hospital grounds and eventually merges with East Main Street/Route 25A when it reaches San Remo. It reaches the end of its almost four-mile journey at Jericho Turnpike near the statue of the Bull, erected in honor of Richard "Bull" Smith, the founder of Smithtown. In an annual report from 1899, it is referred to as the Huntington Road, and it appears as such on a map from 1902. Today, it is mainly referred to as St. Johnland Road.

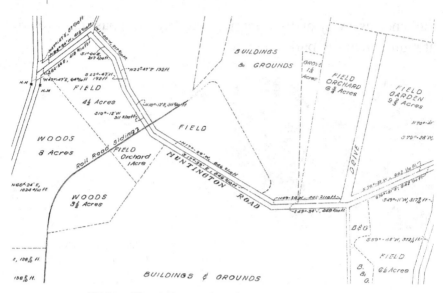

LI State Hospital map, 1902 showing Huntington Rd

On the other side of Old Dock Road heading westbound, the road becomes Sunken Meadow Road. According to a map from the 1700s, it was originally called the Sunk Meadow Road. At some point, it was called the Old Northside Road, since it travels along the north side of the village. It was called the Northside Road long before that. Another map from 1967 shows this part of the road as St. Johnland Road.

Map from the 1700s-1800s,
showing Sunk Meadow Rd

Smithtown Topographical
Geological Survey map, circa 1967

Old Dock Road travels in a north-south direction through the hospital grounds, separating the last reservoir used by the hospital, Potter's Field Cemetery, the dairy farm and piggery, and the buildings of Group 4 from the rest of the hospital grounds. During the 1700s, this road was known as the Cord Wood Road. It became known as Dock Road soon after Cornish Dock was built in 1844. Extensive repair work was done on the road in 1898 near the hospital's dairy farm. On a map from 1902, it actually appears as the Dairy Road because of the hospital's dairy farm. Superintendent Macy refers to it as the Dairy Barn Road in his first annual report from 1904. According to a map from 1917, the road is shown as both Cordwood Road and Dock Road, since it led to the dock. After the 1930s, the road remained with its current name, Old Dock Road.

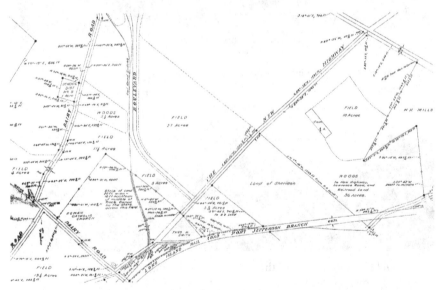

LI State Hospital map from 1902 showing the Dairy Rd

Dairy Rd facing north just before
the dairy barn on April 22, 1925

Near the old school house on the
Dairy Rd on April 22, 1925

Halfway between Sheridan's corner &
the old school house, April 22, 1925

Dairy Rd facing north toward
Group 3, April 22, 1925

Old Dock Rd facing north
on Sept. 9, 2011

Facing south on Old Dock
Rd on Dec. 19, 2012

Old Dock Road continues north past St. Johnland Road, coming to an end at the beach near Kings Park Bluff, but appears to split in two just before reaching it. It actually continues on the left. The road, which begins at the right, is called Upper Dock Road. This one-block-long, inverted C-shaped street once acted as a border for the northern end of the hospital with its staff houses, along the edge of the property line across from private residential homes that belonged to Kings Park villagers.

Old Dock Rd facing north toward
Upper Dock Rd, 1920s

Old Dock Rd facing south from
Upper Dock Rd, 1920s

In 1916, Albert L. Potter Inc. made a business proposal to the hospital. This corporation wished to build a mill on Old Dock Road near the power plant (Building 6). In exchange for obtaining free water for its boiler and the right to conduct its business on hospital property, Albert L. Potter Inc. was willing to provide the best timber at a reasonably discounted price, all slabs of wood, and any sawdust. It would also be the hospital's responsibility to supply men to remove the slabs and sawed lumber each day.

This was not a deal the state wished to accept, so this mill was never constructed at the location. It certainly would have been interesting to see an old mill on the west side of Old Dock Road.

Heading south on Old Dock Road will eventually lead you to Church Street. However, before St. Joseph's Church was erected and the street was renamed, it was the northern part of Indian Head Road. Before that, it was once called Commack Road because it connects to the village of Commack. Old Dock Road continues past it and comes to an end at East Main Street/Route 25A. Afterward, it becomes Pulaski Road.

There was another access road that traveled north and south. It first appears on a map from 1897, but the road is not named on the map. It is the same case with the previously shown map from 1898. The road was called Student Road. It extended from East Main Street/Route 25A right across from Kings Park High School, traveled north through the woods, and intersected East Third Street before connecting with East Fourth Street just south from St. Johnland Road. It basically went along the east side of Buildings 7, 21–23, 1–3, and 82, running parallel to Lawrence Road, called Lover's Lane at the time. By the 1950s, this hospital road begins to fade from the maps and does not appear on any from the 1960s.

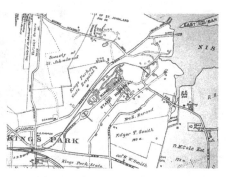

Belcher Hyde map with the Student Road between the boulevard & Lover's Lane, circa 1917

The southernmost portion of the road was abandoned and forgotten. The area near Buildings 7 and 21–23 was merged with another road called Roundtree Road that encircled most of these buildings. A part of the road just north from there was merged with East Third Street, while the northern section near the early female cottages was still very much in use until the 1970s.

During the 1980s, the leftover fragments of this road slowly fell into disrepair. By the 1990s, it was almost completely overgrown. All that remains now is a small portion behind where Building 82 once stood. Soon enough, it will become one with nature.

Student Rd facing north on July 11, 2011   Student Rd facing south on July 11, 2011

One former resident of Kings Park and employee of the KPPC can still remember the road in detail. Barry Charletta, who worked at Group 2 in the 1970s, recalls, *"I remember that the southernmost part of the road, the section between Buildings 7, 21, and 22 and 25A, was also navigable because the hospital safety officers would drive down there. I also remember seeing the road exit from the woods across from Kings Park High School, but it went no farther south, at that time.*

"The first time I made note of its existence was when I was gazing out of the window of a second-floor classroom. There was always a hollow at the wood line at that location, but I saw the front of a hospital Safety Department car sticking out on that day. While working at the hospital many years later, we took a walk up the road with patients.

"It was paved with blacktop, but the portion of road in the woods south of Building 22 was deteriorating rapidly with trees down across it, holes in the pavement, and no discernable edges. Both ends of the road were blocked by piles of demolition debris, likely placed to prevent vehicle traffic."

While most of the Student Road has more or less disappeared, the road it once connected to is still around. East Fourth Street still connects to St. Johnland Road, but it is closed to traffic. This road runs from the boulevard across from Building 93 to the staff cottages behind Macy Home, all abandoned now. It then turns left at Student Road and exits onto St. Johnland Road. It once continued on the north side of St. Johnland Road and led directly to the superintendent or director's residence. That side is also closed to traffic and has been for quite some time.

Postcard of Superintendent's driveway facing south toward St. Johnland Rd

E. Fourth St. facing south on Jan. 2, 2016   E. Fourth St. facing north into the
                                                old driveway on Jan. 2, 2016

Mariner Road is divided in half by trees, although there was a time when it was connected. It leads onto the property from the north side of St. Johnland Road and leads to the sewage disposal plant. The road seemingly ends there, and it is only open to authorized vehicles. In the past, the road used to continue along the south bank of the boat basin and connected to the boulevard, just south of the old dam.

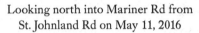

Looking north into Mariner Rd from
St. Johnland Rd on May 11, 2016

Heading east on Mariner Rd from
St. Johnland Rd on Oct. 5, 2015

Lawrence Road borders the hospital on its easternmost side running in a north-south direction. It used to go from East Main Street/Route 25A to St. Johnland Road until it was shortened. It now connects to Yale Lane, which connects to Bowman Lane, and then Squire Lane. It is now Squire Lane that connects to St. Johnland Road.

Lawrence Road is actually a very old road. It goes back to colonial times and appeared on a map from the 1700s. It is possible it was named after Daniel Lawrence, a grandson to Richard "Bull" Smith, the founder of Smithtown. Lawrence died in 1697, which gives us a general idea of when the road acquired the name. Chances are it was not named for him during his lifetime.

The road has gone through several names throughout history. During the 1800s, it was referred to as Rye Lot Road and also as Hog Pond Road. This comes as no surprise, since the area once known as Hog Pond encompassed the surrounding area. By the early 1900s, it became Lover's Lane. Considering how quiet and

Smithtown map from 1909, showing
Lover's Lane on the right

isolated it can be, it was an ideal setting for young couples looking to share an intimate moment. The road shows up as Lover's Lane in E. Belcher Hyde maps, dated from 1909 to 1917. During the 1940s, the road was changed back to its original name, Lawrence Road, which is how it has remained ever since.

According to Barry Charletta, the northern part of Lawrence Road past San Remo Elementary School and going to St. Johnland Road was not paved during the 1960s. It was not even open to traffic. He recalls both ends of the unpaved section being blocked by sandbags and construction debris.

While the hospital was operational, the entrance gate located at Lawrence Road was usually not open to traffic. It was opened daily at six in the morning and closed promptly at five in the evening. After complaints from the inconvenienced employees working the late shift, a new policy was put in place. Beginning in January 1974, this entrance gate was reopened for a short time at night, between the hours of 10:30 p.m. and 11:45 p.m., to accommodate the late shift.

In 1996, the Smithtown Highway Department extended Lawrence Road from Columbus Avenue to Old Northport Road.

There were several short roads that passed through the hospital grounds.

Cottonwood Drive begins on the north side of St. Johnland Road just east of Old Dock Road and behind Building 39 (73Q). It goes north running parallel to Sound View Road until it reaches Building 140 (73P). It then turns right, heading eastbound, until it reaches Sound View Road and

Cottonwood Drive with Bldg 138 (left) & 140 (right) on Dec. 22, 2011

comes to a stop. This road is closed to public access.

Sound View Road also entered the hospital grounds from the north side of St. Johnland Road just east of Cottonwood Drive. It begins near Buildings 39 (73Q) and veers east going past

Buildings 139 (73O), 138 (73N), and 136 (73L) before turning left and heading north toward Kings Park Bluff. It ends at the former site of Building 135 (73K). The road got its name from the Sound View Hotel because it used to lead to it.

Aerial photos showing Sound View Rd on April 10, 1976

Looking north from St. Johnland Rd
at Sound View Rd on Jan. 23, 2013

Sound View Rd facing north toward
Kings Park Bluff on Aug. 21, 2016

Shore Road was a small road that began at Sound View Road and went around the back of Building 137 (73M). At one time, it connected to Upper Dock Road, but now it ends near the fence that marks the property line near Upper Dock Road.

The entrance to Shore Road, shown on the left, on June 20, 2016

Shore Rd stretches behind Buildings 136 (73L) and 137 (73M), 12/22/11

Flynn Road is a one-block-long road that enters the former hospital grounds via Old Dock Road. It was originally called Flynn's Crossing because long ago the Flynn family used it to travel from their home to their jobs at the hospital. The idea for naming the road for the family came about after the unfortunate death of Private Daniel Flynn, who was killed during the Vietnam War. The road is situated diagonally across from William T. Rogers Middle School and leads straight to the area that was once the lower reservoir on the boulevard. Buckman Center used to sit directly across from it before it was demolished.

Flynn Road was established in 1912 to make getting to the train easier from Old Dock Road, since the hospital's passenger platform was located here on the west side of the boulevard. It may have been part of Crooked Tree Road, which can be found on the 1865 map earlier in this chapter.

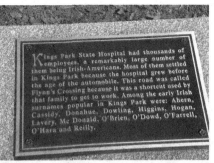

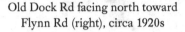

Old Dock Rd facing north toward
Flynn Rd (right), circa 1920s

Hike & Bike Trail sign at
Flynn Rd on July 11, 2011

After the hospital closed, this road was closed to the public for several years. It is currently open.

Just north of Flynn Road along Old Dock Road were a few other entrance roads that led onto the hospital grounds. The first was the long road that leads to Potter's Field Cemetery on the west side of Old Dock Road. As far as I know, this road never had a name. It was just the Cemetery Road. The second road was West Third Street, which entered the grounds on the east side of Old Dock Road behind where Group 1 stood. It also led to the dairy farm on the west side of Old Dock Road. The next road was also on the west side of Old Dock Road. It was called Maple Hill Road. This limited access road made a loop around the buildings of Group 4. Orchard Road was the last entrance road on the east side of Old Dock Road. Named for the nearby apple orchards, it entered the hospital grounds near the power plant area and headed straight toward the storehouse before turning right and meeting up with Industrial Road.

Cemetery Rd heading west toward
the water tower on July 11, 2011

Aerial photo, showing Maple
Rd on April 10, 1976

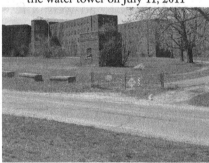

Entrance to Maple Rd on April 16, 2013

Looking down on Maple Rd from
Building 43 on Aug. 31, 2013

West Third Street closed at Old
Dock Rd on June 20, 2016

Facing west on West Third Street
toward Old Dock Rd on Oct. 5, 2015

Closed entrance to Orchard Rd on   Orchard Rd facing the
Old Dock Rd on April 28, 2013   storehouse on May 11, 2011

All three of these roads are currently closed to vehicular traffic. They have been closed since the hospital closed in 1996.

There is one other road that connects to St. Johnland Road. This road has no name to the best of my knowledge. It goes completely around Tiffany Field and originally served as a running track, paved with cinders from the power plant. These days, whenever the field is open to the public, this road becomes accessible to vehicles. However, when the field is closed, an iron bar is put in place to block the road at both ends.

Aerial image from April 21, 1984,   Entrance to Tiffany Field
shows road just around Tiffany Field   on Jan. 23, 2013

Shortly after the hospital closed, so did many of the roads leading onto the hospital grounds. As of March 1997, the Office of Mental Health had begun closing off the roads, restricting vehicular access to the public. Fences and gates were put up, some of which are still in place today.

By early April, access onto the boulevard was closed off at St. Johnland Road but not at East Main Street/Route 25A. However, there was no outlet for vehicles entering there. One could no longer drive through the grounds to St. Johnland Road as before. A security officer was stationed at the boulevard entrance near East Main Street/Route 25A. Only employees were allowed access.

This made traveling from East Main Street/Route 25A to St. Johnland Road an inconvenience for residents of Kings Park. Now, they had to go around the grounds using either Old Dock Road or Lawrence Avenue. Another alternative was where East Main Street/Route 25A and St. Johnland Road meet at San Remo.

Over the next couple of years, the abandoned hospital buildings had already started to deteriorate. Vandals wasted little time in setting a few fires and causing damage to some structures. The Kings Park Fire Department was provided with keys to the locked gates for easy access in the event of fire. Safety officers from the Office of Mental Health patrolled the grounds frequently in vehicles, but they were shorthanded and did not deter the increasing number of trespassers on the grounds.

After protests from the community during the early 2000s, access through Kings Park Boulevard and Flynn Road was permitted once again. The people of Kings Park rejoiced. However, the roads are considered closed at dusk, when the park closes. Driving through the grounds after hours could result in being stopped by law enforcement personnel. Furthermore, vehicular access to any of the other former hospital roads is still not permitted.

There has been talk of closing public access again in hopes of keeping trespassers away from the buildings. However, it would be pointless. If trespassers want to get into the buildings bad enough, they will no matter what roads they need to travel to do so. It would only cause unnecessary inconvenience to the community again.

Entrance to Kings Park
Boulevard on May 21, 2010

Lower end of the boulevard near old
railroad spur route on May 21, 2010

Boulevard facing Buildings 15,
93, and 83 on Dec. 19, 2012

The same view during a
snowy day in Feb. 2015

Facing south where the boulevard
crosses St. Johnland Rd on July 13, 2015

Facing south from the traffic circle &
flagpole at Bldg 125 (73A), 5/11/11

As a small anecdote, there are many old trees that line the sides of the boulevard, planted by the employees and patients many years ago. One of the most popular trees for photographers is an old dead tree that stood across from Building 93 at a slight angle.

This tree dates back to the time when Buildings A–D existed. It was around, at least, since the 1940s. It stood in front of the south side of the entrance walkway, leading to Building B. By the 2000s, this tree became the subject of several photographers who ventured onto the grounds. It even appears on Wikipedia in a photo of Building 93.

After so many years, the tree has finally succumbed to old age and was cut down in the winter of 2015–2016.

| Dead tree across from Building 93 on March 27, 2011 | The tree & Building 93 on Dec. 19, 2012 | My mother looking up at the tree on May 1, 2013 |

Another dead tree on June 22, 2010 that was removed in recent years

Hospital Roads

Or if the path has merely eluded us so far, what indications may we use that might lead us to hope that in renewed attempts we will be luckier than those who have gone before us?
— Immanuel Kant (author and philosopher), *Critique of Pure Reason*, 1781

There were quite a few small roads that only went from one point of the hospital to another, never leaving the grounds. A lot of old maps simply referred to these roads as hospital roads, since they were not significant to the town. However, mostly all of them had names. Many of

This KPPC billboard map stood on the boulevard during the 1990s

these roads are no longer accessible and have been buried by an overgrowth of vegetation, making them barely visible and practically forgotten.

East First Street was just north of the lower reservoir on the east side of the boulevard. It crossed Roundtree Road and passed in front of Building 7, coming to an end when it reached Roundtree Road again. This road was established during the mid-1960s, although it is no longer accessible. In fact, it can barely be seen anymore because grass has grown over it. There was no West First Street.

Roundtree Road was a road built for the sole purpose of circling Buildings 7, 21, and 22. It was established during the mid-1960s, when the buildings were completed and opened. It goes from East First Street around the buildings until it reaches East Second Street. Access to this road was completely blocked when the hospital closed.

Aerial from 1986, showing First-Third Streets

East First Street sign found in
Building 57 in 2010, courtesy
of James Edward Olsen

East First Street closed to
traffic on June 20, 2016

East Second Street was north of East First Street. It led to Building 2 and then curved toward the right, connecting to the west side of Roundtree Road in front of Building 22. The road was built sometime around 1920 to provide easy access to Building 2. After the hospital closed, this road was closed to traffic. The entrance has been converted into a small parking lot. West Second Street was located across the boulevard and looped around the connected buildings from Group 1. Many of the Group 1 roads were built from 1900 to 1901. After Building 56 was demolished in 2012, West First Street was removed.

Closed entrance to East Second Street on June 20, 2016

The former entrance to West Second Street (right) on July 6, 2012

The entrance to East Third Street was located further north on the boulevard, directly across from Building 15. It traveled east from the boulevard past Building 1 before reaching Student Road. East Third Street was still in use during the early 2000s because Building 1 was still being used to treat patients. The building finally closed in 2012. The road was closed about three years later. It leads to the former parking lot for Group 5.

Facing East Third Street from the boulevard on June 20, 2016

Looking west from East Third Street on Jan. 23, 2013

Student Road was next along the boulevard. It was located between Dewing Home and the firehouse. It was used to access the tennis courts. It was actually an extension of the original Student Road that passed by the early female cottages. When that road was no longer used to go straight through to East Main Street/Route 25A, this turnoff leading to the boulevard became the new end of the road. It is no longer accessible to traffic. The entrance from the boulevard no longer exists.

West Fourth Street was across the boulevard on the west side and was accessible between Building 93 and Tiffany Field. It goes to the laundry building and ends at Industrial Road. It used to lead to some of the early male cottages. This road is blocked, but park personnel and police used it often to gain access to Industrial Road.

Industrial Road was once used to access the industrial buildings of the hospital. It begins where West Second Street ends and extends from West Third Street to West Fourth Street, passing behind Buildings 15 and 93. It was once used to reach the power plant area from the boulevard. This road is currently closed to traffic, but police and park personnel use it often.

| South end of Industrial Rd facing the rear of Building 15 on Oct. 5, 2015 | Looking down on Industrial Rd from Building 93 on March 27, 2013 | North end of Industrial Rd turns into West Fourth Street, March 17, 2013 |

There is a path that runs along the south side of the duck pond at the Nissequogue River State Park. This was once a road called Pickle Road. It began at the rear of Building 58, once called the Pickle House. The building originally served as an icehouse. The road continued west until it reached Sound View Road. During the 1930s, this building was used for storing sauerkraut. Afterward, the road became known as Sauerkraut Road. Today, the road is simply a trail at the park, while the building is long gone.

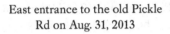

East entrance to the old Pickle   The west entrance to Pickle
Rd on Aug. 31, 2013   Rd on Aug. 31, 2013

The following roads were all added after 1932, when the Veterans' Memorial Hospital Unit was constructed. These roads were placed to make getting around this section of the hospital easier.

In the previous section, I mentioned the first half of Mariner Road, which is currently used to reach the town's sewage treatment plant. The other half of Mariner Road can only be accessed from within the Nissequogue River State Park. It begins on the east side of the boulevard near the boat basin and goes east to the marina, where the boathouse once stood. This road now connects to the Greenbelt Trail at Nissequogue River State Park.

Canal Road runs parallel to Mariner Road but lies on the north side of the boat basin. It leads from the end of the boulevard to where the canal was built, hence the name of the road. This was also the former site of the old barge, which is now gone. Currently, there is a new marina at this location.

| Entrance to Canal Rd & the north marina on Sept. 15, 2014 | Facing north on Canal Rd toward the beach on May 11, 2016 |

There was another small road that led to the old docks near Kings Park Bluff. The road started at the western end of Canal Road near the canal and headed north following the path of the river. This road is also part of the Greenbelt Trail.

Grandview Circle starts at Sound View Road and basically forms a traffic circle, or rather an oval, between Buildings 126 (73B) and 129 (73E). Sea View Court also begins and ends at Sound View Road but loops in front of the former staff cottages numbered Buildings 130 (73F)–134 (73J). Most of these buildings will probably be gone by the time this book is published. The roads here are currently closed to vehicular traffic aside from authorized vehicles.

Aerial from April 30, 1972, showing roads around staff homes

Doctors' cottages at Sea View Court on April 19, 2016

Entrance to Grandview
Circle on April 19, 2016

Grandview Circle quadrangle
on April 19, 2016

And finally, one road that did not have a name was a small road that led to the buildings of Group 2 from the west side of the boulevard. It was more like a driveway than an actual road. It was paved with asphalt and went around to the other side of Building 123, passing in front of Buildings 122, 124, and 40.

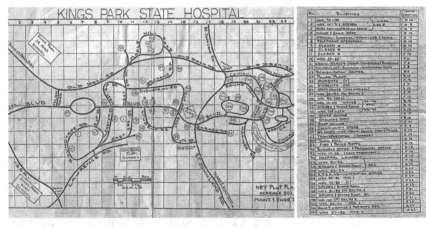

Key Plot Plan, circa 1973

Key Plot Plan
Index, circa 1973

CHAPTER 17

The Underground Tunnel System

Creating the Underground Tunnels

We often used the tunnels to take patients from one building to another during inclement weather. The most common usage was taking them to and from the dining room when rain, snow, or cold were too much outside.
—Barry Charletta (former employee of the Kings Park Psychiatric Center's Mental Retardation Unit [MRU] of Group 2, Building 124)

THE UNDERGROUND STEAM tunnel system beneath the Kings Park Psychiatric Center spans nearly seven miles in length. It is surely one of the most intriguing and mysterious places at Kings Park. The tunnels were constructed for the purpose of connecting the buildings to the power plant's electrical system, the water supply, and the steam pipes while providing easy access for maintenance.

As a bonus, these tunnels became underground passageways that connected the buildings to one another, especially during harsh weather. In some cases, it offered a low-risk solution for transporting patients through certain traffic tunnels that existed under the building groups without having to risk escape attempts by taking them outside instead. There were tunnels like this under Groups 2, 3, and 5 that linked the patient ward buildings to the dining hall buildings.

However, these tunnels were not created overnight. It took a great deal of time to plan, excavate, and build these tunnels. Not to mention installing all of the pipes and connecting them wherever necessary. It was a great deal of work. It began before the first permanent building was erected.

As of December 1887, Patrick J. Carlin had been hired as a contractor to work on the steam heating of the Kings County Farm and Asylum, as it was known back then. After he drew up his plans, he estimated the job to cost about $10,490 more than the original contract price.

As of November 1891, the first of the old steam tunnels were built and in place. The majority of these early tunnels were located under the boulevard and on the east and west sides of the boulevard under the early female and male cottages. At the time, connections were still being made to the boiler house and the newly constructed heating plant.

The tunnels began as trenches that were ten feet deep and twelve feet wide. Wooden frames were placed within the trenches and filled with concrete. Bricks were laid out to form the walls and arched ceilings. The walls were six feet tall and double thick. Dozens of curved wooden support beams shaped the roof, which was finished off with bricks to form magnificent arches. Iron beams were set in place as support. The tunnels were stepped up to about eight feet as they rose up from the heating plant (Building 59) and continued southbound beneath the boulevard and also to the north.

Tunnel arch underneath   Sealed entrance to Building
Building 59 on Nov. 13, 2016   59 on Jan. 10, 2016

Pipes cluttered together in a   Ladder leading up to a higher
tunnel, on Jan. 10, 2016   section, on Jan. 10, 2016

The tunnel gradually slants upward in the distance on Nov. 13, 2016

Brick cradles were built for the steam pipes, and long sections of pipe were laid in place, covered with hot tar to waterproof them. A series of wooden boards with electrical insulators were fastened into place along the walls opposite the pipes. Wires from the electric heating plant carried current to each building of the hospital. Afterward, the new tunnel system was buried with dirt that had been removed for its construction.

A problem occurred with the underground system from the start. The heat was so intense from the uninsulated steam pipes that they caused the electrical insulation on the wires to dry and crack. This became a serious issue by the late 1890s. In 1897, a fan had to be installed at the lower end of the main conduit beneath the boulevard to ventilate and cool the tunnels, but it was not enough. A new solution would have to be provided.

At the time when the early cottages were built, they did not have basements. This would later prove to be another problem. There were no proper partitions set in place to shut off the steam vapor from reaching the wood from underneath the cottages after the tunnels were built. As a result, the cottages became heavily soaked in vapor, and the timber began to rot at an accelerated rate. In time, several of the cottages had to be partially rebuilt. This included Female Cottages 20, 22, and 23. During the mid-1890s, partitions had to be placed between the tunnels and the newly built basements of the cottages to prevent further erosion.

When Buildings A–D were constructed, the tunnels had to be extended further south beneath the boulevard to connect these buildings to the electrical wiring, steam pipes, and water supply.

It was the same for Group 1, built about a year later. A lot of the underground work in connection with these buildings was not completed until the early 1900s. A team of patients did the excavating for these new tunnels. As of the end of 1900, all of the old pipes in the tunnels had been removed as well and replaced with new pipes.

In 1902, a proposal was made by Paul Vacuum System Company to install a new system that would help economize the steam and fuel costs. Within two years, the system was installed and fully operational. At the same time, the old electrical cables in the tunnels, which had been short circuited, cracked, and otherwise damaged by steam, were finally removed and replaced. The new wiring was placed in separate smaller iron underground conduits away from the heat of the steam pipes. All future electrical cables would be installed within these new conduits.

Replacing insulation around the electrical wiring, circa 1960s-1980s

From 1904 to 1910, much work was done with the help of patients. A two-by-four-foot temporary tunnel was added to the auxiliary boiler house at Group 1. Partitions were placed to prevent drafts and the condensation of steam in the main steam conduit under the boulevard. Steam mains were installed from the Group 1 temporary boiler house to the A-B and C-D kitchens. This new line would also provide heat to the hot water tanks of the wards in these buildings. The tunnels underneath these buildings were whitewashed in 1907 and 1910.

Old tunnel can be seen through hole behind Building 93 on March 17, 2013

By 1908, plans were made to create a steam conduit from the boiler house at the new power plant (Building 6), branching out to the rear of Male Cottage 25 and to the front of Male Cottage 29 on the north side. Another conduit would connect to the new laundry and Group 1. Another tunnel would run from the boiler house and laundry toward Building 12, the kitchen for Buildings C and D. The work on these new tunnels began in 1909, but within a year, they had to be torn out and redone because of poor workmanship.

By 1912, the temporary tunnel leading to the Group 1 auxiliary boiler house was dug up, and the steam pipes were removed. The tunnels that led from this boiler house to Building 120 of this group and the C and D kitchen were buried and forgotten. The pipes were all removed and reused elsewhere. In addition, a new extension was excavated for the new power plant.

Within a year, it was deemed sensible to begin placing all telephone lines as well as light and power cables underground. The chaotic mess of wires that connected to the telephone and power poles had become an eyesore. This work was completed near the male and female cottages by the use of a hospital labor force, patients. Afterward, the hospital did away with all unsightly aerial wiring, which previously required considerable maintenance.

In 1916, the steam tunnel line was enlarged, and much work was done. A Worthington two-stage horizontal pump was installed to force steam returns of newly built Groups 2 and 3 from a point in the tunnels near the old electric heating plant to the new power plant much further away. A Connersville vacuum-heating pump was installed for the vacuum heating system of Groups 2 and 3. In addition, control valves were put in to regulate the steam for Group 2, while the pipe in the tunnel beneath the group was properly graded. Material was also purchased to make changes at the refrigeration plant (Building 51) so that pressure could be reduced in the steam pipes running from the new power plant to the original storehouse, also Building 51, causing the pipes to operate on low steam pressure. This would effectively save coal for the hospital. The steam lines for Group 4 were also enlarged when new pipes were installed from 1919 to 1920.

During the 1920s, the Carlson family, a prominent Swedish family of Kings Park with a well-known concrete business, did a great deal of work on the underground tunnels. They excavated new sections for the Veterans' Memorial Hospital Unit and also worked on the foundations, improving them greatly and making them stronger.

Tunnel leading from Building 137
(73M) to 136 (73L) on Dec. 22, 2011

Tunnel underneath Building 136
(73L) facing south on Nov. 15, 2010

Tunnel leading from Building 39
(73Q) to 139 (73O) on April 28, 2015

Dead end beneath Building 139
(73O) on April 28, 2015

By the 1930s, after almost forty years of additions and modifications, the portion of the tunnels under the upper portion of the main boulevard in front of Buildings 93 and A–D had become overcrowded with various pipes that went across its width from floor to ceiling. It became quite a difficult task to conduct maintenance within these particular sections of the tunnels. It also became virtually impossible to walk through some of these areas.

Old brick tunnel under the
boulevard on April 17, 2016

Cluttered pipes in the
old boulevard tunnel
on April 17, 2016

Looking into
the side of the
tunnel from
another tunnel,
April 17, 2016

As a result, a new set of concrete tunnels had to be built around the 1930s parallel to the older brick tunnels under the boulevard, creating dual tunnel corridors. The older tunnels were abandoned but not sealed off. The power and steam were disconnected from that section and redirected through the newer tunnels.

Facing south under the
boulevard on April 17, 2016

An elevated portion of the
boulevard on April 17, 2016

Stairs going
down, as you
head north
past Fourth
St on April
17, 2016

There are many tunnels that were abandoned over the years. Some were sealed off permanently and forgotten. While maps do exist showing the current tunnels, there are numerous sections of the tunnels that do not appear on these incomplete and often inaccurate maps. There were tunnels that connected to the old Group 4 TB cottages, tunnels under Group 1, more connecting to the early cottages, and another that led from Building 60 to the old pumping station near the boat basin. As buildings are demolished, more dead-end tunnels are created. That was the case with Groups 1, 2, 3, and 5.

Heading toward Group 1 under West Second St on Dec. 7, 2011

Sealed Group 1 tunnel under West Second St on Dec. 7, 2011

Heading south toward Group 1 under Industrial Rd on April 17, 2016

Facing southbound under West Third St on April 17, 2016

At one time, even the hospital did not have a map of the tunnels. In an annual report from 1897, general superintendent Oliver M. Dewing made it known that the hospital had no idea of the steam tunnels' layout. He made a suggestion to the state advising them to purchase a map from the engineer that designed the tunnels.

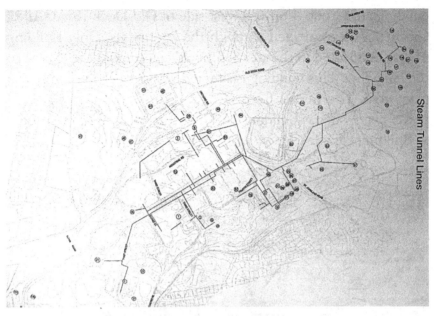

Steam tunnel engineer's map, circa 2002

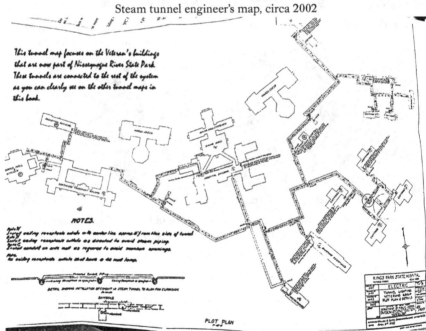

Veterans' Group tunnel lighting plot plan from April 6, 1945

During the early 1930s, new tunnels were added to connect to Building 1 on the east side of the boulevard and to the three buildings of Group 4 on the west side of Old Dock Road. All of Group 4 was connected through the basements. Only Building 41 was connected to the steam tunnels, since it was the closest to the main line. This building is situated across from the last power plant area. The tunnel from Group 4 runs straight to the final power plant, built as Building 29. This power plant then connected to Building 85.

A ladder leading up from the Group 4 tunnels on Aug. 25, 2011

Staircase leading up to Building 41 from the tunnels on Aug. 21, 2013

Tunnel under Group 4 leading to a turn on Aug. 25, 2011

One of many ladders leading to the surface on Aug. 25, 2011

Sewage pipe passing through the tunnel
under Old Dock Rd, Oct. 24, 2011

Approaching the power plant
from Group 4 on Oct. 24, 2011

Tunnel between Buildings
29 & 6 on Oct. 24, 2011

Tunnel in the steam tunnel
junction area on Oct. 24, 2011

This small building was added in 1939 as a steam pipe junction house. It was built near the second power plant and connected several tunnels to one large basement room that could easily be accessed from outside through a door and staircase that led down to this room. It became the fastest way into the tunnels of this area for maintenance crews. After Building 29 was built to serve as the final power plant during the mid-1960s, the older one was subsequently demolished. The steam pipe junction house was partially rebuilt soon afterward and renumbered as the next Building 6.

Several other buildings were added in 1939, requiring extensive work in the tunnels. Buildings 15 and 93 were built on the west side of the boulevard. Tunnels were added from the main boulevard conduit, leading to these buildings. The tunnel beneath Building 93 is parallel to an old tunnel from the early male cottages, some of which had been demolished for the construction of Building 93. It actually led to the old Clubhouse and bowling alley. The tunnel now leads to dead ends on two sides. Additional tunnels were built to connect to the new greenhouse (Building 65) and director's mansion on the north side of the property to the main line under the boulevard.

Dead end brick tunnel under
Building 93 on Oct. 6, 2013

Rusted valve in a tunnel under
Building 93 on Oct. 6, 2013

Concrete tunnel under Building
93 on Oct. 6, 2013

Staircase in the tunnels under
Building 93 on April 17, 2016

Tunnel leading from Building
93 to 5 on Oct. 6, 2013

Concrete beam crossing a tunnel from
Building 93 to 5 on Oct. 6, 2013

Tunnel leading to Building
5 on Oct. 6, 2013

Elevated tunnel going south toward
Building 5 on Oct. 6, 2013

The last large tunnel project undertaken was in the mid-1960s with the completion of Buildings 7, 21, and 22. At the time, these buildings were the farthest to the south. The main boulevard tunnel was extended at an angle to reach these buildings.

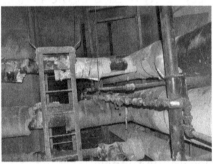

Tunnel in front of Bldg 93 indicating
the direction to 7 on April 17, 2016

Ladder going over pipes at the lower
end of the boulevard on Dec. 7, 2011

Ladder leading into the basement
of Building 7 on Dec. 7, 2011

Valves on pipes between Buildings
7 & 21 on Dec. 7, 2011

Tunnel leading into Building 21 on March 12, 2013

Ladder going up to the basement of Building 21 on March 12, 2013

The portion of old tunnels located under the main boulevard near Tiffany Field and the old heating plant was modernized. They continued to be used until the last power plant was shut down in November 1996. However, the majority of the other tunnels were very rarely used after the 1970s. Many of the tunnels had actually been abandoned years prior to the closing of the hospital.

After the hospital closed, any outside entrances leading to the underground tunnels were sealed off, while most of the entrances located within the buildings were welded shut. However, over the years, since the hospital has been abandoned, many creative urban explorers have found ways to enter, often leaving the path clear for others to follow. Currently, there are dozens of ways to access the tunnels.

Tunnel access in the basement of the Director's mansion on Jan. 1, 2016

Sealed tunnel entrance under the Director's mansion on Jan. 1, 2016

Ventilation shafts on the boulevard, near East Second St on Oct. 5, 2015

Ventilation shafts on the boulevard, in front of Macy Home on Oct. 5, 2015

Ventilation shaft behind Macy Home on Aug. 31, 2013

Ventilation shaft ladder behind Macy Home on Aug. 31, 2013

Ventilation shaft in front of Building 93 on April 16, 2013

Peeking into ventilation shaft in front of Building 93 on April 16, 2013

Tunnel exit on the boulevard on Oct. 5, 2015

Manhole behind Bldg 44 on April 17, 2016 could be sewer or an old tunnel

Locked tunnel entrance near Building 15 on Oct. 24, 2011

Looking up from below the same access hatch on April 17, 2016

The longest, straightest portion of the tunnel is located beneath Kings Park Boulevard, extending from the former location of the lower reservoir all the way up to Fourth Street. This is also the highest point in the tunnels. The lowest would be in the vicinity of the boat basin, near the end of the boulevard. The most southern point is located under Building 21, while the farthest northern point was underneath Building 135 (73K) on the opposite end of the property, prior to its demolition.

The furthest south end of the tunnels under Building 21 on Dec. 7, 2011

The furthest north end of the tunnels was in the basement of 135, 2/7/15

Looking into the tunnel under Building 135 (73K) on Feb. 7, 2015

Before any major demolitions are conducted, there is usually a survey team sent to check the access points of the tunnels beneath the work site. Those points must be sealed first to make sure no one sneaks into the building just as it is about to be demolished.

A survey team uses a tunnel access hatch in May 2009

Survey team checks steam pipe junction area under 6 in May 2009

Steam tunnel is marked on Student Rd on Aug. 3, 2012

Steam tunnel marked on boulevard in front of Group 2 on Aug. 3, 2012

Manhole in front of Group 2 is marked
as tunnel access point, Aug. 3, 2012

Tunnel marked as filled with
soil on Aug. 3, 2012

Metal doors near Building 142 (73R)
are marked on April 19, 2016

Metal doors near Building 142 (73R)
are marked on April 19, 2016

The top of a tunnel unearthed in this
photo by Sean Hardy, circa 2012

Filling in a brick tunnel near
Student Road, circa 2012-2013

Mysteries and Dangers of the Underground Tunnels

The world is indeed full of peril, and in it there are many dark places.
–J. R. R. Tolkien (author), *Lord of the Rings: The Fellowship
of the Ring*, 1954

The tunnels beneath the abandoned psychiatric center sprawl throughout the darkness leading to untold dangers. Ever since the closing of the hospital, the tunnels have been abandoned. They have fallen deeply into disrepair. Inside this darkened maze filled with dead ends, there are pitfalls, tight squeezes, collapsed ceilings, an excessive amount of asbestos, flooded areas, nests of camel crickets, and even wildlife. Someone I know once encountered an angry raccoon underneath the buildings of Group 2.

The skull of what appears to be a cat found on a pipe, early 2000s

A bat sleeping on a pipe near the steam pipe junction area on Oct. 6, 2013

Camel crickets spread across the ceiling of a tunnel on April 17, 2016

Large hole in the ground, as seen in this photo provided by Ray Staten

When the hospital was open, the tunnels provided an isolated location for the mistreatment of patients. There are rumors about patients who were tortured down in the tunnels. Allegedly, there were hidden torture chambers in the tunnels, although none have ever been discovered. So many stories surround places like this, adding to their creepiness and mystique. Some believe the tunnels to be the most haunted area of the former state hospital.

Speaking as a paranormal investigator, I must disagree. While the tunnels are definitely the darkest and most isolated areas, I have very little reason to believe many patients might have been taken down there. It was mainly the maintenance employees that worked in the tunnels or spent any significant amount of time down there.

There are small areas that resemble rooms scattered throughout the underground tunnel system. Whether patients were ever tortured in these rooms is another story. There is no proof or legitimate claims from former patients.

For the most part, the tunnels are dark, cool, and damp. It is ironic considering how hot they used to be when the steam pipes were operational. Some areas have moisture buildup on the ceilings, attracting hundreds of camel crickets. They tend to feed on the asbestos and spiders. Sometimes they will even feed on each other.

Unfortunately, the tunnels were poorly maintained for a very long time, causing them to fall into a dangerous state of disrepair far more quickly as the years went by. Years of rain and snow have caused flooding in some areas. Some are too tight to walk through because of the heavy concentration of pipes. In a few instances, you might even have to crawl or climb over to get by the pipes. The worst danger is the asbestos hanging from the pipes and covering the floors. Exposure to asbestos fibers can lead to life-threatening illnesses such as mesothelioma.

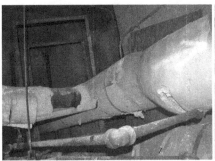 

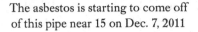

The asbestos is starting to come off of this pipe near 15 on Dec. 7, 2011	Asbestos from these boulevard pipes is already on the floor, April 17, 2016

While there were a few employees that got a thrill from venturing into the tunnels, others were afraid to do so and preferred to avoid them. Entering the tunnels was not encouraged, as the majority of them were not intended for traveling from one building to another.

It is wise to keep in mind that the underground tunnels are a dangerous dark place filled with many long tunnels that lead to dead ends, flooded corridors, asbestos, debris, loose bricks, and weakened support beams. Some of the tunnels have become so difficult to walk through and unbelievably filthy that they are virtually unbearable and claustrophobic. You can barely crawl through the rusted pipes and slimy floor, let alone walk. Why would anyone want to be exposed to this unnecessarily, especially while not wearing protective gear? The older tunnels are by far the worst. The ceilings, walls, and even floors are unstable in some areas.

Beam under East Fourth St ready
to come down on April 17, 2016

Another beam under East Fourth St
being held up by a pipe on 4/17/16

Ceiling collapsed into tunnel under
Building 123 on Aug. 2, 2011

Beams collapsed into tunnel under
Building 123 on Aug. 2, 2011

There is one portion of the tunnels beneath the main boulevard that has been nicknamed Hell Tunnel by urban explorers who have been daring enough to venture through. For the most part, it is an old, narrow brick tunnel with a brick ceiling, although some portions are concrete. The tunnel is partially flooded and cluttered with debris. It extends under the boulevard at Fourth Street in front of Building 93 and goes past St. Johnland Road, where it bends to the left and turns right as it nears the demolished heating plant. This has always been one of the worse sections of the underground tunnels because of heavy flooding, several drops, and limited mobility. Prepared explorers that venture through here usually tie bags around their footwear before entering this area. At one point, you have to climb over rusted old pipes to avoid the flooded ground.

"Hell Tunnel" goes from 4th St beyond the curve in
the boulevard to Bldg 59, Oct. 6, 2013

Asbestos covered pipes in "Hell
Tunnel" on Jan. 10, 2016

One of several flooded
areas on Jan. 10, 2016

Ladder climbing to a higher
section on Jan. 10, 2016

Facing south into an elevated
section on Jan. 10, 2016

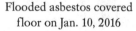

Flooded asbestos covered   Surrounded by asbestos & mushy
floor on Jan. 10, 2016   floors in these photos by Sam
Bartels from Jan. 10, 2016

It can be extremely dangerous to explore these tunnels. It is very easy to get lost and become disoriented if you are not familiarized with the layout of the grounds.

It is no surprise that the underground tunnels remain one of the most popular haunts for adventure-seeking explorers despite the multiple dangers involved. It is inadvisable to enter any of these locations, especially without permission and proper protective gear, including safety-approved asbestos masks, thick-soled waterproof work boots, and gloves. A few good working LED flashlights are also a must!

An interesting fact about the demolished buildings at the hospital is that the rubble was usually buried within the basements of the buildings to save on cleanup costs. This also created dead ends in the tunnels and prevented trespassers from traveling through certain areas and going from building to building while remaining underground.

For example, the brick tunnel leading from the boulevard to the laundry building (Building 94) is a dead end because it actually went to the old tailor shop, demolished in the 1950s. The tunnel that connected Building 1 to Building 2 is another dead end and can only be accessed from the basement of Building 1. There are also dead-end tunnels under where Buildings 143 and 147 of Group 3 were located. Prior to the demolition of Buildings 122 and 123 of Group 2, there was another dead-end tunnel that led to where Building 124 once stood. After the demolition, access to this tunnel from Building 40 was sealed.

Facing north toward sealed access
to demolished Building 6, 4/17/16

Facing west toward sealed access to
demolished Building 6, 4/17/16

Dead end tunnel leading to demolished
Building 12 on April 17, 2016

Facing basement access into
Building 40 on April 12, 2011

Sealed tunnel access from inside
of Building 40 on Aug. 31, 2013

Close up of sealed tunnel
access on Aug. 31, 2013

Tunnel leading to demolished   Sealed wall under site of Building
Building 143 (73S) on Dec. 22, 2011   143 (73S) on Dec. 22, 2011

Tunnel leading to demolished Building 147 (73W) on Dec. 22, 2011

Another area with dead ends is the area under Student Road. The tunnel that once led to the morgue was walled up long ago. Nearby under the hill to the east are more brick tunnels that once led to the female cottages. A few still connect to the staff cottages on East Fourth Street.

Brick tunnel under Student Rd leading to Building 82 on April 17, 2016

Brick tunnel leading into the basement of Building 18, circa 2012-2013

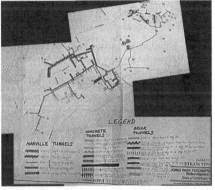

Diagram of tunnel near Student Rd from Jan. 31, 2009

Steam Tunnel Survey map, by Saccardi and Schiff, Inc., circa 2010

It is illegal to enter the tunnels. However, if you insist on taking a risk, please do not go alone. If you are injured falling from a ladder or by a ceiling caving in on you, it could be weeks or months before anyone ever finds you and help arrives. Consider that before putting your life at risk. Also, it might be a good idea to pay heed to the messages spray-painted on the walls. They are usually correct.

Dead end warning under the
Veterans' Group on Feb. 7, 2015

Dead end, just as the message
warned, on Feb. 7, 2015

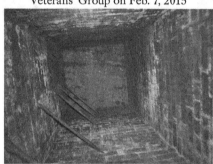

Sealed access hatch under East
Fourth St on April 17, 2016

Sealed door under East Fourth
St on April 17, 2016

Out of reach access hatch under
East Fourth St on April 17, 2016

An urban explorer exiting the tunnels
into a building on April 17, 2016

SECTION VII

The End of an Era

CHAPTER 18

Deinstitutionalization

The Hospital Closes Down

Surely, the hospital was a different place than what it became during the 1970s with all the budget cuts. The taxpayer money was going elsewhere. The staffing ratios were difficult to maintain.

The worst thing to happen to the patients besides deinstitutionalization, in my opinion, was the court system, disallowing patients to work for anything less than minimum wages. This completely killed meaningful occupational therapy. The taxpayers certainly could not afford to pay that to many thousands of patients per institution. Most patients were then left to linger on the wards all day. Sad.

—Barry Charletta (former employee of the Kings Park Psychiatric Center's Mental Retardation Unit [MRU] of Group 2, Building 124)

WHEN THE KINGS Park Psychiatric Center closed its

doors in 1996, it came as a surprise to many employees. They had been hearing rumors for years that the state was shutting it down. Most of them did not believe it would actually happen, but it did.

Throughout the 1970s, the increased costs from Medicare and Medicaid put most of the states into budget crises. New York State began to realize it could no longer finance the growing costs of its many state institutions. In 1955, it completed the Mental Health Study Act. The act called for the abolition of state mental hospitals and the redirecting of federal funds to instead build community centers for the mentally ill while financing research into psychoactive drugs, which subdued patients, making them less dangerous to themselves and others.

Letter from 1972 assuring the director that the hospital is not closing

The costs of maintaining occupational therapy facilities at mental hospitals became far too expensive. It became an unwanted burden for the state, which spent more money on the mentally ill than most other states. The state had already begun diverting its funds to other causes that were deemed more important such as the welfare system. Thus, a transitional period began that led to many large state hospitals closing down. New methods for treating the mentally ill, based out of community mental health centers and clinics, would gradually take over. Emphasis was placed on short-term care and crisis intervention, while long-term patient care would see a gradual decline.

By the late 1960s and early 1970s, society's thoughts regarding mental health care and psychiatry in general changed drastically. This was largely due to the intensity of cultural, political, and social turmoil that characterized this rebellious era filled with protests, civil rights movements, and war. People from many walks of life denounced the very existence of mental health. Psychiatrists were viewed as ruthless oppressors of the weak, whose sole purpose was to dominate and crush the individuality of those opposed to the typical values instilled by society.

Aerial photos from 1968

A sort of hierarchy had developed among the employees in the mid-1900s. Your position and title governed where you dined and where you were allowed to reside on the grounds. If your social status was important enough, you could reside in one of the elite staff cottages that overlooked Kings Park Bluff or perhaps a cottage behind Macy Home.

This was a time when patients were practically being used as slaves, spending more time working as servants in the doctors' homes rather than being treated for their mental illnesses. They did cleaning, cooking, babysitting, and lawn work, and walked dogs. Some doctors would even postpone discharging a cured patient to hold on to their servant a little longer. This information was actually received from a credible former employee who was in a position of authority.

Eventually, the government stepped in, and state hospitals were now compelled to pay working patients a sufficient salary. Around this time, occupational therapy came to an end, as did patient servitude. Soon enough, the hierarchal structure started to crumble as well.

Deinstitutionalization began around the same time and soon spread across the East Coast like wildfire. Patients were released and put into outpatient programs, if they were capable enough. Psychiatric medications were prescribed as needed. Many of the hospital's patients with more-serious mental issues were directed to Pilgrim Psychiatric Center, while the more-capable patients were rapidly discharged and placed in community-based housing.

The patient populations at many state institutions, including at Kings Park, gradually decreased. As a result, the hospital closed its unneeded and unused buildings at a steady pace starting in 1970. In fact, the 1970s became the height of deinstitutionalization across the country. It would continue throughout the 1980s and well into the 1990s.

When nursing homes began to accept the elderly, the patient population was reduced by almost half. There was more of an inclination to medicate and rehabilitate patients so they could be returned to society sooner rather than keeping them institutionalized for extended periods. It was apparent the elderly would be better cared for at nursing homes.

There were quite a few instances when patients were released onto the streets with nowhere else to go. Unfortunately, many of these ill-fated people were added to the homeless population of Long Island and New York City.

Homeless person sleeping in Harlem

These people had very little help from the very welfare system that unintentionally helped to put them out onto the streets.

It seemed deinstitutionalization created just as many problems as it was intended to solve.

Following the end of occupational therapy and the closing of numerous hospital buildings as well as the rise of deinstitutionalization, the KPPC was slowly heading toward its end of days.

When the abandoned buildings of Group 1 burned to the ground, it was truly the end of an era. Buildings were being demolished little by little, leaving behind large empty fields, where fully occupied buildings once bustled with activity.

Home V, Home W, and the old electric heating plant/ occupational therapy offices were abandoned in the 1970s.

In the 1980s, there were both federal and state budget cuts that had a substantial effect on mental health care. By 1983, funding for several Office of Mental Health programs was slashed. One newspaper called the cuts "Draconian." As a result of federal cutbacks, New York State and other states became firmly committed to community-based programs in relation to mental health. It was believed these programs would be less costly in the long run in regard to inpatient care at the much larger state psychiatric centers.

Aerial photo from April 21, 1984

More buildings were abandoned during this decade. Building 2 and all four buildings of Group 2 were vacated by 1983. As of 1985, there were officially only five abandoned buildings. The others were considered to be indefinitely closed and vacant. By my count, the following structures were either vacant or abandoned by this time: Buildings 2, 35 (Home V), 36 (Home W), 40, 59, 68 (original), 72, 78 (White House), and 122–124. None of these buildings were ever used again. Of these buildings, only Building 40 is still standing today, and it is abandoned.

Throughout these trying times, director Shepard Nathan, the hospital's last medical director, ran the hospital. He had taken over after director Charles Buckman retired. After director Nathan retired in the early 1980s, Stephen Goldstein took over as the very last director of the hospital, although he was not a medical doctor. He had previously served as the hospital's business officer. He remained the director until 1986.

By this time, the KPPC had become a mere shell of what it once was with many of its buildings left to abandonment and more than dozen razed. The continuous downsizing of the hospital and discharging of the patients resulted in a virtual "ghost town" at the once longtime overcrowded institution.

Three buildings were slated for demolition in the mid-1980s. Building 2 was used for firefighting practice and demolished around 1985–1986. Building 68 was demolished around 1988–1989, Building 72 was demolished sometime around 1988–1992, and Building 78 was demolished around 1986–1988. Apparently, 1988 is the most common year, so it is likely that year was a busy year for demos.

By the early 1990s, the hospital was barely operating with so many buildings shut down or reduced in usage, including the massive Building 93. At this point, only the lower floors of Building 93 were still being used. The top floors were all empty, which led to early rumors of the upper floors being haunted.

Front of Building 93 on Oct. 6, 2013   Rear of Building 93 on Oct. 6, 2013

Social workers were employed to place patients into less restrictive care and also for the more-serious cases, eventually transferred to Pilgrim. The admission standards were changed, and fewer patients were admitted. In 1988, executive director Robert Hettenbach established a new admissions program that only catered to people from specific areas of Long Island.

In 1991, budget cuts led to a protest in the form of a funeral march, complete with black ribbons, by members of the Civil Service Employees Association (CSEA). On September 19, at ten o'clock in the morning, they began their march at the boulevard entrance and made their way up the boulevard as they mourned the death of mental health care. It was a bold and dramatic statement, to say the least.

Most of the state's psychiatric centers were practically locking their front doors to potential patients while discharging their admittees and pushing them out the back doors to decrease their patient population. Long-term patients were discharged from psychiatric centers that had been their homes for countless years. Patients were being released into society before they were ready.

From the 1980s to 1990s, the decrease in the state's mentally ill patient population was even more dramatic than the numbers at the height of deinstitutionalization in the 1970s. During the early 1980s, there were nearly twenty-two thousand patients residing in all of New York's state psychiatric centers combined. By the 1990s, that number had essentially been cut in half to less than eleven thousand. More than 60 percent of that decrease occurred from 1988 to 1993. The numbers would continue to drop statewide as a few of the state's largest institutions closed during the mid-1990s. These institutions had served their purpose throughout history, but they really were not needed anymore, considering the constant advances in medicine and treatment methods.

The patients were not the only ones getting pushed out the door. Approximately seventy-eight positions were eliminated and more than two hundred employees were laid off as a result of the cuts. Over two hundred more employees were shuffled around to different psychiatric centers on Long Island. The budget cuts affected close to 70 percent of the workforce that were not involved with direct patient care and 30 percent that provided hands-on assistance.

With patient populations at increasingly low levels, the New York State Office of Mental Health began their plan for the closure of the KPPC as well as another Long Island asylum, the Central Islip Psychiatric Center. The plans called for Kings Park and Central Islip to close and have any remaining patients from both facilities transferred to Pilgrim. The closing of these and three other psychiatric centers in the state was expected to free up $210 million in revenue, including funds that would have paid the salaries of employees that were losing their jobs. Nearly $15 million of that money was slated to benefit Long Island for a period of five years.

In January 1995, New York State senator Thomas Libous, chairman of the Senate Mental Health and Developmental Disabilities Committee, wanted to slow the progress of deinstitutionalization. He wanted to make sure the people, whom he felt were being callously tossed out onto the streets, were provided with the appropriate services they required. It was a noble effort, but it would not save the KPPC from its fate.

Throughout its final year, many of the staff began searching for new employment opportunities, but certain opportunities came to only a few fortunate staff members. The Office of Mental Health transferred deputy director Dean Weinstock, brother of CEO Alan Weinstock, to the newly constructed Brooklyn Children's Hospital to serve as director of Facility Administration Services. Dean Weinstock, in turn, offered his friend and colleague Kenneth Marion a job as director of Quality Assurance at the Brooklyn Children's Hospital, to which Marion gladly accepted. He knew his days were numbered, so he did not hesitate.

Marion had been a longtime employee of Kings Park, working there since August 1972. He spent the last decade serving as the director of Quality Assurance and as director of Public Affairs, essentially making him the spokesman and media liaison for the KPPC.

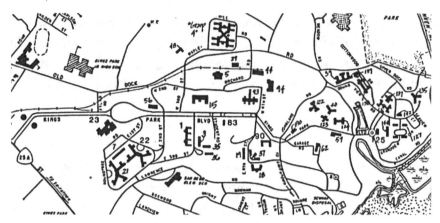

KPPC Site Plan from 1987, by Advertising Unlimited, Inc.

Both men would remain employees of the state. However, not every employee would be as lucky. Layoffs were on the rise, leading union officials to take action.

On Tuesday, July 2, 1996, the Office of Mental Health Safety and Security Officers, led by members of the Local 1790, Council 82, New York State Law Officers Union, protested cutbacks and pending layoffs. The rally took place at Pilgrim Psychiatric Center, which would be the only remaining psychiatric center for them to patrol after the upcoming closings of the facilities at Kings Park and Central Islip. These closures would mean a drastic reduction of their personnel.

At the time, there were thirty-five officers that rotated between the three facilities. There were always two cars at Kings Park, but that would soon change. Plans were to lay off about twenty employees by the end of the month, and even if some could be saved, more would be cut when the hospitals closed.

As it was, the majority of the buildings were already closed. The Office of Mental Health began closing procedures in August and continued into September. Numerous patients were transferred during that time. On October 7, the power at the power plant was shut down, and just like that, the KPPC had completely dissolved, ending its 111-year run. Its remaining 721 patients were loaded onto buses and transported to a newly expanded wing at Pilgrim, where their care would continue.

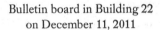

| Bulletin board in Building 22 on December 11, 2011 | Aerial of Pilgrim Psychiatric Center, circa 2001 |

Sadly, the patients were not the only ones to get the boot. About 245 of the 276 remaining staff members lost their jobs when the hospital finally closed. Some were eligible to retire, but many had to find work elsewhere.

Critics of deinstitutionalization maintain that not enough funding or time was spent on sufficient community-based care. They argued that many of the discharged patients ended up on the streets with medication but no follow-up care. Once the medication ran out, they were essentially on their own.

It is likely a good number of these former patients have already succumbed to poverty, disease, frostbite, heatstroke, murder, and at least a dozen other fates that were dealt to the homeless. There was even a time when someone was going around setting fire to homeless people in New York City.

After the KPPC closed, four of its buildings remained open. Pilgrim operated these buildings. Building 1 became a Residential Care Center for Adults (RCCA), housing 140 patients. Buildings 150 and 151 housed another forty-eight patients as Self-Care Centers for Adults (SCCA). Building 23 remained open as an outpatient clinic, referred to as the Buckman Treatment Center.

Four groundskeepers were hired in April 1997 to maintain the grounds. The hospital firehouse was used to store their equipment.

Grounds maintenance workers in front   A grounds maintenance vehicle on
of Building 83 on March 17, 2013   the boulevard in front of 93, 6/22/10

Buckman Treatment Center only stayed open to patients for a year. In October 1997, the clinic was relocated to Pilgrim's Building 47. Afterward, the building was used as a headquarters for the Office of Mental Health safety officers, who patrolled the grounds day and night with vigilance.

The building was officially closed in the early 2000s. Building 1 was closed in November 2012, and its patients transferred to Pilgrim. The two remaining residences (Buildings 150 and 151) are still in use and operated by Pilgrim. The rest of the former hospital grounds have since been converted to state park land.

The loss of this psychiatric center has left a lasting effect on Long Island and the surrounding region. There is a large number of criminally insane that are sent to the Suffolk County jail system for lack of a better place to send them. There simply is not enough space at Pilgrim anymore, so prison has become one of the main providers for mental health in that region of the state.

In a time when most of the big psychiatric centers of yesteryear are now memories of the past, it is difficult to find decent psychiatric care. One nonprofit organization that exists today is called the Citizens Commission on Human Rights (CCHR).

Established in 1969, this organization acts as a "watchdog investigating and exposing psychiatric human rights violations." It is based in Los Angeles, California, although it has numerous chapters all over the world.

Through their efforts, legislation in the United States was enacted to ban the use of electroshock treatment and psychosurgery on children. Deep sleep treatment, a combination of drugs and electroshock treatment, resulting in at least forty-eight deaths, has been banned in Australia. They have even created a Mental Health Declaration of Human Rights. The following are just a few key items from the list.

"No person shall be given psychiatric or psychological treatment against his or her will."

"No person, man, woman or child, may be denied his or her personal liberty by reason of mental illness, so-called, without a fair jury trial by laymen and with proper legal representation."

"No person shall be admitted to or held in a psychiatric institution, hospital or facility because of their political, religious or cultural beliefs and practices."

To learn more, use this link and check out their website:

http://www.cchr.org/about-us/mental-health-declaration-of-human-rights.html

Lost in Time

It's sad that Long Island history isn't taken seriously and becomes forgotten. KPPC, as well as a lot of other sites on the island, are being destroyed because they weren't maintained. KPPC is rich with history and it's just not fair that soon it will be gone, and along with it, the opportunity to remember and learn in the realest sense.

–Amie Bernstein (concerned citizen)

Once the hospital closed down, a lot of things changed for the town of Kings Park. So many people who worked at the hospital were out of work and had to find a way to move on. Former patients became homeless, and the grounds of the hospital were off limits.

There are several roads that went through the hospital grounds, making getting across the town a lot easier. When the hospital closed, those roads were closed too. Barriers were set up, blocking traffic from entering the Kings Park Boulevard, Flynn Road, and many other roads that are still closed to this day. Only a few were eventually reopened. Currently, only Kings Park Boulevard and Flynn Road are open to vehicular traffic.

The abandoned buildings of the hospital were boarded up one by one. Doors were sealed, and large planks of wood covered up most of the windows along the ground level. Entrances into the underground tunnel system were also sealed up. As the years went by, a few areas were even closed using chain-link fences.

| A fence in front of the abandoned dairy farm buildings on March 29, 2011 | Fence in front of the entrance to Building 93 on May 1, 2013 | The fence was put up to deter trespassers, seen here on April 16, 2013 |

Slowly but surely, the hospital began to decay and fade into history. The grounds were no longer kept as well as before. Grass and bushes were allowed to grow wild and thrive. Invasive weeds and vines began to swallow up the structures as they climbed the walls of the buildings and burst through the windows and floors. At times, some buildings literally disappeared from sight. Mother

Nature did her best to erase these once overcrowded buildings from existence. Without maintenance crews to keep the buildings in good condition, she was surely succeeding.

Rainwater flooded the rooftops and eventually broke through the weakened structures, creating gaping holes and causing constant leaks and flooded rooms. When it snowed excessively, the weight of the snow and ice caused a few rooftops to collapse, destroying ceilings and floors below and leaving hazardous holes within some of the older buildings such as Buildings 35, 57, the doctors' cottages behind Macy Home, and the old Group 2 buildings.

Collapsed ceiling in Building 122 of Group 2 on Aug. 2, 2011   Collapsed roof in Building 123 of Group 2 on Aug. 2, 2011   Collapsed front porch of Building 98 on Jan. 2, 2016

Whatever nature did not destroy was destroyed whenever vandals smashed their way into the doors and windows of the buildings to gain access. A few salvageable items were taken from the buildings, while many other things were carelessly destroyed. Sometimes furniture was thrown out of windows or from the rooftops. Walls were covered in graffiti or smashed open so that copper piping could be stolen and sold.

Destroyed wall in Building 93 on Oct. 6, 2013

Garbage pile in the alleyway behind Building 7 on Oct. 5, 2015

Garbage pile in the alleyway behind Building 7 on Oct. 5, 2015

It became necessary to weld doors shut and place iron bars across many of the open doorways and windows. Once again, the place resembled a prison with its iron bars across the windows. This time, people were locked out rather than locked in.

Bars across a door of Building 23 on March 26, 2011

Bars blocking a roll down gate & window at the rear of 93 on July 31, 2009

Cemented windows at the rear of
Building 59 on Dec. 22, 2011

Boarded up windows of Building
132 (73H) on Dec. 22, 2011

Park security patrolling the
grounds on Aug. 14, 2012

A group of teens getting busted
behind Building 93 on Oct. 6, 2013

For a while, a few of the former employees entered the old buildings using their keys, if they retained them. Normally, no one tried to stop them. Former employee Steve Weber actually gave tours of the building exteriors and grounds for several years while he was associated with the Kings Park Heritage Museum. Former employee Al Cibelli, currently of the Pilgrim Psychiatric Center Museum, used to collect artifacts from the buildings to display as museum exhibits. However, after doors were welded shut because of constant trespassers and vandals, those activities came to an end. No one was allowed in the buildings anymore.

Of course, that did not really stop trespassers and vandals. For every new opening they make, it is only a matter of time before it is discovered and sealed by park personnel.

Aerial photo showing Bldg 93, the power plant, & Group 4, circa 2007

Aerial photo from 2007, showing Buildings 7 & 21-23

At first, it might have seemed that the hospital was lost to time. However, with more and more urban exploration Internet websites and books, or ghost hunting shows airing on television, things have changed for the previously forgotten location. A new age has begun. These days, people want to remember the history and pay homage to the countless abandoned locations around the world. Urban exploration and abandoned photography are on the rise as part of that trend. The increase in books over the past decade depicting "Abandoned America" or "Forgotten Long Island" and other such places is proof of that. In fact, this book is also a testament to it.

CHAPTER 19

Abandoned, But Not Forgotten

Trespassing, a Rite of Passage

I came for six years before I even entered a building. The mysterious beauty of everything, it's always interesting to me. This is where I fell in love with photography. In a way, I discovered myself here.
—*Ray Staten* (urban explorer, photographer, and founder of *www.LostinTime.us*)

SINCE CLOSING, SOME of the major concerns regarding the Kings Park Psychiatric Center have been trespassing and vandalism. Between groups of people in search of the paranormal, local teenagers looking for a place to hang out, urban explorers photographing the abandoned for their websites and blogs, and vandals destroying the property or stealing copper piping, it is almost as if the buildings are still in use. They are constantly being visited, although none of it is legal. The former psychiatric center has developed quite a reputation across Long Island as a notorious haunted location. It attracts thrill-seeking and curious individuals from all over New York and even from neighboring states. The thrill of trying not to get caught only adds to the excitement for some.

While the power was shut down after it closed, it remained connected until around 2007–2008. Lights could be seen flickering and blinking on consoles inside of the power plant. Sometimes you were able to actually turn on the lights in the abandoned buildings. That was the case in the Buckman Day Treatment Center.

Abandoned Building 23 with lights on, provided by Ryan McDougall

A humming sound could sometimes be heard coming from the transformers in the basement of some buildings such as Building 7. According to a source of mine, repeaters were placed at the top of this building. These are electronic devices that receive signals and retransmit them at higher levels. After the power was shut down, they operated by generators until a new tower was erected. This is probably what kept the motion sensor alarm powered at the cube/water tower portion at the top of the building.

Basement transformer room of Building 7 on July 11, 2011

Looking up to the top of Building 7 on July 11, 2011

This unit is in the fan room on the tenth floor, circa March 9, 2014

I heard someone actually turned on the power from the power plant (Building 29) and lit up the entire property briefly. Supposedly, this happened more than once until the power was permanently disconnected.

It is quite fortunate no one was hurt and no fires were started. Turning on the power could have resulted in many things going wrong. It is extremely dangerous and reckless. Throughout the many abandoned structures are open fuse boxes, loose wires, puddles of water, stacks of paper, and other flammable and hazardous debris. Someone could have easily been accidentally electrocuted, or a fire could have been started.

One thing that always seems to be true is that people are the one true danger anywhere we exist. As long as the KPPC is devoid of humankind, it is just a complex filled with empty structures, but when foolish and reckless trespassers roam free within the buildings, it can become a deathtrap.

Vandalism has increased dramatically in recent years. Graffiti has been appearing more and more on highly visible locations rather than just on the insides of the buildings as before. There is large-lettered graffiti that adorns the rooftop levels of Buildings 7 and 93. I understand some of these are tributes to dead friends, but there are other ways that can be done so the entire town does not have to see it or so it does not distract from the view of the building.

Graffiti at the top of Bldg 7 makes it resemble a billboard on July 13, 2015

Graffiti at the top of Building 93 on April 17, 2016

Lately, arson has been the main problem. Actually, it has been a concern since the 1970s, when an arsonist burned an entire group of abandoned buildings. It seems like every decade, another building or more is set on fire. In the 1990s, it was Building 124 of Group 2. Building 49 was burned to the ground during the fall of 2000. There were also fires in numerous other buildings since the closing of the hospital. Recently, Buildings 7 and 93 have had several fires, one of the staff cottages was burned right around News Year's Day 2016, and someone started a fire in Building 83 during the fall of the same year, which caused a lot of damage. So far, there have not been any injuries or deaths.

I learned that someone has been arrested in connection with these fires. I can only hope there will be no more fires at this location.

Fire damage to the breezeway behind Building 7 on Oct. 5, 2015

Scorched lobby doors of Building 7 on Oct. 5, 2015

Fire damage within Building 93 on April 17, 2016

Destroyed cottage from Building 18 on Jan. 2, 2016

Fire damage to Building 83 on Sept. 29, 2016

There are also scavengers who tear the place apart so they can steal pipes, roof eaves, and any other objects made of copper, which is very valuable. There is practically no copper left in these buildings anymore. Copper thefts have been going on in these buildings since the 1970s, while the hospital was operational. The damage is quite evident in many photos shown in this book.

One of the earliest reported incidents took place during the mid-1970s, when the copper gutters were stolen from the Group 2 buildings.

These people have absolutely no respect for the historical value of anything. They will destroy walls, floors, and ceilings so they can reach the pipes. They create safety hazards whenever they recklessly destroy the integrity of these structures.

Oftentimes, dangerous dust laden with asbestos and lead paint particles are left lingering in the air or scattered on the floor following the destruction caused by copper thieves. These particles can cling to a person's clothing, skin, and hair. Walking around in these places only helps to kick up more harmful particles into the air. People get these toxic particles all over themselves and their clothing, and then they get into their cars, go home to their families, and sleep in their beds. After prolonged exposure, that person can ultimately become terminally ill.

Mesothelioma is a rare form of cancer that develops from the protective lining that covers most internal body organs. It can be easily contracted through long exposure to asbestos. This form of cancer can take a long time before symptoms become noticeable, and by then, the cancer is in its later stages. Symptoms include coughing, fatigue, fever, night sweats, and weakness of the muscles, which can easily be mistaken for signs of other non-life-threatening illnesses. Therefore, it is often misdiagnosed as such by doctors, allowing it to reach its final stages undetected.

It is very likely an increase in urban exploration has helped to keep this cancer on the rise. Approximately three thousand people are diagnosed with mesothelioma each year in the United

States, and an average of 2,500 die from it each year. In 1999–2010, there have been over thirty-one thousand related deaths.

It is a shame so many young people explore these buildings and are uninformed of the dangers involved.

Asbestos is a white coating that was used to insulate the steam pipes during the early 1900s. At one time, it was great for insulation because of its resistance to heat and was widely used by construction workers and carpenters, especially in power plants, shipbuilding, other building materials, and automotive parts. At the Kings Park facility, it was used in practically every building. In those early days, the risks of using such materials were still unknown. There was a time when asbestos plate covers were used to keep the patients' food warm. The dangers it poses to health only became known by the 1970s.

Asbestos covered clothing & bag on Oct. 24, 2011

Asbestos covered clothing on Nov. 14, 2011

Despite this danger, the derelict buildings have successfully continued to lure curiosity seekers. What exactly is the fascination about an old abandoned psychiatric hospital? Well, that is just it. It was an old psychiatric hospital. One can only imagine the torment that went on there, the intense feelings of loneliness and frustration, and the shock therapy. Not to mention the complete mental anguish of individuals with no true escape from their own miserable existence. This, in some cases, was more real in their minds than in the physical form. The imprinted psychic memories alone that haunt this place probably linger everywhere.

Of course, it can also be a great place to get away for a teenager who feels he or she has no place else to go. There are no movie theaters, arcades, dance clubs, amusement parks, or shopping malls. So, instead, teenagers sneak into the buildings.

Needless to say, teenagers are not the only ones that sneak into the buildings. Places like this attract people of all ages. Some go in on a dare and climb all the way to the top of Buildings 7 or 93, while others might try lying in the old refrigerated drawers of the morgue. The buildings have also attracted former employees and patients. The water tower is a popular attraction for teenagers who go there with the intention of climbing to the top to take in the view.

There are also those who yearn to explore the mysteries of the tunnels beneath the complex. It is less risky to walk where you cannot be seen, and the tunnels connect to mostly every building. The fact that they are dark and spooky only adds to their intrigue.

It is especially unsafe in the tunnels without the proper safety precautions and equipment. Many trespassers do not go out of their way to acquire asbestos safety respirator masks before going to these places. It cannot be just any facemask. The mask *must* be an asbestos-rated mask to provide the proper level of protection needed against asbestos contamination.

A 3M asbestos safety respirator mask from WS Safety Solutions, 1/23/13

Another type of safety mask on Oct. 10, 2011

I have always made certain to be cautious of the dangers that exist throughout the grounds, specifically within the buildings. Aside from breathing in asbestos fibers or lead paint contaminants, there are deadly hazards such as unseen pitfalls, weak floors and ceilings, open elevator shafts, pieces of broken glass, and pointy or edged shards of metal, and there is always the possibility of a collapse. There are plenty of insects and rodents too. They love to hide in dark places.

Some of the more-dangerous locations have already been demolished. The older buildings of Group 2 were among the weakest most dangerous structures, but they are gone now. Some believed the smokestack from the power plant was in danger of collapsing. It is also gone. Building 57, which was nearby, was structurally unsound. The second floor had collapsed onto the first only months before it was demolished. There are still many other dangers out there that some people do not seem to realize when sneaking into these buildings.

Open manhole next to Building 93 on April 29, 2010

Open elevator shaft on Oct. 6, 2013

Jagged branch from a fallen tree on March 17, 2013

Collapsed ceiling & roof in Building 57 on Oct. 27, 2010

Pipe protruding from ground across from Building 93 on May 1, 2013

The Suffolk County Police Department, State Parks Police, and Office of Mental Health patrols have increased their presence in the area in an attempt to ward off trespassers. Most cars observed driving through the boulevard at night are watched closely and pulled over if suspicious. Driving through the boulevard is not allowed at night, since the boulevard is on park property and the park closes at dusk. A word of advice, you are only asking for trouble by doing the obvious.

The Suffolk County Police Department and New York State Police have their hands full with more-serious crimes. Trespassing in abandoned buildings is not high on the list of priorities. As for the State Parks Police, they cover the entire state of New York. Therefore, they are already stretched out thin without having to worry about focusing on an abandoned psychiatric center. Each Halloween and during other high-profile holiday weekends, they have implemented special stepped up patrols.

Door on the floor in Building 22 with bullet holes in it on March 12, 2013

During late October 2009, the FBI conducted several official joint training exercises with the Suffolk County Police Department and their Emergency Services Unit at the KPPC. Explosives were used during the time, so the citizens of Kings Park were warned in advance of the event and advised not to be concerned. They have also conducted shooting exercises in Building 22. There are bullet holes that can be used to verify this information.

On October 14, 2016, the military conducted a drill during the evening. There were more than ten helicopters, several explosions, and gunfire. This time, the police only had about an hour's notice prior to the start of the drill. It was barely enough time to make sure the grounds were clear of trespassers. Many citizens were caught by surprise when they heard what sounded like World War III near their homes. I learned about it through social media, only a half hour after it began, from someone who lives on Old Dock Road.

It is highly probable future training exercises could take place at any time in the future. Believe me, you would not want to accidentally get in the way if that was the case. Fortunately, no one was hurt.

Normally, patrolling the grounds is left to the Office of Mental Health, which monitors the grounds at Kings Park, Central Islip, and Pilgrim Psychiatric Center. The safety officers have their hands full, considering they are understaffed and must divide their patrols between two abandoned hospitals and an active one where trespassing also occurs in its abandoned structures and tunnels.

It is ironic how so many people want to visit the KPPC now that it is abandoned as opposed to when it was still operational, at a time when few people wanted to be there.

It has almost become like a rite of passage for teenagers on Long Island to sneak onto the grounds and enter certain buildings or the tunnels. Graffiti can be found on upper levels proclaiming their success at having reached the top floors or roofs.

Message from Oct. 27, 2007, claiming top floor was conquered on 7/12/02

Top level of Building 93 on July 31, 2009

The rear view from Building 93 on Oct. 22, 2011

These days, it is nearly impossible to keep a child that lives in the area from finding out about the abandoned psychiatric center. Considering the countless photos and videos posted on the Internet and frequent media coverage, it is easy for teenagers and children to learn about it. If not, they surely hear about it from their friends or family members. Even my first book describes the buildings and grounds very thoroughly.

Aside from music video-style video tours of the buildings, rooftops, and tunnels, there have been videos of reckless teens rappelling off the sides of the taller buildings and even climbing to the very top of Buildings 7 and 93. The same person also has a video of himself and his friends spraying graffiti on the walls inside of Building 7 and then carelessly throwing an empty spray can out of the window without even checking to see if anyone might have been walking by outside.

It is reckless and stupid behavior like this that can get someone hurt. There is nothing cool or cute about it. It is careless and dangerous. Be considerate of other people.

In the 1980s, a maintenance worker fell from the top of Building 93. He was wearing safety gear at the time, and he was more experienced, yet he still fell to his death. Luck will not always be on your side. Think before you act.

An old wives' tale told to young people growing up in Kings Park was that there are former patients roaming around the woods and in the abandoned buildings. Some believed former patients might have returned to the only place they knew as home. It is not unlikely for the buildings to attract vagrants or gangs.

According to police, each year there are hundreds of violations tickets issued to trespassers. Dozens of arrests are made for various other infractions, ranging from trespassing to burglary.

One suggestion made by the townspeople to prevent trespassing was to have surveillance cameras installed around the property near the buildings. This could definitely act as a deterrent to trespassers and scavengers. However, it would be expensive, and someone would have to monitor these cameras, so it is unlikely it will ever happen. There is also a chance vandals could steal or damage the cameras, which would also prove to be costly.

Another possible solution offered was to brick up the entrances to the underground tunnels. This would definitely be an effective way of putting a stop to trespassing because those tunnels are an essential link to the buildings, and they can allow for unseen passage throughout the property. With each demolition project, tunnel passages are filled in or blocked off. It is only a matter of time before the tunnels become a series of small passages that lead nowhere. Of course, that could take years, and there will still be accessible tunnels even after the buildings are long gone, as was the case with Edgewood.

That was the case when Edgewood State Hospital was demolished. There are still tunnels beneath that property. It is just harder to get to them now, and they do not lead to anything.

Stephen Weber, former hospital employee and respected resident of the community, has stated that until the fate of the site is finally decided, video cameras should be installed and access to the underground tunnels should be shut down. In an interview, he was quoted saying, "*It's a vital conduit through the system. Just brick it up.*"

Both the New York State Police and Kings Park School District have considered sending literature home to parents to warn them of the dangers their children could face inside the buildings or tunnels. In addition, signs could be posted all around the property warning individuals of the medical dangers they face when trespassing. It is not enough to just post signs stating that trespassing is illegal. They need to know it can also be dangerous.

WARNING!

IF YOU ENTER ANY PROHIBITED AREA, YOU MAY BE SERIOUSLY INJURED, KILLED OR EXPOSED TO HAZARDOUS SUBSTANCES.

YOU WILL BE ARRESTED AND PROSECUTED

 ALL GROUNDS ARE CLOSED AT DUSK
IF YOU OBSERVE ILLEGAL ACTIVITY CALL THE
NY STATE PARK POLICE AT 631-669-2500 OR DIAL 9-1-1

Yellow "No Trespassing" sign

A sign from March 26, 2011   A good example of the kind of signs needed from Nov. 15, 2010

"There are so many risks," according to the Kings Park schools superintendent Martin Brooks. *"You don't want your children to be there. It's not safe."*

He is absolutely right. Yet I have seen young children there without adult supervision.

You should never assume you are alone when inside any abandoned building. Urban explorers tend to forget about potential dangers when they are operating on adrenaline or focusing on taking photos of their exploits. It is amazing more people have not gotten hurt or victimized, but do not be fooled. It does happen.

Someone was robbed while exploring a building at Kings Park. The unknown assailant struck the victim and fled with the victim's camera. To my knowledge, the perpetrator was never caught. It must be kept in mind that these buildings attract people from all over. Not everyone that explores the grounds is a friendly face.

Whenever I go to someplace like this, I am always careful, and I keep a close eye on anyone who is with me. With my experience, I know what kind of dangers to look for, and I am always ready for anything. Safety is never an afterthought for me. It is my first priority.

Back in 2011, a twenty-year-old woman was sexually assaulted on the hike-and-bike trail. This is the sort of thing you would never expect to happen at Kings Park, but it did. This heinous crime occurred early in the evening, while it was still daylight. Even during the day, this place can be dangerous, especially if you are alone.

In the process of writing this book, I have come to know many urban explorers. Despite all of the emphasis I have placed on the dangers of exploring an abandoned location, I know nothing I say will stop them from doing what they love. Some people like to take chances. I hope those that do are, at least, careful and remember these warnings. It is always safer to assume you are never alone and best to keep your wits about you. Be aware of the nearest entrance and exits. Always remember the way you came because you may have to leave the same way. Be cognizant of the condition of the floors, walls, and ceilings. Above all, always wear safety masks when necessary and refrain from eating at these locations. Do you really think you can kick up asbestos while walking around and then eat clean food? Think again.

Be smart and be safe.

Personally, I have always treated each location as if it were sacred ground. I try to avoid damaging property in any way. I show a great deal of respect for the property, and most of all, I never disrespect the spirits of the dead who once resided within the buildings. For me, it is about exploring the past. It is my way of time traveling. I like to look and learn.

To some, the KPPC was a cruel, dark, and lonely place, but for others, it was the only home they ever knew. This must be acknowledged and remembered. It was a different experience for every one of those poor souls. It was not a place of adventure, fun, and excitement. Sometimes there was fear, terror, anger, frustration, loneliness, or extreme depression.

Think about that the next time you go there.

View from Group 4 on Sept. 3, 2011, courtesy of Kat Sederquist

Urban Photographer's Paradise

Let this hell be our heaven.
            –Richard Matheson (author), *What Dreams May Come*,
                                                                    1977

Today, the Kings Park Psychiatric Center sits mostly vacant with just a few buildings either operated by Pilgrim Psychiatric Center or by the New York State Office of Parks, Recreation and Historic Preservation. Its dilapidated buildings, which are slowly being consumed by surrounding trees, now more resemble a long-lost civilization. Scattered here and there are a few mementos of the hospital's glory days such as an old rusty tricycle at the rear of Building 40, the basketball court behind Building 15, or the no-longer-recognizable tennis courts next to the old firehouse.

While the New York State Office of Parks, Recreation and Historic Preservation maintain much of the land, the abandoned buildings have been neglected and left to decay further. The powerful contrast between the decayed graffiti-covered buildings with broken windows and the beautiful parkland located near the picturesque Kings Park Bluff and Long Island Sound has the makings of a surrealistic scene.

Aerial view of lower end
from March 14, 2005

Aerial facing west from March 14, 2005

Aerial facing east from March 14, 2005

Aerial of Vet Group from
March 14, 2005

The state has tried many times to sell the property for redevelopment, but because of the environmental cleanup costs involved and community opposition, so far it has been unsuccessful.

In January 2006, New York State aborted the sale of the property. By the end of that year, the rest of the land was transferred over to the Office of Parks, Recreation and Historic Preservation, but it is unclear whether it will remain part of the park.

There are those like myself who feel it is their historical duty to society to document with the use of cameras what the buildings have become.

This considerably large property has become a testament to the past, composed of dozens of derelict buildings and cottages, vast open grounds of overgrown greenery, a forgotten reservoir, and an intricate system of dark underground steam tunnels that connect most of the buildings on the complex.

Although the buildings have long since been abandoned, the power they possess over those who dare to visit them is indeed truly magnificent. They manage to exude an almost supernatural impression that is dark, eerie, solemn, dizzying, depressing, imposing, and, at times, all too quiet. Yet this old asylum still seems to serve as a great place for exploration, inspiration, and personal reflection.

A chair on a porch of Building
136 (73L) on Dec. 22, 2011

Chairs in one of the turrets of
Group 4 on Aug. 25, 2011

Facing east from the roof of
Building 7 on Nov. 7, 2011

Looking toward Bldg 93 from the roof
of York Hall by Ryan McDougall

The view facing the LI Sound from the roof of Group 4 on Aug. 31, 2013

View facing the LI Sound from the roof of Building 93 on March 27, 2013

A garden in front of Building 125 (73A) on May 11, 2011

Healing garden at Kings Park Bluff on July 13, 2015

When you step onto the hospital grounds in the daytime, a feeling of peace and oneness with nature can easily overtake you. The close proximity to the Long Island Sound and the Nissequogue River provides fabulous views of the water. The water can even be seen from the boulevard, which is at a higher level than the older portion of the Nissequogue River State Park. During the daytime, the smell of freshly cut grass often fills the air as an abundance of beautiful trees and fields of grass surround you. The duck pond and boat basin allow for fantastic photos all year around. Recently, several small gardens have been established, adding to the beauty and serenity.

The wonderful scenic views of the park alone provide a fantastic backdrop for photographers. The opportunity to capture wildlife in natural habitats using still photography or video is an added incentive. Still, there is so much more to capture that is hard to resist even for the average photographer with a simple "point and shoot" camera.

Myself taking photos on Sept. 5, 2012

Members of my team, YGI, on March 17, 2013

Hidden away in plain sight are the mysterious old buildings where life once thrived. People once worked there, and patients were committed to the now empty wards. People laughed and cried. All are now mere echoes of the past. Instead, a ghostlike vacancy has been left behind, creating a strange void that lingers on the verge of destruction.

Toys in Building 40 on Aug. 2, 2011

Clothes in a closet of Building 93 on July 31, 2009

Novels on the floor of a lounge in Building 144 (73T) on Jan. 1, 2016

Inside the buildings, one can find various artifacts of the past. Some belonged to the hospital, while others were patient or employee belongings. This place was home to both. Sometimes you may find rusted bed frames or gurneys that may or may not be covered by filthy, stained mattresses. Broken furniture, mostly chairs, are scattered in every shadowy corner. Abandoned medical equipment can also be found in the different medical buildings around the complex.

Most of the windows are broken, so there is almost always a draft in the halls. Many of the doors are welded shut, locked, or stuck on loose floor tiles and debris. In fact, it has become difficult to ascertain what color the crumbling floor tiles used to be in some places because of the amount of dust, debris, and asbestos on the floors.

On the wards, you may find hairbrushes, books, and clothing. There are also old paintings hanging on the walls of some wards, accompanied by numerous scribbled graffiti drawings, words, and witty phrases written by trespassers over the years. It has become a popular practice for some graffiti artists and explorers to mark the exits with arrows and the word "*Exit.*"

Painting hanging on the wall in Building 21 on March 9, 2014

Exit written on the wall in Building 93 on June 28, 2009

Shakespeare on the wall of Building 44 on March 17, 2013

In certain buildings, patient files can still be found, except they are often scattered across the floor or overflowing from an old cabinet or desk. I found some in the basement of Building 15 and on a second-floor storage room of Building 44, although that particular room was destroyed by fire along with all of the documents within.

Most of the kitchens are still filled with dirty old dishes. A few of the bathrooms even have rolls of toilet paper in them, although vandals have smashed most of the sinks and toilets to pieces.

Kitchen with leftover dishes in Building 15 on March 11, 2010

Semi-decent bathroom with TP in Building 128 on Jan. 5, 2014

Unmolested bathroom in Building 1 on Feb. 7, 2015

Damaged bathroom in Building 93 on June 28, 2009

Destroyed bathroom in Building 90 on March 17, 2013

Destroyed bathroom in Building 39 (73Q) on April 28, 2013

There are so many items that were left behind that one would think everyone left in a hurry. It is as if there was no time to pack. They just rushed off, leaving everything behind.

Venturing onto the grounds at night provides a different set of sensations than during the daytime, although it is not advised because it is illegal. Because of budget cuts, most of the lights along the boulevard are often turned off. This sets the stage for almost complete darkness, allowing many opportunities for infrared photography. Every shadow appears to move as the darkness surrounds you.

Infrared camera set up with an
infrared lamp on Jan. 23, 2013

Photo looking down the hallway taken
with infrared camera on 1/ 23/13

The buildings slowly emerge out of the darkness one by one, as you draw near. You can almost imagine the pain that was once felt throughout the property. Suddenly, feelings of loneliness and dread prevail, and you begin to sense the isolation former patients might have experienced and aching of the lost souls that lived in these now darkened empty buildings who probably never had a chance to live normal lives. Looking through these buildings, you can only imagine what life was like. Some items give the impression that maybe they had some good times. Games and paintings can still be found in a few of the old recreation rooms, which meant they did have some fun.

Parcheesi on a table in the basement
of Building 43 on Aug. 25, 2011

Monopoly on the floor in
Building 43 on Aug. 25, 2011

Sneaking into the buildings only adds to the eerie feelings. Occasionally, one has a feeling that he or she is not alone. It almost feels like someone is watching you. Perhaps, it is the ghost of some patient, nurse, or attendant. Of course, it might just be someone else, who snuck in and is hiding from you. There are so many people who enter these buildings at any given time that you eventually stand the chance of running into someone else who is trespassing. It is easy to jump to conclusions and assume you saw or heard a ghost. The fact is you have no idea who will be there hiding in the shadows. It is a chance you take whenever venturing into dangerous places.

Seeing the World through Broken Windows

While we think we are looking out of these windows, the glass is looking at us . . . judging us and sound-proofing our voices. If only these windows could tell their own stories, then we would really know what it was like to be inside. From these windows we can guess the past, but can never really tell it how these windows saw it . . .

–Michael Confortin (urban explorer, daredevil, and resident of Long Island), 2016

Looking into Building 137 (730) on March 26, 2011

Negative camera effect of a Building 22 ward on Dec. 26, 2011

Looking out from Building 122 in 2012, courtesy of Max Neukirch, Jr.

Looking out from Building 7 on Sept. 2, 2010

The world of urban exploration is growing every day. Each year a new place is abandoned. It opens up countless opportunities for urban explorers to go forth and do their thing.

For the purpose of better understanding the fascination behind the abandoned buildings at Kings Park, I will explain the world of urban exploration. In short, urban exploration is the investigation of abandoned man-made structures or ruins. In a way, it is a combination of archaeology and anthropology, only exploring modern ruins for the average person. No degree is required. There are no permits or training. You learn as you go, and anyone can do it. All you need is a location and the willingness to do whatever has to be done to explore that location. The only real tools needed are a decent camera, a flashlight, and perhaps some safety equipment. Actually, you do not even need those.

Urban explorers walking past Building
5 at night on April 20, 2011

Urban explorers walking near
Building 93 on March 17, 2013

Looking down on a group as they
enter Building 93 on Oct. 6, 2013

Someone inside of Building 43
of Group 4 on Aug. 31, 2013

Urban explorers on the roof of Bldg
41 of Group 4 on Aug. 31, 2013

Urban explorers on the roof of
Building 22 on March 9, 2014

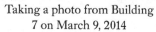

Taking a photo from Building 7 on March 9, 2014

A photographer outside of Building 44 on April 17, 2016

There is definitely a historical interest that goes along with it. There is a certain curiosity that draws a person to an abandoned location in the first place. While exploring, you are digging into the past of any given location. You are searching the environment for clues of the past and trying to learn what life might have been like at that place. Was it a good place? Was it a terrible place? These might be thoughts going through your mind as you find articles that belonged to the people that once occupied or worked at the location.

The main reason for this type of exploration is to find old things. Whether it is antique furniture, clothing, books, paperwork, photographs, old newspapers, toys, vintage tools, or some type of equipment, it is your ultimate goal to find a piece of the past. You want to know what era these things were from and why were they left behind.

Bldg 93 from
Bldg 94 on
10/27/10 by
Mia Dentici

The power plant &
Group 4 from Building
93 on Oct. 6, 2013

The rooftop level of Building
93 on Oct. 6, 2013

Inside of Building 82 on July 5, 2012   Looking into Building 5 on Nov. 7, 2011

Looking into Building 42 of
Group 4 on Aug. 31, 2013

Storage room at Building
44 on April 17, 2016

There are explorers who like to take home souvenirs from their explorations. When you think about the alternative, which is leaving the items to wither away and be covered in mold and mildew, would it not be better to take an item and preserve it? No matter what the item is, someone created it with the intention of it being used and appreciated.

When an abandoned location is demolished, all of the items within are usually destroyed too. Very few things are ever saved. Everything inside is gone forever once it becomes one with the rubble of the building. After it is cleared away, there is absolutely nothing left.

Some items that can be saved from abandoned locations are really not in bad shape. They can be cleaned and repaired. All it may take is a good polishing. Some items may require minor repairs. As the saying goes, "*One man's garbage is another man's treasure.*"

These items have been discarded and left behind, which is the real crime. They are essentially garbage now. Therefore, it is not stealing to take these items. You are not taking anything from anyone. It is salvaging and recycling. It is rescuing.

If a few of these items can end up in a museum, then even better. I have personally donated a stack of hospital paperwork to the Kings Park Heritage Museum. I know urban explorers who have also donated items to that museum and to the Pilgrim Psychiatric Center Museum. It is largely due to urban exploration that these two museums have such wonderful exhibits from the hospitals on display.

Of course, there is more to urban exploration than collecting potential antiques and souvenirs.

For some, it is more about the thrill and excitement involved. They thrive on the potential dangers of getting caught, perhaps getting injured, or just doing something crazy because there is no one there to stop you from doing it. It is an adventure without having to go too far out of your way, unless you choose to do so, and some people certainly do.

"Epic" on a window of Building 7 on July 11, 2011

Looking out of a rear window of Building 136 (73L) on Dec. 22, 2011

In the basement of Building 15 on March 12, 2013

Looking through a door in Building 7 on March 9, 2014

Looking out of a window from Building 1 on Feb. 7, 2015

Truly dedicated urban explorers will travel to other states and even other countries just to explore ruins. It is easy to find new locations by searching the Internet and reading books.

Urban explorers are also interested in photographing abandoned locations. When you enter some of these places, it almost seems like time has stopped and you are transported to another era. Not all abandoned locations are in as bad shape as the buildings at Kings Park. There are places in the world time has truly forgotten. They are not covered in graffiti or destroyed by vandals. They look just as they did when they were first abandoned, only dustier. It is places like this that make you truly appreciate the history of a location, when you can still see it, as if you were there in the past.

At Kings Park, all you can really see is the destruction that has been caused over the years. You have to dig very deep to find the beauty. The unnecessary vandalism has destroyed much of the outer beauty that was once the Kings Park remembered by former employees. At least this book will help to show how it once looked before the graffiti, before the fires, and before the broken and boarded-up windows.

| Bldg 23 on 2/24/11 by Mia Dentici | Inside Building 23 on Nov. 7, 2011 | Outside of Building 23 on Sept. 9, 2011 |

Looking into Bldg 123 of Group 2 in 2008 by Max Neukirch, Jr.   Graffiti around the windows in Building 48 on Oct. 24, 2011

"Something about this vision just seems so troubled, that a person facing mental pain spent their days behind these very windows, as if it was their home. That us, looking through these broken windows, see a clearer vision of what they never got to see," says Matthew Vianna of Long Island.

There is a certain beauty in urban exploration that is difficult to understand unless you have experienced it firsthand. It can be an escape unlike any other–a place where you can leave your reality behind for a short time and enter a world of fantasy, except it is real. Some places will leave you feeling breathless, while others will bring you a tremendous feeling of tranquility. There is so much to experience in this world. Just because a place is abandoned does not mean it should be forgotten.

One lesson learned by all urban explorers is that there can be great beauty in abandonment.

Looking toward Building 93 from Building 15 on March 12, 2013

Open window at Building 136 (73L) on March 27, 2011

Looking out from a basement window on Dec. 22, 2011

Looking toward Building 125 (73A) on Dec. 22, 2011

"We pick up the pieces of our lives . . .
Crawl through the broken glass.
Sunshine came through the pristine windows then,
A false reality protecting human spirits . . .
Purposeful–
And with Dignity.

Gray and blurred now,
Buildings aging but holding on,
The blood of perseverance runs through their veins,
No matter how far they have been shattered and broken.
We must preserve at least a part of them,
This history.
To remind us of their courage,
To remind us of their compassion,
To remind us of their perseverance."

By Pamela Mary Schmidt of Kings Park, 2016

Peeking through a door in
Building 94 on March 17, 2013

Looking through a door in
Building 93 on Oct. 6, 2013

The rear view of Building
93 on March 27, 2013

Looking up from inside of
Building 93 on Oct. 6, 2013

Looking down to the
boulevard on Oct. 6, 2013

Looking down from Group
4 on Aug. 31, 2013

CHAPTER 20

The Nissequogue River State Park

A New State Park

By protecting this valuable property, we are providing New Yorkers with more open space for their enjoyment and ensuring that the most important and environmentally sensitive lands will be preserved for generations to come.

        –George E. Pataki (former governor of New York State)

IT WAS WEDNESDAY, on November 10, 1999, when then N Y S governor George E. Pataki made an announcement that there would be a new state park on Long Island. The park would encompass the 159 acres of land north of St. Johnland Road that once belonged to the Kings Park Psychiatric Center. In the spring of 2000, this waterfront portion of the former hospital reopened as the Nissequogue River State Park.

This large area of land was carved out of the part of the hospital grounds where the remains of the Veterans' Memorial Hospital Unit buildings are located. By turning this area into state parkland, it legally protected the land from commercial and residential development, keeping some semblance of what the hospital used to be.

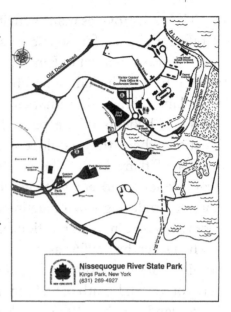

The hospital was originally founded on this land because it was vast open country conveniently situated near the Long Island Sound. It was, and still is, a beautiful parcel of land.

Nissequogue River State Park map from 2011

Of course, this is no ordinary state park. Throughout the park, one can see the abandoned buildings of the hospital, some of which are fenced off for safety reasons, while others such as Buildings 136 and 144 have their boarded-up windows covered by beautifully painted artwork by children of the nearby schools, as seen in earlier chapters.

After this region of land was transferred over to the New York State Office of Parks, Recreation and Historic Preservation, it was like a gift to the townspeople of Kings Park. Ever since the hospital closed several years earlier, the land stood in limbo with several possible futures, all of which stirred ill feelings within the community. It was a good piece of land that was going to waste, and no one could agree on what to do with it. Many ideas were presented, but in the end, only one stuck. Turning it into a park seemed like the best solution. Thus, the Nissequogue River State Park was born.

The park provides many activities for the people of Kings Park. It offers a chance for people to see the true beauty behind the little suburban hamlet of Kings Park. There are many ecosystems within the area, including beaches, tidal and freshwater wetlands, woodlands, brackish estuaries, and a bird sanctuary. All are treasured habitats of the park. The townspeople finally had a location where they could enjoy games and sports activities such as Tiffany Field. The convenience of the boat basin was available for all to enjoy. New ideas for the park are constantly coming up during town meetings, but like many other plans for redevelopment, new suggestions fail because of a lack of funding.

In December 2006, as one of the last acts of his outgoing administration, Governor Pataki transferred the remaining 365 acres of the land south of St. Johnland Road, the bulk of the former KPPC land, to the Office of Parks, Recreation, and Historical Preservation. This area included a hike-and-bike trail, which opened in 2004, under the Rails to Trails Grant. Historical signs were added along the trail to identify the hospital buildings that once stood nearby.

Hike & Bike Trail sign on May 11, 2011   Sign for Building 5 on Sept. 9, 2011

This section is considered the new part of the Nissequogue River State Park, although a sign posted in March 2016 says otherwise. It is as if the park does not wish to acknowledge this portion of land where the majority of large hospital buildings still stand abandoned. Its future remains in question.

Park sign at boulevard entrance
on March 8, 2016

Park entrance sign at St. Johnland
Rd on April 19, 2016

In the early part of 2008, the park banned pets from the grounds in both the new and old portions of the park. Signs were put up near the entrances as warnings. This decision upset many park visitors and members of the community who felt a sense of security and comfort when walking their

"No pets" sign on May 11, 2011

dogs through the park. Despite complaints that went on for more than a year, the signs remain in place nearly a decade later.

Currently, there are plans to demolish several abandoned hospital buildings in the park while renovating two old cottages for use as a comfort station and a potential museum. New rustic scenic paths and trails will be added, while vegetation will be cleared away to enhance the view of the Long Island Sound. There are also plans to build a picnic pavilion and establish a new playing field for visitors.

It seems the people of Kings Park will soon be treated to an even better park. I look forward to seeing some of the changes, especially if they will be an improvement. At the same time, I will be saddened to see some of the structures go. I have developed an attachment to their history. As a frequent visitor to the park, I hope I will not be disappointed.

Nissequogue River State Park Activities

Be healthy by being outdoors in the natural daylight with nature!
–Steven Magee (author and engineer), *Light Forensics*,
2014

The Nissequogue River State Park has plenty of activities to offer for hikers, boat owners, and nature lovers. There are gardens, trails, a bird pond sanctuary, the marina, and an athletic field. While walking through the park, one might also notice a few scattered abandoned hospital buildings. It is illegal to trespass in these buildings.

Close-up of a red dahlia
on Sept. 29, 2016

A bee pollinating some pink
daisies on July 13, 2015

Various flowers in front of Building
125 (73A) on May 11, 2011

Proof that fruit still grows in
the area on Aug. 3, 2012

Former staff houses on May 1, 2013   Buildings of the Veterans'
                                              Group on May 1, 2013

There is one former hospital building that is open to the public. The main office of the park is located within the former main administration building of the hospital, Building 125. Inside is a small museum dedicated to the nature of the park. There are various nature exhibits, including stuffed animals indigenous to the area. Historic photographs of the former hospital grounds are displayed on the wall. As with most museums, the exhibits are subject to change from time to time. Also in this building are restrooms, a water cooler, and useful pamphlets and maps.

 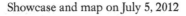 

Showcase and map on July 5, 2012   Close-up of map
                                            on July 5, 2012

Bookshelves &
educational material
in Children's Room
on Jan. 2, 2016

Leaf learning game in
the Children's Room
on Jan. 2, 2016

Bird learning game in
the Children's Room
on Jan. 2, 2016

Closed tree learning
game in the Children's
Room on Jan. 2, 2016

Open tree learning
game in the Children's
Room on Jan. 2, 2016

Birds of the garden
chart in the Children's
Room on Jan. 2, 2016

There are numerous trails throughout the park that take you through the woods, near the Long Island Sound and Nissequogue River, and around the ruins of the former state hospital. One can walk along the thirty-two-acre Greenbelt Trail, which extends through three state parks in Smithtown, or ride along the shorter hike-and-bike trail, which opened in 2004, along the hospital's old railroad spur route. The trails go all along the borders of the park with several lookout points while passing by a few of the former psychiatric center's abandoned buildings. Guided nature walks are available, while other environmental programs are offered throughout the year.

Sign for the Hike & Bike Trail at   Hike & Bike Trail on Sept. 9, 2011
Flynn Rd on Dec. 19, 2012

Entrance to the   A sign on a tree marking   A web-friendly
Greenbelt Trail near the   the location of the trail   informational sign along
canal on Jan. 1, 2016   on May 11, 2016   the trail on May 11, 2016

Facing south on the Greenbelt   Facing north on the trail
Trail on May 11, 2016   on May 11, 2016

The Kings Park Bluff offers a magnificent view of the Long Island Sound looking toward Connecticut, especially from the Long Island Sound Overlook.

Looking toward the canal from
the Old Docks on May 1, 2013

Looking across the river at
Short Beach on May 1, 2013

Looking across the beach toward
the Old Docks on May 11, 2016

The view toward Bridgeport,
Connecticut, on Sept. 17, 2016

The nearby Osprey Overlook offers an impressive view of the Nissequogue River estuary. This lookout point is located just down the hill behind the abandoned two-family doctors' cottages. It runs through a wooded area along the water. The best way to reach it is by taking Canal Road heading east to the marina along the boat basin, make a left, and then head north onto the Greenbelt Trail.

There is a boat launch not far from the main park office, Building 125 (73A), at the boat basin. There was once a boathouse belonging to the state hospital, but that was demolished. The boat launch can also be used to launch canoes and kayaks, which were at one time available for rental. However, since the boathouse was removed, I am uncertain if this is still possible.

The launch is only accessible during certain times of the year because of extremely low tide and mudflats. It is only open four hours before and four hours after high tide. Boats can be stored here during the summer but must be removed by the end of October. The low tide is at its worst during the winter months. One can check with the Long Island/North Shore tide tables, which are available in the main office. The information can also be found online at

http://www.canoerentals.com/Calendar.htm

or

http://www.tide-forecast.com/locations/
Nissequogue-River-entrance-Long-Island-Sound-New-York/tides/latest.

It is always best to travel the river on a rising tide. A round trip along the Nissequogue River can take four to five hours. Therefore, be cognizant of the time when heading out on the river and make sure someone always knows you are there.

Looking south toward Building 93 from Short Beach on May 11, 2016

Looking toward the Old Docks from Short Beach on May 11, 2016

River toward the canal from near the
Osprey Overlook on May 11, 2016

Canadian geese on Sept. 17, 2016

The north marina launching
area on Sept. 17, 2016

Boats docked at the north
marina on May 11, 2011

The Old Docks on May 1, 2013

Boats docked at the mouth of
the river on Sept. 9, 2016

| Marina signs at the entrance to the marina on Oct. 5, 2015 | Park activities sign on July 5, 2012 | This area shown on Oct. 5, 2015 south of boathouse, used to be marshlands |

Fishing is always a great activity. There are numerous fish to be found here. This ecologically sensitive area includes twenty-five acres of saltwater wetlands as well as a coastal habitat, which is home to a variety of reptiles, amphibians, and other animals.

With its many migrating shorebirds, the park is also a bird conservation area complete with several lookout points along the river. There are many different types of birds throughout the park's wooded areas and near the water.

Poison ivy grows in several wooded areas of the park, so try to avoid it. In addition, there are plenty of thorn bushes throughout the grounds. There is also a danger of Lyme disease from deer ticks. Signs have been posted in certain areas to warn visitors. It is also possible to step into an open access hatch or manhole, since there is a vast underground labyrinth of tunnels beneath the former hospital grounds. Sometimes these entrances are carelessly left open by trespassers who venture through the tunnels. A friend of mine once lost his shoe. He was lucky not to fall in.

The park has made use of the former hospital's greenhouse (Building 65), opening it to the public, located just off of the first road north of St. Johnland Road after going toward the right when entering the park. In the greenhouse, one can enjoy the wonderful plants and flowers within, but photos are not allowed.

Looking toward the greenhouse on May 11, 2011

Tiffany Field on Oct. 6, 2013

A large athletic field named Tiffany Field is available for sporting activities but only by permit. It is located where Kings Park Boulevard meets with St. Johnland Road. Parking is available next to the field with additional parking along the boulevard in front of the abandoned Macy Home. The field is equipped with goal posts, bleachers, and portable toilets.

The Nissequogue River State Park is open seven days a week from sunrise to sunset, all year round, unless otherwise noted. The main park entrance is where Kings Park Boulevard meets St. Johnland Road in front of York Hall and across from Tiffany Field. A tollbooth marks the entry point if entering by vehicle. During the warmer months, a parking fee must be paid. Otherwise, free parking is available on the grounds near the main office during the off-season, beginning after Labor Day and ending on Memorial Day weekend.

Guardhouse on July 5, 2012

Picnic & barbecue area on May 11, 2016

As a member of the Nature Conservancy, I care about our state parks and hope many of you do as well. When visiting the park, please do your part to keep the park clean and visitor-friendly. Remember, our state parks are for all of us to enjoy. Please do not ruin the experience for others. Thank you.

Please help enhance the beauty of the park by making a tax-deductible donation to the Nissequogue River State Park Foundation, PO box 159, Kings Park, New York 11754.

www.ourstatepark.com

For more information or for any questions, call the park's main office at (631) 269-4927. For group outings or youth day camp applications, call (631) 669-1000, extension 223. If you wish to make a reservation for a canoe or kayak, call (631) 581-1072. Normal business days are Wednesdays through Sundays from 8:30 a.m. to 5:00 p.m. In case of an emergency, call the Park Police at (631) 669-2500, or simply dial 911.

http://nysparks.com/parks/110/details.aspx

CHAPTER 21

Redevelopment Plans

Development Ideas

It's right next to Sunken Meadow Park and the Nissequogue River and faces Long Island Sound, which we're trying to upgrade. This is a regional resource too precious to put up for development.
— Steve Englebright (NYS Assemblyman)

REDEVELOPING THE BUILDINGS and the land has been something the state and county have been considering long before the hospital closed. There were already several abandoned structures as of the 1970s. This continued into the next decade.

By the early 1980s, there were plans to convert one of the nursing students' residences, Home W (Building 36), into temporary housing for the poor. The residents of Kings Park were in an uproar because this was planned without their knowledge. This came at a time when Suffolk County was housing welfare clients in motels, which were being used as emergency housing. It was estimated that renovations for the building would come to $326,000, and that did not include the cost of food and electricity.

These plans were never fulfilled, but this would not be the only cause for worry the townspeople would have. During the early 1990s, rumors of another proposal led to more feelings of outrage.

In the early part of 1993, there were plans to use two vacant four-apartment residences and one staff house as alternative housing for psychiatric patients from Brooklyn that were ready to be discharged but unable to return to city living. This included Building 126 (73B), another similar building nearby, and, once again, one of the staff houses. This proposal included bringing in outside agencies such as the Federation Employment and Guidance Services (FEGS) to operate the residences.

<table>
<tr><td>Building 126 (73B) on April 19, 2016</td><td>Rear of Building 126 (73B) on April 19, 2016</td></tr>
</table>

While these plans were not definite, the hospital made necessary preparations. The residents of the staff house were given until June 30, 1993, only a few months' time, to vacate the premises and find other living accommodations.

Numerous townspeople were under the impression that the hospital was going to be renting to underprivileged people that would actually arrive from Brooklyn, which was a false notion. Another concern was that these former patients, who could possibly have criminal records and issues with drug abuse, would be allowed to roam the community unsupervised. Residents feared for their safety and believed the crime rate would go up.

No agreement was ever signed, partially because of overwhelming protests from the community. In the end, the staff members that were evicted got the short end of the stick. They were not allowed back.

By the time July arrived, the town of Smithtown had proposed to develop 930 housing units on the property once it closed, consisting of ten single-family homes, ten two-family homes, twenty townhouses, 240 condominiums, 450 apartments, and two hundred senior citizen housing units. Some new buildings would be built for this purpose, while a few of the current structures would also be utilized.

The town board did not adopt this proposal.

KPPC Re-Use Plan artwork

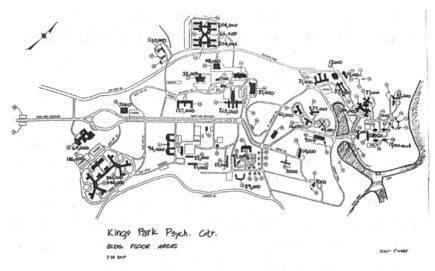

Kings Park Psych. Ctr.
BLDG. FLOOR AREAS
7-74 DMP
SCALE: 1"=400'

KPPC Building Areas, circa 1994

The only definite thing was that the New York State Office of Mental Health planned on closing the hospital by the end of the decade. There was speculation it might even close sooner. The hospital was tentatively set to close in October 1997.

When the hospital closed a year earlier than expected, there were different ideas on what to do with the hundreds of acres of land. The New York State Empire Development Corporation was one of the first to take bids on the site. There were also environmentalists that wanted the land to be used as a park, while developers had hopes to build a shopping mall and residential community. Another idea was to build a golf course like what was done at Letchworth Village in Haverstraw, New York. Many residents opposed this idea because there are already plenty of golf courses in the county. Other proposed ideas included building luxury condos, converting Building 93 into a hotel, creating a nursing home or assisted-living quarters for the elderly, opening a recreation center for children, and establishing a private hospital, a college, or a government office center.

Some of the buildings were painted on the inside and considered for leasing to outside entities such as Building 7 and certain buildings of Group 2. However, there were strict stipulations that included limiting the hours of operation. In addition, the interested parties would never be able to own these buildings. They would only be leased. No deals were ever made.

In 2000, part of the land became the Nissequogue River State Park. Most of the townspeople were pleased by this decision. They got the park they wanted, along with use of the marina and playing field. In time, a trail was added for hiking and biking on the old railroad spur, adding to the beauty of the new park.

Within a year, some of the roads that had been blocked off when the hospital shut down five years earlier were finally reopened to public traffic, much to the delight of daily commuters. It was, once again, possible to drive from East Main Street/Route 25A to St. Johnland Road without having to use side roads to get around the former hospital grounds.

In 2002, a real estate development company, Saccardi & Schiff Inc., published a large study based upon the former state hospital's grounds. This would mark the beginning of the end for some abandoned structures. As part of the study, several redevelopment recommendations were made for the remainder of the land, including dividing it into 185 lots.

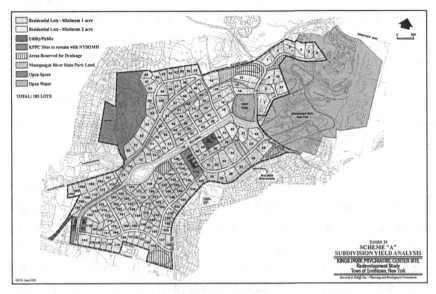

KPPC Redevelopment Scheme "A," circa June 2002

Abandoned Building 125
(73A) by King Pedlar

Broken window at Bldg 40 of Group
2 on 2/24/11 by Mia Dentici

Looking out from inside
Building 23 on Nov. 7, 2011

Upper level windows in Building
136 (73L) on Jan. 5, 2014

Since the closing of the hospital, its buildings stood dormant for the first decade or so. As time went on, the buildings became dilapidated, and some were eventually slated for demolition. However, demolishing old buildings is a costly affair because of the cleanup operation that must go along with the process. First, a survey must be conducted to check what must be done on the site. Afterward, the asbestos has to be safely removed from the site before any demolition can take place.

In 2007, an asbestos study was conducted in the area. The New York State Office of Parks, Recreation Historic Preservation (OPRHP) engineering staff members were able to develop rough estimates for additional buildings based on the study. Detailed asbestos remediation and demolition costs were made available. Next, the OPRHP had to hire a private engineering firm under contract to create detailed demolition plans and specifications for each structure.

There was a project that never left the planning stages, which was to convert Building 15 into government offices. Over the years, the condition of the building has gradually worsened.

Building 15 on March 9, 2015

One environmentalist called this land "*the Central Park of Long Island*," and Assemblyman Steve Englebright was quoted as saying,

"It's right next to Sunken Meadow Park and the Nissequogue River and faces on Long Island Sound, which we're trying to upgrade. This is a regional resource too precious to put up for development."

However, to some other state officials, it is just an extensive piece of developable land that should be used to bring in revenue. State lawmakers were soon flooded with hundreds of letters urging that *"the park be kept in Kings Park."*

For many residents of Kings Park, the abandoned buildings have become an unwanted blight on the town. Yet there are those that have a strange love affair with this place. Call it a love and respect for history or a morbid curiosity. Whatever the case, this place has attracted and drawn in countless people, including myself.

Looking out of a rear window from Building 93 on March 27, 2013

Facing east from the rooftop solarium of Building 138 (73N) on 4/28/13

An open window guard at Group 4 on Aug. 31, 2013

Broken window at Group 3 on March 27, 2011

There are people that wish to save a few structures as a way of preserving the history of the hospital. One such building was Building 135 (73K) of the former Veterans' Memorial Hospital Unit.

Preservationist Pamela M. Schmidt appealed to the state during the first half of 2016 to save the brick arches of the central walkway of Building 135 (73K), which she often referred to as the Y Building because of its shape. Sadly, her appeals fell upon deaf ears, and the arches were demolished later in the year with the rest of the building.

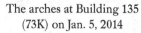

The arches at Building 135 (73K) on Jan. 5, 2014	Most of Building 135 (73K) was demolished by Sept. 29, 2016

Personally, I thought the arches would have looked great surrounded by a garden, but my opinion does not count for much. It is already too late.

It is interesting how many people's lives have been affected by the Kings Park Psychiatric Center. These buildings and the land on which they were built have touched thousands of lives in both positive and negative ways. The site has a true historic significance to Kings Park, Long Island, and the state of New York. It is truly a shame that something was never done to preserve the buildings years earlier before they fell apart.

Once these buildings are all gone, no one else will ever be able to truly appreciate the legacy of what they have become, except through books, photos, and the Internet. This is part of our history as well as an important part of Kings Park culture. If some of these structures can be saved and reused, then no resource should be spared to make this happen.

Demolition Projects

There is great value sitting idle at this facility. Destroying it to me seems like a very negative thing, all loss and very little gain or benefit to the people of New York State. Instead of millions of dollars being used in a negative way to destroy something of such great value, the same (and actually much less) money could be used in a more positive way to remove all of the asbestos from the facilities tunnels and buildings and restore the entire facility and grounds, keeping the park like atmosphere and allowing park visitors to walk on all of the grounds.

—Greg Gusew (concerned citizen)

On the walls within most of the abandoned buildings and along the roads and sidewalks, one can sometimes find spray-painted numbers, arrows, and other specific markings. These are not the work of graffiti artists. Survey teams do this in preparation for the massive cleanup operations that take place before any buildings are demolished.

| Basement room no. 33 (B-33) in Building 93 on April 20, 2011 | Stairway no. 1 (ST-1) in Building 15 on March 12, 2013 | Hallway no.1 (H-1) in Bldg 90 on 3/17/13 |

As of 2009, as many as fourteen structures were scheduled for demolition set to take place in 2010. Because of financial issues, the demolitions were delayed until the fall of 2011. The demolitions were later postponed again until summer of 2012. At that time, preselected structures were razed one by one over the next year.

The following list shows the structures that were scheduled for removal during phase 1. The buildings were chosen because of ongoing safety concerns and a lack of future use. For the most part, they served no purpose other than being safety risks to trespassers.

PHASE 1 DEMOLITIONS
Building 6 – steam pipe junction house
Building 23 – Buckman Hall Recreation Center
Building 29 – the power plant's smokestack and fuel tanks
Building 35 – staff residence
Building 36 – staff residence
Building 46 – slaughterhouse
Building 48 – ground maintenance/former horse barn
Building 55 – boathouse near the marina
Building 56 – community store, a.k.a. Cafe 56
Building 57 – electrical and plumbing maintenance workshops
Building 59 – former power plant/manufacturing and medical records storage
Building 60 – former water pumping station/repair workshop
Building 122 – Mental Retardation Unit/former female adolescent wards
Building 123 – kitchen and dining hall for Group 2
Railroad spur supports – railroad trestle concrete support beams
Road removal – asphalt and concrete from unused hospital roads
Sand Pyramid – salt and sand shed located near Building 5
The Barge – the former yacht clubhouse built on a landlocked barge

At first, local subcontractors in areas such as asbestos removal, concrete restoration, rodent/pest control, and trucking were sought, but in the end, the state settled on using an out-of-state company. As of the early part of 2012, a $6.4 million demolition contract was awarded to the National Salvage and

Service Corporation of Bloomington, Indiana. Out of a total of twenty bids received on the project, this company presented the lowest, making them the most cost-effective choice. Soon after, the company took on the daunting task of removing nineteen buildings and various other structures.

The project was scheduled to begin in mid-May but did not start until July with the abatement and demolition of Building 82, the first to go from this phase of demolitions.

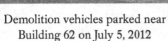

Demolition vehicles parked near Building 62 on July 5, 2012

Demolition forklift in front of Macy Home on Aug. 3, 2012

On July 5, 2012, I paid a visit to Kings Park and saw a couple of construction CAT vehicles parked near Building 62 at the Nissequogue River State Park. A week later, the trees that covered Building 82 from sight had been cleared away, and a fence had been erected around that building. There was also a noticeable increase in security on the property. That was to be expected, considering the amount of construction/demolition equipment that would now be left on the grounds overnight.

I knew by the time I returned to Kings Park on my next visit there would be a significant change, and I was right. Soon enough, more buildings were taken down. I was there to see much of it happen. It was sad to see some of the oldest buildings of Group 2 and the recreation center destroyed, although I knew it was necessary. Those buildings were in terrible shape. It was also a shame to see Cafe 56 torn down because it could have been renovated and repurposed.

Saying goodbye to Group
2 on Aug. 3, 2012

Speaking with a security
guard on Aug. 3, 2012

Ray Staten & Max Neukirch, Jr. across
from Group 2 on Aug. 14, 2012

Myself with Max witnessing demo
of Group 2 on Aug. 14, 2012

Me with Ray & Max photographing
the demo of Bldg 56, Aug. 14, 2012

Ray Staten photographing the demo
of Building 56 on Aug. 14, 2012

Posing with Ray & Max in front of
Macy Home on Aug. 14, 2012

Photographing the demo area of
Building 23 on Dec. 19, 2012

Demolition vehicles at
Building 6, 2012 by Max Neukirch, Jr.

Photographing the demo of
Building 6 on Sept. 5, 2012

The firm hired to demolish the buildings was not using local union workers. This caused an outcry among these workers, who picketed on the former hospital grounds. They even brought out the giant inflatable rat that has become quite popular with union protestors.

There was also talk of a different kind of protest. A group of the urban explorers who understood the importance of the history behind the buildings in question discussed how to protest the demolitions in their own way. There was even talk of disrupting the workers and obstructing them from demolishing the buildings by chaining themselves to the structures, which might have led to other problems. In the end, cooler heads prevailed, and it was agreed to let the buildings go with dignity.

The expected completion date for the entire project was November 2013. The job was done before the end of May. The highlight of the project was the highly publicized demolition of the power plant's smokestack on March 27, 2013.

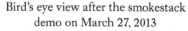

Bird's eye view after the smokestack demo on March 27, 2013

Demolition vehicle parked near Building 44 on April 16, 2013

Another large demolition project referred to as phase 2 was originally set to begin in October 2015. Instead, it would not begin until April 18, 2016. This project would mainly include the razing of buildings on the side of the Nissequogue River State Park and is meant to clear the parkland of unwanted structures. Most of the buildings scheduled for demolition were previously used as staff residences. The most attractive aspect of this project was that the park was going to gain several new additions.

PHASE 2 DEMOLITIONS
Building 7 – medical/surgical building (partial demolition/water tank tower only)
Building 44 – storehouse (no abatement necessary)
Building 89 – comfort station near Tiffany Field (no abatement necessary)
Building 130 (73F) – doctors' residence (abatement only/future comfort station)
Building 131 (73G) – doctors' residence
Building 132 (73H) – doctors' residence (abatement only/future KPPC museum)
Building 133 (73I) – doctors' residence
Building 134 (73J) – doctors' residence

Building 135 (73K) – convalescence building (no abatement necessary)
Building 136 (73L) – medical/surgical building
Building 137 (73M) – Group 3 kitchen/dining area
Building 142 (73R) – staff kitchen/dining area/elderly care building
Steam tunnel segments beneath Veterans' Group

NEW ADDITIONS
Picnic pavilion and picnic areas
Recreational fields
Garden areas
Pathways/rustic overlook trails
Selective thinning of vegetation for improved vistas

Just as with phase 1, the second phase will be compliant with all Occupational Safety and Health Administration (OSHA) and Environmental Protection Agency (EPA) standards.

The anticipated completion of this project was expected to be sometime in January 2017, although it will likely be completed after that projected date, since it began late. Asbestos abatement began on April 18, 2016, with Building 131. Within two months, the first structures were demolished. Demolitions continued throughout the summer and fall.

Construction vehicles parked near
Building 62 on June 20, 2016

Construction vehicles at the former
site of Building 142 (73R) on 9/17/16

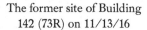

The former site of Building   Construction vehicle at the former site
142 (73R) on 11/13/16   of Building 135 (73K) on 11/13/16

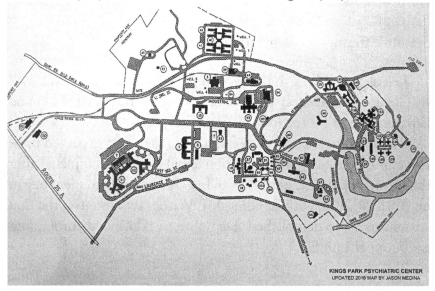

Map of the KPPC, circa 2016, updated by the author

This project is currently scheduled to continue until March 1,
2017. Therefore, it is very possible the bulk of these demolitions
could take place in 2016, with the remaining structures from the
list being finished by spring 2017. JVN Restoration Inc. from Staten
Island was hired to do the job, which should be well under way by
the time this book is published.

To keep informed about the latest developments and
demolitions, check out the following website:

http://www.kppccleanup.com

Cleanup Costs

They just pile up all the trash over the old hill, and then they would come here with the pay loader and just dump dirt over it. And they'd do that over and over, again. So many of these hills and valleys are all old garbage piles. Something that they're going to have to address, if they do anything with this land.

–Stephen Weber (Kings Park activist and former employee of the Kings Park Psychiatric Center's Cafe 56, Building 56)

By March 2009, plans for the demolition of approximately fourteen buildings, structures, and unused roads on the hospital grounds were made official. A significant portion of the steam tunnel system would also be demolished. However, the actual costs would later be determined through the state's normal competitive bidding process.

Estimates at the time for phase 1:
Asbestos abatement and monitoring: $1,500,000
Demolition: $8,200,000
Restoration and landscaping: $1,000,000
Engineering and design: $1,200,000
Construction management: $800,000
Contingency (10 percent)

A question many are wondering, found on a wall on Oct. 6, 2013

Total estimated cost = $14,000,000

One can imagine quite a significant price for the cleanup of this area, which contains more than fifty abandoned buildings that encompass close to 2.5 million square feet on approximately

320 acres of land. Later estimates had increased to $60 million. Currently, the cost is listed as $200 million.

At the time when this plan was formulated, the only available funding was $29 million, which was for Kings Park's remediation activities appropriated in the state budget at the direction of the New York State Senate. A public information meeting was held at the Kings Park High School on March 27, 2009, in an attempt to gain public input from local officials, possible interested organizations, and members of the town.

Most of the attendees at the hearing and sixty written comments were in favor of the demolition, although Smithtown's planning director requested that some of the more historically significant buildings among the eighty-four on the site be spared such as York Hall.

The state of New York was faced with approximately $48 million in bonded debt, which had to be paid on the site. Still, the state planned to put at least three-quarters of the property on the block for development despite protests from preservationists and environmentalists. The intention was for only about 100–150 acres of land to be retained as public land under a plan, including the wetlands at the mouth of the Nissequogue River and the hospital's mile-long frontage of shore land along the Long Island Sound.

Looking towards the park from Short Beach on May 11, 2016

Facing east toward the mouth of the
river from the Bluff on July 21, 2016

Dividing line between the town
& park on March 16, 2016

Several interested parties, including the township of Smithtown, wanted the state to fund a new study before deciding the final fate of the property so it can be determined exactly how marketable the grounds can be. The previous study done several years ago was inadequate in examining the details of access to the site, ground contamination from lead paint, buried debris, and asbestos, as well as other potential problems that could exist.

Some of the main concerns were how many of the old outdated buildings could be converted to modern-day uses and how much it would cost to make that happen, also how the vast underground tunnel system and buried rubble of previously demolished buildings would affect any possible future construction projects. Another major issue was what to do about access to the property, since the main entrance to the grounds is located at East Main Street/Route 25A, which is far too narrow and easily becomes congested with traffic.

These issues have created apprehension in the community of Kings Park that some future developer would have to build high-density housing to cover the environmental cleanup costs just to make a profit. To develop the rest of the land for sale, many buildings would have to be demolished or renovated, and the miles of asbestos piping would need to be carefully removed during the abatement process, as would any other potentially hazardous materials. Any project would likely include a great deal of excavating and grading as well.

Building 93 with rubble from the smokestack on April 16, 2013

The sign from Building 136 (73L) on Dec. 22, 2011

The estimated cleanup costs can be as high as a few hundred million dollars, while the value of the land has only been assessed at being worth $55 million. Some believe the only feasible way of making a profit from this kind of extensive operation would be by building a residential community. However, this is something that is strongly opposed by Kings Park residents and visitors to the Nissequogue River State Park.

One possible solution would be for the state to offer up the land in its present condition and sell it while, at the same time, agreeing to pay for any required environmental cleanup. Another option would be for the state to lease the land out to interested parties. Yet another suggestion was that perhaps the state could pay off the bonded debt, utilizing other means rather than selling the land. It has been noted that if the state sold only 150 acres of land, it could pay off most of the debt that is owed.

Personally, I prefer the idea of leaving it as a park and just improving the area where necessary.

In the meantime, buildings are being demolished little by little with the start of the phase 2 demolitions. After this latest demolition project, there will be about $5.75 million left over from the $25 million that was secured by Senate Majority Leader John Flanagan.

In the future, if you decide to visit the grounds of the former Kings Park Psychiatric Center, you may notice a lot of open space and grassy fields. Perhaps you might take notice of a few heavily wooded areas. As you walk through these areas, you may actually be walking over the site of a former building. Sometimes it gets harder to tell with time, but there are still basements buried in the ground that are filled with rubble and certain portions of the steam tunnels that have been filled in. The buildings are usually never completely demolished. Something always remains underground.

A friend of mine, Kelly Lindner, said it best, *"There is practically a whole other hospital buried on those grounds."*

This ventilation shaft photographed on 4/17/16 led to basement of Bldg C

Basement of Building 135 (73K) on Sept. 29, 2016

Printed in the United States
By Bookmasters